Schizophrenia

World Psychiatric Association *Evidence and Experience in Psychiatry* Series

Series Editor: Helen Herrman, WPA Secretary for Publications, University of Melbourne, Australia

Depressive Disorders, 3e
Edited by Helen Herrman, Mario Maj and Norman Sartorius
ISBN: 9780470987209

Substance Abuse Disorders
Edited by Hamid Ghodse, Helen Herrman, Mario Maj and Norman Sartorius
ISBN: 9780470745106

Posttraumatic Stress Disorder
Edited by Dan J Stein, Matthew J Friedman and Carlos Blanco
ISBN: 9780470688977

Schizophrenia 2e
Edited by Mario Maj, Norman Sartorius
ISBN: 9780470849644

Dementia 2e
Edited by Mario Maj, Norman Sartorius
ISBN: 9780470849637

Obsessive-Compulsive Disorders 2e
Edited by Mario Maj, Norman Sartorius, Ahmed Okasha, Joseph Zohar
ISBN: 9780470849668

Bipolar Disorders
Edited by Mario Maj, Hagop S Akiskal, Juan José López-Ibor, Norman Sartorius
ISBN: 9780471560371

Eating Disorders
Edited by Mario Maj, Kathrine Halmi, Juan José López-Ibor, Norman Sartorius
ISBN: 9780470848654

Phobias
Edited by Mario Maj, Hagop S Akiskal, Juan José López-Ibor, Ahmed Okasha
ISBN: 9780470858332

Personality Disorders
Edited by Mario Maj, Hagop S Akiskal, Juan E Mezzich
ISBN: 9780470090367

Somatoform Disorders
Edited by Mario Maj, Hagop S Akiskal, Juan E Mezzich, Ahmed Okasha
ISBN: 9780470016121

Current Science and Clinical Practice Series

Series Editor: Helen Herrman, WPA Secretary for Publications, University of Melbourne, Australia

Schizophrenia
Edited by Wolfgang Gaebel
ISBN: 9780470710548

Obsessive Compulsive Disorder
Edited by Joseph Zohar
ISBN: 9780470711255

Schizophrenia
Current Science and Clinical Practice

Editor

Wolfgang Gaebel
Heinrich-Heine University, Düsseldorf, Germany

A John Wiley & Sons, Ltd, Publication

Library of Congress Cataloging-in-Publication Data

Schizophrenia : current science and clinical practice / editor, Wolfgang Gaebel.
       p. ; cm.
    Includes bibliographical references and index.
     ISBN 978-0-470-71054-8 (cloth) – ISBN 978-0-470-97868-9 (ePDF)   1. Schizophrenia.
 I. Gaebel, Wolfgang.
    [DNLM: 1. Schizophrenia.   2. Schizophrenia–therapy.   WM 203]
    RC514.S3352 2011
    616.89'8–dc22

                                                                            2010047250

A catalogue record for this book is available from the British Library

This book is published in the following electronic format: ePDF 9780470978689, WileyOnline Library: 9780470978672; Epub 978047097310

Set in 11/13 Times by Aptara Inc., New Delhi, India.
Printed in Malaysia by Ho Printing (M) Sdn Bhd

First Impression 2011

Contents

List of Contributors

Tyrone D. Cannon
Departments of Psychology and Psychiatry and Biobehavioral Sciences and Staglin
Center for Cognitive Neuroscience
University of California, Los Angeles
1285 Franz Hall
Los Angeles
CA 90095-1563
USA

Peter Falkai
Department of Psychiatry and Psychotherapy
University of Göttingen
Von-Siebold-Str. 5
37075 Göttingen
Germany

Philippa Garety
King's College London
Institute of Psychiatry, Department of Psychology
16 De Crespigny Park
Denmark Hill
London, SE5 8AF
UK

Sherilyn Goldstone
Centre for Youth Mental Health
Orygen Youth Health Research Centre
University of Melbourne
Parkville, VIC 3052
Australia

Michael F. Green
VA Desert Pacific Mental Illness Research Education and Clinical Center UCLA
Semel Institute for Neuroscience and Human Behavior
VA Greater Los Angeles Healthcare System
11301 Wilshire Blvd.
Bldg. 210, Mail Code: 210A, Rm. 115
Los Angeles, CA 90073
USA

Philippe-Olivier Harvey
VA Desert Pacific Mental Illness Research Education and Clinical Center UCLA
Semel Institute for Neuroscience and Human Behavior
VA Greater Los Angeles Healthcare System
11301 Wilshire Blvd.
Bldg. 210, Mail Code: 210A, Rm. 115
Los Angeles, CA 90073
USA

William P. Horan
VA Desert Pacific Mental Illness Research Education and Clinical Center UCLA
Semel Institute for Neuroscience and Human Behavior
VA Greater Los Angeles Healthcare System
11301 Wilshire Blvd.
Bldg. 210, Mail Code: 210A, Rm. 115
Los Angeles, CA 90073
USA

Assen Jablensky
Centre for Clinical Research in Neuropsychiatry
The University of Western Australia
35 Stirling Highway
Crawley WA 6009
Perth, Australia

Suzanne Jolley
King's College London
Institute of Psychiatry, Department of Psychology
16 De Crespigny Park
Denmark Hill
London, SE5 8AF
UK

Robert S. Kern
VA Desert Pacific Mental Illness Research Education and Clinical Center UCLA
Semel Institute for Neuroscience and Human Behavior
VA Greater Los Angeles Healthcare System
11301 Wilshire Blvd.
Bldg. 210, Mail Code: 210A, Rm. 115
Los Angeles, CA 90073
USA

Patrick D. McGorry
Centre for Youth Mental Health
Orygen Youth Health Research Centre
University of Melbourne
Parkville, VIC 3052
Australia

Stephen R. Marder
Semel Insitute for Neuroscience at UCLA
The VA Greater Los Angeles Healthcare Center, and the VA Desert Pacific Mental
Illness Research, Education, and Clinical Center
Los Angeles, California, CA 90024
USA

Michael O'Donovan
MRC Centre for Neuropsychiatric Genetics and Genomics
Cardiff University School of Medicine
Heath Park
Cardiff, CF14 4XN
UK

Michael J Owen
MRC Centre for Neuropsychiatric Genetics and Genomics
Cardiff University School of Medicine
Heath Park
Cardiff, CF14 4XN
UK

Wulf Rössler
Department of General and Social Psychiatry
University of Zurich
Militärstrasse 8
8021 Zürich
Switzerland

Andrea Schmitt
Department of Psychiatry
University of Göttingen
Von-Siebold-Str. 5
37075 Göttingen
Germany

Jonathan E. Sherin
Mental Health and Behavioral Science, Miami VA Healthcare System
1201 NW 16th Street
Miami, FL
33125
Psychiatry and Behavioral Science, University of Miami
1120 NW 14th Street
Miami, FL, CA 90073
33136

James TR Walters
MRC Centre for Neuropsychiatric Genetics and Genomics
Cardiff University School of Medicine
Heath Park
Cardiff, CF14 4XN
UK

Preface

This book is the successor to *Schizophrenia*, edited by Mario Maj and Norman Sartorius, published in 1999 in the Evidence and Experience in Psychiatry series of the World Psychiatric Association (WPA). Given the considerable development in various areas of research and practice concerning schizophrenia, an updated edition was required. It was decided to revise the format, focusing on new scientific findings and their translation into clinical applications: therefore a new WPA series has been created, Current Science and Clinical Practice, of which this is the first volume.

The term 'schizophrenia', coined by Eugen Bleuler, celebrates its 100th anniversary in 2011. Since his ground-breaking monograph, *Dementia praecox or the Group of Schizophrenias*, researchers around the world have struggled to unravel myth and reality in this heterogeneous group of disorders. Is schizophrenia still an intractable illness, inevitably leading to mental deterioration and social exclusion? Is it a 'real' illness, an illness entity, or just a construct of psychiatrists' minds', a stigmatising label, the consequences of which are more deleterious than the illness itself?

The search for the truth, the reality, the causes, preconditions and antecedents of schizophrenia has been pursued ever since, rapidly increasing our knowledge from molecular basics to clinical practice. While discussions about renaming the illness continue—hoping to give it a name less stigmatising and more related to the underlying pathophysiology—expert opinion on its value and status as a concept is still divided across the world.

In this context, the present volume provides updated information on the diagnosis, the neurobiological foundations, and the management of schizophrenia, including aspects ranging from aetiology and pathophysiology to early recognition and rehabilitation.

One topic is the current revision of the international psychiatric classification systems ICD-11 and DSM-5, including the diagnostic criteria for schizophrenia and related disorders. While, at first glance, novel findings on the pathophysiology of schizophrenia, including a large range of new genetic observations, may suggest that a radical new approach to the diagnosis of schizophrenia is imminent, closer inspection shows that they are not yet specific and sensitive enough to warrant inclusion in psychiatric classification systems for clinical use. Ongoing discussions involve the putative role of novel "dimensional" specifiers for diagnostic assessment, which may also facilitate the future development of a new classification framework (Research Domain Criteria, RDoC) for research on schizophrenia and related syndromes.

Although the aetiology of 'the schizophrenias' is still unknown, current research shows that biological factors like genetic risk, psychological factors like information processing, and social factors like environmental stressors all play decisive roles. Regarding the pathophysiology of schizophrenia, research demonstrates that the hierarchical organization of functional brain networks is altered, that some degree of cortical atrophy occurs, and that altered information processing takes place, involving both basic functions like visual information processing and complex functions like semantic processing. The most pressing current issue is to relate such findings to the clinical phenotype and to functional outcome measures.

Research in the field of cognition has shown that cognitive dysfunctions are among the major determinants of general psychosocial functioning in schizophrenia. Research initiatives like MATRICS and CNTRICS are beginning to identify those areas of cognition which are of major importance for functional outcome, determining the best ways to assess cognition in patients with schizophrenia, and investigating the neurobiological basis of cognitive dysfunctions. A novel aspect here is that social cognition, ranging from basic concepts like facial affect recognition to complex social constructs like empathy, is beginning to yield systematic insight into schizophrenia, thereby triggering the development of specific psychotherapeutic training strategies and pharmacological cognitive enhancers to improve cognitive functions and functional outcome.

While many studies have shown that genetic factors play a role in determining the development of schizophrenia, little is known about the differential contribution of genetic and environmental factors towards disease development or the determination of the clinical subtype that will develop. Obviously, there is considerable genetic overlap of the schizophrenias with affective disorders. There appears to be a clinical continuum from health to fully developed psychosis, the determinants of risk and progression obviously involving a highly complex interaction between genetic and environmental factors. Currently, much research focuses on these interactions with the hope to advance both diagnosis and treatment of schizophrenia.

Early recognition and prevention of schizophrenia are hotly debated areas of research because international studies show different degrees of progression from prodromal states to overt schizophrenia, depending on the criteria used for detecting and assessing individuals at high risk of developing schizophrenia. Another issue is the question at which time during the prodromal phase treatment should be initiated. Also, ethical issues arise in the context of the revision of the international classification criteria because individuals may be labelled as "pre-psychotic" without ever progressing to schizophrenia. While these questions need to be addressed, the benefits of early detection and possibly complete prevention of schizophrenia are obvious. Standardized methods of risk assessment are warranted in order to identify the best approach for early recognition and prevention of schizophrenia.

While pharmacological treatment was characterized mainly by a discussion of whether first or second generation antipsychotics were preferable, nowadays the differential side-effect profiles of these substances have come to the fore. There are also novel pharmacological agents acting on transmitters beyond the dopamine system, with most recent progress having been made in the area of glutamate receptor agonists. Then there are novel pharmacological agents under development for improving cognition in schizophrenia. These pharmacological innovations are accompanied by an increasing interest in questions of efficacy and efficiency, which are now addressed in large multi-center studies.

With the current emphasis on the neurobiology of schizophrenia, an important aspect is still the behavioural one and the role that cognitive-behavioral interventions play in treatment. These cover not only acute crisis intervention or the management of clinical symptoms such as delusions and hallucinations, but also complex cognitive training programmes to improve cognitive functions in the long term. We need not only to develop optimal psychotherapeutic strategies for patients with schizophrenia, but also to address the side-effects of cognitive-behavioral interventions, placebo-like unspecific learning effects and their contributions to therapeutic efficacy, and interactions of psychotherapy with pharmacological treatment.

While research on the diagnosis and pathophysiology of schizophrenia is yielding important new insights almost daily, the management of schizophrenia in routine clinical settings has yet to profit from such insights. Major progress has been made in the field of managing schizophrenia with the help of case management or in novel therapeutic settings. The field of schizophrenia rehabilitation has profited from studies showing that cognitive training programmes improve functional outcomes. Patients with schizophrenia and their professional caretakers are often subject to stigmatization to such a degree that it has been called the 'second disorder'. Research has shown that some anti-stigma measures are more effective than others, and that the construct of social distance may be a key component of stigmatization. Taken together, while researchers are still striving to understand the pathophysiology of schizophrenia, everyday clinical routine management may still profit more from evidence-based pragmatic approaches.

Schizophrenia: Current Science and Clinical Practice clearly synthezies recent information on the diagnosis, the neurobiological foundations, and the treatment and management of schizophrenia, ranging from early recognition to rehabilitation. It reviews the findings obtained with modern techniques like magnetic resonance imaging, genetics, network analyses, and others.

I would like to thank the WPA President, Mario Maj, and the WPA Secretary for Publications, Helen Herman, for giving me the opportunity to edit this new volume. I thank the authors for their excellent scientific contributions and their cooperation in keeping to deadlines. My thanks also go to the staff at John Wiley & Sons, in particular to Joan Marsh for her continued support. Finally, I want to thank Juergen

Zielasek for his help in drafting the book exposé, as well as Ricarda Albrecht and Sonja Schmidt for contributing to a smooth publication process.

I sincerely hope that this volume will be a valuable successor to the first WPA volume on schizophrenia published 10 years ago – both as an up-to-date knowledge base and a helpful practice tool.

Wolfgang Gaebel
Chair, WPA Section on Schizophrenia

CHAPTER 1

Diagnosis and revision of the classification systems

Assen Jablensky
*Centre for Clinical Research in Neuropsychiatry, The University
of Western Australia, Perth, Australia.*

Information Box

- Like most of psychiatry's diagnostic concepts represented in ICD-10 and DSM-IV, the 'disease' schizophrenia is a working hypothesis that may not meet the criteria of unitary aetiology or pathogenesis, and its diagnostic criteria should be regarded as provisional.
- There is a growing understanding that the complex syndromal spectrum of schizophrenia comprises end-point phenotypes for heterogeneous gene networks, pathophysiological pathways and environmental modifiers.
- There is little evidence that schizophrenia is a discrete category, separated from other disorders by 'natural' boundaries, yet proposals to replace the category with a dimensional construct are premature.
- Although schizophrenia cannot yet be described as a valid disease category, the diagnostic concept of schizophrenia and its spectrum provides information of great utility to clinicians and continues to generate testable research hypotheses.

INTRODUCTION

There is a broad consensus that schizophrenia is a complex mental disorder with variable phenotypic expression and poorly understood multifactorial aetiology, involving a significant but likely heterogeneous genetic contribution; environmental factors interacting with the genetic susceptibility; and – in many cases – early

Schizophrenia: Current Science and Clinical Practice, First Edition. Edited by Wolfgang Gaebel.
© 2011 John Wiley & Sons, Ltd. Published 2011 by John Wiley & Sons, Ltd.

neurodevelopmental aberrations that precede the onset of overt psychotic symptoms. Schizophrenia occurs in diverse populations at comparable rates [1,2], with a lifetime prevalence of ~0.4% [3] and, as far as archival data are available, without significant secular changes in its incidence [4]. This is consistent with an ancient origin of the disorder. At present, schizophrenia accounts for at least 2.3% of the global burden of disease and disability, yet, globally, a large proportion of the people affected by the disorder still remain untreated [5].

Diagnostic concepts play a critical role in the management and treatment of schizophrenia patients: in research aiming to identify risk factors and causal mechanisms; and in attempts at resolving contentious issues, such as the nature of comorbidity and the relationships between schizophrenia and other, partly overlapping disorders. A major difficulty hampering progress in this work is the inherent weakness of the diagnostic concept of schizophrenia, in that it remains predicated on the assumption of an underlying but still unknown disease process. Most of the criteria defining schizophrenia are symptom-based, relying on the clinician's interpretation of patients' subjective experiences. As yet, there is no objective diagnostic test or a validated biological marker that could unequivocally support clinical decision-making or biological and epidemiological research. Notwithstanding the current availability of explicit diagnostic criteria, incorporated in the World Health Organisation classification of mental disorders, ICD-10 [6] and the Diagnostic and Statistical Manual of the American Psychiatric Association, DSM-IV [7], disagreements persist regarding the delimitation of schizophrenia from other psychoses, and from affective and neurodevelopmental disorders. Similarly, there is no consensus on the classification of its subclinical forms, such as schizotypal disorder, or its pre-clinical manifestations, such as the putative schizophrenia risk syndrome. Other contentious issues concern the utility of a categorical classification of the disorder as compared to descriptive symptom dimensions or subtypes based on quantitative cognitive traits. The present chapter provides an overview of the origin, evolution, and current state of the concept of schizophrenia, and aims to foreshadow some of the options worth considering in the process of revision of the major diagnostic classifications.

ORIGIN AND EVOLUTION OF THE CONCEPT OF SCHIZOPHRENIA

The disease concept of schizophrenia is relatively recent, as compared with mental afflictions known since antiquity, such as melancholia, mania, or 'insanity'. Only by mid-nineteenth century did European psychiatrists begin singling out from the bulk of 'insanity' a particular disorder of unknown causation, typically affecting young people, and often progressing to chronic deterioration. In France, Morel [8] referred to such cases as '*démence précoce*', while in Scotland, Clouston [9] coined the term 'adolescent insanity'. In Germany, Kahlbaum [10] delineated the catatonic syndrome, and his disciple Hecker [11] described hebephrenia. However, it was

Emil Kraepelin (1856–1926) who integrated those quite varied clinical pictures into a single nosological entity under the name of *dementia praecox* [12] on the basis of his systematic observations of a large number of clinical cases presenting with variable cross-sectional features but commonly tending towards a course that ultimately resulted in cognitive and behavioural decline.

Kraepelin's 'clinical forms'

Kraepelin acknowledged the diversity of the clinical pictures subsumed under *dementia praecox* and articulated nine different 'clinical forms' (Table 1.1). He emphasised that 'we meet everywhere the *same fundamental disorders* in the

Table 1.1 Emil Kraepelin's 'clinical forms'

- **Dementia praecox simplex**
  (*'Impoverishment and devastation of the whole psychic life which is accomplished quite imperceptibly'*)
- **Hebephrenia**
  (*Insidious change of personality with shallow capricious affect, senseless and incoherent behaviour, poverty of thought, occasional hallucinations and fragmentary delusions, progressing to profound dementia*)
- **Depressive dementia praecox (simple and delusional form)**
  (*Initial state of depression followed by slowly progressive cognitive decline and avolition, with or without hypochondriacal or persecutory delusions*)
- **Circular dementia praecox**
  (*Prodromal depression followed by gradual onset of auditory hallucinations, delusions, marked fluctuations of mood and aimless impulsivity*)
- **Agitated dementia praecox**
  (*Acute onset, perplexity or exaltation, multimodal hallucinations, fantastic delusions*)
- **Periodic dementia praecox**
  (*Recurrent acute, brief episodes of confused excitement with remissions*)
- **Catatonia**
  (*'Conjunction of peculiar excitement with catatonic stupor dominates the clinical picture' in this form, but catatonic phenomena frequently occur in otherwise wholly different presentations of dementia praecox*)
- **Paranoid dementia (mild and severe form)**
  (*The essential symptoms are delusions and hallucinations. The severe form results in a 'peculiar disintegration of psychic life', involving especially emotional and volitional disorders. The mild form is a very slowly evolving 'paranoid or hallucinatory weak-mindedness' which 'makes it possible for the patient for a long time still to live as an apparently healthy individual'*)
- **Schizophasia (confusional speech dementia praecox)**
  (*Cases meeting the general description of dementia praecox but resulting in an end state of 'an unusually striking disorder of expression in speech, with relatively little impairment of the remaining psychic activities'*)

different forms of *dementia praecox* . . . in very varied conjunctions, even though the clinical picture may appear at first sight ever so divergent'. [13]. The 'fundamental disorders' included cognitive deficit (a 'general decay of mental efficiency') and executive dysfunction ('loss of mastery over volitional action'). Kraepelin never issued a definitive list of diagnostic criteria for *dementia praecox* and was rather sceptical about the existence of 'pathognomonic' symptoms. He believed that the validation of the provisional disease entity, which he always regarded as provisional, would ultimately come from neuropathology, physiology, and biological chemistry of the brain. Towards the end of his career, he even considered abandoning the categorical disease formulation of schizophrenia and manic-depressive illness as distinct disorders and replacing the dichotomy with an essentially dimensional model in which schizophrenic and affective syndromes 'do not represent the expression of particular pathological processes, but rather indicate the areas of our personality in which these processes unfold' [14]. In the same paper Kraepelin proposed three hierarchically arranged 'registers' or strata of psychopathology – affective, schizophrenic and encephalopathic – which would recombine in many different ways to produce the manifold syndromes of the major mental disorders. Later, this concept became known in German psychiatry as the *'Schichtenregel'* (the *strata* rule).

Bleuler's 'group of schizophrenias'

Eugen Bleuler (1857–1939) modified Kraepelin's original concept by adding to the scope of *dementia praecox* clinical illnesses that did not evolve into a 'terminal state' of deterioration, which Kraepelin considered to be the hallmark of the disease. Having coined the term schizophrenia to replace *dementia praecox*, Bleuler [15] stated that schizophrenia 'is not a disease in the strict sense, but appears to be a group of diseases . . . Therefore we should speak of schizophrenias in the plural'. Bleuler introduced a fundamental distinction between *basic* (obligatory) and *accessory* (supplementary) symptoms of the disorder. While the accessory symptoms comprised the delusions and hallucinations which today are given preeminent diagnostic prominence in both ICD-10 and DSM-IV as 'positive' symptoms, Bleuler's basic symptoms included thought and speech derailment ('loosening of associations'), volitional indeterminacy ('ambivalence'), affective incongruence, and withdrawal from reality ('autism'). It was the basic symptoms that, according to Bleuler, gave schizophrenia its distinctive diagnostic profile. Along with the 'latent' schizophrenias, which represented attenuated forms of the basic symptoms and were mainly manifested as aberrant personality traits, he also added to the 'broader concept' of schizophrenia atypical depressive or manic states, Wernicke's motility psychoses, reactive psychoses, and other non-organic, non-affective psychotic disorders, on grounds that 'this is important for the studies of heredity', thus foreshadowing the notion of schizophrenia spectrum disorders.

Leonhard's 'endogenous psychoses'

In a clinical tradition originating with Wernicke and Kleist, who had proposed grouping psychotic illnesses on the basis of a presumed localised cerebral dysfunction, Karl Leonhard (1904–88) [16] developed an elaborate classification of the 'endogenous' psychoses which departed substantially from the Kraepelinian and Bleulerian nosology. Leonhard defined sharply delineated disease entities, based on a detailed psychopathology that emphasised objective signs, such as psychomotor behaviour, course and outcome, as well as family history. The nonaffective psychoses were split into 'systematic' and 'unsystematic' forms of schizophrenia, and a third group of 'cycloid' psychoses, each containing further subtypes (Table 1.2). While the 'unsystematic' schizophrenias were considered to be primarily genetic, hereditary factors played a secondary role in the cycloid psychoses and in the 'systematic' schizophrenias, which were presumed to be exogenously determined, for example, by maternal obstetric complications or early failure of social learning. Leonhard's classification neither expanded, nor constricted the boundaries of schizophrenia, but carved the schizophrenia spectrum in a different way.

Classification of psychoses in French psychiatry

At the time when Kraepelin's ideas were gaining wide, though not uncontested, acceptance in Europe and North America, French psychiatrists [17] maintained a distance from the prevailing *dementia praecox* trend. Following the French tradition of a refined nosography, the non-affective psychotic disorders were divided into three major classes: (i) '*bouffée délirante polymorphe aiguë*' (acute polymorphic delusional psychosis); (ii) '*psychose hallucinatoire chronique*' (chronic hallucinatory psychosis); and (iii) '*schizophrenie chronique*' (chronic schizophrenia). The latter category, though influenced by Bleuler, was only reserved for the late, presumably irreversible, stages of the chronic hallucinatory psychosis. French psychiatrists placed much emphasis on the age at onset and the mode of onset (acute versus insidious). In ICD-10 (but not in DSM-IV), the French concept of acute polymorphic delusional psychosis was considered to be closely similar to Leonhard's cycloid psychoses and was incorporated as an inclusion term in the classification.

Other post-Kraepelinian and post-Bleulerian subtypes and dichotomies

During the next several decades, there was a growing realisation that schizophrenia was indeed a broad grouping of clinically heterogeneous disorders. A number of

Table 1.2   Karl Leonhard's classification of the non-affective endogenous psychoses

I. Group of systematic schizophrenias
(Insidious onset, auditory and somatic hallucinations, delusions, early blunting of affect, continuous unremitting course, personality deterioration)

Paraphrenias
(Auditory hallucinosis, audible thoughts, thought broadcast, passivity experiences, delusional misidentifications, falsifications of memory)
Hebephrenias
(Extreme autistic withdrawal, flat affect, impoverished or disorganised speech and behaviour)
Catatonias
(Excessive parakinesias, mannerisms, verbigeration, posturing, stereotypies, mutism, auditory hallucinations)

II. Group of unsystematic (atypical) schizophrenias
(Rapid onset, relatively preserved affect, remitting course, mild personality deterioration)

Affect-laden paraphrenia
(Paranoid delusions with affective loading)
Cataphasia (schizophasia)
(Incoherent, pressured speech but well-organised behaviour)
Periodic catatonia
(Episodic hyper- or hypokinesia, mixed excitatory and hallucinatory symptoms)

III. Group of cycloid psychoses
(Sudden onset, pervasive delusional mood, multimodal hallucinations, labile affect, polarity of manifestations, typically complete recovery from episode)

Anxiety-happiness psychosis
(Extreme shifts of affect, polarity intense fear – ecstatic elation)
Motility psychosis
(Impulsive hypermotility – psychomotor inhibition)
Confusion psychosis
(Incoherent pressure of speech – mutism)

sub-nosological distinctions were proposed, based on a mix of criteria that included symptomatology, course, or presumed aetiology (Table 1.3). [18,19,20,21,22,23]

In what could be regarded as prototype diagnostic criteria, Kurt Schneider [24] proposed that nine groups of psychotic manifestations, designated as 'first-rank symptoms' (FRS), had a 'decisive weight' in the diagnosis of schizophrenia: audible thoughts; voices arguing about, or discussing the patient; voices commenting on the patient's actions; experiences of influences on the body; thought withdrawal

Table 1.3 Post-Kraepelinian and post-Bleulerian subtypes and dichotomies

Schizophrenia subtypes	Descriptive features	Authors
Schizoaffective disorder	Acute onset of hallucinations and delusions accompanied by distinct and prominent manic or depressive symptoms	Kasanin [18]
Schizophreniform psychoses	Cases initially diagnosed as schizophrenia but lacking features such as affective flattening, autistic withdrawal, disturbances of volition and chronic course	Langfeld [19]
Process / non-process schizophrenia	Process: introverted premorbid personality, insidious onset, affective blunting, primary delusions (often bizarre), somatic delusions. Non-process: extroverted premorbid personality, absence of gradual personality changes, acute onset with marked excitement, elation, anxiety or depression, good prognosis	Stephens & Astrup [20]
Paranoid-nonparanoid schizophrenia	Paranoid: later age of onset, well-organised delusions or hallucinations, absence of affective changes. Non-paranoid: earlier age of onset, flat or inappropriate affect, formal thought disorder, poorer prognosis	Tsuang & Winokur [21]
Positive-negative schizophrenia ("Type I" and "Type II"	Type I: positive symptoms (hallucinations, delusions, formal thought disorder). Type II: negative symptoms (social withdrawal, loss of volition, affective flattening, poverty of speech)	Crow [22]
Deficit-nondeficit schizophrenia	Deficit subtype: enduring primary negative symptoms that cannot be explained as sequelae of depression or other psychopathology	Carpenter et al. [23]

and other interference with thought; thought broadcast (diffusion of thought); delusional perception; and other experiences involving 'made' impulses and feelings experienced as caused by an outside agency. Due to the specificity with which they were described, the FRS were later adopted and incorporated in the Research Diagnostic Criteria, RDC [25]; DSM III [26]; and ICD-10 [6].

The schizophrenia spectrum concept

The observation that several different disorders tend to cluster among biological relatives of individuals with clinical schizophrenia has been supported by epidemiological and family studies suggesting that the genetic liability to schizophrenia is shared with liability to other related syndromes [26,27]. The most prominent among these syndromes is schizotypal disorder. The term 'schizotypy', introduced by Rado [27] and Meehl [28], refers to a personality characterised by anhedonia, ambivalence, 'interpersonal aversiveness', body image distortion, 'cognitive slippage', and sensory, kinaesthetic or vestibular aberrations. Chapman *et al.* [29] designed scales to measure perceptual aberrations and 'magical ideation' as traits predicting 'psychosis proneness'. These constructs were later incorporated into the DSM-III category of schizotypal personality disorder (SPD). The frequent occurrence of SPD among first-degree relatives of individuals with schizophrenia has been replicated in the Roscommon epidemiological study [30], which added to the schizophrenia spectrum further disorders co-segregating within families. The resulting 'continuum of liability' includes: (i) 'typical' schizophrenia; (ii) schizotypal and paranoid personality disorders; (iii) schizoaffective disorder, depressed type; (iv) other non-affective psychotic disorders (schizophreniform, atypical psychosis); and (v) psychotic affective disorders. Evidence from family and twin data suggests that the manifestations of SPD fall into two genetically separate clusters: a 'negative' cluster (odd speech and behaviour, inappropriate affect and social withdrawal), more common among relatives of schizophrenic probands, and a 'positive' cluster (magical ideation, brief quasi-psychotic episodes), associated with increased incidence of affective disorders in relatives. 'Negative' schizotypy may indeed represent a subclinical *forme fruste* of schizophrenia with attenuated cognitive deficits and mild brain structural abnormalities.

Statistically derived clusters and symptom dimensions

Factor analysis and related statistical methods have been used to extract covariances from a small number of latent factors which could account for the interrelationships of symptoms and explain a proportion of their variance. A three-factor solution has been proposed [31] and subsequently replicated [32–34], based on a relatively small number of input variables (SANS/SAPS scores). In this model, negative symptoms load on a single factor of 'psychomotor poverty', while positive symptoms split into a delusions-and-hallucinations factor ('reality distortion') and a thought-and-speech disorder factor ('disorganisation'). In a large sample of schizophrenia probands, McGrath *et al.* [35] identified five factors (positive, negative, disorganised, affective and early onset/developmental). In another series of factor analyses based on an expanded list of 64 psychopathological symptoms, Cuesta and Peralta

[36] concluded that a hierarchical 10-dimensional model provided the best fit on statistical and clinical grounds. However, the output of factor analyses of symptomatology depends on the content of the input, for example, studies using SANS and SAPS produce different solutions from those based on scales such as PANSS, BPRS or OPCRIT. Factor solutions, therefore, are not unique and the number of factorial dimensions that describe parsimoniously the clinical presentation varies, depending on the particular selection of symptoms and measurement methods. Therefore, factor-analytical studies suggesting 'established' dimensions or syndromes of schizophrenia should be viewed with caution, considering the diversity of clinical populations and the limitations of the instruments used to generate the input data. Similar considerations apply to the methods of cluster analysis which group individuals on the basis of maximum shared characteristics.

Latent class analysis (LCA) assumes the existence of a finite number of mutually exclusive and jointly exhaustive groups of individuals. A latent class typology of schizophrenia, proposed by Sham *et al.* [37], using data on 447 patients with nonaffective psychoses, ended up with three subgroups: a 'neurodevelopmental' subtype resembling the hebephrenic form of the disorder (poor premorbid adjustment, early onset, prominent negative and disorganised features); a 'paranoid' subtype (less severe, better outcome); and a 'schizoaffective' subtype (dysphoric symptoms). In an epidemiological sample of 343 cases of schizophrenia and affective disorders, Kendler *et al.* [38] identified six latent classes, broadly corresponding to the clinical forms of 'Kraepelinian' schizophrenia: major depression, schizophreniform disorder; schizoaffective disorder (manic), schizoaffective disorder (depressed) and hebephrenia. Similar results, using a combination of principal component analysis and LCA in a sample of 387 patients with psychoses have been reported by Murray *et al.* [39].

In contrast to conventional LCA, a form of latent structure analysis, known as grade of membership (GoM), allows individuals to be members of more than one disease class and represents the latent groups as 'fuzzy sets' [40,41]. The GoM model simultaneously extracts from the data matrix a number of latent 'pure types' and assigns to each individual a set of numerical weights quantifying the degree to which that individual resembles each one of the identified pure types. When applied to the symptom profiles of 1065 cases in the WHO International Pilot Study of Schizophrenia [42], the method identified eight pure types of which five were related to schizophrenia, two to affective disorders and one to patients in remission, all showing significant associations with course and outcome variables used as external validators.

SCHIZOPHRENIA IN ICD-10 AND DSM-IV

While both DSM-IV and ICD-10 are widely regarded as authoritative documents providing evidence-based definitions and diagnoses of mental disorders, they have

evolved in different contexts and address partially overlapping but different con-
stituencies [43].

Origins of the two classifications

The International Classification of Diseases (ICD), of which Chapter 5, Mental and
Behavioural Disorders is a part, is a statutory responsibility of the World Health
Organisation (WHO) as an intergovernmental agency that aims to provide a common language for the reporting of all known diseases and health states across
the world's populations. The DSM is essentially a national diagnostic classification of mental disorders, developed by a non-governmental professional body, the
American Psychiatric Association (APA), and widely adopted by US government
agencies, such as the Food and Drugs Administration and the Social Security Administration, as well as by the health insurance industry and the American legal
system. A major difference between the two classifications is that, in contrast to
DSM-IV, which provides a single set of 'operational' diagnostic criteria for all
potential users, ICD-10 was designed as a 'family' of inter-related versions, addressing different users. While the ICD-10 Clinical Descriptions and Diagnostic
Guidelines (ICD-10 CDDG) is the conceptual core of the system, the more restrictive Diagnostic Criteria for Research (ICD-10 DCR) are designed for use in a more
narrowly constrained context.

Both DSM-IV and ICD-10 are descendants of the Kraepelinian nosology

The basic concept underlying Kraepelin's classification of psychoses was the disease entity, postulating close relationships between clinical symptoms, the longitudinal course and outcome, and brain pathology. Notwithstanding decades of
clinical, neuroscience and genetic research, the validating criteria of the nosological
entity of schizophrenia remain to this day essentially restricted to the internal cohesion of the clinical picture and the regularities of course and outcome. There are both
similarities and differences in the way the two classifications define schizophrenia
(Tables 1.4 and 1.5). While ICD-10 explicitly acknowledges schizophrenia as a
group of disorders, the DSM-IV criteria implicitly suggest a unitary view of the
disorder. However, both sets of criteria refer to: (i) characteristic symptoms present
in the cross-section of the clinical picture, weighted differentially for diagnostic
significance ('at least one. . .' or 'two or more. . .'); (ii) the duration of symptoms
required for a reliable ascertainment; and (iii) the longitudinal pattern of course.
While both systems require persistence of 'active phase' diagnostic symptoms for
at least one month, ICD-10 lays greater emphasis on the presence of Schneiderian
first-rank symptoms. An important difference is the DSM-IV requirement of at

Table 1.4 ICD-10 / F2 group of disorders

Schizophrenia (F20): Diagnostic Criteria for Research
At least one...
(a) thought echo, insertion, withdrawal or broadcasting
(b) delusion of control, influence or passivity
(c) hallucinatory voices – running commentary or discussing the patient
(d) persistent delusions – culturally inappropriate and completely impossible

Or at least two...
(a) persistent hallucinations in any modality, when accompanied by delusions
(b) neologisms, breaks or interpolations in the train of thought, incoherence
(c) catatonic behaviour
(d) 'negative' symptoms: apathy, paucity of speech, emotional blunting or
   incongruity

...should be present for most of the time during an episode of psychotic illness
lasting for at least one month

Pattern of course (period of observation at least one year)
Continuous (no remission of psychotic symptoms)
Episodic with progressive deficit ('negative' symptoms in the intervals)
Episodic with stable deficit (persistent but non-progressive 'negative' symptoms)
Episodic remittent (complete remissions between psychotic episodes)
Incomplete remission
Complete remission
Other
Course uncertain, period of observation too short

Clinical subtypes
Paranoid
Hebephrenic
Catatonic
Undifferentiated
Post-schizophrenic depression
Residual
Simple
Other
Unspecified

Other F2 disorders
Schizotypal disorder (F21)
Persistent delusional disorders (F22)
Acute and transient psychotic disorders (F23)
Induced delusional disorder (F24)
Schizoaffective disorders (F25)
Other nonorganic psychotic disorders (F28)
Unspecified nonorganic psychosis (F29)

Table 1.5   DSM-IV-TR Schizophrenia and other psychotic disorders

A. Two (or more) *characteristic symptoms*, each present for a significant portion of
time during a one-month period (or less if successfully treated):
(1) delusions; (2) hallucinations; (3) disorganised speech (derailment or
incoherence); (4) grossly disorganised or catatonic behaviour; (5) negative
symptoms (affective flattening, alogia, or avolition). (*Only one symptom is
required if delusions are bizarre or hallucinations consist of a voice keeping up a
running commentary...or two or more voices conversing with each other*).
B. Social/occupational dysfunction
C. Duration: Continuous signs of the disturbance persist for at least six months,
including at least one month of active-phase symptoms and may include periods
of prodromal or residual symptoms. During prodromal or residual periods, the
signs of the disturbance may be manifested by only negative symptoms or two or
more *Criterion A* symptoms in an attenuated form (for example, odd beliefs,
unusual perceptual experiences).
D. Schizoaffective and mood disorder exclusion
E. Substance/general medical condition exclusion
F. Relationship to a pervasive developmental disorder: If there is a history of
Austistic Disorder or another pervasive developmental disorder, the additional
diagnosis of schizophrenia is made only if prominent delusions or hallucinations
are also present for at least a month.

Subtypes:
Paranoid (295.30)
Disorganised (295.10)
Catatonic (295.20)
Undifferentiated (295.90)
Residual (295.60)

Longitudinal course:
Episodic with interepisode residual symptoms (prominent negative symptoms may
be added)
Episodic with no interepisode residual symptoms
Continuous (prominent negative symptoms may be added)
Single episode in partial remission (prominent negative symptoms may be added)
Single episode in full remission
Other unspecified pattern

Other disorders within the same group:
Schizophreniform disorder (with / without good prognostic features) (295.40)
Schizoaffective disorder (bipolar or depressive type) (295.70)
Delusional disorder (297.1)
Brief psychotic disorder (with / without stressor, or with postpartum onset) (298.8)
Shared psychotic disorder (297.3)
Psychotic disorder due to a general medical condition (293.xx)
Substance-induced psychotic disorder (291xx or 292.xx)
Psychotic disorder not otherwise specified (298.9)

least six months duration of *any* disturbances (including prodromal and residual symptoms) for a confident diagnosis, relegating cases of shorter duration to a diagnosis of schizophreniform disorder that could be revised at a later stage. A period of four weeks is considered in ICD-10 to be sufficient to eliminate the majority of acute, non-schizophrenic psychotic episodes associated with substance use. Another difference between the two classifications is related to the DSM-IV Criterion B which requires the presence of significant social or occupational dysfunction as part of the definition of schizophrenia. In contrast, the explicit principle applying to all ICD-10 diagnoses is that social and occupational functioning is context-dependent and not an invariant attribute of the clinical syndrome. On the whole, it is assumed, though not empirically demonstrated, that the DSM-IV criteria of six months duration and social/occupational dysfunction tend to select cases of more severe or chronic illness than the ICD-10 criteria.

Importantly, DSM-IV and ICD-10 are not systematic classifications in the usual sense in which that term is applied in biology. Essentially, they are augmented *nomenclatures*, that is, lists of names for conditions and behaviours, supplied with explicit rules about how these names should be assigned and used. As such, they are useful tools of communication and can play a pragmatically useful role in psychiatric research, clinical management and teaching.

CRITERIA FOR ASSESSING THE DIAGNOSTIC CLASSIFICATION OF SCHIZOPHRENIA

Positive impact and unintended adverse effects

Four decades after the introduction of explicit diagnostic criteria and rule-based classifications such as DSM-III [26], ICD-10 [6] and DSM-IV [7], it is now possible to examine the impact of these tools on psychiatric practice and research. The worldwide adoption of these classification systems has influenced several domains of professional practice: (i) a standard frame of reference is now available to clinicians, enabling them to achieve better diagnostic agreement; (ii) more rigorous diagnostic standards have become the norm in psychiatric research; (iii) the teaching of psychiatry to medical students, trainee psychiatrists and other mental health workers is based on an international reference system which provides a 'common language'; (iv) open access to the criteria used by mental health professionals has improved communication with the users of services, carers, and the public at large. These achievements, however, have not been without a downside.

First, once a diagnostic concept like schizophrenia has been 'operationalised' for general use, it tends to become reified. Professionals and members of the general public too easily assume that it is an entity which explains the patient's symptoms and whose validity need not be questioned. The mere fact that a diagnostic concept is listed in an influential official nomenclature and provided with an operational definition tends to encourage this insidious reification.

Secondly, for most of the diagnostic rubrics of DSM-IV and ICD-10 (which clearly do not qualify as diseases), both classifications avoid discussing precisely what is being classified. DSM-IV explicitly rejects the 'misconception that a classification of mental disorders classifies people' and states that 'actually what are being classified are *disorders* that people have' [7]. The term 'disorder', first introduced in DSM-I in 1952, circumvents the problem that the information from which most of the diagnostic rubrics are constructed consists primarily of reported subjective experiences and patterns of behaviour. Some of those rubrics correspond to syndromes in the medical sense, but many appear to be isolated symptoms, habitual behaviours, or personality traits.

Thirdly, the fragmentation of psychopathology into a very large number of 'disorders' – of which many are merely symptoms – leads to a proliferation of comorbid diagnoses which clinicians are forced to use in order to describe their patients. This blurs the distinction between true comorbidity (co-occurrence of aetiologically independent disorders) and spurious comorbidity. masking complex but essentially unitary *syndromes*. It is not surprising, therefore, that recent epidemiological and clinical research leads to the conclusion that disorders, as defined in the current versions of DSM and ICD, have a strong tendency to co-occur, which suggests that 'fundamental assumptions of the dominant diagnostic schemata may be incorrect' [44].

Fourthly, while eminently useful for specific purposes of communication, the DSM-IV and ICD-10 criteria are no substitute for clinical acumen. The belief that 'operationalised' criteria have once and for all resolved the problem of reliability of psychiatric diagnosis may be illusory, if the validity of the assessment of symptoms and signs in actual clinical practice can be shown to be questionable. An unfortunate adverse effect of both classifications is the alienation of the practice of clinical psychiatry from its roots in psychopathology and phenomenology. To quote a perceptive commentator [45], 'since the publication of DSM-III in 1980, there has been a steady decline in the teaching of careful clinical evaluation that is targeted to the individual person's problems and social context and that is enriched by a good general knowledge of psychopathology... by 2005, the decline has become so severe that it could be referred to as 'the death of phenomenology in the United States.'

Clinical relevance and cognitive ease of use

The clinical relevance of a diagnostic concept refers to its scope (coverage), capacity to describe attributes of individuals (such as clinical severity of the disorder, impairments and disabilities), and its ease of application in the various settings in which people with mental health problems present for assessment or treatment.

In the instance of schizophrenia, the diagnostic system should be capable of not only identifying the broad syndrome but also differentiating between degrees and variants of its expression in individual patients and the severity of the associated impairments and disabilities. This implies that the DSM / ICD multiaxial models of diagnostic formulation should not be abandoned but rather further refined. By and large, a multiaxial arrangement allowing separate and independent assessment of psychopathological syndromes, personality characteristics, somatic morbidity, psychosocial precipitants or complicating factors, cognitive functioning and over-all impairment or disability, should be capable of 'individualising' the diagnostic assessment. However, the content of information to be recorded on individual axes will require substantial refinement. For example, the axes that are particularly prob-lematic in the present ICD and DSM multiaxial systems are those concerned with the level of cognitive functioning and personality.

As classifications are basically devices for reducing cognitive load, a diagnostic classification in psychiatry should also be examined from the point of view of its capacity to integrate diverse observations with a minimum number of assumptions, concepts and terms [46] and ease of evocation of its categories in clinical situations. The system should also allow the clinician to use the type of knowledge usually described as clinical experience or judgement, and enable appropriate decisions to be made under conditions of uncertainty, incomplete data, and time pressure.

Utility in research

Both DSM-III and its successors and, to a lesser extent, ICD-10, were quickly adopted by researchers as rigorous diagnostic standards. However, the performance of a classification as a research tool needs to be evaluated against a number of different requirements that are not always compatible – for example, the type of diagnostic criteria needed for clinical trials or for biological research may not be suitable for epidemiological surveys.

The use of restrictive DSM-IV or ICD-10 definitions, rather than of broader clinical concepts, as sampling criteria in recruiting subjects for clinical or epidemi-ological research, carries the risk of systematic error due to a selective exclusion of segments of the syndrome. For example, the DSM-IV requirement of at least six months duration of symptoms plus the presence of social or occupational dysfunc-tion for a diagnosis of schizophrenia is likely to bias the selection of populations for biological, therapeutic, or epidemiological longitudinal studies. It would certainly make little sense to study the variation in course and outcome in a clinical popu-lation that had already been pre-selected for chronicity by applying the six-month duration criterion. Studies of the molecular genetics of psychoses, usually involving collaborative consortia of investigators and a considerable investment of resources, are predicated on the validity of DSM-IV criteria. However, so far no susceptibility genes have been definitively identified and few of the many reported linkage or association findings have been replicated [47]. In the absence of genes of major effect, the chances of detecting multiple genes of small or moderate effect depend critically on the availability of phenotypes mapping onto characteristic brain dysfunction or morphology. The 'disorders' of current symptom-based classifications may be masking substantial phenotypic variation in symptomatology and outcome which would hinder genetic analysis. In addition to a better syndromal definition at the clinical symptom and course level, future developments of diagnostic systems for research are likely to involve supplementing the clinical diagnosis with measures of brain morphology and quantitative traits such as cognitive or neurophysiological dysfunction. Such enriched syndromes or endophenotypes [48] may substantially increase the informativeness of patient samples for genetic and other biological research.

Reliability

Psychiatric research and communication among clinicians have long been impeded by the low reliability of diagnostic assessment and by the fact that key terms like schizophrenia were used in different ways in different countries, or even in different centres within a single country [49]. The situation has changed radically since the introduction of explicit or 'operational' diagnostic criteria in DSM-III [26] in 1980 and in the research version of ICD-10 [6] in 1993. DSM-III and its successors, as well as ICD-10, have undergone extensive field trials and their final versions have been shown to be highly reliable. It can be assumed that the diagnostic criteria of future classifications will be similarly field-tested to remove ambiguous elements in them, but it is unlikely that improving further the reliability of classification will remain a major goal – in contrast to issues of validity which now dominate the agenda. However, by and large, reliability imposes a ceiling on the evaluation of validity in the sense that validity would be extremely difficult to determine if the diagnostic category was unreliable [50].

Concepts of validity

If future versions of ICD and DSM are to be a significant improvement on their predecessors, it will be because the validity of the diagnostic concepts they incorporate has been enhanced. However, what exactly is meant by the validity of a diagnostic concept, or of a system of classification in psychiatry, is rarely discussed and few studies have addressed this question explicitly and directly. There is no simple measure of the validity of a diagnostic concept that is comparable to the established procedures for the assessment of reliability. Four types of validity are often mentioned in the discourse on psychiatric diagnosis – construct, content, concurrent and predictive – all of them being borrowed from psychometric theory where they apply to the validation of psychological tests. A diagnostic category which: (i) is based on a coherent, explicit set of defining features (construct validity); (ii) has empirical referents, such as verifiable observations for establishing its presence (content validity); (iii) can be corroborated by independent procedures such as biological or psychological tests (concurrent validity); and (iv) predicts future course of illness or treatment response (predictive validity) is more likely to be useful than a category failing to meet these criteria. Few diagnostic concepts in psychiatry meet at present these criteria, and many of them are of uncertain applicability outside the setting in which they were generated [50].

Despite these ambiguities, a number of *procedures* have been proposed to enhance the validity of psychiatric diagnoses in the absence of a simple single measure. Robins and Guze [51] outlined a 'validation' programme with five components: (i) clinical description (symptomatology, demography and typical precipitants); (ii) laboratory studies (psychological tests, radiology and post mortem findings); (iii) delimitation from other disorders (by means of exclusion criteria); (iv) follow-up studies (including evidence of stability of diagnosis); and (v) family studies. Subsequently, Kendler [52] proposed to distinguish between antecedent validators (familial aggregation, premorbid personality, precipitating factors); concurrent validators (for example, psychological tests); and predictive validators (diagnostic consistency over time, rates of relapse and recovery, response to treatment). More recently, Andreasen [53] proposed 'a second structural program for validating psychiatric diagnosis' which includes additional validators such as molecular genetics and molecular biology, neurochemistry, neuroanatomy, neurophysiology and cognitive neuroscience.

The weakness of these procedural criteria is that they implicitly assume that psychiatric disorders are distinct entities, and that the role of the validating criteria and procedures is to determine whether a putative disorder is a valid entity in its own right or a variant of some other entity. The possibility that disorders might merge into one another with no valid boundary in between – what Sneath [54] called a 'point of rarity' – is rarely considered. In fact, several DSM/ICD disorders, such as bipolar affective disorder and depression, cluster non-randomly among the relatives of individuals with schizophrenia. Findings like these have given rise to the concepts of 'schizophrenia spectrum' and 'affective spectrum' disorders. It will not be surprising if such findings of overlapping genetic predisposition to seemingly unrelated disorders become the rule rather than the exception. It is equally likely that the same environmental factors contribute to the genesis of several different syndromes [55].

Predictive validity: course and outcome

Studies conducted over many decades consistently demonstrate that schizophrenia presents a spectrum of outcomes and course patterns, ranging from nearly complete recovery after acute episodes of psychosis to continuous, unremitting illness leading to deterioration of cognitive performance and social functioning [56]. Between these extremes, a substantial proportion of patients show an episodic course with psychotic relapses and partial remissions during which affective and cognitive impairments become increasingly conspicuous and may progress to gross deficits. Although no less than one-third of all patients with schizophrenia have relatively benign outcomes, in the majority the illness still has a profound, lifelong impact on personal growth and development. The initial symptoms of the disorder are not strongly predictive of the pattern of course but the mode of onset (acute or insidious), the duration of illness prior to diagnosis and treatment, the presence or absence of substance use, as well as background variables such as premorbid adjustment, educational and occupational achievement, and availability of a supportive social network allow a reasonable accuracy of prediction in the short- to medium term (two to five years).

Longitudinal studies suggest that the characteristic symptoms of schizophrenia tend to 'breed true', that is, only a minority of patients are eventually reclassified into other disease categories because of a significant and lasting change in the predominant symptoms. Schneiderian 'first-rank' symptoms at first presentation, such as thought broadcast or insertion, passivity ('replacement of will') experiences and hallucinatory third-person 'voices' [24], which are given special diagnostic weight in both ICD-10 and DSM-IV, exhibited in the WHO 10-country study [1] a strong tendency to recur during subsequent psychotic episodes, but were not associated with a poorer outcome as compared to patients with no first-rank symptoms on initial examination.

The evidence that each of the 'classic' subtypes of schizophrenia is associated with a characteristic pattern of course is generally weak but surprisingly good for some of the subtypes. Consistent differences have been reported between paranoid, hebephrenic and undifferentiated schizophrenia (diagnosed according to DSM-III) on a long-term follow-up of 19 years [57]. Paranoid schizophrenia tended to have a remittent course, and to be associated with less disability, in contrast to hebephrenia which had an insidious onset and poor long-term prognosis. Undifferentiated schizophrenia occupied an intermediate position. In the WHO International Pilot Study of Schizophrenia [58], four alternative groupings of the ICD-9 subtypes were examined for differences with regard to several course and outcome measures. Clear discrimination was achieved between simple and hebephrenic schizophrenia grouped together, on the one hand, and the schizoaffective subtype on the other.

The course and outcome data on schizoaffective disorders seem to support their placement within the broad category of schizophrenia. A retrospective and prospective study of 150 schizoaffective patients and 95 bipolar affective patients [59] established general similarities between the two groups but the schizoaffective cases were less likely to achieve a full remission and more likely to develop a residual state. An intermediate outcome between that of schizophrenia and bipolar affective disorder is a common finding in schizoaffective disorders.

The current focus on early detection and treatment of first episodes of psychosis is supported by evidence suggesting that the course and outcome of the earliest stages of a schizophrenic illness may have a pathoplastic effect on its subsequent course. Specifically, the duration of untreated psychosis, (DUP) has been shown to correlate with prolonged time to remission and poor treatment response. [60,61].

What determines the long-term outcome of schizophrenic illnesses is far from clear but the stereotype view of the disorder as invariably progressive and leading to profound deterioration does not accord well with the evidence. In a significant proportion of cases, the disorder exhibits the features of a shift-like process with acute exacerbations and remissions which may progress to severe deterioration or come to a standstill at any stage. Whether a single underlying pathophysiology can explain the variety of clinical outcomes, or several different pathological processes are at work, remains obscure. It has been suggested that the longitudinal course of schizophrenia should be seen as an open-ended, dynamic life process with multiple, interacting biological and psychosocial determinants. Such issues cannot be resolved by clinical follow-up studies alone, and require a strong involvement of neurobiological research in prospective investigations of representative samples of cases spanning the entire spectrum of course and outcomes.

Criterion validity: genetics

The rapid advances in molecular genetics and genomics have given rise to expectations that genetic research will provide robust biological criteria for the validation (or refutation) of the current nosology of schizophrenia and its boundaries relative to other psychotic disorders. While this hope may ultimately come true, the present evidence is neither unequivocal nor consistent. In the light of recent findings, the genetic architecture of schizophrenia now appears to be far more complex than previously thought. In addition to the likely genetic heterogeneity of schizophrenia and other psychiatric disorders across and within populations, it appears possible that 'current nosology, now embodied in DSM-IV, although useful for other purposes, does not define phenotypes for genetic study' [62]. Most of the 'first generation' genetic linkage studies were predicated on the assumption that schizophrenia and bipolar disorder are 'natural' disease entities with distinct aetiology and pathogenesis, and that current diagnostic criteria, all the way from RDC and DSM-III to DSM-IV and ICD-10, identify 'real', biologically anchored phenotypes suitable for genetic analysis [63]. This assumption has failed to find unequivocal support from family, twin and population-based studies which often produce inconsistent or contradictory results [47]. On the one hand, a number of studies support the view that schizophrenia and bipolar disorder tend to 'breed true' in families and populations. In a large population-based sample from the Danish Psychiatric Register, most of the risk factors aggregating in families and previously reported to be associated with schizophrenia, were not found to be associated with bipolar affective disorder, which supports at least a partial aetiological separation of the two disorders [64]. On the other hand, another population-wide study [65] linking a large number of Swedish pedigrees reported overlapping heritabilities and recurrent risks for schizophrenia and bipolar disorder, suggesting that the two disorders, at least in part, share common genetic causes.

The existence of a shared genetic susceptibility between schizophrenia and bipolar disorder has been further supported by results from 'second generation' genome-wide linkage and association studies. One of those studies [65] demonstrated that two candidate genes which had previously been implicated in schizophrenia, *DISC1* and *COMT,* map to regions on chromosomes 1q42 and 22q11 which were found to be significantly linked to both schizophrenia and bipolar disorder, suggesting that they may predispose to psychotic illness across the nosological schizophrenia-bipolar border. Similar findings of shared, trans-nosological effects have been reported for a number of other candidate genes, including *NRG1, DTNBP1, GRM4* and *G30/G72* [66]. Such findings have led to a proposal of a genetic susceptibility continuum spanning across schizophrenia and bipolar disorder and including, at its two extreme ends, unique genetic factors associated with each disorder and a middle zone of overlap, occupied by schizoaffective disorder and containing shared genetic factors [67]. This model was suggested as an alternative to the traditional nosology of the psychoses, replacing the 'Kraepelinian dichotomy'. However, it is extremely doubtful that the present state of knowledge about the genetic basis of schizophrenia and related disorders could provide a definitive evidence base for a meaningful revision of the classification of psychotic disorders.

First, the presence of shared genetic factors across complex disorders is neither a new discovery, nor is it limited to the schizophrenia – bipolar dichotomy. It is well known, for instance, that ischaemic heart disease and cerebrovascular disease share many risk factors and multiple susceptibility genes; yet such commonality has not led to their amalgamation into a single disease or a continuum because of the existence of specific differences in clinical symptoms, pathology, pathophysiology, and treatment. Complex disorders, such as schizophrenia, are likely to involve a very large number of genes operating in multiple functional networks, as well as significant interactions with the environment, including epigeneic effects [68]. This makes it extremely unlikely that a conceptually sound and practically useful classification of psychotic illnesses could be based solely on current genetic data.

Secondly, and more importantly, a real understanding of the genetic architecture of schizophrenia is at present simply lacking. It is important to realise that there are no simple linear relationships between specific genes and clinical, behavioural or cognitive outcomes. Genes do not specify particular symptoms or cognitive processes – they code for regulatory factors, signalling molecules, receptors and enzymes, which interact within complex networks, modulated by environmental influences. The concepts and technologies of molecular genetic and genomic research are evolving rapidly and, correspondingly, the views of the nature of the genetics underlying this group of disorders are likely to change dramatically in the next decade, that is, long before the expiry of the useful shelf life of both DSM-V and ICD-11. Recent evidence supports a likely aetiological role for copy number variation (CNV), which includes rare, highly penetrant mutations in multiple genes, as well as a role for gene networks shared among schizophrenia, autism and certain forms of mental retardation [69]. Together with the prospect of cost-effective sequencing of entire individual genomes, these developments signal the emergence of a 'third generation' of genetic studies which are likely to have far-reaching implications for the future classification of psychotic disorders – especially if genomics is successfully linked with neural circuit analysis [70].

Aspects of culture

Current classifications tend to obscure the complex relationships between culture and mental disorder. Although both ICD-10 and DSM-IV acknowledge the existence of cultural variation in psychopathology, they essentially regard culture as a pathoplastic influence that distorts or otherwise modifies the presentation of the 'disorders' defined in the classification. Both systems ignore the existence of 'indigenous' languages in mental health [43] and this limits the relevance and value of the classification in many cultural settings. Although the essential syndromal structure of schizophrenia is discernible in quite varied cultural contexts [1,71], there are many instances of its difficult diagnostic differentiation from the so-called culture-bound syndromes or the variations in the expression of acute reactive psychoses in traditional societies and indigenous populations [72].

Reducing stigma

Countering the socially harmful negative stereotypes associated with the concept of schizophrenia should be an important objective of diagnostic classifications. The theory and practice of psychiatric diagnosis and classification cannot be divorced from their social context [73]. In the past this has rarely been a primary consideration in the development of classifications but there are good reasons to include 'stigma avoidance' among the criteria on which the merits of psychiatric classifications and nomenclatures should be assessed. The risk of misuse of diagnostic categories and classifications for political or economic purposes is not buried with the past. Misinterpretations of advances in neuroimaging and genetics in the form of simplistic determinism may again make psychiatry vulnerable to political ideologies, market forces and various forms of abuse. Concepts concerning the nature and classification of psychiatric illness and specifically schizophrenia will always attract ideological and political attention that can translate into laws or policies that may have unforeseen consequences for the human rights of patients suffering from the disorder.

REVISION OF THE CLASSIFICATIONS: PROSPECTS FOR SCHIZOPHRENIA

One classification or many?

For the last thirty years there have been two widely used classifications of mental disorders, the World Health Organisation's ICD and the American Psychiatric Association's DSM. Fundamentally, the two are similar, though there are some important conceptual differences, as well as differences in the definitions and diagnostic criteria for individual disorders. For a variety of reasons both classifications will continue to produce new editions or revisions and in some respects to compete with one another. It is, of course, uncomfortable to have two rival classifications, particularly as many of the differences between them are minor or accidental. On the other hand, the existence of two parallel classifications and diagnostic criteria does help to emphasise that most of the concepts of psychiatric disorders are still provisional and their definitions arbitrary. It is likely that the minor differences between the classifications will be reduced in future revisions, but where conceptual differences are involved, they should be explicated to stimulate research testing the advantages and disadvantages of the alternative concepts or definitions. Individual research groups may well produce novel concepts and definitions for specific purposes and should not be discouraged from doing so. Innovation is essential to progress and sooner or later radical changes are going to be needed [50].

CRITICAL ISSUES IN THE REVISION PROCESS

Disease or a broad syndrome?

Psychopathological syndromes are dynamic patterns of intercorrelated symptoms and signs that have a characteristic evolution over time. Although the range and number of aetiological factors that may give rise to psychiatric disorders is very wide, the range of psychopathological syndromes is limited. The syndromes of schizophrenia – paranoid, hebephrenic, schizoaffective, catatonic – to mention just a few – occur with impressive regularity in different individuals and settings, although in each case their presentation is imprinted by personality and cultural differences. Since a variety of aetiological factors may produce the same syndrome (heterogeneity) and conversely, a single aetiological factor may give rise to a spectrum of different syndromes (pleiotropy), the relationship between aetiology and clinical syndrome is an indirect one. In contrast, the relationship between the syndrome and the underlying pathophysiology, or specific brain dysfunction, is likely to be much closer. In the complex psychiatric disorders, where aetiology is multifactorial, future research into specific pathophysiological mechanisms could be considerably facilitated by a sharper delineation of the syndromal status of many current diagnostic categories. In addition to their clinical utility, syndromes can also serve as a gateway to elucidating the pathogenesis of psychiatric disorders. This provides a strong rationale for reinstating the concept of the *syndrome* as the basic Axis I unit of future versions of psychiatric classifications.

'Deconstructing' schizophrenia: categories or dimensions?

Psychiatric classifications, such as DSM-IV and ICD-10, are eclectic in the sense that they are organised along several different classes of criteria (symptoms, behaviours or traits, age at onset, course and, occasionally, causes) without a clear-cut hierarchical arrangement among them. There are many different ways in which current classifications can be revised and modified, but one of the fundamental choices to be made is that between a categorical and a dimensional arrangement. It is worth recalling that, although most sciences start with a categorical classification of their subject matter, they often replace this with dimensions as more accurate measurement becomes possible [74].

Whether psychotic disorders can be better described dimensionally or categorically remains an open, researchable question [75]. The difficulties with dimensional models stem from their novelty; lack of agreement on the number and nature of the dimensions required to account adequately for clinically relevant variation; the absence of an established, empirically grounded metric for evaluating severity or change; and, perhaps most importantly, the complexity and cumbersomeness of dimensional models in everyday clinical practice.

These considerations seem to preclude, at least for the time being, a radical restructuring of psychiatric classification from a predominantly categorical to a predominantly dimensional model. However, if psychiatric classification ought to be eclectic and pragmatic, such restructuring may not be necessary or even desirable. Moreover, categorical and dimensional models need not be mutually exclusive, as demonstrated by so-called mixed or class-quantitative models [76] which combine qualitative categories with quantitative trait measurements. For example, there is increasing empirical evidence that should make it attractive to supplement a retained and refined categorical clinical description of the syndrome of schizophrenia with selected quantitative traits such as attention or memory dysfunction and volumetric deviance of cerebral structures.

Endophenotypes

Endophenotypes (intermediate, elementary, alternative, or correlated phenotypes) offer a novel approach to reducing the complexity and heterogeneity of schizophrenia that could provide either an alternative or a complement to symptom-based phenotypes. As 'measurable components unseen by the unaided eye along the pathway between disease and distal genotype' [77], endophenotypes must meet criteria of being: (i) associated with the clinical disorder but not necessarily part of its diagnosis; (ii) heritable; (iii) state-independent (that is, present before the onset of active illness or during remissions); (iv) cosegregating with illness in families; and (v) found in unaffected family members at a higher rate than in the general population.

'Candidate' endophenotypes in schizophrenia research may include: (i) neurophysiological markers (for example, the P50 sensory gating potential, the P300 wave, antisaccade error rate, prepulse inhibition of the startle reflex); (ii) neuroimaging markers (for example, fronto-thalamic-cerebellar grey matter deficit, frontal hypoactivation in response to cognitive tasks); and (iii) cognitive markers (for example, continuous performance tasks, verbal memory deficit, prefrontal executive/working memory, spatial working memory). At present, the balance of the evidence suggests that cognitive dysfunction meets most of the criteria of an endophenotype in schizophrenia. This conclusion is underscored by the meta-analysis by Heinrichs and Zakzanis [78] of 204 studies published between 1980 and 1994 (a total of 7,420 schizophrenia patients and 5,865 controls), in which effect sizes (Cohen's d) and the U statistic (degree of non-overlap) were calculated for 22 neurocognitive test variables ranging from IQ, verbal memory and attention to executive function and language. Neurocognitive deficit was found to be a reliable and well replicated finding in schizophrenia. The dissection of the schizophrenia syndrome into modular endophenotypes with specific neurocognitive or neurophysiological underpinnings is beginning to be perceived as a promising approach in schizophrenia genetics. The study of endophenotypes cutting across the conventional diagnostic boundaries may reveal unexpected patterns of associations with symptoms, personality traits, or behaviour which may in the future substantially recast the psychiatric nosology [63].

The concept of utility

Most contemporary psychiatric disorders, even those like schizophrenia with a pedigree stretching back to the nineteenth century, cannot yet be described as valid disease categories. This does not mean, though, that they are not valuable concepts, and it is crucial to maintain a clear distinction between validity and utility. Kendell and Jablensky [50] proposed that a diagnostic rubric may be said to possess utility if it can be shown to provide non-trivial information about prognosis and likely treatment outcomes, and/or testable propositions about biological and social correlates. The term utility was first used in the sense proposed by Meehl (79) who wrote that 'the fundamental argument for the utility of formal diagnosis ... amounts to the same kind of thing one would say in defending formal diagnosis in organic medicine. One holds that there is a sufficient amount of aetiological and prognostic homogeneity among patients belonging to a given diagnostic group so that the assignment of a patient to this group has probability implications which it is clinically unsound to ignore'.

Many, though not all, of the diagnostic concepts represented by the categories of disorder listed in contemporary nomenclatures like DSM-IV and ICD10 are extremely useful to practicing clinicians, and most clinicians would be hard put to cope without them. Diagnostic categories provide invaluable information about the likelihood of future recovery, relapse, deterioration and social handicap; they are often essential for decisions about treatment; and they provide a wealth of information about similar patients encountered in clinical populations or community surveys throughout the world – their frequency and demographic characteristics, their family backgrounds and pre-morbid personalities, their symptomatology and its evolution over time; the results of clinical trials of several alternative therapies; and research into the aetiology of the syndrome. This is all useful and sometimes invaluable information whether or not the category in question is valid. How useful it is depends mainly on two things: the quantity and quality of the information available in the literature, which will depend on how long the category has been recognised and provided with adequate diagnostic criteria, and how much competent research it has generated; and how different the implications of that information, particularly about aetiology, prognosis and treatment, are from the implications of analogous information about other related syndromes. The DSM-IV definition of schizophrenia, for example, is particularly useful for predicting outcome, largely because some degree of chronicity is in-built. But a much broader definition, embracing a heterogeneous 'schizophrenia spectrum', may be more useful for defining a syndrome with high heritability [50].

CONCLUSION

It is important to maintain awareness of the fact that most of psychiatry's disease concepts are merely working hypotheses and their diagnostic criteria provisional. The protagonist of modern psychiatric nosology Emil Kraepelin wrote, late in his career, that 'it is now necessary to turn away from arranging illnesses in orderly, well defined groups and to set ourselves instead the undoubtedly higher and more satisfying goal of understanding their essential structure' [14].

Nine decades later, both the arrangement of psychiatric disorders and the understanding of their essential structure is an unending quest, despite spectacular advances in neuroscience, genetics and therapeutics. The basic construct underlying current psychiatric classifications remains that of nosological entity, retained in modern psychiatry more or less in the form in which it was first formulated by Kahlbaum (1874) and elaborated by Kraepelin, postulating correspondences between clinical symptoms, course, brain pathology and aetiology as criteria defining a 'natural disease entity'. In actual practice, the validating criteria remained restricted to the cohesion of the clinical picture and disease outcome as a proxy for brain pathology.

Today, both DSM-IV and ICD-10 are essentially classifications of diagnostic concepts, and not of 'natural kinds', such as people or diseases. Despite historical and recent assumptions to the contrary, there is little evidence that most currently recognised mental disorders are separated by natural boundaries. Diagnostic categories defined by their syndromes should be regarded as valid only if they have been shown to be discrete entities with natural boundaries separating them from other disorders. Most diagnostic concepts in psychiatry have not been shown to be valid in this sense, though many possess utility by virtue of the information about outcome, treatment response and aetiology which they convey. Researchers are increasingly assuming that variation in symptomatology is continuous and therefore questioning the validity of contemporary classifications. Although the evidence is far from being consistent or definitive, there is a growing understanding that the broad syndromal spectrum of schizophrenia, a complex disorder comprising multimodal cortical abnormalities and cognitive dysfunctions with or without frank psychotic manifestations, is the end-point phenotype for heterogeneous gene networks, pathophysiological pathways and environmental modifiers.

Recent proposals to deal with biological heterogeneity by linking genomics with neural circuitry analyses that may cut across conventional disease categories [70] resonate – surprisingly – with Kraepelin's late views on pre-existing response templates of the human brain and 'registers' of continuous variation replacing the 'natural disease entity' concept.

REFERENCES

1. Jablensky A, Sartorius N, Ernberg G et al. (1992) Schizophrenia: manifestations, incidence and course in different cultures. *Psychological Medicine* (Monograph Suppl 20) 1–97.
2. Jablensky A (2000) Epidemiology of schizophrenia: the global burden of disease and disability. *Eur Arch Psychiatry Clin Neurosci* **250**, 274–285.
3. Lichtenstein P, Björk C, Hultman CM et al. (2006) Recurrence risks for schizophrenia in a Swedish National Cohort. *Psychological Medicine* **36**, 1417–1425.
4. Nixon NL, Doody GA (2005) Official psychiatric morbidity and the incidence of schizophrenia 1881–1994. *Psychological Medicine* **35**, 1145–1153.
5. The WHO World Mental Health Survey Consortium. (2010) Prevalence, severity, and unmet need for treatment of mental disorders in the World Health Organization World Mental Health Surveys. *JAMA* **291**, 2581–2590.
6. World Health Organization (1993) *The ICD-10 Classification of Mental and Behavioural Disorders*. Diagnostic Criteria for Research. World Health Organization, Geneva.
7. American Psychiatric Association (1994) *Diagnostic and Statistical Manual of Mental Disorders*, 4th edition. American Psychiatric Association, Washington DC.

8. Morel BA (1860) *Traité des maladies mentales*. (Treatise on mental diseases), Masson, Paris.

9. Clouston TS (1904) *Clinical Lectures on Mental Diseases*, 6th edition. J&A Churchill, London.1904.

10. Kahlbaum KL (1863) Die Gruppierung der psychischen Krankheiten und die Einteilung der Seelenstörungen (The Grouping of Psychiatric Diseases and the Classification of Mental Disturbances). Kafemann, Danzig.

11. Hecker E (1871) Die Hebephrenie: ein Beitrag zur klinischen Psychiatrie. (Hebephrenia: a contribution to clinical psychiatry). Archiv für pathologische Anatomie und für klinische Medizin **52**, 394–429.

12. Kraepelin E (1899) Psychiatrie. Ein Lehrbuch für Studiernede und Aerzte. 6. Auflage. Barth, Leipzig 1899. English translation by H. Metoui and S. Ayed: Psychiatry, A Textbook for Students and Physicians, 6th edition (1990). Volumes 1 and 2. Science History Publications, Canton MA, 1990.

13. Kraepelin E (1909) Psychiatrie. 8 Auflage. Barth: Leipzig 1909. Reprinted English translation: Dementia praecox and paraphrenia. Krieger Publishing: Huntington, New York, 1971.

14. Kraepelin E (1920) Die Erscheinungsformen des Irreseins. *Zeitschrift für die gesammte Neurologie und Psychiatrie* 62,1-29. English translation by H. Marshall: Patterns of mental disorder. In SR Hirsch & M Shepherd (eds.) *Themes and Variations in European Psychiatry: An Anthology* (1974). John Wright & Sons, Bristol, pp. 7–30.

15. Bleuler E (1920) Lehrbuch der Psychiatrie. Springer Verlag, Berlin. English translation: *Textbook of Psychiatry*. Arno Press: New York.

16. Leonhard K (1999) *Classification of Endogenous Psychoses and Their Differential Etiology*, 2nd edition. Springer, Vienna and New York (1976).

17. Pull CB, Pull MC, Pichot P, Licet S (1981) Une liste intégrée de critères d'evaluation taxonomique pour les psychoses nonaffectives. *Journal de Psychiatrie Biologique et Thérapeutique* **1**, 27–33.

18. Kasanin J (1933) The acute schizoaffective psychosis. *Am J Psychiatry* **90**: 97–126.

19. Langfeld G (1956) The prognosis of schizophrenia. *Acta Psychiatr Neurol Scand* Suppl*110)*. Munksgaard, Copenhagen.

20. Stephens JH, Astrup C (1963) Prognosis in "process" and "non-process" schizophrenia. *Am J Psychiatry* **119**, 945–953.

21. Tsuang MT, Winokur G (1974) Criteria for subtyping schizophrenia. *Arch Gen Psychiatry* **31**: 43–47.

22. Crow T (1985) The two-syndrome concept: origin and current status. *Schizophr Bull* **11**, 471–486.

23. Carpenter WT, Heinrichs DW, Wagman AMI (1988) Deficit and non-deficit forms of schizophrenia: the concept. *Am J Psychiatry* **145**, 578–583.

24. Schneider K (1950) *Klinische Psychopathologie*, 8th edition. Thieme, Stuttgart. English translation by Hamilton MW & Anderson EW *Clinical Psychopathology*. Grune and Stratton, New York (1959).

25. Spitzer RL, Endicott J, Robins E (1978) Research diagnostic criteria. Rationale and reliability. *Arch Gen Psychiatry* **35**, 773–782.

26. American Psychiatric Association (1980) *Diagnostic and Statistical Manual of Mental Disorders*, 3rd edition. American Psychiatric Association, Washington DC.

27. Rado S (1960). Theory and therapy: the theory of schizotypal organization and its application to treatment of decompensated schizotypal behavior. In Scher SC, Davis HR, eds. *The Outpatient Treatment of Schizophrenia*. Grune & Stratton, New York.

28. Meehl PE (1962) Schizotaxia, schizotypy, schizophrenia. *American Psychologist* **17**, 827–838.

29. Chapman LJ, Chapman JP (1980) Scales for rating psychotic and psychotic-like experiences as continua. *Schizophr Bull* **6**, 476–489.

30. Kendler KS, Neale MC, Walsh D (1995) Evaluating the spectrum concept of schizophrenia in the Roscommon Family Study. *Am J Psychiatry* **152**, 749–754.

31. Liddle PF (1987) The symptoms of chronic schizophrenia. A re-examination of the positive-negative dichotomy. *Br J Psychiatry* **151**, 145–151.

32. Johnstone EC, Frith CD (1996) Validation of three dimensions of schizophrenic symptoms in a large unselected sample of patients. *Psychological Medicine* **26**, 669–679.

33. Smith DA, Mar CM, Turoff BK (1998) The structure of schizophrenic symptoms: a meta-analytic confirmatory factor analysis. *Schizophr Res* **31**, 57–70.

34. Arndt S, Andreasen NC, Flaum M, Miller D, Nopoulos P (1995) A longitudinal study of symptom dimensions in schizophrenia. Prediction and patterns of change. *Arch Gen Psychiatry* **52**, 352–360.

35. McGrath JA, Nestadt G, Liang KY *et al.* (2004) Five latent factors underlying schizophrenia: analysis and relationship to illnesses in relatives. *Schizophr Bull* **30**, 855–873.

36. Cuesta MJ, Peralta V (2001) Integrating psychopathological dimensions in functional psychoses: a hierarchical approach. *Schizophr Res* **52**, 215–229.

37. Sham PC, Castle DJ, Wessely S, Farmer AE, Murray RM (1996) Further exploration of a latent class typology of schizophrenia. *Schizophr Res* **20**, 105–115.

38. Kendler KS, Karkowski LM, Walsh D (1998) The structure of psychosis. Latent class analysis of probands from the Roscommon Family Study. *Arch Gen Psychiatry* **55**, 492–499.

39. Murray V, McKee I, Miller PM *et al.* (2005) Dimensions and classes of psychosis in a population cohort: a four-class, four-dimension model of schizophrenia and affective psychoses. *Psychol Med* **35**, 499–510.

40. Woodbury MA, Clive J, Garson A (1978) Mathematical typology: a Grade of Membership technique for obtaining disease definition. *Comput Biomed Res* **11**, 277–298.

41. Manton KG, Woodbury MA, Tolley DH (1994) *Statistical Applications Using Fuzzy Sets*. New York, John Wiley.

42. Manton KG, Korten A, Woodbury MA, Anker M, Jablensky A (1994) Symptom profiles of psychiatric disorders based on graded disease classes: an illustration using data from the WHO International Pilot Study of Schizophrenia. *Psychol Med* **24**, 133–144.

43. Jablensky A (2009) Towards ICD-11 and DSM-V: issues beyond 'harmonisation'. *British Journal of Psychiatry* **195**, 379–381.

44. Sullivan PF, Kendler KS (1998) Typology of common psychiatric syndromes. *British Journal of Psychiatry* **173**, 312–319.

45. Andreasen NC (2007) DSM and the death of phenomenology in America: an example of unintended consequences. *Schizophr Bull* **33**, 108–112.

46. Millon T (1991) Classification in psychopathology: rationale, alternatives, and standards. *J Abnorm Psychol* **100**, 245–261.
47. Sullivan PF (2005) The genetics of schizophrenia. *PLoS Medicine* **2**, 614–618.
48. Gottesman II, Gould TD (2003) The endophenotype concept in psychiatry: etymology and strategic intentions. *Am J Psychiatry* **160**, 636–645.
49. Stengel E (1959) Classification of mental disorders. *WHO Bulletin* **21**, 601–663.
50. Kendell R, Jablensky A (2003) Distinguishing between the validity ad utility of psychiatric diagnoses. *Am J Psychiatry* **160**, 4–12.
51. Robins E, Guze SB (1970) Establishment of diagnostic validity in psychiatric illness: its application to schizophrenia. *Am J Psychiatry* **126**, 983–987.
52. Kendler KS (1980) The nosologic validity of paranoia (simple delusional disorder). A review. *Arch Gen Psychiatry* **37**, 699–706.
53. Andreasen NC (1995) The validation of psychiatric diagnosis: new models and approaches. *Am J Psychiatry* **152**, 161–162.
54. Sneath PHA (1975) A vector model of disease for teaching and diagnosis. *Medical Hypotheses* **1**, 12–22.
55. Brown GW, Harris TO, Eales MJ (1996) Social factors and comorbidity of depressive and anxiety disorders. *British Journal of Psychiatry* **168** Suppl 30, 50–57.
56. Jablensky A (2009) Course and outcome of schizophrenia and their prediction. In Gelder MG, Andreasen NC, López-Ibor JJ & Geddes JR, eds. *New Oxford Textbook of Psychiatry*, 2nd edition. Volume **1**. Oxford University Press, Oxford, pp. 568–578.
57. Fenton WS, McGlashan TH (1991) Natural history of schizophrenia subtypes. I. Longitudinal study of paranoid, hebephrenic, and undifferentiated schizophrenia. *Arch Gen Psychiatry* **48**, 969–977.
58. World Health Organization (1979) *Schizophrenia. An international follow-up study*. Wiley, Chchester.
59. Angst J, Felder W, Lohmeyer B (1980) Course of schizoaffective psychoses: results of a follow-up study. *Schizophr Bull* **6**, 579–585.
60. Perkins D, Gu H, Boteva K *et al.* (2005) Relationship between duration of untreated psychosis and outcome in first-episode schizophrenia: a critical review and meta-analysis. *Am J Psychiatry* **162**, 1785–1804.
61. Marshall M, Lewis S, Lockwood A *et al.* (2005) Association between duration of untreated psychosis and outcome in cohorts of first-episode patients: a systematic review. *Arch Gen Psychiatry* **62**, 975–983.
62. Ginsburg BE, Werick TM, Escobar JL *et al.* (1996) Molecular genetics of the psychopathologies; a search for simple answers to complex problems. *Behav Genet* **26**, 325–333.
63. Jablensky A (2006) Subtyping schizophrenia: implications for genetic research. *Molecular Psychiatry* **11**, 815–836.
64. Mortensen PB, Pedersen CB, Melbye M *et al.* (2003) Individual and familial risk factors for bipolar affective disorders in Denmark. *Arch Gen Psychiatry* **60**, 1209–1215.
65. Lichtenstein P, Yip BH, Björk C *et al.* (2009) Common genetic determinants of schizophrenia and bipolar disorder in Swedish families: a population-based study. *The Lancet* **373**, 234–239.

66. Cradock N, O'Donovan MC, Owen MJ. (2006) Genes for schizophrenia and bipolar disorder? Implications for psychiatric nosology. *Schizophr Bull* **32**, 9–16.

67. Owen MJ, Craddock N, Jablensky A (2007) The genetic deconstruction of psychosis. *Schizophr Bull* **33**, 905–911.

68. Petronis A (2010) Epigenetics as a unifying principle in the aetiology of complex traits and diseases. *Nature* **465**, 721–727.

69. Rzhetsky A, Wajngurt D, Park N, Zheng T (2007) Probing genetic overlap among complex human phenotypes. *PNAS* **104**, 11694–11699.

70. Akil H, Brenner S, Kandel E *et al.* (2010) The future of psychiatric research: genomes and neural circuits. *Science* **327**, 1580–1581.

71. Jablensky A (1975) Culture and schizophrenia. *Psychological Medicine* **5**, 113–124.

72. Murphy HBM (1982) *Comparative Psychiatry*. Springer, Berlin, pp. 91–114.

73. Jablensky A (1999) The nature of psychiatric classification: issues beyond ICD-10 and DSM-IV. *Australian and New Zealand Journal of Psychiatry* **33**, 137–144.

74. Hempel CG (1961) Introduction to problems of taxonomy. In Zubin J, ed. *Field Studies in the Mental Disorders*. Grune & Stratton, New York, pp. 3–22.

75. Grayson DA (1987) Can categorical and dimensional views of psychiatric illness be distinguished? *British Journal of Psychiatry* **26**, 57–63.

76. De Boeck P, Wilson M, Scott Acton G (2005) A conceptual and psychometric framework for distinguishing categories and dimensions. *Psychological Review* **112**, 129–158.

77. Gottesman II, Gould TD (2003) The endophenotype concept in psychiatry: etymology and strategic intentions. *Am J Psychiatry* **160**, 636–645.

78. Heinrichs RW, Zakzanis KK (1998) Neurocognitive deficit in schizophrenia: a quantitative review of the evidence. *Neuropsychology* **12**, 426–445.

79. Meehl PE (1959) Psychodiagnosis. In *Selected Papers*. University of Minnesota Press, Minneapolis.

CHAPTER 2

Pathophysiology of schizophrenia

Peter Falkai and Andrea Schmitt

Department of Psychiatry and Psychotherapy University of Göttingen, von-Siebold-Str. 5, Göttingen, Germany.

Tyrone D. Cannon

Departments of Psychology and Psychiatry and Biobehavioral Sciences and Staglin Center for Cognitive Neuroscience, University of California, Los Angeles, 1285 Franz Hall, Los Angeles, CA, USA.

Information Box

- Neurotransmitter disturbances are postulated by the dopamine and glutamate hypothesis of schizophrenia
- Frontotemporal brain regions and dysfunctional neuronal networks are involved in the pathophysiology of the disease and related to symptom dimensions
- Neurodevelopmental disturbances and additional neurodegenerative processes in subgroups of patients are hypothesised to be underlying pathophysiological mechanisms
- Synaptic pathology, oligodendrocyte dysfunction and decreased neurogenesis may lead to a disconnection syndrome as a basis of symptoms and cognitive deficits

---

INTRODUCTION

Schizophrenia has a worldwide prevalence of 1% and mainly strikes young adults between the ages of 20 and 35. It is a severe psychiatric disorder leading to lifelong disability in more than 50% of the sufferers and therefore belongs to the ten most

---

Schizophrenia: Current Science and Clinical Practice, First Edition. Edited by Wolfgang Gaebel.
© 2011 John Wiley & Sons, Ltd. Published 2011 by John Wiley & Sons, Ltd.

costly illnesses worldwide [1]. The course of the disease is heterogeneous with approximately 50% of the patients requiring one or more readmissions during follow-up [2]. Only 20% of the patients will be able to reach full employment and only 30% to keep up a stable relationship [3].

Even if an early diagnosis of schizophrenia was favourable and helped initiate early intervention, reliable biological disease markers are still lacking and little is known about the pathophysiological basis of the disease. It has been hypothesised that the disorder originates from brain neurodevelopmental neuropathology with symptoms and neuropsychological deficits arising from alterations in described brain regions or functional neuronal circuits.

MAJOR FINDINGS AND RELATED PATHOPHYSIOLOGICAL HYPOTHESES

Symptom domains and neurotransmitter hypotheses

Symptoms of schizophrenia: classification of disturbed functional domains

Due to the heterogeneity of symptoms and the course of the disease, schizophrenia has been regarded as a syndrome. Thus, the classification of a defined phenotype which shares a common pathophysiology has been regarded as evident. Nevertheless, the definition of a clinical phenotype of the disorder is difficult due to the diversity of individual symptoms. Symptom dimensions actually reflect groups of symptoms that generally occur together and may explain a part of the phenotypic variation between patients [4,5,6,7,8]. First concepts to classify symptomatology stem from Kraepelin's original distinction between affective and non-affective psychoses with 'dementia praecox' [9].

In the last decades, symptom classifications have been calculated in four or five main domains. These include positive symptoms with exaggeration of normal function, such as hallucinations, delusions, disorganised speech, and disorganised behaviour. Thought disorganisation may be regarded as a separate dimension. The negative symptoms comprise a diminution of mental functions, such as affective blunting, avolition, alogia, anhedonia and a deficit in social interaction [10,11]. Beside affective symptoms (for example, depressive mood), another domain refers to cognitive symptoms in episodic and working memory as well as attention which possess special relevance for schizophrenia [12,13,14,15,16]. Interestingly, a correlation between working memory dysfunction, but not the general level of symptoms, and vocational functioning has recently been described [17,18].

Each patient has an individual mix of positive symptoms, affective symptoms, negative symptoms and cognitive deficits, while the relation between these factors changes over time depending on the disease stage. Schizophrenia is characterised by phases of acute illness where mainly positive symptoms prevail, followed by phases of remission of psychosis, in which negative symptoms are more prominent. In particular, persistent cognitive deficits are very reliable predictors for a relapse and therefore an unfavourable long-term outcome [19,20]. Further concepts of phenotypes include the appearance of neurological soft signs such as dysdiadochokinese or deficits in motor coordination [21,22,23] and eye tracking abnormalities with deficits in smooth pursuit eye movements [24,25]. Additionally, schizophrenia patients show deficits in sensory processing. Prepulse inhibition (PPI) of the acoustic startle response, which is disrupted in schizophrenia patients and restored by antipsychotics, mainly clozapine, serves as a reliable model of sensorimotor gating in vertebrates [26]. Each of these domains can be well measured clinically and by neuropsychological and neurophysiological tests and it is assumed that they are linked to specific pathophysiological cascades, genetic networks and/or disturbances in neurotransmitter systems.

Neurotransmitter hypotheses of schizophrenia

The dopamine hypothesis

Currently available therapeutic practices with antipsychotic medications are based on monoamines, the dopaminergic and serotonergic systems which mainly influence positive symptoms. Dopamine is involved in the control of locomotion, cognition, affect and neuroendocrine secretion [27] and its receptors can be categorised as D1- and D2-like receptors with D2-receptors possessing high affinity for the butyrophenone class of neuroleptics such as haloperidol [28]. The dopamine hypothesis of schizophrenia postulating a dopaminergic hyperactivity in the limbic circuitry is based on the evidence of typical neuroleptics with a D2-dopamine antagonism being effective in the treatment of positive symptoms [29] and on the fact that this antagonism is correlated with the clinical potency of these drugs [30]. Accordingly, dopamine enhancing drugs like amphetamine, which increase dopamine activity, generally worsen the positive symptoms of schizophrenia [31,32]. The initial Photon Emission Computed Tomography and Positron Emission Tomography (PET) studies showed that an amphetamine challenge increases the release of dopamine from the basal ganglia and that this release is exaggerated in patients with schizophrenia [33,34,35] (Table 2.1).

However, due to the large variation, dysfunction of dopamine might be restricted to a subgroup of patients. Furthermore, these patients underwent an acute episode of the disorder and used an amphetamine challenge. Laruelle *et al.* [36] showed a hyperdopaminergic state during the acute episode, but not in periods of remission. Despite these findings, documentation of abnormalities in the dopaminergic system of schizophrenia patients has revealed inconsistent results. Post-mortem studies measuring dopamine, its metabolites and receptors in brains of schizophrenia

Table 2.1 Summary of hypotheses of the pathophysiology of schizophrenia and findings from the literature

Hypotheses	Findings	Author(s)
Neurotransmitter hypotheses of schizophrenia		
The dopamine hypothesis (dopaminergic hyperactivity in the limbic circuitry)		
	Typical neuroleptics with a D2-dopamine antagonism effective in the treatment of positive symptoms	[29]
	Antagonism correlated with clinical potency of drugs	[30]
	Dopamine enhancing drugs like amphetamine generally worsen positive symptoms	[31,32]
	Amphetamine challenge increases the release of dopamine from the basal ganglia	[33,34,35]
Restrictions of the dopamine hypothesis		
	Hyperdopaminergic state during the acute episode, but not in periods of remission	[36]
	Post-mortem studies show no consistent alterations independent of D2 receptor upregulation by antipsychotic medication	[37]
	No appearance of negative and cognitive symptoms	[10]
The glutamate hypothesis (Hypofunction of the NMDA receptor and hypoglutamatergic state in projection neurons)		
	Antagonists of the glutamatergic NMDA receptor like phencyclidine or ketamine precipitate psychosis with positive symptoms and negative symptoms in healthy subjects and schizophrenia patients	[40,41]
	Schizophrenia risk genes like neuregulin-1, DAAO, G72 and dysbindin are responsible for hypofunction of NMDA receptor	[47,48,49]
Schizophrenia is a disturbance of neuronal networks		
Central role of frontotemporal regions in pathophysiology		
	Subtle, but robust volume deficits in medial temporal (hippocampus) and prefrontal	[52,53]
	Lesions of medial temporal lobe induce fear, aggression, anxiety, irritability, paranoid symptoms and hallucinations	[57,58]
	Volume loss in hippocampal subregions are related to positive symptoms	[58]

Table 2.1 Summary of hypotheses of the pathophysiology of schizophrenia and findings from the literature (*Continued*)

Hypotheses	Findings	Author(s)
	Prefrontal cortex critical for executive control of cognition, disturbed in schizophrenia patients leading to deficits in working memory, perception, attention, smooth pursuit eye movements and PPI	[75]
	Hypofrontality	[79,80]
Schizophrenia is a disconnection of neuronal networks		
	Decreased white matter anisotropy in schizophrenia key regions	[90]
	Disturbed functional integrity of brain systems underlying working memory, attention and sensory information processing	[105,106, 107,122]
	Dysfunction of the cortico-cerebellar-thalamic-cortical neuronal circuit leading to cognitive symptoms	[116,117]
Schizophrenia is a disturbance on the microscopic level		
	Parvalbumine-positive interneurons decreased	[136]
	No alteration of total neuronal numbers	[144,146, 148]
	Decrease oligodendrocyte numbers in the hippocampus and prefrontal cortex induce deficits in propagation of nerve impulses (macroconnectivity)	[144,159, 160]

Neurodevelopmental disturbances or neurodegenerative changes?
Schizophrenia is a neurodevelopmental disorder (abnormal perinatal brain development)

	Volume deficits at first episode	[178,179]
	Absence of classical neurodegenerative process with astrogliosis	[143,144]
	No progression of cognitive symptoms during a five and ten years follow-up period	[14,15]

In a subgroup of patients, an additional neurodegenerative process is evident

	Progression of volume deficits, e.g. ventricular volumes or grey matter deficits in a subgroup of patients during course of disease	[180,182]
	Progressive volume loss in patients with a worse clinical outcome of the disease and persisting symptoms	[183,184, 185,186, 191,192, 193,194, 195]

Table 2.1 Summary of hypotheses of the pathophysiology of schizophrenia and findings from the literature (*Continued*)

Hypotheses	Findings	Author(s)
	Grey matter reduction in prefrontal regions in prodromal patients who convert to psychosis compared with those who do not and first-episode patients	[196,197]
Schizophrenia is a synaptopathy		
	Increased neuronal density based on decreased volume of neuropil (dendrites and axons)	[155,156]
	Axon terminals and dendritic spines reduced	[201]
	Alterations in synaptic proteins	[210,216,220,221]
Schizophrenia is a disturbance of neurogenesis		
	Decreased cell proliferation in dentate gyrus	[223]

patients showed no consistent alterations which would allow them to be regarded independently of D2-like receptor upregulation of the antipsychotic medication [37]. Moreover, elevation of dopamine levels is related to positive symptoms [36], and negative or cognitive symptoms are not a prominent feature of this pharmacological model [38].

The glutamate hypothesis

The glutamate hypothesis of schizophrenia is based on the observation that phencyclidine and ketamine, which block the ion channel of the glutamatergic N-methyl-D-aspartate (NMDA) receptor and initiate NMDA hypofunction, precipitate psychosis. This psychosis not only models the positive symptoms of schizophrenia, but some patients even develop a chronic deteriorative psychosis which resembles the deficit state of schizophrenia [39,40]. In contrast to dopamine agonists, phencyclidine and ketamine induce positive and negative symptoms in both healthy subjects and schizophrenia patients [41,42] (Table 2.1). Thus, to date, the NMDA hypofunction pharmacologically models schizophrenia most reliantly. Additionally, the elevated dopamine level in the basal ganglia of schizophrenia patients may be the consequence of a glutamatergic deficit in cortico-striatal projection neurons [43,44,45] (Figures 2.1, 2.2).

Cortical NMDA receptor hypofunction on gamma-butyric acid (GABA)ergic interneurons induces reduced GABAergic inhibitory tone on glutamatergic pyramidal neurons. In the long-term, these neurons could be incrementally injured by an increased neurotransmission at non-NMDA ionotropic glutamatergic and cholinergic receptors resulting in a final hypoglutamatergic state of corticostriatal

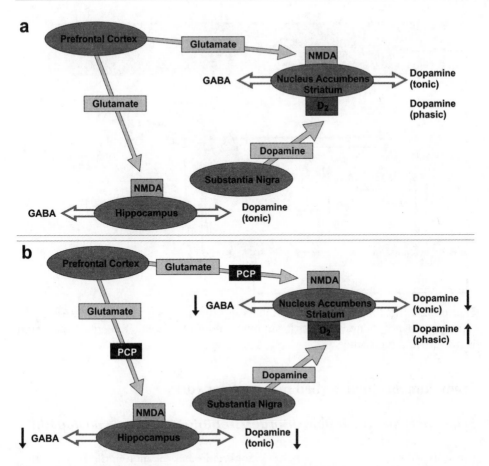

Figure 2.1 a) Glutamatergic, GABAergic and dopaminergic projections from cortical areas and substantia nigra to the nucleus accumbens and striatum as well as hippocampus. b) Effects of the NMDA receptor antagonist PCP in this network; decreased GABAergic innervations, decreased tonic dopamine and increased phasic dopamine release in the striatum.

projections [44,46]. Further evidence for the involvement of the NMDA receptor in the pathophysiology of schizophrenia evolves from recent genetic studies depicting the influence of risk genes of schizophrenia such as neuregulin-1, D-amino-acid oxidase (DAAO), G72, and dysbindin on NMDA receptor function [47]. For example, the neuregulin-β isoform of neuregulin-1 is known to induce the gene expression of the NR2C subunit of the NMDA receptor in cerebellar neurons [48], and a null mutation in the dysbindin gene produces reductions in paired-pulse facilitation, and evoked and miniature excitatory post-synaptic currents in cortical pyramidal cells, indicating a difference in the function of pre-synaptic glutamatergic terminals as well as elevated spike thresholds [49].

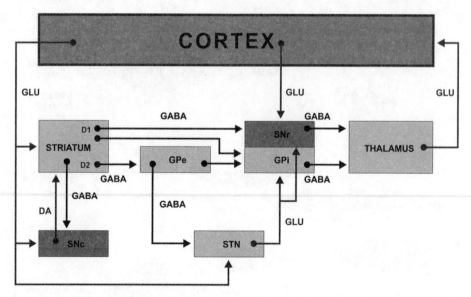

Figure 2.2   The thalamus receives projections from the basal ganglia. In case of a glutamatergic hypofunction, it loses its inhibitory control and glutamatergic stimulation is overflowing the cortex.

From domains to disturbed neuronal networks

Schizophrenia as a limbic disorder/frontotemporal encephalopathy

Since Bleuler and Kraepelin [9] schizophrenia has been regarded as a brain disease. However, during the first half of the twentieth century, little progress was made given the lack of tools with adequate resolution and reliability. For example, post-mortem findings could only be described qualitatively while solid methods for systematic quantification were developed later. The first computer tomography investigations initiated by Johnstone *et al.* [50], who detected increased ventricle volumes in schizophrenia patients, raised and enhanced the interest in morphological and post-mortem studies [51]. The use of improved methods and quantification tools nourished the conviction of schizophrenia being a neurobiological brain disease. Subsequently, the development of magnetic resonance imaging (MRI) was beneficial with respect to detailed morphological studies, with segmentation of brain regions into grey and white matter and cerebrospinal fluid (CSF) spaces. Its introduction supported the discovery of specific alterations in schizophrenia, since deficits are subtle and have been detected in precisely defined brain regions.

Meta-analyses of structural magnetic resonance imaging (MRI) studies reveal grey matter volume deficits in a number of different brain regions in schizophrenic patients. Affected regions are the medial temporal lobe including the hippocampus and parahippocampal gyrus (limbic system), the heteromodal association

Table 2.2 Summary of structural and functional findings in schizophrenia

Type of studies	Findings	Author(s)
Structural MRI and post-mortem studies		
	Increased volumes of ventricles	[50]
	Decreased hippocampal volumes	[58,59,60,61]
	Decreased volume of the posterior hippocampus	[61,64,65,66, 67,68,69]
	Decreased volume of the anterior hippocampus	[70,71]
	Decreased grey matter volume of the temporal and prefrontal cortex	[52,53,54,55,56, 76,77,78]
	Disturbed gyrification index	[82,83,84,85,86]
Functional PET, SPECT and fMRI studies		
	Decreased activation of the posterior hippocampus	[72,73]
	Metabolic hypofrontality	[79,80,89]
	Decreased prefrontal asymmetry	[81]
	Decreased prefronto-parietal activation	[122,123,124]
	Decreased superior temporal, occipital activation	[104,105,106]
	Decreased activation of the thalamus	[116,117, 119,120,121, 124]
	Hypofunction of the thalamus	[119,120,121]
	Reduced metabolic activity of the thalamus	[118]
DTI: connectivity		
	Decreased fractional anisotropy of the hippocampus	[91,92,93,94,95]
	Decreased connectivity of the entorhinal cortex	[96]
	Decreased fractional anisotropy of the prefronto-temporal network	[97,98,92]

cortex including the prefrontal and parietal cortex, and superior temporal gyrus (Table 2.2). The degree of grey matter reduction is in the range of 5–10% in the frontotemporolimbic network [52,53]. Additionally, asymmetries of the temporal and prefrontal cortices have been reported to be disturbed in schizophrenia [54,55,56].

In their early stages, lesions involving the medial temporal region produce emotional symptoms of fear, aggression, anxiety, irritability and over-attention to external stimuli, sometimes even paranoid symptoms and hallucinations. Such presentations may be difficult to differentiate from ideopathic schizophrenia [57,58]. Structural MRI and post mortem schizophrenia studies have shown volume loss in the medial temporal lobe, especially in the hippocampus, as one of the most consistent structural abnormalities [59]. Additionally, post mortem studies showed volume loss in hippocampal subregions, which possibly are related to positive symptoms [60,61,58]. The human hippocampus is involved in memory and regulation of affect, which are both compromised in schizophrenia [62]. Behavioural and anatomical studies reveal that the posterior hippocampus performs primarily cognitive functions, while the anterior part relates to emotion, affect and stress [63]. A large number of structural MRI studies has shown a reduced volume in the posterior part of the hippocampus [61,64,65,66,67,68,69], while a few other studies reported a pronounced reduction in the anterior part [70,71]. In functional MRI studies, decreased activation of the posterior part of the hippocampus has been related to smooth pursuit eye movement deficits [72] and impaired verbal learning in schizophrenia [73].

The prefrontal cortex is critical for executive control of cognition, mediating specific functions carried out by other cortical and subcortical regions. Many indicators for executive functions are disturbed in schizophrenia patients, including working memory, perception, attention and smooth pursuit eye movements [74]. Thus the prefrontal cortex has been regarded as a key region for the pathophysiology of this disease [75]. Detailed volumetric investigations detected reductions mainly in the dorsolateral prefrontal cortex [76,77]. Concerning structural MRI studies, about 70% of them reported decreased volumes in this region [78]. Functional PET studies revealed a suitable metabolic hypofrontality [79,80]. Moreover, the normal asymmetry of the prefrontal cortex (right>left) is decreased in schizophrenia patients [81] which has been interpreted as a sign of disturbed perinatal neurodevelopment. A further sign of early developmental deficit consists in the disturbed gyrification index as a measure of disturbed cortical folding [82,83,84,85,86], moreover, regional brain volumes correlate with symptoms like decreased visual and verbal memory and semantic fluency [87,88]. Negative symptoms, again, have been associated with decreased prefrontal glucose uptake [89,80]. However, results from recent investigations suggest that not only a deficit in one circumscribed region is underlying cognitive or positive/negative symptom dimensions, but alterations in neuronal networks controlling cognition and higher sensory processing.

The dysconnection hypothesis

Newer developments in neuroimaging techniques such as *in vivo* functional MRI (fMRI) and diffusion tensor imaging (DTI) afforded the investigation of disturbances in connectivity and neuronal networks. Namely magnetic transfer imaging (MTI) and DTI showed decrease in the myelin or axonal membrane in cortical regions and decreased white matter anisotropy (a measurement of the coherence along white matter tracts), respectively [90]. DTI studies of white matter tracts of the fornix body and hippocampus in schizophrenia showed decreased fractional anisotropy and support the hypothesis of structural and functional dysconnectivity [91,92,93,94]. Moreover, cognitive function such as verbal declarative memory is correlated with the fractional anisotrophy of the hippocampus in schizophrenia [95]. In the entorhinal cortex, a combined high-resolution MRI and DTI study showed decreased volumes of the ERC and reduction of diffusional anisotropy, suggesting disturbed connectivity to the hippocampus [96] (Table 2.2).

This disruption of connectivity in prefronto-temporal neuronal networks could result in cognitive as well as clinical negative symptoms [97,98,92]. This assumption is based on the fact that neuronal fibrer traversing the limbic pathways from the posterior part of the hippocampus are connected to prefrontal regions, anterior thalamic complex and anterior cingulate cortex, and pathways involved in higher cognition and information processing [99,63]. On the system level, schizophrenia patients are thought to experience primary disturbances in the early stages of information processing occurring during the first few hundred milliseconds maybe leading to 'downstream' effects on higher cortical functions, such as cognitive deficits. Disturbed information processing has been regarded as a stable marker in patients with good and poor prognosis [100]. In contrast, projections from the anterior part of the hippocampus target to the amygdalar nuclei and medial prefrontal and agranular insular cortices, regions involved in emotion and stress. An intermedial part of the hippocampus is projecting to the medial prefrontal cortex as well as to olfactory cortical areas [63]. The anterior cingulate cortex is part of the medial prefrontal cortex and receives processed multimodal sensory information from insular, temporal and parietal association cortices and emotional information from the amygdala and orbitofrontal cortex and serves as modulator of the dorsolateral prefrontal cortex [101,102].

The prefrontal cortex and hippocampus belong to a neuronal network showing disturbances in schizophrenia, most likely of neurodevelopmental origin. The dorsolateral prefrontal cortex, like the superior temporal gyrus and inferior parietal cortex, belongs to the heteromodal association cortex, which is responsible for cognitive processing and influences complex behaviour in a multifocal neuronal network [103]. It has been suggested that the temporo-parietal association cortices are linked to positive symptoms in schizophrenia, while neuropsychological deficits in executive function are related to the dorsolateral prefrontal cortex [75]. In a series of fMRI studies, we investigated the functional integrity of distinguishable brain systems underlying maintenance-related subprocesses of working memory (articulatory rehearsal, non-articulatory maintenance of phonological information, maintenance of visuospatial information) in patients with schizophrenia. Schizophrenia patients showed reduced activation of the fronto-opercular, intraparietal, and anterior cingulate cortex during the nonarticulatory maintenance of phonological information, as well as attenuated deactivation of the hippocampus. During visuospatial maintenance, patients showed impaired activation of the superior parietal, temporal and occipital cortex, combined with enhanced activation of the frontal eye field and the inferior parietal cortex. This study with fine-grained analysis of dysfunctions, in particular aspects of working memory circuitry, provides evidence for a differential impairment of the brain systems supporting working memory subcomponents in schizophrenia [104,105,106]. During nonarticulatory maintenance of phonological information, patients showed reduced connectivity of the prefrontal cortex with intraparietal cortex and hippocampus [106]. A recent meta-analysis of fMRI studies of executive function in schizophrenia revealed reduced activation of the dorsolateral and ventrolateral prefrontal cortex, anterior cingulate cortex, and thalamus [107].

A reduction in thalamic volumes in schizophrenia has been shown in structural MRI studies [108,109]. Because the thalamus is heterogeneous, schizophrenia-related changes would likely occur in specific thalamic subregions. This brain structure is composed of various subnuclei that received attention in schizophrenia research by reason of their unique location and connectivity to the cortex and hippocampus [110,111,112,113,114,155] (Figure 2.2). The thalamus acts as a central relay station, transferring peripheral sensory inputs to the cortex. It plays a critical role in filtering sensory information, in regulating cognitive input to the cortex, and mediating corticocortical connections between areas particularly implicated in schizophrenia, such as frontal and temporal regions. In schizophrenia patients, positron emission tomography (PET) studies show a dysfunction of the cortico-cerebellar-thalamic-cortical neuronal circuit contributing to 'cognitive dysmetria', that is, impaired cognition and other symptoms of the disease [116,117]. Similarly, reduced levels of metabolic activity in the thalamus as measured by PET and single-photon emission computed tomography (SPECT) of cerebral perfusion have been linked to cognitive deficits and increased severity of both positive and negative symptoms [118]. Functional MRI studies show sensory processing and attention deficits in schizophrenia patients that involve a thalamic hypofunction [119,120,121]. An fMRI study using visual and acoustic stimuli revealed thalamic as well as prefronto-parietal dysfunctions in neuroleptic-naive, first-episode schizophrenia patients [122]. Even in chronic schizophrenia patients the anterior cingulate cortex, which serves as modulator of the dorsolateral prefrontal cortex [101,102], showed reduced activation [123]. Furthermore, a disturbed prefronto-parietal-thalamic network has been shown to be involved in disease-related working memory deficits in schizophrenia [124]. In summary, results from fMRI and DTI studies confirm the dysfunction of cortico-prefrontal-thalamo-temporolimbic networks and the hypofrontality hypothesis of schizophrenia [177]. However, resolution of *in vivo* MRI investigations does not allow conclusions on cellular networks or on the cellular level to be drawn.

From networks to the cellular level

The neuropathological evidence

The small amount of tissue reduction of approximately 5% in schizophrenia patients suggests that some cellular subfractions within these structures might be lost, reduced in volume or the ratio between different cell types (for example, neuron to glia ratio) is changed. Besides the noninvasive neuroimaging methods, actual morphological post-mortem investigations are also based on computer-derived analysis. The development of design-based stereology provides the advantage to estimate volumes of defined regions and cell numbers of a total structure [125]. This method avoids disadvantages of two-dimensional cell counting in only a few sections without considering the volume of the region but carries methodological limitations because of the influence of volume differences (for example, mediated by neuropil degeneration) and tissue shrinkage by fixation procedures. Additionally, problems may be caused by irregular cell shape and size, nonrandom orientation and cutting of cells during sectioning [126]. Microscopic studies of post-mortem tissue from schizophrenic patients showed decreased neuronal or glial density and reduced neuronal size in regions and neuronal networks involved in the pathophysiology of schizophrenia such as hippocampus and entorhinal cortex, prefrontal cortex, anterior cingulate cortex, superior temporal cortex and thalamus (Table 2.3).

Hippocampus and entorhinal cortex

Earlier quantitative studies of the hippocampus and entorhinal cortex described reduced glial cells as well as unchanged neuron-glia ratios [127,128,129]. The entorhinal cortex is closely connected to the hippocampal formation, linking cortical areas to the hippocampus [130]. In the entorhinal cortex, abnormalities of positioning of neuronal clusters (pre-alpha-cells) have been repeatedly reported and support the hypothesis of migrational disturbances in schizophrenia [131,132,133] (Figure 2.3). However, number or volume of neurons in pre-alpha-cell clusters or other layers of the entorhinal cortex are unknown.

A recent post-mortem study of hippocampal grey matter using grey-level-index (GLI) showed no cytoarchitectonic alterations suggesting no changes of neuronal perikarya-neuropil ratio [134]. Earlier quantitative studies of the hippocampus described reduced density of interneurons, mainly of parvalbumin-immunoreactive cells, without alterations of pyramidal neurons [135,136]. While most of these studies reported no alterations in cell density [137,138], the density of pyramidal neurons has been shown to be decreased in schizophrenia [127]. Additionally, there are findings of both smaller [139,140] or unchanged [141] pyramidal neuron volumes in schizophrenia. Although some authors have noted a reduction of glial cells in the hippocampus of male patients with schizophrenia [127], astrogliosis has not been detected in the hippocampus of post-mortem brains from patients with schizophrenia [142,143,144]. However, one study showed increased S100B positive astroglial or oligodendroglial cells in patients with paranoid schizophrenia [145].

Two stereological estimates of total cell number reported no differences in the hippocampus of schizophrenic patients. However, one study investigated only total numbers of neurons [146] whereas the subdivision of parvalbumin-positive

Table 2.3 Summary of cellular alterations in schizophrenia

Type of studies	Findings	Author(s)
Hippocampus and Entorhinal Cortex		
Density studies	No alterations in grey-level index (GLI)	[134]
	Unchanged neuron-glia-ratio	[128,129]
	No alteration in cell density	[137,138]
	No astrogliosis	[142,143]
	Reduced density of interneurons	[135,136]
	Reduced density of pyramidal neurons	[127]
	Reduction of glia cells	[127]
	Increased glia cells	[145]
	Smaller volumes of pyramidal neurons	[139,140]
	Unchanged volumes of neurons	[141]
	Abnormalities of positioning of neuronal clusters in the entorhinal cortex	[131,132, 133]
Stereology studies	No change in total cell number	[146,148]
	Decreased interneurons	[147]
	Decreased oligodendrocytes in CA4	[144]
	No astrogliosis	[144]
Prefrontal and Temporal cortex		
Density studies	Reduced Grey-level-index (GLI)	[152,153]
	No change in GLI	[154]
	Increased neuronal density BA9	[155,156]
	Decreased density of astrocytes BA9	[158]
	Reduced volumes of neurons BA9	[157,158]
	No alterations in cell density BA22	[165]
Stereology studies	Reduced number of neurons and glia cells BA24	[161,162]
	Decreased number of oligodendrocytes BA9	[149,160]
	Deficit of perineuronal oligodendrocytes PFC	[164]
	No alterations of oligodendrocytes in white matter BA24	[163]
	No alteration in cell density BA22	[166]
Thalamus		
Stereology studies	Reduced neuronal number	[171,173, 174]

interneurons has been reported to be decreased [147]. The second study also did not differentiate between different cell types and included schizophrenic as well as schizoaffective patients [148]. Nevertheless, there is still evidence for a subtle neurodegeneration without gliosis. Namely, the pathophysiological processes in schizophrenia could be interpreted as an arrest of the developmental process of

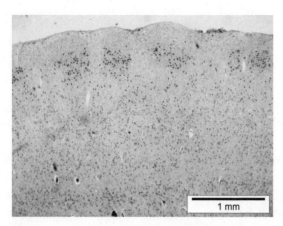

Figure 2.3 Histological figure of the entorhinal cortex of a schizophrenia patient. Close to the surface, pre-alpha cell clusters are situated.

myelination [149]. White matter myelination plays a crucial role in rapid impulse conduction and also supports the brain's structural synchrony and connectivity. Direct investigation of post-mortem tissue showed structural abnormalities of myelin sheath and regressive changes in oligodendrocytes in the prefrontal cortex and hippocampus, suggesting apoptotic or necrotic cell death [150]. We investigated the posterior hippocampus of patients with chronic schizophrenia using design-based stereology and found decreased numbers of oligodendrocytes in right and left CA4 subregions [144]. The results indicate disturbed connectivity of the CA4 of the posterior part of the hippocampus and thus contribute to the growing number of studies showing the involvement of posterior hippocampal pathology in the pathophysiology of the disease. In schizophrenia, a reduced number and abnormalities in or death of oligodendrocytes influence or harm myelin integrity and connectivity in neuronal networks.

Prefrontal and temporal cortex

In post-mortem studies of the cortex, regions mainly have been dissected according to the cytoarchitectural criteria of Brodman [151]. In BA (Brodman area) 10 and BA9, no change and a decrease of GLI points to a circumscribed disturbance of cytoarchitecture in schizophrenia [152,153,154]. Along these lines, neuronal density has been reported to be increased in BA9 [155,156]. In this region in layer III, pyramidal neurons and neuronal cells showed reduced somal size [157,158]. Astrocyte density has been reported to be decreased in layer V [158]. A stereological study of total cell numbers described decreased numbers of oligodendrocytes in layer III of BA9 in schizophrenia [159,160]. Stereological studies of the anterior cingulate cortex (BA24) measuring the total number of neurons and glial cells reported reduced number of glial cells and reduced volume of pyramidal cells in schizophrenia [161,162]. However, in the white matter of this region, no alterations in olgodendrocyte numbers have been detected [163]. Since in the prefrontal cortex a deficit of perineuonal oligodendrocytes has been described [164], alterations in the white matter may be lacking. Using GLI, we detected a decrease of neuronal density in the right superior temporal gyrus in female subjects suffering from schizophrenia (Falkai unpublished results). The superior temporal gyrus (BA22) is a heteromodel association cortex and includes the planum temporale. It has been investigated using two-dimensional cell counting methods which failed to demonstrate differences in neuronal density [165]. A stereological study also reported unaltered neuronal and glial density in schizophrenia [166]. However, this study did not differentiate between different cell types.

Apoptosis and necrosis of oligodendrocytes have both been reported in the frontal cortex and caudate nucleus in association with schizophrenia [167]. In addition to apoptosis and necrosis, ultrastructural investigations of oligodendrocytes in schizophrenia revealed atrophy of axons and swelling of periaxonal processes in the prefrontal cortex, caudate nucleus and hippocampus [168]. Oligodendrocytes are involved in the myelination process of axonal projections during development. Myelination of projections in the frontal and temporal lobes, including the hippocampus, in turn peaks in late adolescence and early adulthood, occurring in close temporal proximity with the onset of schizophrenia [169].

Thalamus

On the cellular level, the densities of parvalbumine-immunoreactive varicosities in the middle layer of the prefrontal cortex were lower in schizophrenia patients, suggesting fewer projections from the thalamus to the prefrontal cortex [170]. Post-mortem findings of reduced volume, neuron number, and size of the entire thalamus [171], of the mediodorsal nucleus, pulvinar and ventral posterior thalamic nucleus [172,173,174,175,176] support the hypothesis of disturbed function and dysconnection of different thalamic nuclei in schizophrenia.

Neurodevelopmental disturbances versus neurodegenerative hypothesis

During the last decades, schizophrenia has been regarded as a developmental disorder. The so-called 'neurodevelopmental hypothesis' proposes that schizophrenia is related to adverse conditions leading to abnormal brain development during the pre- or postnatal period, whereas symptoms of the disease appear in early adulthood [177] (Figure 2.4). Meta-analyses of structural MRI studies revealing volume deficits of the hippocampus or increased ventricular volumes in first-episode patients confirm this hypothesis [178,179]. On the other hand, it is possible, that at

Developmental Model

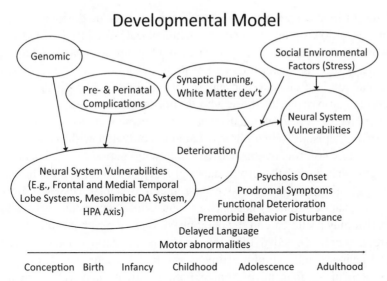

Figure 2.4 The neurodevelopmental hypothesis of schizophrenia: risk genes and environmental factors such as perinatal complications act during neurodevelopment, whereas symptoms of the disease occur in young adulthood after the synaptic pruning process.

least in some patients, an additional neurodegenerative process, beginning at the time of symptom onset, may play a role in the pathophysiology of the disease. This consequently would lead to long-term changes in the brain structure causing brain malfunction and predisposing functional deficits and symptoms which are based on pathophysiological processes in the brain [177] (Table 2.1). A recent meta-analysis of voxel-based MRI studies comparing first-episode and chronic schizophrenia patients revealed no evidence for a progression of pathology of hippocampus, but evidence for progression of grey matter of cortical areas, namely insular and anterior cingulate cortex [180].

Several studies have investigated the progression of volume deficits during the course of the disease. Out of these studies, progressive investigation of first-episode schizophrenia patients considering the distinct outcome are valuable to assess the effects of symptom dimensions on progressive changes in brain volumes. Some of these studies showed a specific progression of ventricular enlargement in subgroups of patients [181,182], especially in patients with a chronic course of the disease and persisting negative symptoms [183,184,185,186]. However, in a longitudinal study over 10 years from the first episode, data are heterogenous and do not confirm ventricular enlargement in patients with worse outcome [187]. Other studies showed a progressive volume loss of cortical grey matter, mainly in the frontal-temporal and parietal region as well as the anterior cingulate gyrus [186,188,189,190,191,192,193] with poor outcome patients showing more brain tissue loss during follow-up than good outcome patients [194,195]. Grey matter loss of the insular cortex was associated with severity of positive and negative symptoms at follow-up and related to functional outcome [191,192]. The UCLA team, working collaboratively with investigators in a prodromal program based in Melbourne, Australia, has recently demonstrated a significantly steeper rate of grey matter reduction in prefrontal cortical regions in prodromal patients who convert to psychosis compared with those who do not over a one-year follow-up period [196]. This pattern of accelerated change in prefrontal regions is mirrored in a sample of first-episode schizophrenia patients compared with age- and gender-matched healthy controls over a two-year follow-up period [197]. Together, these data suggest that during the prodromal and early phases of schizophrenia, there is an exaggeration of the regressive neuromaturational processes (programmed cell death, synaptic pruning) normative to late adolescence and early adulthood, changes that may participate in the pathophysiology of psychosis onset.

Future research is needed focusing on the relationship between longitudinal structural changes and symptom dimensions in schizophrenia. The progressive changes seen in a subgroup of schizophrenia patients may reflect neurodevelopmental and /or degenerative changes. However, a further precondition for a neurodegenerative process is the increment of symptoms during the course of the disorder. In fact, follow-up studies after five and ten years do not confirm the increase in cognitive symptoms such as deficits in working memory, verbal and spatial memory and concentration skills. Mainly those patients with low deficits at onset of the disease do not develop an increment in neuropsychological deficits [15]. Additionally, in post-mortem studies no signs for astrogliosis and loss of neurons in general have been detected. Therefore, pathological processes in schizophrenia are not regarded as a classical neurodegeneration. In contrast, the neuropathological process may be related to a pre-existing neurodevelopmental loss of synaptic contacts as well as, in subgroups of patients, to ongoing deficits on the synaptic and molecular level, resulting in an excessive loss of neuronal connectivity.

Hypothesis of disturbed synaptogenesis and neurogenesis

In the prefrontal cortex of schizophrenia patients, neuronal density has been reported to be increased in BA9 [155,156]. Findings of increased cell package density without a change in neuronal number [198,199] suggest that the volume reduction may be due to disturbances of the surrounding neuropil, these are dendrites and axons [200]. Axon terminals and dendritic spines are the main substrate for synapses and have been reported to be reduced in the prefrontal cortex of schizophrenia patients [201]. In schizophrenia, a hypofunction of the glutamatergic NMDA receptor may decrease synaptic plasticity [202]. There is strong support for the assumption of disturbed glutamatergic and gamma-amino-butyric acid (GABA)ergic microcircuitry on the molecular level, mainly affecting the expression of presynaptic vesicle proteins including the synaptosome-associated protein 25 (SNAP-25) and syntaxin, which form the soluble N-ethylmaleimide-sensitive factor attachment protein receptor (SNARE) complex [203,204,205,206,207,208,209,210,211,212]. The trimeric SNARE complex consists of the vesicle protein synaptobrevin (VAMP) and the plasma membrane proteins syntaxin (STX1A) and synaptosomal associated protein SNAP-25, which drive membrane fusion by guiding the vesicle and plasma membrane proteins in close proximity, thus overcoming the energy barrier for fusion. Synaptophysin, Complexin 1 (in inhibitory and excitatory synapses) and complexin 2 operate at a post-priming step in synaptic vesicle exocytosis by stabilising the SNARE complex [213].

Levels of six synaptic mRNAs including SNAP-25 were increased in the temporal cortex of the younger (58-79 years) subgroup of schizophrenic patients compared to control subjects and older (80-95 years) subgroup of schizophrenic patients [212]. A recent microarray study in the prefrontal area 10 of two schizophrenia cohorts showed altered gene sets associated with synaptic vesicle recycling [214]. Reduced synaptophysin immunoreactivity has been reported in the prefrontal cortex in schizophrenia [215,216]. Protein analyses also indicated a significant reduction in SNAP-25 immunoreactivity in the schizophrenia nonsuicide group [217,207,218]. In another study, however, quantitative immunoblotting in the prefrontal cortex revealed that there were no differences in the immunoreactivity of proteins measured in schizophrenia patients as compared to matched controls [219]. An immunocytochemical study indicated reduced SNAP-25 protein in schizophrenia compared to controls, particularly in the terminal fields of entorhinal cortex projections [220]. Normal levels of SNAP-25 are noted in schizophrenia patients in Brodman area 17, decreased levels in areas 10 and 20, and an elevated level in area 9 [218]. Those findings strongly support the notion of regionally distinct expressions prevailing in schizophrenia.

In the hippocampus it was shown that neuron populations had fewer dendritic spines and reduced dendritic arborisation. Evidence for reduced presynaptic markers was also reported. Another finding within the hippocampus is abnormal synaptic connectivity, as shown by decreased expression of the presynaptic proteins synapsin, synaptophysin and SNAP-25 [221]. In addition, disturbances of complexins in the hippocampus were associated with the severity of ante mortem cognitive impairment [210]. In recent years it has become evident that in addition to the subventricular zone [222] the subgranular layer of the hippocampal dentate gyrus also contains progenitor cells possessing the capacity to proliferate until and throughout adulthood (neurogenesis). Dysconnectivity of the hippocampus in schizophrenia may also be related to disturbances in neurogenesis [223]. Additionally, risk genes of schizophrenia like Disrupted in schizophrenia-1 (DISC1) may contribute to disturbed development of dendrites in neuronal stem cells [224]. The DISC1 gene appears to play a role in reduced dendritic complexity and synaptic density. Inherited variations in DISC1 associate with schizophrenia and reduced grey matter density in prefrontal cortex and hippocampus [225]. Experimentally altered DISC1 function (specifically interfering with DISC1-Nudel protein complexes) produces neurons that have less dendritic complexity, produce smaller amplitude responses to electrical stimulation, and produce disrupted behaviour paralleling that observed in patients with schizophrenia, including reduced social preference and impaired working memory [226].

Effects of antipsychotics

By comparing patients treated with typical neuroleptics to patients receiving the (atypical) antipsychotic clozapine we found that elderly patients treated with cloza-pine showed stronger activation in the dorsolateral prefrontal and posterior parietal cortex as well as in the anterior cingulate cortex compared with those treated with typical neuroleptics [123]. This confirms the results of improved BOLD-response in the prefrontal and parietal cortex after a three-week treatment period with olan-zapine in younger patients [227] and improved activation of the anterior cingulate cortex after short-term treatment with atypical antipsychotics [228,229,230]. Re-garding the prefrontal cortex, such restoring effects on brain activation have not been observed in association with typical neuroleptics [231]. Using a working mem-ory task, prefrontal and posterior parietal activation was increased after switching from typical neuroleptics to risperidone [232]. Additionally, decreased activation of these regions as well as the anterior cingulate gyrus are involved in attention deficits in schizophrenia [233,234]. Typical neuroleptics such as haloperidol are known to interfere with attentional skills [235] by tonic antidopamine D_2 recep-tor modulation of higher cognitive function, as shown in healthy volunteers and rodents [236,237,238].

As the majority of schizophrenia patients in post mortem studies had been on antipsychotic medication over long time periods, medication effects have to be considered as a possible influential factor. In macaque monkeys, antipsychotics reduced astrocytes and, to a nonsignificant degree, also oligodendrocytes, while increasing neuronal density [239,240]. In animal studies of the hippocampus, cell proliferation has been reported to be increased after treatment with atypical an-tipsychotics [241]. In the rat forebrain, complexin I was increased after olanzapine treatment [242]. Animal studies using haloperidol, clozapine and risperidone re-veal conflicting results with regard to antipsychotic action on NMDA receptor binding and subunit gene expression [232]. An increased NMDA receptor bind-ing with elevated glutamate neurotransmission in the striatum may be related to side-effects associated with haloperidol, such as altered oral movements in tar-dive dyskinesia. On the other hand, it may counteract the hypothesised impaired prefronto-striato-thalamic pathway in schizophrenia [244]. In contrast, clozapine may increase glutamate levels in cortical synapses by downregulating glutamate transporters [245,247].

SUMMARY AND CONCLUSIONS

In summary, we can conclude that schizophrenia is not a classical neurodegenerative disorder with astrogliosis, neuronal loss and an increment of cognitive deficits during its course. However, on the functional level, deficits are evident in symptom dimensions, a subtle loss of volumes in specific brain regions, and in the activation pattern of neuronal networks. The disturbed function is related to decreased macro- and microconnectivity with disturbed connections in neuronal networks and a deficit on the synaptic level. Insight from stereological microscopic studies revealed decreased numbers of oligodendrocytes in several brain regions. On the molecular level, a dysfunction of these glia cells is evident. Additionally, dysfunction of the glutamatergic system, in cytoskeletal proteins, in proteins related to energy metabolism, and membrane phospholipid components are subject to molecular alterations with consequences on the functional capacity of brain regions in complex networks. The question arising from these findings is the possible influence of therapeutic approaches on the deficits underlying symptom dimensions. New substances improving synaptic plasticity and cognition in schizophrenia patients are erythropoietin [246] and glutamate agonists [247] as well as agonists of the nicotinergic acetylcholine receptor [248]. But also well established add-on therapy forms such as physical exercise (cycling) have been shown to increase hippocampus volumes in schizophrenia patients and healthy probands. Accordingly, the patients' short-term memory ameliorated. Moreover, in the schizophrenia exercise group, the ratio NAA/creatine has been shown to be increased, suggesting improvement of neuronal function [249]. In animal models, exercise entailed increased synaptic plasticity and cognitive skills [250]. These results give hope for future studies aiming at improvement of macro- and microconnectivity in neuronal circuits. As a consequence, new treatment options should be investigated with respect to their influence on neuroplasticity to achieve progress in effects on pathophysiological processes in schizophrenia.

REFERENCES

1. Murray CJ, Lopez AD. (1996) Evidence-based health policy–lessons from the Global Burden of Disease Study. *Science* **274**(5288), 740–743.
2. Watt DC, Katz K, Sheperd M (1983) The natural history of schizophrenia: a 5-year prospective follow-up of a representative sample of schizophrenics by means of a standardized clinical and social assessment. *Psychol Med* **13**(3), 663–670.
3. Häfner H, an der Heiden W (2003) Course and outcome of schizophrenia. In: Hirsch & Weinberger (Hrsg.). *Schizophrenia*, Blackwell Publishing, Oxford, pp. 101–139.
4. Andreasen NC, Arndt S, Alliger R *et al.* (1995) Symptoms of schizophrenia. Methods, meaning, and mechanisms. *Arch Gen Psychiatry* **52**, 341–351.

5. Liddle PF (1987) The symptoms of chronic schizophrenia. A re-examination of the positive-negative dichotomy. *Br J Psychiatry* **161**, 861.

6. Lindenmayer JP, Grochowski S, Hyman RB (1995) Five factor model of schizophrenia: replication across symples. *Schizophr Res* **14**, 229–234.

7. Toomey R, Kremen WS, Simpson JC *et al.* (1997) Revisiting the factor structure for positive and negative symptoms: evidence from a large heterogeneous group of psychiatric patients. *Am J Psychiatry* **154**, 371–377.

8. Toomey R, Faraone SV, Simpson JC *et al.* (1998) Negative, positive and disorganized symptom dimensions in schizophrenia, major depression, and bipolar disorder. *J Nerv Ment Dis* **186**, 470–476.

9. Kraepelin E (1919) *Dementia praecox and paraphrenia*. Edinburgh: Livingstone.

10. Crow TJ (1980) Molecular pathology of schizophrenia: more than one disease process? *Br Med J* **280**, 66–68.

11. Andreasen NC (1982) Negative symptoms in schizophrenia: definition and reliability. *Arch Gen Psychiatry* **39**, 784–788.

12. Albus M, Hubmann W, Scherer J *et al.* (2002) A prospective 2-year follow-up study of neurocognitive functioning in patients with first-episode schizophrenia. *Eur Arch Psychiatry Clin Neurosci* **252**(6), 262–267.

13. Albus M, Hubmann W, Mohr F *et al.* (2006) Neurocognitive functioning in patients with first-episode schizophrenia: results of a prospective 5-year follow-up study. *Eur Arch Psychiatry Clin Neurosci* **256**(7), 442–451.

14. Hoff AL, Harris D, Faustman WO *et al.* (1996) A neuropsychological study of early onset schizophrenia. *Schizophr Res* **20**(1–2), 21–28.

15. Hoff AL, Svetina C, Shields G *et al.* (2005) Ten year longitudinal study of neuropsychological functioning subsequent to a first episode of schizophrenia. *Schizophr Res* **78**(1):27–34.

16. Heinrichs RW, Zakzanis KK (1998) Neurocognitive deficit in schizophrenia: a quantitative review of the evidence. *Neuropsychology* **12**(3), 426–445.

17. McGurk SR, Meltzer HY (2000) The role of cognition in vocational functioning in schizophrenia. *Schizophr Res* **45**, 175–184.

18. Holthausen EA, Wiersma D, Cahn W *et al.* (2007) Predictive value of cognition for different domains of outcome in recent-onset schizophrenia. *Psychiatry Res* **149**(1–3), 71–80.

19. Robinson DG, Woerner MG, Alvir JM *et al.* (2002) Predictors of medication discontinuation by patients with first-episode schizophrenia and schizoaffective disorder. *Schizophr Res* **57**(2–3): 209–219.

20. Andreasen NC, Carpenter WT Jr, Kane JM *et al.* (2005) Remission in schizophrenia: proposed criteria and rationale for consensus. *Am J Psychiatry* **162**(3):441–449.

21. Heinrichs DW, Buchanan RW (1988) Significance and meaning of neurological signs in schizophrenia. *Am J Psychiatry* **145**, 11–18.

22. Tsuang MT, Faraone SV (1999) The concept of target features in schizophrenia research. *Acta Psychiatr Scand* Suppl **395**, 2–11.

23. Chen EY, Shapleske J, Luque R *et al.* (1995) The Cambridge Neurological Inventory: a clinical instrument for assessment of soft neurological signs in psychiatric patients. *Psychiatry Res* **56**, 183–204.

24. Levy DL, Holzman PS, Matthyse S *et al.* (1994) Eye tracking and schizophrenia: a selective review. *Schizophr Bull* **20**, 47–62.
25. Thaker GK, Ross DE, Cassady SL *et al.* (2000) Saccadic eye movement abnormalities in relatives of patients with schizophrenia. *Schizophr Res* **45**, 235–244.
26. Braff DL, Geyer MA, Swerdlow NR (2001) Human studies of prepulse inhibition of startle: normal subjects, patient groups, and pharmacological studies. *Psychopharmacology* **156**, 234–258.
27. Jaber M, Robinson SW, Missale C *et al.* (1996) Dopamine receptors and brain function. *Neuropsychopharmacology* **35**(11), 1503–1519.
28. Kebabian JW, Calne DB (1979) Multiple receptors for dopamine. *Nature* **271**, 93–96.
29. Carlsson A (1995) The dopamine theory revisited. In: Hirsch SR, Weinberger DR (eds.) *Schizophrenia*, Blackwell Science, Oxford, pp. 379–400.
30. Seeman P, Lee T, Chau-Wong M *et al.* (1976) Antipsychotic drug doses and neuroleptic/DA receptors. *Nature* **261**, 717–719.
31. Angrist B, van Kammen DP (1984) CNS stimulants as a tool in the study of schizophrenia. *Trends Neurosci* **7**, 388–390.
32. Lieberman JA, Kane JM, Alvir J (1987) provocative tests with psychostimulant drugs in schizophrenia. *Psychopharmacology* **91**, 415–433.
33. Laruelle M, Abi-Dargham A, van Dyck CH *et al.* (1996) Single photon emission computerized tomography imaging of amphetamine-induced dopamine release in drug-free schizophrenic subjects. *Proc Natl Acad Sci USA* **93**(17), 9235–9240.
34. Breier A, Su T-P, Saunders R *et al.* (1997) Schizophrenia is associated with elevated amphetamine-induced synaptic dopamine concentrations: evidence from a novel positron emission tomography method. *Proc Natl Acad Sci USA* **94**, 2569–2574.
35. Abi-Dargham A, Gil R, Krystal J *et al.* (1998) Increased striatal dopamine transmission in schizophrenia: confirmation in a second cohort. *Am J Psychiatry* **155**, 761–767.
36. Laruelle M, Abi-Dargham A, Gil R *et al.* (1999) Increased dopamine transmission in schizophrenia: Relationship to illness phases. *Biol Psychiatry* **46**, 56–72.
37. Davis KL, Kahn RS, Ko G *et al.* (1991) Dopamine in schizophrenia: a review and reconceptualization. *Am J Psychiatry* **148**, 1474–1486.
38. Crow TJ (1980) Molecular pathology of schizophrenia: More than one disease process? *Br Med J* **280**, 66–68.
39. Javitt DC, Zukin SR (1991) Recent advances in the phencyclidine model of schizophrenia. *Am J Psychiatry* **148**, 1301–1308.
40. Jentsch JD, Roth RH (1999) The neuropsychopharmacology of phencyclidine: from NMDA receptor hypofunction to the dopamine hypothesis of schizophrenia. *Neuropsychopharmacology* **20**, 201–225.
41. Krystal JH, Karper LP, Seibyl JP *et al.* (1994) Subanesthetic effects of the noncompetitive NMDA antagonist, ketamine, in humans. Psychotomimetic, perceptual, cognitive, and neuroendocrine responses. *Arch Gen Psychiatry* **51**, 199–214.
42. Lahti AC, Koffel B, LaPorte D *et al.* (1995) Subanesthetic doses of ketamine stimulate psychosis in schizophrenia. *Neuropsychopharmacology* **13**, 9–19.
43. Grace AA (1991) Phasic versus tonic dopamine release and the modulation of dopamine system resposivity: A hypothesis for the etiology of schizophrenia. *Neuroscience* **41**(1), 1–24.

44. Olney JW, Farber NB (1995) Glutamate receptor dysfunction and schizophrenia. *Arch Gen Psychiatry* **52**, 998–1007.
45. Jentsch JD, Redmond DE Jr, Elsworth JD *et al.* (1997) Enduring cognitive deficits and cortical dopamine dysfunction in monkeys after long-term administration of phencyclidine. *Science* **277**(5328), 953–955.
46. Farber NB, Newcomer JW, Olney JW (1999) Glycine agonists: what can they teach us about schizophrenia? *Arch Gen Psychiatry* **56**, 13–17.
47. Harrison PJ, Weinberger DR (2005) Schizophrenia genes, gene expression, and neuropathology: on the matter of their convergence. *Mol Psychiatry* **10**(1), 40–68.
48. Ozaki M, Sasner M, Yano R *et al.* (1997) Neuregulin-beta induces expression of an NMDA-receptor subunit. *Nature* **390**(6661), 691–694.
49. Jentsch JD, Trantham-Davidson H, Jairl C (2009) Dysbindin modulates prefrontal cortical glutamatergic circuits and working memory function in mice. *Neuropsychopharmacology* **34**(12), 2601–2608.
50. Johnstone EC, Crow TJ, Frith CD *et al.* (1976) Cerebral ventricular size and cognitive impairment in chronic schizophrenia. *Lancet* **2**(7992), 924–926.
51. Kovelman JA, Scheibel AB (1984) A neurohistological correlate of schizophrenia. *Biol Psychiatry* **19**(12), 1601–1621.
52. Wright IC, Rabe-Hesketh S, Woodruff PW *et al.* (2000) Meta-analysis of regional brain volumes in schizophrenia. *Am J Psychiatry* **157**(1), 16–25.
53. Shenton ME, Dickey CC, Frumin M *et al.* (2001) A review of MRI findings in schizophrenia. *Schizophr Res* **49**, 1–52.
54. Crow TJ (1990) Temporal lobe asymmetries as the key to the etiology of schizophrenia. *Schizophr Bull* **16**, 433–443.
55. Falkai P, Bogerts B, Schneider T (1995) Disturbed planum temporale asymmetry in schizophrenia. A quantitative post-mortem study. *Schizophr Res* **14**, 161–176.
56. Falkai P, Honer WG, Alfter D, Schneider-Axmann, T *et al.* (2002) The temporal lobe in schizophrenia from uni- and multiply affected families. *Neurosci Lett* **325**, 25–28.
57. Greenwood R, Bhalla A, Gordon A *et al.* (1983) behavior disturbances during recovery from herpes simplex encephalopathy. *J Neurol Neurosurg Psychiatry* **46**, 809–817.
58. Bogerts B (1997) The temporolimbic system theory of positive schizophrenic symptoms. *Schizophr Bull* **23**, 423–435.
59. Heckers S (2001) Neuroimaging studies of the hippocampus in schizophrenia. *Hippocampus* **11**, 520–528.
60. Bogerts B, Falkai P, Haupts M *et al.* (1990) Post-mortem volume measurements of limbic system and basal ganglia structures in chronic schizophrenics. Initial results from a new brain collection. *Schizophr Res* **3**, 295–301.
61. Bogerts B, Lieberman JA, Ashtari M *et al.* (1993) Hippocampus-amygdala volumes and psychopathology in chronic schizophrenia. *Biol Psychiatry* **33**, 236–246.
62. Heckers S, Konradi C (2002) Hippocampal neurons in schizophrenia. *J Neural Transm* **109**, 891–905.
63. Fanselow MS, Dong HW (2010) Are the dorsal and ventral hippocampus functionally distinct structures? *Neuron* **65**, 7–19.

64. Becker T, Elmer K, Schneider F *et al.* (1996) Confirmation of reduced temporal limbic structure volume on magnetic resonance imaging in male patients with schizophrenia. *Psychiatry Res* **67**, 135–143.

65. Hirayasu Y, Shenton ME, Salisbury DF *et al.* (1998) Lower left temporal lobe MRI volumes in patients with first-episode schizophrenia compared with psychotic patients with first-episode affective disorder and normal subjects. *Am J Psychiatry* **155**, 1384–1391.

66. Narr KL, Thompson PM, Sharma T *et al.* (2001) Three-dimensional mapping of temporo-limbic regions and the lateral ventricles in schizophrenia: gender effects. *Biol Psychiatry* **50**, 84–97.

67. Velakoulis D, Stuart GW, Wood SJ, *et al.* (2001) Selective bilateral hippocampal volume loss in chronic schizophrenia. *Biol Psychiatry* **50**, 531–539.

68. Yamasue H, Iwanami A, Hirayasu Y, *et al.* (2004) Localized volume reduction in prefrontal, temporolimbic, and paralimbic regions in schizophrenia: an MRI parcellation study. *Psychiatry Res* **131**, 195–207.

69. Rametti G, Segarra N, Junque C, *et al.* (2007) Left posterior hippocampal density reduction using VBM and stereological MRI procedures in schizophrenia. *Schizophr Res* **96**, 62–71.

70. Pegues MP, Rogers LJ, Amend D, *et al.* (2003) Anterior hippocampal volume reduction in male patients with schizophrenia. *Schizophr Res* **60**, 105–115.

71. Szeszko PR, Goldberg E, Gunduz-Bruce H, *et al.* (2003) Smaller anterior hippocampal formation volume in antipsychotic-naive patients with first-episode schizophrenia. *Am J Psychiatry* **160**, 2190–2197.

72. Tregellas JR, Tanabe JL, Miller DE, *et al.* (2004) Neurobiology of smooth pursuit eye movement deficits in schizophrenia: an fMRI study. *Am J Psychiatry* **161**, 315–321.

73. Eyler LT, Jeste DV, Brown GG (2008) Brain response abnormalities during verbal learning among patients with schizophrenia. *Psychiatry Res* **162**, 11–25.

74. Kinney DK, Levy DL, Yurgelun-Todd DA *et al.* (1998) Inverse relationship of perinatal complications and eye tracking dysfunction in relatives of patients with schizophrenia: evidence for a two-factor model. *Am J Psychiatry* **155**, 976–978.

75. John JP (2009) Fronto-temporal dysfunction in schizophrenia: A selective review. *Indian J Psychiatry* **51**(3), 180–190.

76. Schlaepfer TE, Harris GJ, Tien AY *et al.* (1994) Decreased regional cortical gray matter volume in schizophrenia. *Am J Psychiatry* **151**(6), 842–848.

77. Cannon TD, Thompson PM, van Erp TG *et al.* (2002) Cortex mapping reveals regionally specific patterns of genetic and disease-specific gray-matter deficits in twins discordant for schizophrenia. *Proc Natl Acad Sci U S A* **99**(5):3228–3233.

78. Schmitt A, Weber-Fahr W, Jatzko A *et al.* (2001) Aktueller Überblick über strukturelle Magnetresonanztomographie bei Schizophrenie. *Fortschritte der Neurologie Psychiatrie* **69**(3), 105–115.

79. Carter CS, Perlstein W, Ganguli R *et al.* (1998) Functional hypofrontality and working memory dysfunction in schizophrenia. *Am J Psychiatry* **155**(9), 1285–1287.

80. Schröder J, Buchsbaum MS, Siegel BV *et al.* (1996) Cerebral metabolic activity correlates of subsyndromes in chronic schizophrenia. *Schizophr Res* **19**(1), 41–53.

81. Bilder RM, Wu H, Bogerts B *et al.* (1994) Absence of regional hemispheric volume asymmetries in first-episode schizophrenia. *Am J Psychiatry* **151**(10), 1437–1447.
82. Vogeley K, Tepest R, Schneider-Axmann T *et al.* (2003) Automated image analysis of disturbed cytoarchitecture in Brodmann area 10 in schizophrenia. *Schizophr Res* **62**, 133–140.
83. Sallet PC, Elkis H, Alves TM *et al.* (2003) Rdeuced cortical folding in schizophrenia: an MRI morphometric study. *Am J Psychiatry* **160**(9), 1606–1613.
84. Falkai P, Honer WG, Kamer T *et al.* (2007) Disturbed frontal gyrification within families affected with schizophrenia. *J Psychiatry Res* **41**(10), 805–813.
85. Stanfield AC, Moorhead TW, Harris JM *et al.* (2008) Invreased right prefrontal cortical folding in adolescents at risk of schizophrenia for cognitive reasons. *Biol Psychiatry* **63**(1), 80–85.
86. McIntosh AM, Moorhead TW, McKirdy J *et al.* (2009) prefrontal gyral folding and its cognitive correlates in bipolar disorder and schizophrenia. *Acta Psychiatr Scand* **119**(3), 192–198.
87. Noga JT, Aylward E, Barta PE, Pearlson GD (1995) Cingulate gyrus in schizophrenic patients and normal volunteers. *Psychiatry Res* **61**(4), 201–208.
88. Baare WF, Pol HE, Hijman R *et al.* (1999) Volumetric analysis of frontal lobe regions in schizophrenia: relation to cognitive function and symptomatology. *Biol Psychiatry* **45**(12):1597–1605.
89. Corcoran R, Frith CD (1993) Neuropsychology and neurophysiology in schizophrenia. *Current Opinion in Psychiatry* **6**, 74–9.
90. Davis KL, Stewart DG, Friedman JI *et al.* (2003) White matter changes in schizophrenia: evidence for myelin-related dysfunction. *Arch Gen Psychiatry* **60**, 443–56.
91. Kalus P, Buri C, Slotboom J, *et al.* (2004) Volumetry and diffusion tensor imaging of hippocampal subregions in schizophrenia. *Neuroreport* **15**, 867–871.
92. Kuroki N, Kubicki M, Nestor PG *et al.* (2006) Fornix integrity and hippocampal volume in male schizophrenic patients. *Biol Psychiatry* **60**, 22–31.
93. White T, Kendi AT, Lehericy S *et al.* (2007) Disruption of hippocampal connectivity in children and adolescents with schizophrenia–a voxel-based diffusion tensor imaging study. *Schizophr Res* **90**, 302–307.
94. Zhou Y, Shu N, Liu Y *et al.* (2008) Altered resting-state functional connectivity and anatomical connectivity of hippocampus in schizophrenia. *Schizophr Res* **100**, 120–132.
95. Lim KO, Ardekani BA, Nierenberg J *et al.* (2006) Voxelwise correlational analyses of white matter integrity in multiple cognitive domains in schizophrenia. *Am J Psychiatry* **163**, 2008–2010.
96. Kalus P, Slotboom J, Gallinat J *et al.* (2005) New evidence for involvement of the entorhinal region in schizophrenia: a combined MRI volumetric and DTI study. *Neuroimage* **24**, 1122–1129.
97. Rajarethinam R, DeQuardo JR, Miedler J *et al.* (2001) Hippocampus and amygdala in schizophrenia: assessment of the relationship of neuroanatomy to psychopathology. *Psychiatry Res* **108**, 79–87.
98. Harrison PJ (2004) The hippocampus in schizophrenia: a review of the neuropathological evidence and its pathophysiological implications. *Psychopharmacology* (Berl) **174**, 151–162.

99. Goldman-Rakic PS, Selemon LD, Schwartz ML (1984) Dual pathways connecting the dorsolateral prefrontal cortex with the hippocampal formation and parahippocampal cortex in the rhesus monkey. *Neuroscience* **12**, 719–743.

100. Saccuzzo DP, Braff DL (1981) Early information processing deficit in schizophrenia. New findings using schizophrenic subgroups and manic control subjects. *Arch Gen Psychiatry* **38**, 175–179.

101. Kerns JG, Cohen JD, MacDonald AW *et al.* (2004) Anterior cingulate conflict monitoring and adjustments in control. *Science* **303**, 1023–1026.

102. Fincham JM, Anderson JR (2006) Distinct roles of the anterior cingulate and prefrontal cortex in the acquisition and performance of a cognitive skill. *Proc Natl Acad Sci U S A* **103**, 12941–12946.

103. Pearlson GD, Petty RG, Ross CA, Tien AY (1996) Schizophrenia: a disease of heteromodal association cortex? *Neuropsychopharmacology* **14**, 1–17.

104. Gruber O, von Cramon DY (2003) The functional neuroanatomy of human working memory revisited. Evidence from 3-T fMRI studies using classical domain-specific interference tasks. *Neuroimage* **19**, 797–809.

105. Gruber O, Gurber E, Falkai P (2006) Articulatory rehearsal in verbal working memory: A possible neurocognitive endophenotype that differentiates between schizophrenia and schizoaffective disorder. *Neurosci Lett* **405**, 24–28.

106. Henseler I, Falkai P, Gruber O (2009) Disturbed functional connectivity within brain networks subserving domain-specific subcomponents of working memory in schizophrenia: Relation to performance and clinical symptoms. *J Psychiatr Res* Oct 16 [Epub ahead of print]

107. Minzenberg MJ, Laird AR, Thelen S *et al.* (2009) meta-analysis of 41 functional neuroimaging studies of executive function in schizophrenia. *Arch Gen Psychiatry* **66**(8), 811–822.

108. Gaser C, Nenadic I, Volz HP *et al.* (2004) Neuroanatomy of 'hearing voices': a frontotemporal brain structural abnormality associated with auditory hallucinations in schizophrenia. *Cereb Cortex* **14**(1):91–96.

109. Brickman AM, Buchsbaum MS, Shihabuddin L *et al.* (2004) Thalamus size and outcome in schizophrenia. *Schizophr Res* **71**, 473–484.

110. Gur RE, Maany V, Mozley PD *et al.* (1998) Subcortical MRI volumes in neuroleptic-naïve and treated patients with schizophrenia. *Am J Psychiatry* **155**(12), 1711–1717.

111. Carlsson A, Waters N, Carlsson ML (1999) Neurotransmitter interactions in schizophrenia-therapeutic implications. *Eur Arch Psychiatry Clin Neurosci* **249**(Suppl 4), IV37–IV/43.

112. Tekin S, Cummings JL. (2002) Frontal-subcortical neuronal circuits and clinical neuropsychiatry: an update. J Psychosom *Res* **53**(2), 647–654.

113. Taber KH, Wen C, Khan A, Hurley RA (2004) The limbic thalamus. *J Neuropsychiatry Clin Neurosci* **16**(2), 127–132.

114. Lang DJ, Khorram B, Goghari VM, *et al.* (2006) Reduced anterior internal capsule and thalamic volumes in first-episode psychosis. *Schizophr Res* **87**, 89–99.

115. Ettinger U, Picchioni M, Landau S *et al.* (2007) Magnetic resonance imaging of the thalamus and adhesio interthalamica in twins with schizophrenia. *Arch Gen Psychiatry* **64**(4), 401–409.

116. Andreasen NC, Arndt S, Swayze V, 2nd *et al.* (1994) Thalamic abnormalities in schizophrenia visualized through magnetic resonance image averaging. *Science* **266**, 294–298.

117. Andreasen NC, Nopoulos P, O'Leary DS *et al.* (1999) Defining the phenotype of schizophrenia: cognitive dysmetria and its neural mechanisms. *Biol Psychiatry* **46**, 908–920.

118. Min SK, An SK, Jon DI, Lee JD (1999) Positive and negative symptoms and regional cerebral perfusion in antipsychotic-naive schizophrenic patients: a high-resolution SPECT study. *Psychiatry Res* **90**(3), 159–168.

119. Takahashi H, Koeda M, Oda K *et al.* (2004) An fMRI study of differential neural response to affective pictures in schizophrenia. *Neuroimage* **22**, 1247–1254.

120. Butler PD, Zemon V, Schechter I *et al.* (2005) Early-stage visual processing and cortical amplification deficits in schizophrenia. *Arch Gen Psychiatry* **62**, 495–504.

121. Kiehl KA, Stevens MC, Celone K *et al.* (2005) Abnormal hemodynamics in schizophrenia during an auditory oddball task. *Biol Psychiatry* **57**, 1029–1040.

122. Braus DF, Weber-Fahr W, Tost H *et al.* (2002) Sensory information processing in neuroleptic-naive first-episode schizophrenic patients: a functional magnetic resonance imaging study. *Arch Gen Psychiatry* **59**, 696–701.

123. Schmitt A, Otto S, Jatzko A *et al.* (2009) [Parieto-prefrontal dysfunction during visuo-auditory information processing in elderly, chronic schizophrenic patients and medication effects]. *Revista de Psiquiatria Clinica* **36**(3), 89–96.

124. Schneider F, Habel U, Klein M *et al.* (2007) Neural correlates of working memory dysfunctions in first-episode schizophrenia patients: An fMRI multicenter study. *Schizophrenia Research* **89**, 198–210.

125. Gundersen HJ, Bagger P, Bendtsen TF *et al.* (1988) The new stereological tools: disector, fractionator, nucleator and point sampled intercepts and their use in pathological research and diagnosis. *Apmis* **96**, 857–881.

126. Williams RW, Rakic P (1988) Three-dimensional counting: an accurate and direct method to estimate numbers of cells in sectioned material. *J Comp Neurol* **278**, 344–352.

127. Falkai, P, Bogerts B (1986) Cell loss in the hippocampus of schizophrenics. *Eur Arch Psychiatry Neurol Sci* **236**, 154–161.

128. Benes FM, Bird ED (1987) An analysis of the arrangement of neurons in the cingulate cortex of schizophrenic patients. *Arch Gen Psychiatry* **44**, 608–616.

129. Falkai, P, Bogerts, B, Rozumek M (1988) Limbic pathology in schizophrenia: the entorhinal region–a morphometric study. *Biol Psychiatry* **24**, 515–521.

130. Weinberger DR (1999) Cell biology of the hippocampal formation in schizophrenia. *Biol Psychiatry* **45**, 395–402.

131. Jakob H, Beckmann H (1986) Prenatal developmental disturbances in the limbic allocortex in schizophrenics. *J Neural Transm* **65**, 303–326.

132. Falkai P, Schneider-Axmann T, Honer WG (2000) Entorhinal cortex pre-alpha cell clusters in schizophrenia: quantitative evidence of a developmental abnormality. *Biol Psychiatry* **47**, 937–943.

133. Kovalenko S, Bergmann A, Schneider-Axmann T *et al.* (2003) Regio entorhinalis in schizophrenia: more evidence for migrational disturbances and suggestions for a new biological hypothesis. *Pharmacopsychiatry* **36** Suppl 3, S158–16.1

134. Hurlemann R, Tepest R, Maier W *et al.* (2005) Intact hippocampal gray matter in schizophrenia as revealed by automatized image analysis postmortem. *Anat Embryol* (Berl) **210**, 513–517.

135. Benes FM, Kwok EW, Vincent SL, Todtenkopf MS (1998) A reduction of nonpyramidal cells in sector CA2 of schizophrenics and manic depressives. *Biol Psychiatry* **44**, 88–97.

136. Zhang ZJ, Reynolds GP (2002) A selective decrease in the relative density of parvalbumin-immunoreactive neurons in the hippocampus in schizophrenia. *Schizophr Res* **55**, 1–10.

137. Arnold SE, Franz BR, Gur RC, *et al.* (1995) Smaller neuron size in schizophrenia in hippocampal subfields that mediate cortical-hippocampal interactions. *Am J Psychiatry* **152**, 738–748.

138. Dwork AJ (1997) Postmortem studies of the hippocampal formation in schizophrenia. *Schizophr Bull* **23**, 385–402.

139. Benes FM (1991) Evidence for neurodevelopment disturbances in anterior cingulate cortex of post-mortem schizophrenic brain. *Schizophr Res* **5**, 187–188.

140. Zaidel DW, Esiri MM, Harrison PJ (1997) Size, shape, and orientation of neurons in the left and right hippocampus: investigation of normal asymmetries and alterations in schizophrenia. *Am J Psychiatry* **154**, 812–818.

141. Highley JR, Walker MA, McDonald B, *et al.* (2003) Size of hippocampal pyramidal neurons in schizophrenia. *Br J Psychiatry* **183**, 414–417.

142. Casanova MF, Stevens JR, Kleinman JE (1990) Astrocytosis in the molecular layer of the dentate gyrus: a study in Alzheimer's disease and schizophrenia. *Psychiatry Res* **35**, 149–166.

143. Falkai P, Honer WG, David S, *et al.* (1999) No evidence for astrogliosis in brains of schizophrenic patients. A post-mortem study. *Neuropathol Appl Neurobiol* **25**, 48–53.

144. Schmitt A, Steyskal C, Bernstein HG, *et al.* (2009) Stereologic investigation of the posterior part of the hippocampus in schizophrenia. *Acta Neuropathologica* **117**(4), 395–407.

145. Steiner J, Bernstein HG, Bielau H *et al.* (2008) S100B-immunopositive glia is elevated in paranoid as compared to residual schizophrenia: a morphometric study. *J Psychiatr Res* **42**(10), 868–876.

146. Heckers S, Heinsen H, Geiger B, *et al.* (1991) Hippocampal neuron number in schizophrenia. A stereological study. *Arch Gen Psychiatry* **48**, 1002–1008.

147. Zhang Z, Sun J, Reynolds GP (2002) A selective reduction in the relative density of parvalbumin-immunoreactive neurons in the hippocampus in schizophrenia patients. *Chinese Medical Journal* **115**, 819–823.

148. Walker MA, Highley JR, Esiri MM, *et al.* (2002) Estimated neuronal populations and volumes of the hippocampus and its subfields in schizophrenia. *Am J Psychiatry* **159**, 821–828.

149. Bartzokis G, Nuechterlein KH, Lu PH, *et al.* (2003) Dysregulated brain development in adult men with schizophrenia: a magnetic resonance imaging study. *Biol Psychiatry* **53**, 412–421.

150. Kolomeets NS, Uranova NA (2008) [Pathology of oligodendroglia and myelinated fibers of the hippocampus in schizophrenia (an ultrastructural and morphometric study)]. *Zh Nevrol Psikhiatr Im S S Korsakova* **108**, 52–60.

151. Brodmann K (1025) Vergleichende Lokalisationslehre der Groβhirnrinde. Barth.
152. Kawasak Y, Vogeley K, Jun V *et al.* (2000) Automated image analysis of disturbed cytoarchitecture in Brodmann area 10 in schizophrenia: a post-mortem study. *Prog Neuropsychopharmacol Biol Psychiatry* **24**, 1093–1111.
153. Vogeley K, Tepest R, Schneider-Axmann T *et al.* (2003) Automated image analysis of disturbed cytoarchitecture in Brodmann area 10 in schizophrenia. *Schizophr Res* **62**, 133–140.
154. Tepest R, Vogeley K, Viebahn B *et al.* (2008) Automated gray level index measurements reveal only minor cytoarchitectonic changes of Brodmann area 9 in schizophrenia. *Psychiatry Res* **163**(2), 183–192.
155. Selemon LD, Rajkowska G, Goldman-Rakic PS (1995) Abnormally high neuronal density in the schizophrenic cortex. A morphometric analysis of prefrontal area 9 and occipital area 17. *Arch Gen Psychiatry* **52**, 805–818; discussion 819-820.
156. Selemon LD, Mrzljak J, Kleinman JE *et al.* (2003) Regional specificity in the neuropathologic substrates of schizophrenia: a morphometric analysis of Broca's area 44 and area 9. *Arch Gen Psychiatry* **60**, 69–77.
157. Pierri JN, Volk CL, Auh S *et al.* (2001) Decreased somal size of deep layer 3 pyramidal neurons in the prefrontal cortex of subjects with schizophrenia. *Arch Gen Psychiatry* **58**, 466–473.
158. Rajkowska G, Miguel-Hidalgo JJ, Makkos Z *et al.* (2002) Layer-specific reductions in GFAP-reactive astroglia in the dorsolateral prefrontal cortex in schizophrenia. *Schizophr Res* **57**, 127–138.
159. Hof PR, Haroutunian V, Copland C *et al.* (2002) Molecular and cellular evidence for an oligodendrocyte abnormality in schizophrenia. *Neurochem Res* **27**, 1193–1200.
160. Hof PR, Haroutunian V, Friedrich VL, Jr. *et al.* (2003). Loss and altered spatial distribution of oligodendrocytes in the superior frontal gyrus in schizophrenia. *Biol Psychiatry* **53**, 1075–1085.
161. Bouras C, Kovari E, Hof PR *et al.* (2001) Anterior cingulate cortex pathology in schizophrenia and bipolar disorder. *Acta Neuropathol* (Berl) **102**, 373–379.
162. Stark AK, Uylings HB, Sanz-Arigita E *et al.* (2004) Glial cell loss in the anterior cingulate cortex, a subregion of the prefrontal cortex, in subjects with schizophrenia. *Am J Psychiatry* **161**, 882–888.
163. Segal D, Schmitz C, Hof PR (2009) Spatial distribution and density of oligodendrocytes in the cingulum bundle are unaltered in schizophrenia. *Acta Neuropathol* **117**(4), 385–394.
164. Vostrikov VM, Uranova NA, Orlovskaya DD (2007) Deficit of perineuronal oligodendrocytes in the prefrontal cortex in schizophrenia and mood disorders. *Schizophr Res* **94**(1–3), 273–280.
165. Beasley CL, Chana G, Honavar M *et al.* (2005) Evidence for altered neuronal organisation within the planum temporale in major psychiatric disorders. *Schizophr Res* **73**, 69–78.
166. Cotter D, Mackay D, Frangou S *et al.* (2004) Cell density and cortical thickness in Heschl's gyrus in schizophrenia, major depression and bipolar disorder. *Br J Psychiatry* **185**, 258–259.
167. Uranova N, Orlovskaya D, Vikhreva O *et al.* (2001) Electron microscopy of oligodendroglia in severe mental illness. *Brain Res Bull* **55**, 597–610.

168. Uranova NA, Vostrikov VM, Vikhreva OV *et al.* (2007) The role of oligodendrocyte pathology in schizophrenia. *Int J Neuropsychopharmacol* **10**, 537–545.
169. Yakovlev PI, Lecours AR (1967) The myelogenetic cycles of regional maturation of the brain. Blackwell Scientific Publications, 3–70.
170. Lewis DA, Cruz DA, Melchitzky DS, Pierri JN (2001) Lamina-specific deficits in parvalbumin-immunoreactive varicosities in the prefrontal cortex of subjects with schizophrenia: evidence for fewer projections from the thalamus. *Am J Psychiatry* **158**, 1411–1422.
171. Pakkenberg B (1990) Pronounced reduction of total neuron number in mediodorsal thalamic nucleus and nucleus accumbens in schizophrenics. *Arch Gen Psychiatry* **47**, 1023–1028.
172. Danos P, Baumann B, Bernstein HG *et al.* (2002) The ventral lateral posterior nucleus of the thalamus in schizophrenia: a post-mortem study. *Psychiatry Res* **114**, 1–9.
173. Popken GJ, Bunney WE Jr, Potkin SG, Jones EG (2000) Subnucleus-specific loss of neurons in the medial thalamus of schizophrenics. *PNAS* **97**, 9276–9280.
174. Young KA, Manaye KF, Liang C *et al.* (2000) Reduced number of mediodorsal and anterior thalamic neurons in schizophrenia. *Biol Psychiatry* **47**, 944–953.
175. Byne W, Buchsbaum MS, Mattiace LA *et al.* (2002) Postmortem assessment of thalamic nuclear volumes in subjects with schizophrenia. *Am J Psychiatry* **159**, 59–65.
176. Danos P, Baumann B, Krämer A *et al.* (2003) Volumes of association thalamic nuclei in schizophrenia: a postmortem study. *Schizophr Res* **60**, 141–155.
177. Weinberger DR (1996) On the plausibility of 'the neurodevelopmental hypothesis' of schizophrenia. *Neuropsychopharmacology* **14**, 1S–11S.
178. Steen RG, Mull C, McClure R *et al.* (2006) Brain volume in first-episode schizophrenia: systematic review and meta-analysis of magnetic resonance imaging studies. *Br J Psychiatry* **188**, 510–518.
179. Vita A, De Peri L, Lilenzi C, Dierci M (2006) Brain morphology in first-episode schizophrenia: a meta-analysis of quantitative magnetic resonance imaging studies. *Schizophr Res* **82**(1), 75–88.
180. Ellison-Wright I, Glahn DC, Laird AR *et al.* (2008) The anatomy of first-episode and chronic schizophrenia: an anatomical likelihood estimation meta-analysis. *Am J Psychiatry* **165**(8), 1015–1023.
181. DeLisi LE, Tew W, Xie S *et al.* (1995) A prospective follow-up study of brain morphology and cognition in first-episode schizophrenic patients: preliminary findings. *Biol Psychiatry* **38**, 349–360.
182. DeLisi LE, Sakuma M, Tew W (1997) Schizophrenia as a chronic active brain process: a study of progressive brain structural change subsequent to the onset of schizophrenia. *Psychiatry Res* **74**, 129–140.
183. Nair TR, Christensen JD, Kingsbury SJ *et al.* (1997) progression of cerebroventricular enlargement and the subtyping of schizophrenia. *Psychiatry Res* **74**(3), 141–150.
184. Gur RE, Cowell P, Turetsky BI *et al.* (1998) A follow-up magnetic resonance imaging study of schizophrenia. Relationship of neuroanatomical changes to clinical and neurobehavioral measures. *Arch Gen Psychiatry* **55**(2), 145–152.
185. Woods BT (1998) is schizophrenia a progressive neurodevelopmental disorder? Toward a unitary pathogenetic mechanism. *Am J Psychiatry* **155**, 1661–1670.

186. Ho BC, Andreasen NC, Nopoulos P *et al.* (2003) Progressive structural brain abnormalities and their relationship to clinical outcome: a longitudinal magnetic resonance imaging study early in schizophrenia. *Arch Gen Psychiatry* **60**(6), 585–594.

187. DeLisi LE, Sakuma M, Maurizio AM *et al.* (2004) Cerebral ventricular change over the first 10 years after the onset of schizophrenia. *Psychiatry Res* **130**, 57–70.

188. Whitford TJ, Grieve SM, Farrow TF *et al.* (2006) Progressive grey matter atrophy over the first 2-3 years of illness in first-episode schizophrenia: A tensor-based morphometry study. *Neuroimage* **32**(2), 511–519.

189. Koo MS, Levitt JJ, Salisbury DF *et al.* (2008) A cross-sectional and longitudinal magnetic resonance imaging study of cingulate gyrus gray matter volume abnormalities in first-episode schizophrenia and first-episode affective psychosis. *Arch Gen Psychiatry* **65**(7), 746–760.

190. Hulshoff Pol HE, Kahn RS. (2008) What happens after the first episode? A review of progressive brain changes in chronically ill patients with schizophrenia. *Schizophr Bull* **34**(2), 354–366.

191. Takahashi T, Wood SJ, Soulsby B *et al.* (2009) Follow-up MRI study of the insular cortex in first-episode psychosis and chronic schizophrenia. *Schizophr Res* **108**(1–3), 49–56.

192. Mane A, Falcon C, Mateos JJ *et al.* (2009) progressive gray matter changes in first-episode schizophrenia: A 4-year longitudinal magnetic resonance study using VBM. *Schizophr Res* **114**(1–3), 136–143.

193. Takahashi T, Suzuki M, Zhou SY *et al.* (2010) A follow-up MRI study of the superior temporal subregions in schizotypal disorder and first-episode schizophrenia. *Schizophr Res* Jan 3 [Epub ahead of print].

194. Van Haren NE, Hulshoff Pol HE, Schnack HG *et al.* (2008) progressive brain volume loss in schizophrenia over the course of the illness. Evidence of maturational abnormalities in early adulthood. *Biol Psychiatry* **63**(1), 106–113.

195. Kasparek T, Prikryl R, Schwarz D *et al.* (2009) Gray matter morphology and the level of functioning in one-year follow-up of first-episode schizophrenia patients. *Prog Neuropsychopharmacol Biol Psychiatry* **33**(8), 1438–1446.

196. Sun D, Phillips L, Velakoulis D *et al.* (2009) Progressive brain structural changes mapped as psychosis develops in 'at risk' individuals. *Schizophr Res* **108**(1–3): 85–92.

197. Sun D, Stuart GW, Jenkinson M *et al.* (2009) Brain surface contraction mapped in first-episode schizophrenia: a longitudinal magnetic resonance imaging study. *Mol Psychiatry* **14**(10):976–986.

198. Akbarian S, Kim JJ, Potkin SG *et al.* (1995) Gene expression for glutamic acid decarboxylase is reduced without loss of neurons in prefrontal cortex of schizophrenics. *Arch Gen Psychiatry* **52**, 258–266.

199. Thune JJ, Hofsten DE, Uylings HBM *et al.* (1998) Total neuron numbers in the prefrontal cortex in schizophrenia. *Soc Neurosci Abstracts* **24**, 437–458.

200. Goldman-Rakic PS, Selemon LD (1997) Functional and anatomical aspects of prefrontal pathology in schizophrenia. *Schizophr Bull* **23**, 437–358.

201. Glantz LA, Lewis DA (2000) Decreased dendritic spine density on prefrontal cortical pyramidal neurons in schizophrenia. *Arch Gen Psychiatry* **57**, 65–73.

202. Stephan KE, Baldeweg T, Friston KJ (2006) Synaptic plasticity and dysconnection in schizophrenia. *Biol Psychiatry* **59**, 929–939.

203. Eastwood SL, Cairns NJ, Harrison PJ (2000) Synaptophysin gene expression in schizophrenia. Investigation of synaptic pathology in the cerebral cortex. *Br J Psychiatry* **176**, 236–242.
204. Eastwood SL, Harrison PJ (2000) Hippocampal synaptic pathology in schizophrenia, bipolar disorder and major depression: a study of complexin mRNAs. *Mol Psychiatry* **5**(4):425–432.
205. Eastwood SL, Harrison PJ (2001) Synaptic pathology in the anterior cingulate cortex in schizophrenia and mood disorders. A review and a Western blot study of synaptophysin, GAP-43 and the complexins. *Brain Res Bull* **55**(5):569–578.
206. Eastwood SL, Harrison PJ (2005) Decreased expression of vesicular glutamate transporter 1 and complexin II mRNAs in schizophrenia: further evidence for a synaptic pathology affecting glutamate neurons. *Schizophr Res* **73**(2–3):159–172.
207. Honer WG, Falkai P, Bayer TA *et al.* (2002) Abnormalities of SNARE mechanism proteins in anterior frontal cortex in severe mental illness. *Cereb Cortex* **12**(4):349–356.
208. Knable MB, Barci BM, Webster MJ, Meador-Woodruff J, Torrey EF, Stanley Neuropathology Consortium. (2004) Molecular abnormalities of the hippocampus in severe psychiatric illness: postmortem findings from the Stanley Neuropathology Consortium. *Mol Psychiatry* **9**(6):609–620.
209. Kuromitsu J, Yokoi A, Kawai T *et al.* (2001) Reduced neuropeptide Y mRNA levels in the frontal cortex of people with schizophrenia and bipolar disorder. *Brain Res Gene Expr Patterns* **1**(1):17–21.
210. Sawada K, Barr AM, Nakamura M *et al.* (2005) Hippocampal complexin proteins and cognitive dysfunction in schizophrenia. *Arch Gen Psychiatry* **62**(3):263–272.
211. Sawada K, Young CE, Barr AM *et al.* (2002) Altered immunoreactivity of complexin protein in prefrontal cortex in severe mental illness. *Mol Psychiatry* **7**(5):484–492.
212. Sokolov BP, Tcherepanov AA, Haroutunian V, Davis KL (2000) Levels of mRNAs encoding synaptic vesicle and synaptic plasma membrane proteins in the temporal cortex of elderly schizophrenic patients. *Biol Psychiatry* **48**(3):184–196.
213. Brose N (2008) Altered complexin expression in psychiatric and neurological disorders: cause or consequence? *Mol Cells* **25**(1):7–19.
214. Maycox PR, Kelly F, Taylor A *et al.* (2009) Analysis of gene expression in two large schizophrenia cohorts identifies multiple changes associated with nerve terminal function. *Mol Psychiatry* **14**(12), 1083–1094.
215. Glantz LA, Lewis DA (1997) Reduction of synaptophysin immunoreactivity in the prefrontal cortex of subjects with schizophrenia. *Arch Gen Psychiatry* **54**, 943–952.
216. Honer WG, Falkai P, Chen C (1999) Synaptic and plasticity-associated proteins in anterior frontal cortex in severe mental illness. *Neuroscience* **91**(4), 1247–1255.
217. Fatemi SH, Earle JA, Stary JM, Lee S, Sedgewick J (2001) Altered levels of the synaptosomal associated protein SNAP-25 in hippocampus of subjects with mood disorders and schizophrenia. *Neuroreport* **12**(15), 3257–3262.
218. Thompson PM, Sower AC, Perrone-Bizzozero NI (1998) Altered levels of the synaptosomal associated protein SNAP-25 in schizophrenia. *Biol Psychiatry* **43**(4), 239–243.
219. Halim ND, Weickert CS, McClintock BW *et al.* (2003) Presynaptic proteins in the prefrontal cortex of patients with schizophrenia and rats with abnormal prefrontal development. *Mol Psychiatry* **8**(9), 797–810.

220. Young CE, Arima K, Xie J *et al.* (1998) SNAP-25 deficit and hippocampal connectivity in schizophrenia. *Cereb Cortex* **8**(3), 261–268.
221. Harrison PJ, Eastwood SL (2001) Neuropathological studies of synaptic connectivity in the hippocampal formation in schizophrenia. *Hippocampus* **11**(5), 508–519.
222. Conover JC, Allen RL (2002) The subventricular zone: new molecular and cellular developments. *Cell Mol Life Sci* **59**(12), 2128–2135.
223. Reif A, Fritzen S, Finger M *et al.* (2006) Neural stem cell proliferation is decreased in schizophrenia, but not in depression. *Mol Psychiatry* **11**, 514–522.
224. Kalkman HO (2009) Altered growth factor signalling pathways as the basis of aberrant stem cell maturation in schizophrenia. *Pharmacology and Therapeutics* **121**, 115–122.
225. Cannon TD, Hennah W, van Erp TG *et al.* (2005) Association of DISC1/TRAX haplotypes with schizophrenia, reduced prefrontal gray matter, and impaired short- and long-term memory. *Arch Gen Psychiatry* **62**(11), 1205–1213.
226. Li W, Zhou Y, Jentsch JD *et al.* (2007) Specific developmental disruption of disrupted-in-schizophrenia-1 function results in schizophrenia-related phenotypes in mice. *Proc Natl Acad Sci U SA* **104**(46), 18280–18285.
227. Braus DF, Brassen S (2005) [Functional magnetic resonance imaging and antipsychotics. Overview and own data]. *Radiologe* **45**, 178–185.
228. Jones HM, Brammer MJ, O'Toole M *et al.* (2004) Cortical effects of quetiapine in first-episode schizophrenia: a preliminary functional magnetic resonance imaging study. *Biol Psychiatry* **56**, 938–942.
229. Snitz BE, MacDonald A, 3rd, Cohen JD *et al.* (2005) Lateral and medial hypofrontality in first-episode schizophrenia: functional activity in a medication-naive state and effects of short-term atypical antipsychotic treatment. *Am J Psychiatry* **162**, 2322–2329.
230. Davis CE, Jeste DV, Eyler LT (2005) Review of longitudinal functional neuroimaging studies of drug treatments in patients with schizophrenia. *Schizophrenia Research* **78**, 45–60.
231. Braus DF, Ende G, Hubrich-Ungureanu P, Henn FA (2000) Cortical response to motor stimulation in neuroleptic-naive first episode schizophrenics. *Psychiatry Res* **98**, 145–54.
232. Honey GD, Bullmore ET, Soni W *et al.* (1999) Differences in frontal cortical activation by a working memory task after substitution of risperidone for typical antipsychotic drugs in patients with schizophrenia. *Proc Natl Acad Sci U S A* **96**, 13432–13437.
233. Ojeda N, Ortuno F, Arbizu J *et al.* (2002) Functional neuroanatomy of sustained attention in schizophrenia: contribution of parietal cortices. *Hum Brain Mapp* **17**, 116–130.
234. Weiss EM, Siedentopf C, Golaszewski S *et al.* (2007) Brain activation patterns during a selective attention test–a functional MRI study in healthy volunteers and unmedicated patients during an acute episode of schizophrenia. *Psychiatry Res* **154**, 31–40.
235. Tost H, Meyer-Lindenberg, Klein S *et al.* (2006) D2 antidopaminergic modulation of frontal lobe functions in healthy subjects. *Biol Psychiatry* **60**(11), 1196–1205.

236. Mehta MA, Manes FF, Magnolfi G *et al.* (2004) Impaired set-shifting and dissociable effects on tests of spatial working memory following the dopamine D2 receptor antagonist sulpiride in human volunteers. *Psychopharmacology (Berl)* **176**, 331–342.

237. Goto Y, Grace AA (2005) Dopaminergic modulation of limbic and cortical drive of nucleus accumbens in goal-directed behavior. *Nat Neurosci* **8**, 805–812.

238. Floresco SB, Magyar O (2006) Mesocortical dopamine modulation of executive functions: beyond working memory. *Psychopharmacology (Berl)* **188**, 567–585.

239. Konopaske GT, Dorph-Petersen KA, Pierri JN *et al.* (2007) Effect of chronic exposure to antipsychotic medication on cell numbers in the parietal cortex of macaque monkeys. *Neuropsychopharmacology* **32**, 1216–1223.

240. Konopaske GT, Dorph-Petersen KA, Sweet RA *et al.* (2008) Effect of chronic antipsychotic exposure on astrocyte and oligodendrocyte numbers in macaque monkeys. *Biol Psychiatry* **63**, 759–765.

241. Newton SS, Duman RS (2007) Neurogenic actions of atypical antipsychotic drugs and therapeutic implications. *CNS Drugs* **21**(9), 715–725.

242. Eastwood SL, Brunet PWJ, Harrison PJ (2000) Expression of complexin I and II mRNAs and their regulation by antipsychotic drugs in the rat forebrain. *Synapse* **36**, 167–177.

243. Schmitt A, Zink M, Müller B *et al.* (2003) Effects of long-term antipsychotic treatment on NMDA receptor binding and gene expression of subunits. *Neurochemical Research* **28**(2), 235–241.

244. Carlsson A (2001) A paradigm shift in brain research. *Science* **294**, 1021–102.

245. Schmitt A, Zink M, May B *et al.* (2003) Decreased gene expression of glial and neuronal glutamate transporters after antipsychotic treatment in rat brain. *Neuroscience Letters* **347**(2), 81–84.

246. Adamcio B, Sargin D, Stradomska A *et al.* (2008) Erythropoietin enhances hippocampal long-term potentiation and memory. *BMC Biol* **9**, 6–37.

247. Millan MJ (2005) N-methyl-D-aspartate receptors as target for improved antipsychotic agents: novel insights and clinical perspectives. *Psychopharmacology* **179**(1):30–53.

248. Hajos M, Rogers BN (2009) Targeting alpha7 nicotinic acetylcholine receptors in the treatment of schizophrenia. *Curr Pharm Des* Nov 12 [Epub ahead of print].

249. Pajonk F, Wobrock T, Gruber O *et al.* (2009) Hippocampal plasticity in response to exercise in schizophrenia. *Arch Gen Psychiatry* **67**(2), 133–143.

250. Hu S, Ying Z, Gomez-Pinilla F, Frautschy SA (2009) Exercise can increase small heat shock proteins (sHSP) and pre- and post-synaptic proteins in the hippocampus. *Brain Research* **1249**, 191–201.

CHAPTER 3

Neurocognition, social cognition and functional outcome in schizophrenia

William P. Horan, Philippe-Olivier Harvey, Robert S. Kern and Michael F. Green

VA Desert Pacific Mental Illness Research Education and Clinical Center, UCLA Semel Institute for Neuroscience and Human Behavior

---

Information Box Summary Statements

- Neurocognitive and social cognitive impairments are distinctive, core features of schizophrenia that are not secondary to factors such as clinical symptoms, medication-related effects, or illness chronicity.
- Neurocognitive and social cognitive impairments each uniquely contribute to poor functional outcome in schizophrenia – they are among the most important determinants of poor outcome.
- Recent evidence indicates that social cognition mediates the relation between neurocognition on the one hand, and functional outcome on the other hand.
- Neurocognition and social cognition are both viewed as highly promising targets for novel pharmacological and psychosocial interventions that enable people with schizophrenia to achieve functional recovery.

INTRODUCTION

People with schizophrenia experience very high levels of disability and poor community outcome [1,2]. Despite major advances in treating the acute psychotic symptoms of schizophrenia, most patients continue to function poorly between episodes

Schizophrenia: Current Science and Clinical Practice, First Edition. Edited by Wolfgang Gaebel.
© 2011 John Wiley & Sons, Ltd. Published 2011 by John Wiley & Sons, Ltd.

in the areas of work, independent living and social relations, and residual clinical symptoms are typically rather weak predictors of outcome. Thus, improvements in functioning are unlikely to come about through better symptom management alone. Instead, new treatments are needed that address the key determinants of poor functional outcome. This recognition is central to prevailing recovery-oriented approaches to treatment, which reflect a fundamental shift from a focus on symptom reduction to a focus on functional recovery and pursuit of personally meaningful goals and aspirations.

The rational development of new recovery-oriented treatments requires a clear understanding of the key determinants of poor functioning. Considerable evidence indicates that cognitive factors, including neurocognition (defined in this chapter as non-social cognition) and social cognition, are among the most important determinants of how well people with schizophrenia are able to function in the community. Although neurocognition has been a long-standing focus in schizophrenia research, social cognition has emerged more recently as a high priority topic for exploration. This change reflects rapidly growing evidence that social cognition holds a unique role in amplifying our understanding of cognitive processes involved in the social functioning of persons with schizophrenia. Researchers have also begun to develop and test integrative models of the relationship among neurocognition, social cognition, and functioning, which provide important guidance for treatment development efforts aimed at promoting functional recovery.

This chapter provides an overview of neurocognition and social cognition in schizophrenia and their linkages to functional outcome. We begin by reviewing the major domains of neurocognition and social cognition that are affected in schizophrenia, including commonly used assessment methods, their distinctiveness from other features of schizophrenia, their functional correlates, and current research trends. We then review statistical modeling studies that suggest social cognition mediates the relation between neurocognition on the one hand and functional outcome on the other. We conclude with a brief discussion of the treatment implications of these findings and efforts to translate this body of research into new clinical intervention approaches.

NEUROCOGNITION IN SCHIZOPHRENIA

The clinical observation that neurocognitive impairment was a primary feature of schizophrenia can be traced back to the early writings of Emil Kraepelin at the turn of the twentieth century and his use of the term Dementia Praecox to describe the disorder (3). He noted that onset typically occurred in early adulthood (praecox) and resulted in progressive functional and intellectual decline (dementia) in most cases. In his writings on the clinical presentation of dementia praecox, Kraepelin described a wide range of neurocognitive impairments that included disturbances in attention, learning, and problem solving. These disturbances were noted to have marked effects on social behaviour, independent living, and work functioning.

Neurocognition is a term that has been used very broadly to describe functions subsumed by regions of the brain or its networks, and how these relate to thought processes (for example, reasoning) and human behaviour. It encompasses abilities such as perception, processing speed, attention, memory, language processing, visuospatial ability, and executive functions used to interact with and make sense of the environment. The neurocognitive deficits of schizophrenia have been examined and documented in scores of studies using a wide array of tasks derived from traditional clinical neuropsychological batteries as well as cognitive and experimental psychology.

Domains, measurement and magnitude of impairment

Schizophrenia is typically characterised as a disorder with generalised neurocognitive dysfunction that includes specific domains that are more adversely affected than others [5,6]. The breadth of impairment is large, spanning from basic perceptual and speeded motor functions to complex memory, attention, and executive functions. In chronic, stable outpatient samples, clinically meaningful differences are found between patients and healthy controls across these domains with effect sizes typically ranging between .75 and 1.5. This literature was summarised in a large meta-analytic study by Heinrichs and Zakzanis [5], which included 204 studies involving 7420 patients and 5865 controls. The tasks included in this analysis were remarkably diverse, ranging from computerised to pencil-and-paper performance-based tasks of general abilities, derived standardised neuropsychological batteries and specialised cognitive paradigms. Across measures, results indicated that: (a) virtually all areas of cognition are impaired in schizophrenia to some degree, with a preponderance of measures demonstrating a medium–large effect size deficits relative to controls; (b) measures of episodic memory, ideational fluency and aspects of complex attention appear to be most impaired; and (c) measures of semantic knowledge and visual perceptual skills appear to be least impaired. More recent research has highlighted processing speed as an area of impairment with effect sizes comparable, if not higher than, those found for episodic memory [7]. As discussed below, the diverse assessment methods used to document this cognitive profile have created some practical obstacles to making significant advances in clinical therapeutics.

Neurocognition as a core deficit of schizophrenia

Neurocognitive deficits appear to be a core feature of schizophrenia. In the current context, a "core" feature means that these deficits represent a fundamental aspect of the illness, not simply the result of symptoms or the current treatments. Several lines of evidence support this conceptualisation:

1. Neurocognitive deficits are relatively common in schizophrenia. One influential study estimated that 90% of patients have clinically meaningful deficits in at least one domain and that 75% have deficits in at least two [8]. Even these relatively high rates may be underestimates of the frequency of neurocognitive impairment in schizophrenia. It is possible that almost all schizophrenia patients are performing at a level below what would be expected in the absence of illness, based, for example, on the fact that affected monozygotic twins perform more poorly than their unaffected co-twin on neurocognitive tests [9].

2. Neurocognitive deficits appear to be relatively independent of the clinical symptoms of the disorder. Although it is somewhat intuitive to expect neurocognitive functioning to be adversely affected by positive symptoms of psychosis (for example, hallucinations, delusions), the correlations between psychotic symptom severity and measures of cognitive performance are typically small [10–13]. Neurocognitive deficits show a stronger, more consistent relationship with disorganised and negative symptoms (for example, avolition, alogia, apathy, anhedonia) [14,15], but the amount of shared variance remains relatively small (often 5-10%).

3. The time course of neurocognitive deficits differs considerably from acute psychotic episodes. Psychotic symptoms tend to fluctuate from states of acute exacerbation to relative stability or remission. In contrast, for a number of areas of neurocognitive functioning the level of impairment when patients are in psychotic episode is similar to that seen when their symptoms are under control or in remission, indicating stability across the clinical state.

4. The scope and severity of neurocognitive deficits seen in persons with schizophrenia do not appear to be fully explained by treatment with antipsychotic medications or concomitant anticholinergic medications for side-effects. Both first- and second-generation antipsychotic treatments have much stronger effects on psychotic symptoms as compared to neurocognition, suggesting that antipsychotic medications act on different neural systems from those that underlie neurocognitive impairments. Recent studies suggest first- and second-generation antipsychotics convey similarly modest neurocognitive benefits compared to conventional agents [16–18].

5. As documented in a recent meta-analysis [19] the profile of neurocognitive deficits found in chronic patients is similar to that found during the early-onset period of schizophrenia, suggesting that deficits seen in chronic patients are not simply due to factors associated with chronicity. The level of neurocognitive impairment remains relatively stable during the adult years (ages 21–55), and persists into late-life when there may be further decline.

6. Many patients demonstrate neurocognitive impairments before the onset of psychotic symptoms and other more prominent clinical features as evidenced by

results from studies of prodromal samples and meta-analyses of family studies of at-risk children and adolescents [20–22].

7. Milder neurocognitive impairment can be detected in first-degree relatives of schizophrenic patients who have no evidence of psychosis [23]. The presence of such deficits in relatives suggests that certain neurocognitive deficits are likely to be components of genetic vulnerability to schizophrenia.

8. Finally, schizophrenia has a modal pattern of neurocognitive deficits that is different from that seen in other disorders, such as dementia and depression [5,24].

Thus, neurocognitive impairments reflect a primary deficit and are not secondary to other features of the illness or treatment-related factors, are common to most (if not all) persons with schizophrenia, and show linkages to genetic vulnerability. In addition, neurocognitive deficits in schizophrenia have considerable functional significance.

Associations with functional outcome

Neurocognitive deficits are intimately related to the functional outcome of people with schizophrenia. Importantly, functional outcome can be measured in several different ways using ratings from clinical interviewers, informants, or patients [25]. Commonly assessed aspects of functioning include: (a) Real world-functioning, which indexes one's actual level of functional attainment in areas such as work, independent living and activities of daily living, and social activities/networks; (b) Quality of Life, or subjective sense of well-being and satisfaction with life; (c) Psychiatric rehabilitation success; (d) Functional capacity, which assesses social competence or skill in the context of role play tasks to index what one is capable of doing, regardless of what one actually does in the community.

The neurocognitive deficits of schizophrenia show highly consistent cross-sectional relationships to each type of functional outcome listed above [26,27]. Reviews identify learning and memory, attention, working memory, reasoning and problem-solving abilities, and processing speed as individual domains that yield strong relationships with functional outcome. These relationships are typically stronger than those found between psychotic symptoms and functional outcome. One review showed that these findings extend beyond cross-sectional relationships and are present in longitudinal studies as well [28]. In terms of the magnitude of these relations, although modest amounts of variance are explained at the individual domain level, the amount can be quite large when the effects of neurocognitive functioning are considered more broadly. For example, when multiple neurocognitive domains are included in a summary score as much as 30% of the variance in functional outcome can be explained [29]. Hence, neurocognitive impairments reflect "rate limiting factors" for functional recovery.

In summary, a large body of evidence indicates that neurocognitive deficits are distinctive features of schizophrenia and key determinants of real world functioning. These characteristics provide a compelling rationale for intervening at the level of neurocognition as a means to improve functional outcome. However, until recently there were a number of major obstacles to developing new pharmacological treatments for neurocognitive impairment in schizophrenia; two of them involved the definition and measurement of neurocognition for clinical trials. First, there had never been any consensus on what the relevant domains of neurocognition should be for clinical trials of cognition enhancing treatments. Second, there had been no widely accepted, standardised assessment battery to evaluate the efficacy of new cognition-enhancing drugs that is recognised by regulatory agencies. In 2002 the NIMH established the Measurement and Treatment Research to Improve Cognition in Schizophrenia (MATRICS) initiative to address these obstacles and thereby stimulate the development of new cognition enhancing treatment approaches.

The NIMH-MATRICS initiative and current research directions

The NIMH-MATRICS initiative was established to achieve empirically guided consensus on the key domains of cognition in schizophrenia that are relevant for intervention as a foundation for establishing a standardised assessment battery for use in clinical trials. The mandate of MATRICS was to reach consensus on the methods and measures that would be used to evaluate promising new drugs so they could be considered for regulatory approval for cognition enhancement in schizophrenia. The expectation was that once a pathway to drug approval was constructed, the pharmaceutical industry would travel it.

Given the range of neurocognitive impairments in schizophrenia, a fundamental question was whether it was possible to identify reliably separable domains of neurocognitive deficit. To accomplish this task, a team of experts carefully evaluated all known exploratory and confirmatory factor analytic studies of neurocognitive performance in schizophrenia. Because the intent was to develop a consensus based cognitive performance battery for clinical trials of promising pro-cognitive agents for schizophrenia, consideration was also given to the potential for 'pharmacologic sensitivity'. For example, general verbal ability was found to be a replicable factor but was not included as a relevant domain for this purpose because of its likely resistance to change [30]. It was concluded that six separable factors could be identified based on replicated findings from multiple independent studies and were appropriate for inclusion in a consensus cognitive battery for clinical trials: attention/vigilance, speed of processing, working memory, verbal learning, visual learning, reasoning and problem-solving [31]. A seventh domain, social cognition, was added due to recent increased interest in this area and other evidence of its relevance for clinical trials, as described below.

Table 3.1   Seven neurocognitive domains assessed by the MATRICS Consensus Cognitive Battery (MCCB)

Neurocognitive domain	MCCB test
Attention/vigilance	• Continuous Performance Test – Identical Pairs version [164,165]
Speed of processing	• Trail Making Test – Part A [166] • Brief Assessment of Cognition in Schizophrenia - Symbol Coding subtest [167] • Category fluency – animal naming [168]
Working memory	• Letter-Number Span [169] • Wechsler Memory Scale – III Spatial Span subtest [170]
Verbal learning	• Hopkins Verbal Learning Test – Revised [171]
Visual learning	• Brief Visuospatial Memory Test – Revised [172]
Reasoning and problem solving	• Neuropsychological Assessment Battery - Mazes subtest [173]
Social cognition	• Mayer-Salovey-Caruso Emotional Intelligence Test-Managing Emotions [45]

The next step was to select appropriate tests to include in a consensus neurocognitive assessment battery that would provide a standard endpoint for clinical trials of cognition-enhancing drugs for schizophrenia. To establish the consensus battery, a thorough multistep process was carried out [32] to select from over 90 initially nominated tests based primarily on the following criteria: (a) test-retest reliability, (b) utility as a repeated measure, (c) relationship with functional outcome, and (d) practicality and tolerability. Thirty-six of the initially nominated tests were intensively scrutinised and rated by an independent group of diverse experts using the RAND/UCLA Appropriateness Method ([3], which led to the formulation of the beta version of the battery that included 20 tests across the seven domains. The beta version of the battery was then evaluated in a prospective study of 176 schizophrenia and schizoaffective disorder outpatients at five participating sites in the US. The results from the study led to the selection of ten tests for inclusion in the final MATRICS Consensus Cognitive Battery (MCCB), which are summarised in Table 3.1

The final MCCB was then co-normed in a sample of 300 community residents drawn from the same five research sites, and the data were used to develop a scoring program that provides standard scores based on these normative data. Since the MCCB became available for distribution in April 2006, two published reports have shown a relatively similar pattern of results with effect sizes ranging from .75 to 1.8 across tests in a young, adolescent schizophrenia spectrum disorder and chronically ill patient samples [34,35]. The MCCB has been translated and adapted into a variety of languages – simplified Chinese, Russian, German, Spanish for Spain, Spanish for Latin America, Hindi, Italian, Hebrew, Japanese and Croatian – and is currently being used in dozens of studies around the world.

One of the challenges the MATRICS Initiative faced was the need to produce a practical consensus-based set of cognitive measures for use in large clinical trials in a rapid time frame. Thus, MATRICS focused upon tasks with well-established and strong measurement properties (test-retest reliability, low practice effects, and so on), although considerations of construct and neural validity were also of high importance. Measures derived from cognitive neuroscience were considered, but many were not included primarily because they did not have already established psychometric properties. The Cognitive Neuroscience Treatment Research to Improve Cognition in Schizophrenia (CNTRICS; [36]) project grew out of the final MATRICS meeting, in which the potential interpretive benefits of using tasks and tools from cognitive neuroscience were broadly acknowledged. Measuring the function of specific cognitive subsystems that are linked to specific neural systems using a cognitive neuroscience approach offers unique advantages, especially for translational research. One key advantage is the ability to use the results of animal, as well as human, studies to identify molecular targets that modulate specific cognitive systems. The primary goal of CNTRICS is to formally address this limitation and to help the field better integrate the tools and constructs of cognitive neuroscience into translational research focusing on developing therapies for impaired cognitive and emotional processing in schizophrenia.

In contrast to MATRICS, which focused on the needs of large-scale clinical trials and the later stages of drug development (phase 3), the initial products of CNTRICS will likely have their most immediate impact upon earlier phases of drug discovery and testing, such as initial human studies and proof of concept studies seeking preliminary evidence of efficacy (that is, phase 1 and 2 studies). Following a similar consensus-based approach as MATRICS, key cognitive neuroscience constructs have been identified and the most promising methods for assessment have been selected (see [37]. These steps set the stage for on-going translational research to develop performance based tasks and biomarkers that are more sensitive to specific neural systems that contribute to the cognitive deficits of schizophrenia.

SOCIAL COGNITION

Although (non-social) neurocognition has been a long-standing focus in schizophrenia research, social cognition has emerged more recently as a high priority topic for exploration. Social cognition is a multifaceted construct that broadly refers to the mental operations underlying social interactions, including perceiving, interpreting and generating responses to the intentions, dispositions and behaviours of others [38,39]. It includes the ways in which we decipher an emotion on another person's face and how we draw inferences about another's intentions. Simply put, social cognition is a set of skills that people use to understand and effectively interact with other people. Therefore, problems in social cognition, such as mis-perceptions and unexpected reactions to and from other people, can be expected to adversely impact functioning across a variety of domains. Research on social cognition in schizophrenia has expanded exponentially over the past 5-10 years and now clearly indicates that this disorder is characterised by substantial, wide-ranging social cognitive impairments that are separate from basic neurocognitive deficits. As noted above, the investigators of the NIMH-MATRICS identified it as one of seven key cognitive domains that should be routinely assessed in clinical trials of new cognitive enhancers for schizophrenia [31]. This section of the chapter provides a brief overview of the major domains of social cognition studied in schizophrenia.

Domains, measurement and magnitude of impairment

The rapid expansion of social cognition research in schizophrenia has resulted in the use of an increasingly diverse range of terminology and assessment techniques. In light of the diverse range of terms and paradigms used across studies, the NIMH recently sponsored a consensus-building workshop to integrate research in this area and guide future research efforts [40]. This section is organised in terms of the five broad domains of social cognition suggested by this work group, which are summarised in Table 3.2 along with commonly used assessment measures. Importantly, these domains capture the way the field is covered in the literature and are not generally considered to be pure subprocesses. As will become apparent, the distinctions among these areas are not always clear-cut. In addition, some of the areas (for example, emotion processing) are routinely divided into subprocesses in studies with healthy subjects. Nonetheless, this listing of domains captures the current state of the schizophrenia research literature, and maps reasonably well onto other models of social cognition that are based on neuroimaging findings in healthy samples [41].

Emotional processing

Emotional processing refers broadly to aspects of perceiving and using emotion to facilitate adaptive functioning. One influential model of emotional processing defines 'emotional intelligence' as a set of skills that combines emotions and cognition. The model is comprised of four emotional processing components, including identifying emotions, facilitating emotions, understanding emotions, and managing emotions [42,43]. Affect perception, which falls in the identifying emotions component of this model, has been the most extensively studied social cognitive process in schizophrenia. Deficits have been most frequently documented in paradigms that

Table 3.2 Domains of social cognition studied in schizophrenia

Domain	Representative tasks
Emotional Processing	• Facial Emotion Identification Test [174] • Voice Emotion Identification Test [174] • Penn Computerized Neurocognitive Battery – Emotion Recognition Test [175] • The Awareness of Social Inference Test – Part 1 [80] • Mayer-Salovey-Caruso Emotional Intelligence Test [45]
Social Perception	• Profile of Non-Verbal Sensitivity [53] • Social Cue Recognition Test [51]
Social Knowledge	• Situational Features Recognition Test [60] • Schema Comprehension Sequencing Test-Revised [61]
Attributional Bias	• Attributional Style Questionnaire [67] • Internal, Personal, and Situational Attributions Questionnaire [63] • Ambiguous Intentions Hostility Questionnaire [69]
Theory of Mind	• False belief stories [74] • False belief picture sequencing [77] • Hinting task [75] • Reading the Mind in the Eyes test [76] • The Awareness of Social Inferences Test – Parts 2 & 3 [80]

require subjects to identify or discriminate between emotions displayed in still photographs of a single person's face. Similar deficits are found in studies of perceiving emotion in vocalizations or videotaped monologues, with deficits sometimes found to be more severe for certain negative (fear, disgust) compared to positive emotions. The magnitude of patient versus control differences is large; a recent meta-analysis of 86 studies using diverse tasks reported an overall effect size of .91 [44].

Other aspects of emotion processing have been much less extensively studied and the measures used vary widely. For example, the social cognitive measure included in the MCCB, the Managing Emotions subtest of the Mayer-Salovey-Caruso Emotional Intelligence Test (MSCEIT; [45]), involves reading brief social/emotional vignettes and responding to questions about how individuals manage, regulate, or facilitate emotion in themselves and others. Deficits on the Managing Emotions and the other performance-based MSCEIT subtests have been documented in schizophrenia [46,47]. Patients have also shown abnormalities on various self-report measures of emotional processing and on experimental paradigms that assess how patients regulate (for example, intentionally suppress, reappraise) their responses to evocative stimuli [48–50].

Social perception

Social perception refers to a person's ability to judge social cues from contextual information and communicative gestures, including awareness of the roles, rules and goals that typically characterise social situations and guide social interactions [51,52]. In social perception tasks, participants must process nonverbal, paraverbal, and/or verbal cues to make inferences about complex or ambiguous social situations. Individuals may be asked to identify interpersonal features in a situation such as intimacy, status, mood state and veracity. The most commonly used tasks in this domain were developed nearly twenty years ago. For example, the Profile of Nonverbal Sensitivity [53] involves watching two second videos of a Caucasian woman that include facial expressions, vocal intonations, and /or body gestures, and selecting from two labels (for example, saying a prayer, talking to a lost child) the one that best described the most likely context for the social cue(s). Similarly, the Social Cue Recognition Test [51] involves watching videotaped vignettes of two to three actors engaged in low emotion (for example, two friends assembling a puzzle) or high emotion (for example, a husband and wife fighting about their children) situations, and answering true-false questions about concrete and abstract cues displayed during the interactions.

A handful of studies using more contemporary stimuli have assessed the impact of contextual information on social perception in schizophrenia. For example, a series of studies by M.J. Green and colleagues used paradigms in which subjects evaluate the emotions or mental states of people shown in pictures either in isolation (that is, no social context) or embedded in a surrounding social context. Schizophrenia patients' socioemotional judgements were significantly less influenced by contextual information than those of healthy controls [54,55]. Along these lines, a few other research groups have reported deficits in extracting information from complex emotional scenes, and orienting to and visual scanning of social contextual information in schizophrenia [56,57]. These skills required to successfully perform social perception tasks rely on subjects' knowledge about the rules that typically govern social situation, which overlaps with the following domain.

Social knowledge

This area refers to awareness of the roles, rules and goals that characterise social situations and guide social interactions [52,58,59]. Social knowledge (also called social schema) can be measured with paper-and-pencil tests that assess one's awareness of what is socially expected in different situations (for example, in a doctor's office versus in a restaurant). It has been studied somewhat less than the other areas in schizophrenia, and it overlaps with social perception; successful social knowledge requires awareness of which cues occur typically in specific social situations (that is, social perception) and how one is supposed to respond to them. Tasks in this area primarily assess awareness of what is socially expected in different situations. For example, compared to controls, schizophrenia patients have shown impairment on the Social Features Recognition Test [60], a multiple-choice test that assesses participants' knowledge of the characteristics (for example, roles, rules) of different social situations. Similarly, impairments have been found on the Schema Comprehension Sequencing Test-Revised [61,62], which requires subjects to sort index cards describing actions into meaningful sequences of social behaviour.

Attributional bias

Attributional style refers to how individuals characteristically explain the causes for positive and negative events in their lives. Attributions can be measured by questionnaires [63] or rated from transcripts of interactions [64]. In research involving both psychiatric and non-psychiatric samples, key distinctions are typically made between external personal attributions (that is, causes attributed to other people), external situational attributions (that is, causes attributed to situational factors), and internal attributions (that is, causes due to oneself). In schizophrenia research, this aspect of social cognition has been studied primarily in the context of understanding the psychological mechanisms of persecutory delusions and paranoid beliefs. For example, individuals with persecutory delusions may tend to blame others rather than situations for negative events, an attributional style known as a 'personalizing bias' [65,66]. Individuals characterised by this style may also be prone to attribute ambiguous events to hostile intentions of others or to jump quickly to conclusions when forming impressions about others without modifying their impressions based on contextual information.

Instrumentation in this area is limited and results have been somewhat mixed. However, associations between paranoid beliefs and attributional style have been found using socioemotional information processing tasks and self-report measures, such as Attributional Style Questionnaire [67] or the Internal, Personal, and Situational Attributions Questionnaire; [63,68], which describes various hypothetical situations and asks participants to generate explanations for why the events occurred [66,68]. A recently developed self-report measure, the Ambiguous Intentions Hostility Questionnaire [69], and alternative systems for coding attributions from narratives provided by subjects [70, 71], may help address these issues.

Theory of mind

Theory of Mind (also called mental state attribution or mentalising) typically involves the ability to infer intentions, dispositions and beliefs of others [72,73]. Processes typically associated with Theory of Mind involve the ability to understand false beliefs, hints, intentions, humour, deceptions, metaphor and irony. Theory of Mind studies in schizophrenia have relied heavily on paper-and-pencil measures, such as short stories or sequential picture sets of line drawings [74–78], several of which were passed down from the developmental literature examining the social development of healthy children and those with autism spectrum disorders. For example, false belief tasks involve reading short stories and answering questions to assess whether individuals are capable of understanding basic first-order false beliefs (that is, that someone can hold a false belief about a state of the world) or more complex second-order false beliefs (that is, that someone can have a false belief about the belief of another person). Other paradigms evaluate whether subjects can arrange cartoon panels in a coherent fashion by using knowledge about the complex mental states (for example, intention to deceive) of the characters depicted in the pictures [79].

Some more developmentally appropriate and alternative paradigms have recently been applied to schizophrenia. For example, patients have been found to show deficits on The Awareness of Social Inferences Test (Part 3; [80]), a paradigm specifically developed for adults that assesses mentalising processes depicted in videotaped interactions between adults, such as forming inferences about others' intentions and beliefs, and detecting sarcasm and white lies [81]. Another recent study found mentalising impairment in schizophrenia using a computerised paradigm derived from social psychology that depicts dynamic 'interactions' among animated figures [82]. These dynamic types of paradigms may more directly assess theory of mind related processes required for effective every day interactions. Schizophrenia patients consistently show deficits on a variety of tasks believed to involve Theory of Mind-related abilities [83,84], with meta-analyses reporting overall effect sizes based on over 30 studies ranging .90 - 1.25 [85,86].

Social cognition as a core feature of schizophrenia

Although the research literature on social cognition is considerably smaller than the literature on neurocognition in schizophrenia, there is growing evidence that social cognition also demonstrates the characteristics of a core feature of this disorder. For example, several studies have reported social cognitive impairments in prodromal, unmedicated, or recent-onset patients, suggesting impairments are not merely attributable to medication effects or factors associated with chronicity [87–92]. Longitudinal studies have shown that impairments in emotional processing, social perception and Theory of Mind are relatively stable over time and are present even after the remission of psychotic symptoms, suggesting they are trait-like and not merely secondary to clinical symptoms. There is also emerging evidence for the presence of social cognitive deficits across different phases of illness [93–95]. Social cognitive impairments have been found in some studies of unaffected relatives of schizophrenia patients, suggesting links to genetic vulnerability

[96–101]. Importantly, social cognitive deficits can be distinguished from nonsocial neurocognitive deficits, a topic to which we return in a later section. Finally, as is the case for neurocognition, social cognitive deficits appear to have considerable functional significance.

Association with functional outcome

A key motivation to study social cognition in schizophrenia is to explain heterogeneity of functional outcome. For example, misperceptions during social interactions could adversely impact how people with schizophrenia interpret the behaviour of others, which may result in interpersonal conflicts and/or social withdrawal. In support of this expectation, a growing literature demonstrates consistent patterns of association between social cognition and various aspects of community functioning. In a recent comprehensive literature review of 23 studies, Couture and colleagues [102] documented significant relationships with actual community functioning, quality of life, social behaviours in therapeutic settings, and performance measures of social competence (for example, social role-play tasks). The majority of relevant studies examined emotion perception and social perception. Theory of Mind and Attributional style have received considerably less attention in terms of their functional significance, though support for associations with social competence and community functioning continues to emerge.

In summary, it is increasingly clear that people with schizophrenia show substantial impairments across multiple domains of social cognition. These appear to be enduring deficits that show meaningful links to social functioning. Hence, like neurocognition, social cognition appears to be a consistent correlate of functional outcome. As discussed further below, these findings have lead to considerable excitement about the possibility of intervening at the level of social cognition as a means of improving functional outcome.

Current research directions

Although social cognition holds considerable promise for explaining functional outcome in schizophrenia, research into social cognition is much less mature than the literature on neurocognition and a number of key issues remain to be addressed. First, optimal parsing of social cognitive domains in schizophrenia remains an important issue. The boundaries between the social cognitive areas reviewed above are clearly not absolute and further information on the structure of social cognition in schizophrenia is needed. A few factor analytic studies suggest that subdomains can be distinguished [103–105] but additional studies that include larger social cognitive test batteries are needed to address this issue. Second, the psychometric properties of several social cognitive measures are often less than ideal. For example, many tasks adapted from other conditions (for example, childhood autism) show ceiling effects or poor reliability in schizophrenia. Along these lines, the majority of the tasks were not developed for use in clinical trials and their utility as repeated measures and sensitivity to change in the context of treatment trials is unclear. Third, the ecological validity of many tasks has been questioned. Many commonly used tasks (for example, involving static pictures, cartoons, written vignettes) may be quite limited in their ability to capture the complexity and dynamic nature of stimuli that convey meaning in daily social interactions.

Fourth, social cognition is a very broad domain and research in schizophrenia has focused on a narrow subset of the constructs subsumed within this domain. For example, processes such as empathy and self-versus-other related processing are central constructs in social cognition in healthy individuals [106–108] but have received minimal attention in schizophrenia. Fifth, there is much work to be done on examining the neural correlates of social cognitive impairments in schizophrenia. Fortunately, the burgeoning field of social cognitive neuroscience provides a rich conceptual and methodological foundation for expanding the range of constructs studied in schizophrenia and their neural correlates. Finally, as described in the following section, the relationship between neurocognition and social cognition, particularly in terms of understanding the processes that lead to poor functional outcome, is an area of considerable current research interest and clinical relevance.

RELATIONSHIPS AMONG NEUROCOGNITION, SOCIAL COGNITION AND FUNCTIONAL OUTCOME

Neurocognition and social cognition are both clearly impaired and related to poor functional outcome in schizophrenia. A fundamental question is whether neurocognition and social cognition are separable domains; if there is very large overlap between them in schizophrenia it would raise questions about the value of considering social cognition as a separate domain. A related question is whether neurocognition and social cognition uniquely contribute to our understanding of outcome; information about the mechanistic relations between different aspects of cognition and outcome is of considerable importance for optimal treatment development. We now turn to an overview of literature pertinent to these questions.

Distinctiveness of neurocognition and social cognition

The distinctiveness of neurocognition and social cognition in schizophrenia can be considered at several levels. Conceptually, neurocognition is relatively affect-neutral whereas social cognition involves the interface of socio-emotional and cognitive processing [109,110]. Methodologically, the distinction between these processes depends largely on the types of stimuli (for example, people or faces versus objects) and the type of judgement being made (for example, attributing a mental state to another person versus basic tests of attention, speed of processing, or memory). Neurocognitive and social cognitive tasks often share cognitive processes, such as working memory and perception, and therefore are clearly associated. Indeed, significant correlations are found between performance on measures of social cognition and neurocognition in schizophrenia (for example, [111–114]). However, the magnitude of these relations is generally moderate. Furthermore, studies using confirmatory factor analysis in schizophrenia patients [115–117] or exploratory factor analysis in participants with psychosis or heightened vulnerability to psychosis [104,118] indicate that models fit better when the two domains are separated compared to when they are combined. The general conclusion from these studies is that social cognition in schizophrenia is associated with neurocognition, but is not redundant with it.

The question of the distinctiveness of neurocognition and social cognition is not specific to schizophrenia research, but also applies to social cognitive neuroscience research in healthy samples. Evidence increasingly suggests that the processing of social and nonsocial stimuli rely on semi-independent neural systems. For example, dissociations between aspects of social cognition and neurocognition are evident in various clinical conditions, such as prosopagnosia, Williams syndrome, and patients with certain prefrontal cortex lesions [119–121]. Functional neuroimaging research also increasingly suggests that the processing of social and nonsocial stimuli rely on semi-independent neural systems, with growing evidence of a neural network composed of the prefrontal cortex, fusiform gyrus, superior temporal sulcus, and amygdala that is specialised for processing social information [110,122,123]. Thus, the conclusion of partial overlap in schizophrenia is fully consistent with studies from non-clinical social neuroscience that reveal partially overlapping and partially distinctive patterns of neural activation between neurocognitive and social cognitive tasks [124].

A related question is whether social cognition shows unique relationships to functional outcome in schizophrenia. That is, does social cognition account for additional variance in outcome above and beyond the contribution of neurocognition? Several studies using correlation and regression techniques have now evaluated this issue. It does indeed appear from several data sets that social cognition contributes incremental validity for both real-world functioning and functional capacity beyond that provided by neurocognition ([113,125–130]). Notably, social cognition accounts for comparable, or sometimes larger, overall proportions of variance in outcome than neurocognition (for example, [131,132]). Thus, neurocognition and social cognition appear to be separable domains that uniquely contribute to the prediction of functional outcome in schizophrenia.

Social cognition as a mediator

Linkages between neurocognition, social cognition and functional outcome are well documented. However, the pathway(s) through which neurocognitive deficits

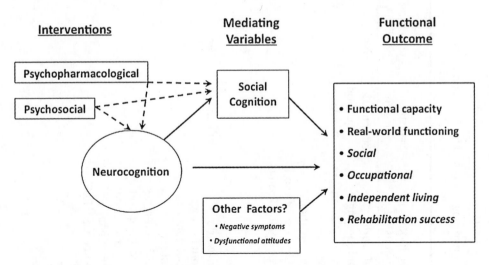

Figure 3.1 Model of Relations among Neurocognition, Social Cognition, and Functional Outcome in Schizophrenia

ultimately lead to poor functioning are complex and likely to involve a host of intervening and interacting variables. A number of potential mediating variables have been proposed to contribute to this causal pathway. For example, as displayed in Figure 3.1, M.F. Green and Nuechterlein [133] proposed that social cognition functions as a key mediator between neurocognition on the one hand, and functional outcome on the other. Using statistical modeling approaches, such as path analysis and structural equation modeling, researchers have begun to empirically test whether social cognition mediates the link between neurocognitive impairments and functional outcome.

To our knowledge, 12 published studies from 10 independent data sets have evaluated whether social cognitive variables mediate the relation between neurocognition and one or more aspects of functional outcome in schizophrenia. These studies are summarised in chronological order in Table 3.3. The sample sizes range from 26–151 individuals in inpatient and/or outpatient settings. Regarding functional outcome domains, eight studies evaluated aspects of real-world functioning, three examined functional capacity, one examined a combination of real-world functioning and functional capacity, and one focused on 12-month psychosocial rehabilitation success. Across the diverse samples, statistical methods, neurocognitive and social cognitive measures, and outcome domains reflected in these 12 studies, 11 reported support for a mediating role for social cognition. The hypothesis that social cognition serves as a mediator in explaining outcome has thus received remarkably consistent support to date.

Although the available evidence supports the conceptualisation of social cognition as a mediator, some methodological aspects of these studies warrant comment. First, the majority of studies was cross-sectional and included somewhat

Table 3.3 Studies examining whether social cognition mediates the relation between neurocognition and functional outcome in schizophrenia

Study	Sample	Design	Neurocognitive and social cognitive measures	Functional outcome domain(s)	Statistical approach	Social cognition mediates?
Vauth et al., 2004 [131]	133 schizophrenia inpatients	Cross-sectional	**Neurocognition:** Vigilance: DS-CPT; Executive functions: WCST; Cognitive flexibility: Trails A/B; Working memory: LNS; Verbal memory: WMS-2 Logical Memory. **Social cognition:** Social knowledge: SFRT; SCST.	**Real-world functioning:** Social skills and personal presentation subscales of Work Personality Profile	Structural Equation Modeling	Yes
Brekke et al., 2005 [134]	139 schizophrenia or schizoaffective outpatients (100 completed the 12-month protocol)	12-month longitudinal	**Neurocognition:** Letter fluency: COWAT; Distractibility: Digit span distractibility test; Verbal memory: CVLT; Vigilance: DS-CPT; Executive functions: WCST. **Social cognition:** Affect perception: FEIT, VEIT, Videotape Affect Perception Test.	**Real-world functioning:** Social competence subscale of the CAF, self-report social support scale, and global functional outcome – RFS	Path analysis	Yes

Study	Sample	Design	Measures	Outcome	Analysis	
Addington et al., 2006 [176]	103 outpatients: 50 first-episode psychosis, 53 multi-episode schizophrenia	Cross-sectional analyses at baseline and at 12-month follow-up assessments	**Neurocognition:** Letter fluency: COWAT, Category fluency; Verbal memory: LMI/LMII/RAVLT; Visual memory: RCF; Working memory: LNS; Executive functions: WCST; Vigilance: DS-CPT; Early visual processing: SPAN; Visual-constructional ability: RCF; Visuomotor sequencing: Trails A/B; Psychomotor speed: Grooved pegboard; Stroop. **Social cognition:** Social perception: SCRT; Social knowledge: SFRT.	**Real-world functioning:** QLS	Regression analyses	Yes
Nienow et al., 2006 [135]	56 schizophrenia or schizoaffective forensic inpatients	Cross-sectional	**Neurocognition function:** Vigilance: DS-CPT, auditory CPT; Early visual processing: SPAN. **Social cognition:** Affect perception: BLERT.	**Functional capacity:** AIPSS	Regression analyses, Sobel test	No
Sergi et al., 2006 [177]	75 schizophrenia outpatients	Cross-sectional	**Neurocognition:** Early visual processing; Forward & backward visual masking **Social Cognition:** Social Perception: Half-PONS.	**Real-world functioning:** RFS	Structural Equation Modeling	Yes

(Continued)

Table 3.3 (Continued)

Study	Sample	Design	Neurocognitive and social cognitive measures	Functional outcome domain(s)	Statistical approach	Social cognition mediates?
Horton & Silverstein, 2008 [178]	65 schizophrenia or schizoaffective outpatients (34 deaf & 31 hearing patients)	Cross-sectional	**Neurocognition:** Early visual processing: SPAN; Vigilance: DS-CPT, Verbal memory: RAVLT; Visual memory – CFT. **Social Cognition:** Affect perception: FEIT, FEDT; Theory of Mind: Hinting test.	**Real-world functioning:** MCAS	Regression analyses, Sobel test	Yes
Vaskinn et al., 2008 [179]	26 schizophrenia patients	Cross-sectional	**Neurocognition:** Semantic fluency – D-KEFS; Processing speed: Digit symbol, Grooved Pegboard; Vigilance: CPT-II, Working memory: Digit span; Executive functions: Color-Word Interference Test; Verbal memory: CVLT; Visual memory: CVMT; Problem solving: Matrix reasoning; Learning Potential: Test-train-test version of WCST. **Social cognition:** Affect perception: FEIT, VEIT, FEDT, VEDT.	**Functional capacity:** AIPPS	Regression analyses	Yes

| Bell et al., 2009 [117] | 151 schizophrenia or schizoaffective patients | 6-month longitudinal (work therapy program) | **Neurocognition:** Executive functions: WCST; Verbal Memory: HVLT; Working memory: Digit span; Processing speed: Digit Symbol; Thought disorder: Gorham's Proverbs Test. **Social cognition:** Affect perception: BLERT; Theory of Mind: Hinting Task; BORI Egocentricity Scale; Social Discomfort on the Job: Weekly evaluation. | **Rehabilitation outcome:** Measures of work performance (WBI), job complexity, & consistency of working. | Path Analysis | Yes |
| Gard et al., 2009 [138] | 91 schizophrenia outpatients | Cross-sectional | **Neurocognition:** Processing speed: Digit Symbol, Trails A; Category Fluency; Working memory: Digit span; Visual memory: Visual memory span; Verbal memory: CVLT; Stroop. **Social Cognition:** Affect perception: Facial Affect Recognition Test; Face memory: Test of Memory and Learning facial memory test; Prosody: Florida Affect Battery. | **Real-world outcome:** GAF scores | Path analysis | Yes |

(Continued)

Table 3.3 (Continued)

Study	Sample	Design	Neurocognitive and social cognitive measures	Functional outcome domain(s)	Statistical approach	Social cognition mediates?
Meyer & Kurtz, 2009 [180]	53 schizophrenia or schizoaffective outpatients	Cross-sectional	**Neurocognition:** Verbal intelligence: WAIS-III Vocabulary; Vigilance: Penn CPT; Problem-solving: PCET; Verbal memory: HVLT. **Social Cognition** Affect perception: Penn Emotion Acuity Test Emotion-Differentiation Task.	**Functional capacity:** Social Skills Performance Assessment	Regression analyses	Yes
Addington et al., 2010 [181]	93 first episode and multiple-episode schizophrenia patients (Overlapping sample with Addington et al., 2006)	Cross-sectional	**Neurocognition:** Letter fluency: COWAT, Category fluency; Verbal memory: LMI/LMII/RAVLT; Visual memory: RCF, Working memory: LNS; Executive functions: WCST; Attention: DS-CPT; Early visual processing: SPAN; Visual-constructional ability: RCF copy; Visuomotor sequencing: Trails A/B; Psychomotor speed: Grooved pegboard: Stroop. **Social cognition:** Affect perception: FEIT, FEDT; Social knowledge: SCRT, SFRT.	**Combination of Real-world functioning** (SFS, QLS) and **Functional capacity** (AIPPS)	Structural Equation Modeling	Yes

Rassovsky et al., in press [141]	174 schizophrenia outpatients (Overlapping sample with Sergi et al., 2006)	Cross-sectional	**Neurocognition:** Early visual processing: Forward & backward visual masking **Social Cognition:** Social Perception: Half-PONS.	**Real-world functioning:** RFS	Structural Equation Modeling	Yes

AIM = Affect Intensity Measure; AIPPS = Assessment of Interpersonal Problem Solving; BACS = Brief Assessment of Cognition in Schizophrenia; BADS = Behavioral Assessment of the Dysexecutive Syndrome battery; BLERT = Bell Lysaker Emotion Recognition Test; BORI = Bell Object Relations Inventory; CAF = Community Adjustment Form; CFT = Complex Figure Test; COWAT = Controlled Oral Word Association Test; CPT = Continuous Performance Test; CVLT = California Verbal Learning Test; CVMT = Continuous Visual Memory Test; DES-MOD = Differential Emotion Scale-Modified; DANVA-2 = The Diagnostic Analysis of Non-Verbal Accuracy II; D-KEFS = Delis-Kaplan Executive Function System; DS-CPT = Degraded Stimulus Continuous Performance Test; EVP = Early Visual Processing; FEDT = Facial Emotion Discrimination Task; FEIT = Facial Emotion Identification Task; GAF = Global Assessment of Functioning; HAWIE-R = Hamburg-Wechsler-Intelligence-Test, revised; HVLT = Hopkins Verbal Learning Test; LMI and LMII = Logical memory subtests of the Wechsler Memory Scale-Revised; LNS = Letter-Number Span; MCAS = Multnomah Community Ability Scale; MSCEIT = Mayer-Salovey-Caruso Emotional Intelligence Test; MWT = "Mehrfachwahlwortschatztest", best translated as "Multiple Choice Verbal Comprehension Test"; PCET = Penn Conditional Exclusion Test; PSP = The Personal and Social Performance Scale; QLS = Quality of Life Scale; RAVLT = Rey Auditory Verbal Learning Test; RCF = Rey Complex Figure; RFS = Role Functioning Scale; RPAS and RSAS = Revised Physical Anhedonia Scale / Revised Social Anhedonia Scale; SAS = Social Adjustment Scale; SBS = Social Behaviour Scale; SCRT = Social Cue Recognition Test; SEM = Structural Equation Modeling; SFS = Social Functioning Scale; SFRT = Situational Features Recognition Test; SPAN test = Partial Report Span of Apprehension test; TASIT = The Awareness of Social Inference Test; WAIS = Wechsler Adult Intelligence Scale; WBI = Work Behavior Inventory; WCST = Wisconsin Card Sorting Test; WMS = Wechsler Memory Scale; WPP = Work Personality Profile.

small sample sizes, which limits any inferences that can be made about causality. Notably, two of the largest studies incorporated longitudinal analyses of real-world functioning and rehabilitation outcome [117,134], which permits stronger causal inferences; additional longitudinal studies are needed. Second, the studies vary in exactly how mediation was assessed and whether evidence of full or partial mediation was found (or even reported). For example, one study that reported results consistent with mediation did not formally test whether social cognition acted as a mediator [131]. Third, it may be relevant to consider certain subject characteristics in order to understand these mechanistic relations. For example, the one study that failed to support a mediating role for social cognition used a unique inpatient forensic sample that had been hospitalised as an alternative to incarceration [135]. Fourth, the range of social cognitive variables considered has been fairly narrow, focusing largely on affect and social perception, and the role of other social cognitive variables remains to be explored. Fifth, there are open questions about the optimal assessment and modeling of functional outcome variables. For example, it remains unclear whether functional capacity measures, which assess what one can do under ideal laboratory conditions, should be modeled either together with or separate from measures of actual real-world functioning. It is also possible that different causal pathways lead to different aspects of outcome (for example, functional capacity, social functioning, vocational functioning, quality of life). The optimal assessment of outcome remains an active area of research [25,136].

To contextualise these findings, a final consideration is that these models typically leave over half the variance in outcome unaccounted for. Thus, incorporating additional variables believed to impact on outcome into these models (which will require larger sample sizes) will more comprehensively account for outcome. This type of work has already begun by examining the interactive contributions of variables such as negative symptoms, motivational processes, emotional experience and reactivity, dysfunctional attitudes, and metacognition [137–141].

In summary, schizophrenia researchers are developing a clearer understanding of the steps through which neurocognitive deficits ultimately lead to poor functioning in the real world. Social cognition appears to be a distinctive domain that uniquely accounts for variance in outcome and also sheds light on the mediating mechanism of the neurocognition – outcome link. Having that information does more than implicate social cognition as an intervening step leading to functional outcome in schizophrenia – it also strongly suggests that social cognition is a rational target for intervention. Social cognition appears to be more proximal to outcome than is neurocognition in the chain of causal factors that ultimately lead to poor functional outcome and, hence, could be a better target for intervention. The proximity of social cognition to community outcome also suggests that improvements in this domain may generalise better to improvement in daily functioning than improvements in neurocognition alone.

FUTURE DIRECTIONS

The associations between neurocognition, social cognition and outcome in schizophrenia described in this chapter have generated considerable interest in the possibility of enhancing cognition as a means to ultimately improve real-world functioning. Neurocognition and social cognition are viewed as highly promising targets for novel treatments using both pharmacological and psychosocial approaches. We conclude by briefly describing treatment development efforts to translate neurocognitive and social cognitive research into clinically potent interventions.

As a part of the MATRICS initiative, experts were convened to identify the highest priority pharmacological mechanisms that could be targeted by adjunctive medications to enhance cognition [142]. Very early findings for add-on pharmacological strategies targeting some of these mechanisms have thus far generally been mixed (see [143,144] for recent reviews). As a way to utilise the products of MATRICS, the NIMH established a clinical trials network called Treatment Units for Research on Neurocognition and Schizophrenia (TURNS) to test promising compounds or mechanisms nominated through the MATRICS process. The TURNS network has completed two studies examining a neuroprotective peptide and a $GABA_A$ $\alpha2/\alpha3$ partial agonist. Results from both studies are currently under review. In addition, a substantial number of separate industry-sponsored trials of novel compounds and their effects on cognition in schizophrenia are currently underway. A listing of these studies can be obtained at clinicaltrials.gov.

More success in improving neurocognition has been reported in the area of psychiatric rehabilitation using neurocognitive remediation. Recent modifications in the way that these interventions are delivered, particularly using computer-based programs, have been generally encouraging for improving attention, memory and problem-solving [145–148]. Treatment benefits have been found to generalise improvements in functioning. For example, studies using three different approaches have demonstrated real-world functional gains, particularly in the area of employment success [145,149,150]. Furthermore, these treatment gains were found to persist up to three years after the intervention ended [151–153]. An important feature of these interventions was that neurocognitive remediation was provided in conjunction with supportive interventions aimed at vocational and/or social functioning, making it difficult to evaluate the specific contribution of the neurocognitive remediation exercises. In addition, many variations of neurocognitive remediation are currently being used and there have been few replicated findings using similar methods in different research groups (for example, [154]).

Regarding social cognition, a much smaller number of studies have examined the modifiability of impairments through pharmacological or psychosocial interventions. Pharmacological interventions that included social cognitive outcome measures (mostly facial affect perception) are summarised in Table 3.4. Despite

Table 3.4 Pharmacological trials including social cognitive outcome measures

Study	Sample	Design	Social cognitive domain(s) & measure(s)	Results
Kee et al., 1998 [182]	18 chronic schizophrenia inpatients	8-week double-blind study with random assignment to risperidone (6 mg/day) versus haldol (15 mg/day). Flexible dosing during weeks 5–8. Assessments at baseline and 8 weeks.	**Facial and vocal affect perception:** Facial Emotion Identification Test; Voice Emotion Identification Test; Videotape Affect Perception Test	**Positive:** Risperidone group showed significantly larger improvements than haldol group.
Littrell et al., 2004 [183]	52 schizophrenia or schizoaffective outpatients	12-month open label trial of olanzapine. Trial was offered to patients who had received a conventional antipsychotic for at least three months. Compared patients who remained on conventional antipsychotics (n = 30) to those who agreed to trial of olanzapine (n = 20; mean dose = 15.3 mg/day). Assessment at baseline and 12 months.	**Social Perception:** Interpersonal Perception Task	**Positive:** Olanzapine group showed significant improvement on IPT (evident by 3 months) that was not present in conventional antipsychotics group.
Herbener et al., 2005 [184]	13 acutely ill first episode schizophrenia patients.	Open administration of risperidone to all patients (mean 3.38 mg/day) – four were switched to other atypical or typical antipsychotics. Assessments at baseline and 4 weeks.	**Facial affect perception:** Penn Emotional Acuity and Discrimination Tests	**Negative:** No significant improvement.

Harvey et al., 2006 [185]	289 schizophrenia outpatients (initially hospitalized 1 week)	8-week double-blind study with randomization to flexible dose of quetiapine (200 – 800 mg/day) versus risperidone (2 – 8 mg/day). Assessments at baseline and 8 weeks.	**Facial affect perception:** Penn Emotional Acuity Test	**Negative:** No significant improvements for either group.
Kohler et al., 2007 [159]	26 schizophrenia or schizoaffective outpatients	16-week double-blind study with randomization to adjunctive donepezil versus placebo; all patients taking atypical antipsychotics (except clozapine). Donepezil 5 mg/day for 4 weeks and then 10 mg/day for 8 weeks. Assessments at baseline and 16 weeks.	**Facial affect perception:** Emotion discrimination or differentiation	**Negative:** No significant improvements for either group.
Sergi et al., 2007 [157]	111 schizophrenia or schizoaffective outpatients	8-week double-blind study with randomization to risperidone (4 mg/day), olanzapine, (15mg/day), or haldol (8 mg/day). Assessments at baseline, 4 weeks, and 8 weeks.	**Facial affect perception and social perception:** Facial Emotion Identification Test; Voice Emotion Identification Test; Half-Profile of Nonverbal Sensitivity; Interpersonal Perception Test-15	**Negative:** No significant improvement for any group.

(Continued)

Table 3.4 *(Continued)*

Study	Sample	Design	Social cognitive domain(s) & measure(s)	Results
Behere et al., 2009 [186]	25 antipsychotic naïve schizophrenia outpatients	7-week open administration of risperidone 4mg/day plus trihexyphenidal 2mg/day to all patients. Assessments at baseline and approximately 7 weeks.	**Facial affect perception:** Tool for Recognition of Emotions in Neuropsychiatric Disorders (TRENDS)	**Positive:** Significant improvement, accounted for primarily perception of disgust expressions.
Penn et al., 2009 [156]	873 schizophrenia outpatients	Clinical Antipsychotic Trials of Intervention Effectiveness (CATIE): 18-month double-blind study with randomization to flexible dosages of olanzapine, perphenazine, quetiapine, risperidone, or ziprasidone. Assessments at baseline and 8 weeks.	**Facial affect perception:** Facial Emotion Discrimination Test	**Negative:** No significant improvement for any group.
Roberts et al., in press [158]	223 schizophrenia or schizoaffective outpatients with prominent negative symptoms	6-month double blind study with randomization to flexible dosages of olanzapine (10-20 mg/day) versus quetiapine (300-700 mg/day). Assessments at baseline and 6 months.	**Social perception:** Social Cue Recognition Test	**Positive:** Significant improvement in both groups.

a few positive findings, studies comparing whether different antipsychotics lead to social cognitive improvements are predominantly negative. Notably, the three largest controlled trials (sample sizes greater than 100) examining facial affect perception were all negative [155–157]. The two largest controlled studies examining social perception were mixed [157,158], though the one with positive findings reported very small effect sizes (d's less than .10 [158]). The one study that examined the efficacy of an add-on agent (donepezil) failed to find significant effects [159]. Although the handful of studies to date show minimal effects of antipsychotic medications on social cognition, novel compounds that may target specific neural systems involved in social cognition are an active area of interest.

As is the case for neurocognitive deficits, the more promising results to date come from psychosocial interventions (see [160] for a recent review). Improvement on social cognitive tasks has been found in studies that embedded social cognitive training exercises within multi-component treatment packages aimed at improving multiple treatment targets, as well as targeted treatment studies that specifically used social cognitive enhancement techniques without other intervention components. The majority of targeted treatment studies focus on a single component (commonly facial affect perception) using inpatient samples (for example, [161]). However, initial evidence from targeted treatments that focus on multiple components of social cognition demonstrate efficacy in stabilised outpatients, with treatment benefits that can persist up to six months beyond the conclusion of treatment [162,163]. Although this type of intervention is in its infancy, initial results are encouraging.

The past decade has been an exciting period for research into the nature, functional significance, and plasticity of neurocognitive and social cognitive impairments in schizophrenia. As translational research into the measurement and neural correlates of neurocognition and social cognition in schizophrenia continues to progress, our interventions will become increasingly effective. The emerging work in cognitive interventions represents a promising approach to treatment that goes beyond the traditional focus on symptom management to include a focus on achieving more complete and satisfying functional outcomes.

REFERENCES

1. Murray CJL, Lopez AD, eds. (1996) *The Global Burden of Disease*. Boston, MA: Harvard School of Public Health.
2. Marder SR, Fenton WS (2004) Measurement and treatment research to improve cognition in schizophrenia: NIMH MATRICS Initiative to support the development of agents for improving cognition in schizophrenia. *Schizophrenia Research* **72**: 5–10.
3. Kraepelin E (1971) *Dementia praecox and paraphrenia*. Huntington, NY: Robert E. Krieger Publishing Co. Inc.

4. Nuechterlein KH, Barch DM, Gold JM, Goldberg TE, Green MF, Heaton RK (2004) Identification of separable cognitive factors in schizophrenia. *Schizophrenia Research*. **72**:29–39.

5. Heinrichs RW, Zakzanis KK (1998) Neurocognitive deficit in schizophrenia: A quantitative review of the evidence. *Neuropsychology*. **12**:426–445.

6. Palmer BW, Dawes SE, Heaton RK (2009) What do we know about neuropsychological aspects of schizophrenia? *Neuropsychol Rev*. Sep; **19**(3):365–384.

7. Dickinson D, Ramsey ME, Gold JM (2007) Overlooking the obvious: a meta-analytic comparison of digit symbol coding tasks and other cognitive measures in schizophrenia. *Arch Gen Psychiatry*. May; **64**(5):532–542.

8. Palmer BW, Heaton RK, Paulsen JS, Kuck J, Braff D, Harris MJ, *et al.* (1997) Is it possible to be schizophrenic yet neuropsychologically normal? *Neuropsychology*. **11**:437–46.

9. Goldberg TE, Ragland JD, Torrey EF, Gold JM, Bigelow LB, Weinberger DR (1990) Neuropsychological assessment of monozygotic twins discordant for schizophrenia. *Archives of General Psychiatry*. **47**:1066–1072.

10. Nieuwenstein MR, de Haan EHF (2001) Relationship between symptom dimensions and neurocognitive functioning in schizophrenia: A meta-analysis of WCST and CPT studies. *Journal of Psychiatric Research*. **35**:119–125.

11. Mohamed S, Paulsen JS, O'Leary DS, Arndt S, Andreasen NC (1999) Generalized cognitive deficits in schizophrenia. *American Journal of Psychiatry*. **156**:749–754.

12. Heydebrand G, Weiser M, Rabinowitz J, Hoff AL, DeLisi LE, Csernansky JG (2004) Correlates of cognitive deficits in first episode schizophrenia. *Schizophrenia Research*. **68**:1–9.

13. Bilder RM, Goldman RS, Robinson D, Reiter G, Bell L, Bates JA, *et al.* (2000) Neuropsychology of first-episode schizophrenia:initial characterization and clinical correlates. *American Journal of Psychiatry*. 157.

14. Addington J, Addington D, Maticka-Tyndale E (1991) Cognitive functioning and positive and negative symptoms in schizophrenia. *Schizophrenia Research*. **5**:123–134.

15. Addington J (2000) Cognitive functioning and negative symptoms in schizophrenia. In: Sharma T, Harvey P, editors. *Cognition in Schizophrenia*. Oxford, UK: Oxford University Press pp. 193–209.

16. Bilder RM, Goldman RS, Volavka J, Czobor P, Hoptman M, Sheitman B, *et al.* (2002) Neurocognitive effects of clozapine, olanzapine, risperidone, and haloperidol in patients with chronic schizophrenia and schizoaffective disorder. *American Journal of Psychiatry*. **159**:1018–1028.

17. Woodward ND, Purdon SE, Meltzer HY, Zald DH (2005) A meta-analysis of neuropsychological change to clozapine, olanzapine, quetiapine, and risperidone in schizophrenia. *The International Journal of Neuropsychopharmacology*. **8**:457–472.

18. Keefe RS, Bilder RM, Davis SM, Harvey PD, Palmer BW, Gold JM, *et al.* (2007) Neurocognitive effects of antipsychotic medications in patients with chronic schizophrenia in the CATIE Trial. *Arch Gen Psychiatry*. Jun;**64**(6):633–647.

19. Mesholam-Gately RI, Giuliano AJ, Goff KP, Faraone SV, Seidman LJ (2009) Neurocognition in first-episode schizophrenia: a meta-analytic review. *Neuropsychology*. May;**23**(3):315–336.

20. Cornblatt B, Lenzenweger MF, Dworkin R, Erlenmeyer-Kimling L (1992) Childhood attentional dysfunction predicts social deficits in unaffected adults at risk for schizophrenia. *British Journal of Psychiatry*. **161**(Suppl. 18):59–64.

21. Jahshan C, Heaton RK, Golshan S, Cadenhead KS (2010) Course of neurocognitive deficits in the prodrome and first episode of schizophrenia. *Neuropsychology*. Jan;**24**(1):109–120.

22. Hawkins KA, Keefe RS, Christensen BK, Addington J, Woods SW, Callahan J, *et al.* (2008) Neuropsychological course in the prodrome and first episode of psychosis: findings from the PRIME North America Double Blind Treatment Study. *Schizophr Res*. Oct;**105**(1–3):1–9.

23. Snitz BE, MacDonald AW, Carter CS (2006) Cognitive deficits in unaffected first-degree relatives of schizophrenia patients: a meta-analytic review of putative endophenotypes. *Schizophrenia Bulletin*. **32**:179–194.

24. Buchanan RW, Davis M, Goff D, Green MF, Keefe RSE, Leon AC, *et al.* (2005) A summary of the FDA-NIMH-MATRICS workshop on clinical trial design for neurocognitive drugs for schizophrenia. *Schizophrenia bulletin*. **31**:5–19.

25. Bellack AS, Green MF, Cook JA, Fenton W, Harvey PD, Heaton RK, *et al.* (2007) Assessment of community functioning in people with schizophrenia and other severe mental illnesses: a white paper based on an NIMH-sponsored workshop. *Schizophr Bull*. May;**33**(3):805–822.

26. Green MF. (1996) What are the functional consequences of neurocognitive deficits in schizophrenia? *American Journal of Psychiatry*. **153**(3):321–330.

27. Green MF, Kern RS, Braff DL, Mintz J (2000) Neurocognitive deficits and functional outcome in schizophrenia: Are we measuring the "right stuff"? *Schizophrenia Bulletin*. **26**:119–136.

28. Green MF, Kern RS, Heaton RK (2004) Longitudinal studies of cognition and functional outcome in schizophrenia: implications for MATRICS. *Schizophrenia Research*. **72**:41–51.

29. Green MF, Kern RS, Braff DL, Mintz J Neurocognitive deficits and functional outcome in schizophrenia: Are we measuring the "right stuff"?. *Schizophrenia Bulletin*. **26**(1):119–136.

30. Lezak MD (1995) *Neuropsychological Assessment*, 3rd ed. New York: Oxford University Press.

31. Nuechterlein KH, Barch DM, Gold JM, Goldberg TE, Green MF, Heaton RK (2004) Identification of separable cognitive factors in schizophrenia. *Schizophr Res*. Dec 15;**72**(1):29–39.

32. Green MF, Nuechterlein KH, Gold JM, Barch DM, Cohen J, Essock S, *et al.* (2004) Approaching a consensus cognitive battery for clinical trials in schizophrenia: the NIMH-MATRICS conference to select cognitive domains and test criteria. *Biol Psychiatry*. Sep 1; **56**(5):301–307.

33. Fitch K, Bernstein SJ, Aguilar MD, Burnand B, LaCalle JR, Lazaro P, *et al.* (2001) The RAND/UCLA Appropriateness Method User's Manual. In: RAND, editor. Santa Monica, CA: RAND.

34. Pietrzak R, Oliver J, Norman T, Piskulic C, Maruff P, Snyder P (2009) A comparison of the CogState Schizophrenia Battery and the Measurement and Treatment Research to Improve Cognition in Schizophrenia (MATRICS) Battery in assessing

cognitive impairment in chronic schizophrenia. *Journal of Clinical and Experimental Neuropsychology* **14**:1–12.

35. Holmen A, Juuhl-Langseth M, Thormodsen R, Melle I, Rund B (2009) Neuropsychological Profile in Early-Onset Schizophrenia-Spectrum Disorders: Measured With the MATRICS Battery. *Schizophrenia Bulletin.*

36. Carter CS, Barch DM (2007) Cognitive neuroscience-based approaches to measuring and improving treatment effects on cognition in schizophrenia: the CNTRICS initiative. *Schizophr Bull.* Sep;**33**(5):1131–1137.

37. Barch DM, Carter CS, Arnsten A, Buchanan RW, Cohen JD, Geyer M, *et al.* (2009) Selecting paradigms from cognitive neuroscience for translation into use in clinical trials: proceedings of the third CNTRICS meeting. *Schizophr Bull.* Jan;**35**(1):109–114.

38. Kunda Z (1999) *Social cognition: Making sense of people.* Cambridge, MA: MIT Press.

39. Fiske ST, Taylor SE (1991) *Social cognition.* 2nd ed. New York, NY: McGraw-Hill Book Company.

40. Green MF, Penn DL, Bentall R, Carpenter WT, Gaebel W, Gur RC, *et al.* (2008) Social cognition in schizophrenia: an NIMH workshop on definitions, assessment, and research opportunities. *Schizophr Bull.* Nov; **34**(6):1211–1220.

41. Ochsner KN (2008) The social-emotional processing stream: Five core constructs and their translational potential for schizophrenia and beyond. *Biological Psychiatry.* **64**:48–61.

42. Mayer JD, Salovey P, Caruso DR, Sitarenios G (2001) Emotional intelligence as a standard intelligence. *Emotion.* **1**:232–242.

43. Salovey P, Sluyter DJ (1997) *Emotional Development and Emotional Intelligence.* New York: Basic Books.

44. Kohler CG, Walker JB, Martin EA, Healey KM, Moberg PJ (2009) Facial Emotion Perception in Schizophrenia: A Meta-analytic Review. *Schizophr Bull.* Mar **27**.

45. Mayer JD, Salovey P, Caruso DR, Sitarenios G (2003) Measuring emotional intelligence with the MSCEIT V2.0. *Emotion.* **3**:97–105.

46. Eack SM, Greeno CG, Pogue-Geile MF, Newhill CE, Hogarty GE, Keshavan MS (2008) Assessing Social-Cognitive Deficits in Schizophrenia With the Mayer-Salovey-Caruso Emotional Intelligence Test. *Schizophr Bull.* Jul 22.

47. Kee KS, Horan WP, Salovey P, Kern RS, Sergi MJ, Fiske AP, *et al.* (2009) Emotional intelligence in schizophrenia. *Schizophr Res.* Jan; **107**(1):61–68.

48. Henry JD, Green MJ, de Lucia A, Restuccia C, McDonald S, O'Donnell M (2007) Emotion dysregulation in schizophrenia: reduced amplification of emotional expression is associated with emotional blunting. *Schizophr Res.* Sep; **95**(1–3):197–204.

49. Henry JD, Rendell PG, Green MJ, McDonald S, O'Donnell M (2008) Emotion regulation in schizophrenia: affective, social, and clinical correlates of suppression and reappraisal. *J Abnorm Psychol.* May; **117**(2):473–478.

50. Horan WP, Blanchard JJ, Clark LA, Green MF (2008) Affective traits in schizophrenia and schizotypy. *Schizophrenia Bulletin.* **34**:856–874.

51. Corrigan PW, Green MF (1993) Schizophrenic patients' sensitivity to social cues: The role of abstraction. *American Journal of Psychiatry.* **150**:589–594.

52. Corrigan PW, Wallace CJ, Green MF (1992) Deficits in social schemata in schizophrenia. *Schizophrenia Research.* **8**:129–135.

53. Rosenthal R, Hall JA, DiMatteo MR, Rogers PL, Archer D (1979) *Sensitivity to nonverbal communication: The PONS test.* Baltimore: Johns Hopkins University Press.

54. Monkul ES, Green MJ, Barrett JA, Robinson JL, Velligan DI, Glahn DC (2007) A social cognitive approach to emotional intensity judgment deficits in scihzophrenia. *Schizophrenia Research.* **94**:245–252.

55. Green MJ, Waldron JH, Coltheart M (2007) Emotional context processing is impaired in schizophrenia. *Cognitive Neuropsychiatry.* **12**:259–280.

56. Sasson N, Tsuchiya N, Hurley R, Couture SM, Penn DL, Adolphs R, *et al.* (2007) Orienting to social stimuli differentiates social cognitive impairment in autism and schizophrenia. *Neuropsychologia.* **45**:2580–2588.

57. Bigelow NO, Paradiso S, Adolphs R, Moser DJ, Arndt S, Heberlein A, *et al.* (2006) Perception of socially relevant information in schizophrenia. *Schizophrenia Research.* **83**(257–267).

58. Corrigan PW, Green MF (1993) Schizophrenic patients' sensitivity to social cues: The role of abstraction. *American Journal of Psychiatry.* **150**(4):589–594.

59. Subotnik KL, Nuechterlein KH, Green MF, Horan WP, Nienow TM, Ventura J, *et al.* (2006) Neurocognitive and social cognitive correlates of formal thought disorder in schizophrenia patients. *Schizophr Res.* Jul; **85**(1–3):84–95.

60. Corrigan PW, Green MF (1993) The Situational Feature Recognition Test: A measure of schema comprehension for schizophrenia. *International Journal of Methods in Psychiatric Research.* **3**:29–35.

61. Corrigan PW, Addis I (1995) The effects of cognitive complexity on a social sequencing task in schizophrenia. *Schizophrenia Research.* **16**:137–144.

62. Penn DL, Ritchie M, Francis J, Combs D, Martin J (2002) Social perception in schizophrenia: the role of context. *Psychiatry Research.* **109**:149–159.

63. Kinderman P, Bentall RP (1996) A new measure of causal locus: the internal, personal, and situational attributions questionnaire. *Personality and Individual Differences.* **20**:261–264.

64. Lee DA, Randall F, Beattie G, Bentall RP (2004) Delusional discourse: an investigation comparing the spontaneous causal attributions of paranoid and non-paranoid individuals. *Psychol Psychother.* Dec; **77**(Pt 4):525–540.

65. Bentall RP, Corcoran, R., Howard, R., Blackwood, N., Kinderman, P (2001) Persecutory delusions: a review and theoretical integration. *Clinical Psychology Review.* **21**:1143–1192.

66. Garety PA, Freeman D (1999) Cognitive approaches to delusions: A critical review of theories and evidence. *British Journal of Clinical Psychology.* **38**:113–154.

67. Peterson C, Semmel A, von Baeyer C, Abramson L, Metalsky GI, Seligman MEP (1982) The Attributional Style Questionnaire. *Cognitive Therapy & Research.* **3**:287–300.

68. Bentall RP, Corcoran R, Howard R, Blackwood N, Kinderman P (2001) Persecutory delusions: a review and theoretical integration. *Clinical Psychology Review* **21**:1143–1192.

69. Combs DR, Penn DL, Wicher M, Waldheter E (2007) The ambiguous intentions hostility questionnaire (AIHQ): A new measure for evaluating hostile social-cognitive biases in paranoia. *Cognitive Neuropsychiatry*. 12; 128–143.

70. Stratton P, Munton AG, Hanks H, Heard DH, Davidson C (1988) Leeds Attrributional Coding System. Leeds, UK: Leeds Family Research Centre.

71. Aakre JM, Seghers JP, St-Hilaire A, Docherty NM (2009) Attributional style in delusional patients: A comparison of remitted paranoid, remitted nonparanoid, and current paranoid patients with nonpsychiatric controls. *Schizophrenia Bulletin*. **35**:994–1002.

72. Baron-Cohen S, Wheelwright S, Hill J, Raste Y, Plumb I (2001) The "Reading the mind in the eyes" test revised version: A study with normal adults, and adults with Asperger syndrome or high-functioning autism. *Journal of Child Psychology & Psychiatry & Allied Disciplines*. **42**:241–251.

73. Frith CD (1992) *The cognitive neuropsychology of schizophrenia*. Hove, UK: Lawrence Erlbaum Associates, Publishers.

74. Frith CD, Corcoran R (1996) Exploring 'theory of mind' in people with schizophrenia. *Psychol Med*. May; **26**(3):521–530.

75. Corcoran R, Mercer G, Frith CD (1995) Schizophrenia, symptomatology and social inference: investigating "theory of mind" in people with schizophrenia. *Schizophrenia Research*. **17**:5–13.

76. Baron-Cohen S, Wheelwright S, Hill J, Raste Y, Plumb I (2001) The "Reading the mind in the eyes" test revised version: A study with normal adults, and adults with Asperger syndrome or high-functioning autism. *Journal of Child Psychology and Psychiatry and Allied Disciplines*. **42**:241–251.

77. Langdon R, Michie PT, Ward PB, McConaghy N, Catts S, Coltheart M (1997) Defective self and/or other mentalising in schizophrenia: A cognitive neuropsychological approach. *Cognitive Neuropsychiatry*. **2**:167–193.

78. Happe F (1994) An advanced test of theory of mind: Understanding of story characters' thoughts and feelings by able austics, mentally handicapped and normal children and adults. *Journal of Autism and Developmental Disorders*. **24**:129–154.

79. Brüne M (2003) Social cognition and behaviour in schizophrenia. In: Brune M, Ribbert H, Schiefenhovel W, editors. *The social brain-evolution of psychology*. Chichister: John Wiley & Sons pp. 277–313.

80. McDonald S, Flanagan S, Rollins J (2002) *The Awareness of Social Inference Test*. Suffolk, UK: Thames Valley Test Company, Ltd.

81. Kern RS, Green MF, Fiske AP, Kee KS, Lee J, Sergi MJ, *et al.* (2009) Theory of mind deficits for processing counterfactual information in persons with chronic schizophrenia. *Psychol Med*. Apr; **39**(4):645–654.

82. Horan WP, Nuechterlein KH, Wynn JK, Lee J, Castelli F, Green MF (in press) Disturbances in the spontaneous attribution of social meaning in schizophrenia. *Psychology Medicine*.

83. Corcoran R (2001) Theory of mind and schizophrenia. In: Corrigan PW, Penn DL, editors. *Social Cognition and Schizophrenia*. Washington, DC: American Psychological Association pp. 149–174.

84. Brüne M (2005) 'Theory of Mind' in Schizophrenia: A Review of the Literature *Schizophr Bull*. **31**:21–42.

85. Bora E, Yucel M, Panteli C (2009) Theory of mind impairment in schizophrenia: Meta-analysis. *Schizophrenia Research*. **109**:1–9.
86. Sprong M, Schothorst P, Vos E, Hox J, Van Engeland H (2007) Theory of mind in schizophrenia: Meta-analysis. *British Journal of Psychiatry*. 191; 5–13.
87. Chung YS, YKang DH, N.Y. S, Yoo SY, Kwon JS (2008) Deficit of theory of mind in individuals at ultra-high-risk for schizophrenia. *Schizophrenia Research*. 99:111–118.
88. Marjoram D, Miller P, McIntosh AM, Cunningham Owens DG, Johnstone EC, Lawrie S (2006) A neuropsychological investigation into 'Theory of Mind' and enhanced risk of schizophrenia. *Psychiatry Res*. Sep 30; **144**(1):29–37.
89. Addington J, Penn DL, Woods SW, Addington D, Perkins DO (2008) Facial affect recogntion in individuals at clincal high risk for psychosis. *British Journal of Psychiatry*. 192; 67–68.
90. Pinkham AE, Penn DL, Perkins DO, Graham KA, Siege M (2007) Emotion perception and social skill over the course of psychosis: A comparison of individuals "At-risk" for psychosis and individuals with early and chronic schizophrenia spectrum illness. *Cognitive Neuropsychiatry*. 12; 198–212.
91. Herbener ES, Hill SK, Marvin RW, Sweeney JA (2005) Effects of antipsychotic treatment on emotion perception deficits in first-episode schizophrenia. *Am J Psychiatry*. Sep; **162**(9):1746–1748.
92. Wolwer W, Streit M, Polzer U, Gaebel W (1996) Facial affect recognition in the course of schizophrenia. *European Archives of Psychiatry and Clinical Neuroscience*. **246**:165–170.
93. Addington J, Penn DL, Woods SW, Addington D, Perkins D (2008) Facial affect recognition in individuals at clinical high risk for psychosis. *British Journal of Psychiatry*. 192; 67–68.
94. Pinkham AE, Penn DL, Perkins DO, Graham K, Siegel M (2007) Emotion perception and the course of psychosis: A comparison of individuals at risk, and early and chronic schizophrenia spectrum illness. *Cognitive neuropsychiatry*. 12; 198–212.
95. Couture SM, Penn DL, Woods SW, Addington J, Perkins DO (2008) Assessment of social judgments and complex mental states in the early phases of psychosis. *Schizophrenia Research*. 100; 237–241.
96. Kee KS, Horan WP, J. Mintz, Green MF (2004) Do the siblings of schizophrenia patients demonstrate affect perception deficits? *Schizophrenia Research*. **67**:87–94.
97. Gur RE, Nimgaonkar VL, Almasy L, Calkins ME, Ragland JD, Pogue-Geile MF, *et al.* (2007) Neurocognitive endophenotypes in a multiplex multigenerational family study of schizophrenia. *Am J Psychiatry*. May; **164**(5):813–819.
98. Toomey R, Seidman LJ, Lyons MJ, Faraone SV, Tsuang MT (1999) Poor perception of nonverbal social-emotional cues in relatives of schizophrenic patients. *Schizophr Res*.40(2):121–130.
99. Eack SM, Mermon DE, Montrose DM, Miewald J, Gur RE, Gur RC, *et al.* (2010) Social Cognition Deficits Among Individuals at Familial High Risk for Schizophrenia. *Schizophr Bull*. **36**:1081–1088.
100. Mazza M, Di Michele V, Pollice R, Casacchia M, Roncone R (2008) Pragmatic language and theory of mind deficits in people with schizophrenia and their relatives. *Psychopathology*. **41**(4):254–263.

101. Leppanen JM, Niehaus DJ, Koen L, Du Toit E, Schoeman R, Emsley R (2008) Deficits in facial affect recognition in unaffected siblings of Xhosa schizophrenia patients: evidence for a neurocognitive endophenotype. *Schizophr Res.* Feb; **99**(1–3):270–273.

102. Couture SM, Penn DL, Roberts DL (2006) The functional significance of social cognition in schizophrenia: a review. *Schizophrenia bulletin.* Oct;32 Suppl **1**:S44–S63.

103. Eack SM, Pogue-Geile MF, Greeno CG, Keshavan MS (2009) Evidence of factorial variance of the Mayer-Salovey-Caruso Emotional Intelligence Test across schizophrenia and normative samples. *Schizophr Res.* Oct; **114**(1–3):105–109.

104. van Hooren S, Versmissen D, Janssen I, Myin-Germeys, I., Campo J, Mengelers R, van Os J, *et al.* (2008) Social cognition and neurocognition as independent domains in psychosis. *Schizophrenia Research.* 103; 257–265.

105. Woodward TS, Mizrahi R, Menon M, Christensen BK (2009) Correspondences between theory of mind, jumping to conclusions, neuropsychological measures and the symptoms of schizophrenia. *Psychiatry Res.* Dec 30; **170**(2–3):119–123.

106. Decety J, Jackson, PL (2006) A social neuroscience perspective on empathy. *Current Directions in Psychological Science.* 15; 54–58.

107. Iacoboni M, Dapretto M (2006) The mirror neuron system and the consequences of its dysfunction. *Nat Rev Neurosci.* Dec; **7**(12):942–951.

108. Lieberman MD (2007) Social Cognitive Neuroscience: A Review of Core Processes. *Annual Reviews of Psychology.* **58**:259–289.

109. Adolphs R The neurobiology of social cognition. *Current Opinion in Neurobiology.* 11; 231–239.

110. Adolphs R The social brain: Neural basis of social knowledge. *Annual Review of Psychology.* **60**:693–716.

111. Kee KS, Kern RS, Green MF (1998) Perception of emotion and neurocognitive functioning in schizophrenia: What's the link? *Psychiatry Research.* **81**:57–65.

112. Greig TC, Bryson, GJ, Bell, MD (2004) Theory of mind performance in schizophrenia: diagnostic, symptom, and neuropsychological correlates. *Journal of Nervous and Mental Disease.* 192; 12–18.

113. Pinkham AE, Penn DL (2006) Neurocognitive and social cognitive predictors of interpersonal skill in schizophrenia. *Psychiatry Research.* Aug 30; **143**(2–3):167–178.

114. Sergi MJ, Green MF (2002) Social perception and early visual processing in schizophrenia. *Schizophrenia Research.* **59**:233–241.

115. Sergi MJ, Rassovsky Y, Widmark C, Reist C, Erhart S, Braff DL, *et al.* (2007) Social cognition in schizophrenia: relationships with neurocognition and negative symptoms. *Schizophr Research.* **90**(1–3):316–324.

116. Allen DN, Strauss GP, Donohue B, van Kammen DP (2007) Factor analytic support for social cognition as a separable cognitive domain in schizophrenia. *Schizophr Res.* Jul; **93**(1–3):325–333.

117. Bell M, Tsang HW, Greig TC, Bryson GJ (2009) Neurocognition, social cognition, perceived social discomfort, and vocational outcomes in schizophrenia. *Schizophr Bull.* Jul; **35**(4):738–747.

118. Williams LM, Whitford TJ, Flynn G, Wong W, Liddell BJ, Silverstein S, *et al.* (2008) General and social cognition in first episode schizophrenia: identification of separable factors and prediction of functional outcome using the IntegNeuro test battery. *Schizophr Res.* Feb; **99**(1–3):182–191.

119. Jones W, Bellugih U, Lai Z, Chiles M, Reilly J, Lincoln A, Adolphs R (2000) II: hypersociability in Williams syndrome. *Journal of Cognitive Neuroscience.* **12**: 30–46.

120. Anderson SW, Bechara A, Damasio H, Tranel D, Damasio AR (1999) Impairment of social and moral behavior related to early damage in human prefrontal cortex. *Nature Neuroscience.* **2**:1032–1037.

121. Kanwisher N (2000) Domain specificity in face perception. *Nature Neuroscience.* **3**:759–763.

122. Pinkham AE, Penn DL, Perkins DO, Lieberman J (2003) Implications for the neural basis of social cognition for the study of schizophrenia. *American Journal of Psychiatry.* **160**:815–824.

123. Brunet-Gouet E, Decety J (2006) Social brain dysfunctions in schizophrenia: a review of neuroimaging studies. *Psychiatry Res.* Dec 1; **148**(2–3): 75–92.

124. Van Overwalle F (2009) Social cognition and the brain: a meta-analysis. *Human Brain Mapping.* **30**(3):829–858.

125. Poole JH, Tobias FC, Vinogradov S (2000) The functional relevance of affect recognition errors in schizophrenia. *Journal of the International Neuropsychological Society.* **6**(6):649–658.

126. Corrigan PW, Toomey R (1995) Interpersonal problem solving and information processing in schizophrenia. *Schizophrenia Bulletin.* **21**(3):395–403.

127. Penn DL, Spaulding WD, Reed D, Sullivan M (1996) The relationship of social cognition to ward behavior in chronic schizophrenia. *Schizophrenia Research.* 20; 327–335.

128. Ihnen GH, Penn DL, Corrigan PW, Martin J (1998) Social perception and social skill. *Psychiatry Research.* **80**:275–286.

129. Roncone R, Falloon IR, Mazza M, De Risio A, Pollice R, Necozione S, *et al.* (2002) Is theory of mind in schizophrenia more strongly associated with clinical and social functioning than with neurocognitive deficits? *Psychopathology.* Sep-Oct; **35**(5):280–288.

130. Pan YJ, Chen SH, Chen WJ, Liu SK (2009) Affect recognition as an independent social function determinant in schizophrenia. *Compr Psychiatry.* Sep-Oct; **50**(5):443–452.

131. Vauth R, Rusch N, Wirtz M, Corrigan PW (2004) Does social cognition influence the relation between neurocognitive deficits and vocational functioning in schizophrenia? *Psychiatry Research.* **128**:155–165.

132. Brune M, Abdel-Hamid M, Lehmkamper C, Sonntag C (2007) Mental state attribution, neurocognitive functioning, and psychopathology: what predicts poor social competence in schizophrenia best? *Schizophr Res.* May; **92**(1–3):151–159.

133. Green MF, Nuechterlein KH (1999) Should schizophrenia be treated as a neurocognitive disorder? *Schizophrenia Bulletin.* **25**; 309–319.

134. Brekke JS, Kay DD, Kee KS, Green MF (2005) Biosocial pathways to functional outcome in schizophrenia. *Schizophrenia Research.* **80**:213–225.

135. Nienow TM, Docherty NM, Cohen AS, Dinzeo TJ (2006) Attentional dysfunction, social perception, and social competence: what is the nature of the relationship? *J Abnorm Psychol.* Aug; **115**(3):408–417.

136. Leifker FR, Patterson TL, Heaton RK, Harvey PD (in press) Validating Measures of Real-World Outcome: The Results of the VALERO Expert Survey and RAND Panel. *Schizophrenia Bulletin.*

137. Tso IF, Grove TB, Taylor SF (2009) Emotional experience predicts social adjustment independent of neurocognition and social cognition in schizophrenia. *Schizophr Res.* Jan 3.

138. Gard DE, Fisher M, Garrett C, Genevsky A, Vinogradov S (2009) Motivation and its relationship to neurocognition, social cognition, and functional outcome in schizophrenia. *Schizophr Res.* Nov; 115(1):74–81.

139. Mathews JR, Barch DM (2010) Emotion responsivity, social cognition, and functional outcome in scihzophrenia. *Journal of Abnormal Psychology.* 119:50–59.

140. Lysaker PH, Shea AM, Buck KD, Dimaggio G, Nicolo G, Procacci M, *et al.* (2009) Metacognition as a mediator of the effects of impairments in neurocognition on social function in schizophrenia spectrum disorders. *Acta Psychiatr Scand.* Mar 16.

141. Rassovsky Y, Horan WP, Lee J, Sergi MJ, Green MF (in press) Pathways between early visual processing and functional outcome in schzophrenia. *Psychological Medicine.*

142. Geyer MA, Tamminga CA (2004) Measurement and treatment research to improve cognition in schizophrenia: Neuropharmacological aspects. *Psychopharmacology.* 174; 1–2.

143. Harvey PD (2009) Pharmacological cognitive enhancement in schizophrenia. *Neuropsychol Rev.* Sep; 19(3):324–335.

144. Galletly C (2009) Recent advances in treating cognitive impairment in schizophrenia. *Psychopharmacology (Berl).* Jan;202(1–3): 259–273.

145. McGurk SR, Twamley EW, Sitzer DI, McHugo GJ, Mueser KT (2007) A meta-analysis of cognitive remediation in schizophrenia. *Am J Psychiatry.* Dec; 164(12):1791–1802.

146. Medalia A, Choi J (2009) Cognitive remediation in schizophrenia. *Neuropsychol Rev.* Sep; 19(3):353–364.

147. Lindenmayer JP, McGurk SR, Mueser KT, Khan A, Wance D, Hoffman L, *et al.* (2008) A randomized controlled trial of cognitive remediation among inpatients with persistent mental illness. *Psychiatr Serv.* Mar; 59(3):241–247.

148. Fisher M, Holland C, Merzenich MM, Vinogradov S (2009) Using neuroplasticity-based auditory training to improve verbal memory in schizophrenia. *Am J Psychiatry.* Jul; 166(7):805–811.

149. Hogarty GE, Flesher S, Ulrich R, Carter M, Greenwald D, Pogue-Geile M, *et al.* (2004) ognitive enhancement therapy for schizophrenia. *Archives of General Psychiatry.* 61:866–876.

150. Wexler BE, Bell MD (2005) Cognitive remediation and vocational rehabilitation for schizophrenia. *Schizophrenia Bulletin.* 31:931–941.

151. McGurk SR, Mueser KT, Feldman K, Wolfe R, Pascaris A (2007) Cognitive training for supported employment: 2-3 year outcomes of a randomized controlled trial. *Am J Psychiatry.* Mar; 164(3):437–441.

152. Hogarty GE, Greenwald DP, Eack SM (2006) Durability and mechanism of effects of cognitive enhancement therapy. *Psychiatr Serv.* Dec; 57(12):1751–1757.

153. Bell MD, Zito W, Greig T, Wexler BE (2008) Neurocognitive enhancement therapy with vocational services: work outcomes at two-year follow-up. *Schizophr Res.* Oct;105(1–3): 18–29.

154. Dickinson D, Tenhula W, Morris S, Brown C, Peer J, Spencer K, *et al.* (in press) A randomized, controlled trial of computer-assisted cognitive remediation for schizophrenia. *American Journal of Psychiatry.*

155. Harvey PD, Patterson TL, Potter LS, Zhong K, Brecher M Improvement in social competence with short-term atypical antipsychotic treatment: A randomized, double-blind comparison of quetiapine versus risperidone for social competence, social cognition, and neuropsychological functioning. *American Journal of Psychiatry.* 163; 1918–1925.

156. Penn DL, Keefe RS, Davis SM, Meyer PS, Perkins DO, Losardo D, *et al.* (2009) The effects of antipsychotic medications on emotion perception in patients with chronic schizophrenia in the CATIE trial. *Schizophr Res.* Nov; 115(1):17–23.

157. Sergi MJ, Green MF, Widmark C, Reist C, Erhart S, Braff DL, *et al.* (2007) Social cognition [corrected] and neurocognition: effects of risperidone, olanzapine, and haloperidol. *Am J Psychiatry.* Oct; 164(10):1585–1592.

158. Roberts DL, Penn DL, Corrigan P, Lipkovich I, Kinon B, Black RA (in press) Antipsychotic medication and social cue recognition in chronic schizophrenia. *Psychiatry Research.*

159. Kohler CG, Martin EA, Kujawski E, Bilker W, Gur RE, Gur RC (2007) No effect of donepezil on neurocognition and social cognition in young persons with stable schizophrenia. *Cogn Neuropsychiatry.* Sep; 12(5):412–421.

160. Horan WP, Kern RS, Penn DL, Green MF (2008) Social cognition training for individuals with schizophrenia: Emerging evidence. *American Journal of Psychiatric Rehabilitation.* 11; 205–252.

161. Wölwer W, Frommann N, Haufmann S, Piaszek A, Streit M, Gaebel W (2005) Remediation of impairments in facial affect recognition in schizophrenia: Efficacy and specificity of a new training program. *Schizophrenia Research.* 80:295–303.

162. Roberts DL, Penn DL (2009) Social cognition and interaction training (SCIT) for outpatients with schizophrenia: A preliminary study. *Psychiatry research.* 166(2–3): 141–147.

163. Horan WP, Kern RS, Sergi MJ, Shokat-Fadai K, Wynn JK, Green MF (2009) Social cognitive skills training in schizophrenia: An initial efficacy study of stabilized outpatients. *Schizophrenia Research.* 107:47–54.

164. Cornblatt B, Risch N, Faris G, Friedman D, Erlenmeyer-Kimling L (1988) The Continuous Performance Test-Identical Pairs (CPT-IP): I. New findings about sustained attention in normal families. *Psychiatry Research.* 26; 223–238.

165. Cornblatt BA, Lenzenweger MF, Erlenmeyer-Kimling L (1989) The continuous performance test, identical pairs version: II. Contrasting attentional profiles in schizophrenic and depressed patients. *Psychiatric Research.* 29; 65.

166. Army Individual Test Battery: Manual of Directions and Scoring. Washington, DC: Adjutant General's Office, War Department; 1944.

167. Keefe RSE (1999) Brief Assessment of Cognition in Schizophrenia (BACS) Manual - A: Version 2.1. Durham: Duke University Medical Center.

168. Spreen O, Strauss E (1991) *A Compendium of Neuropsychological Tests.* New York: Oxford University Press.

169. Gold JM, Carpenter C, Randolph C, Goldberg TE, Weinberger DR (1997) Auditory working memory and Wisconsin Card Sorting Test performance in schizophrenia. *Archives of General Psychiatry.* **54**:159–165.

170. Wechsler D. (1997) *Wechsler Memory Scale.* 3rd ed. San Antonio, TX: The Psychological Corporation.

171. Brandt J, Benedict RHB (2001) *The Hopkins Verbal Learning Test - Revised: Professional Manual.* Odessa: Psychological Assessment Resources, Inc.

172. Benedict RHB (1997) *Brief Visuospatial Memory Test - Revised: Professional Manual.* Odessa: Psychological Assessment Resources, Inc.

173. White T, Stern RA (2003) *Neuropsychological Assessment Battery: Psychometric and Technical Manual.* Lutz: Psychological Assessment Resources, Inc..

174. Kerr SL, Neale JM (1993) Emotion perception in schizophrenia: specific deficit or further evidence of generalized poor performance? *Journal of Abnormal Psychology.* 102; 312–318.

175. Kohler CG, Turner TH, Bilker WB, Brensinger CM, Siegel SJ, Kanes SJ, *et al.* (2003) Facial emotion recognition in schizophrenia: intensity effects and error pattern. *American Journal of Psychiatry.* 160; 1768–1774.

176. Addington J, Saeedi H, Addington D (2006) Facial affect recognition: a mediator between cognitive and social functioning in psychosis? *Schizophr Res.* Jul; **85**(1–3): 142–150.

177. Sergi MJ, Rassovsky Y, Nuechterlein KH, Green MF (2006) Social perception as a mediator of the influence of early visual processing on functional status in schizophrenia. *American Journal of Psychiatry.* 163; 448–454.

178. Horton HK, Silverstein SM (2008) Social cognition as a mediator of cognition and outcome among deaf and hearing people with schizophrenia. *Schizophr Res.* Oct; **105**(1– **3**): 125–137.

179. Vaskinn A, Sundet K, Friis S, Simonsen C, Birkenaes AB, Jonsdottir H, *et al.* (2008) Emotion perception and learning potential: mediators between neurocognition and social problem-solving in schizophrenia? *J Int Neuropsychol Soc.* Mar; **14**(2):279–288.

180. Meyer MB, Kurtz MM (2009) Elementary neurocognitive function, facial affect recognition and social-skills in schizophrenia. *Schizophr Res.* May; **110**(1–3): 173–179.

181. Addington J, Girard TA, Christensen BK, Addington D (Social cognition mediates illness-related and cognitive influences on social function in patients with schizophrenia-spectrum disorders. *J Psychiatry Neurosci.* Jan; **35**(1):49–54.

182. Kee KS, Kern RS, Marshall BD, Jr., Green MF (1998) Risperidone versus haloperidol for perception of emotion in treatment-resistant schizophrenia: preliminary findings. *Schizophr Res.* May 25; **31**(2–3):159–165.

183. Littrell KH, Petty RG, Hilligoss NM, Kirshner CD, Johnson CG Improvement in social cognition in patients with schizophrenia associated with treatment with olanzapine. *Schizophrenia Research.* **66**:201–202.

184. Herbener ES, Hill KS, Marvin R, Sweeney J (2005) Effects of Antipsychotic Treatment on Emotion Perception Deficits in First-Episode Schizophrenia. *American Journal of Psychiatry.* 162; 1746–1748.

185. Harvey PD, Patterson TL, Potter LS, Zhong K, Brecher M (2006) Improvement in social competence with short-term atypical antipsychotic treatment: a randomized, double-blind comparison of quetiapine versus risperidone for social competence, social cognition, and neuropsychological functioning. *Am J Psychiatry*. Nov; **163**(11):1918–1925.

186. Behere RV, Venkatasubramanian G, Arasappa R, Reddy N, Gangadhar BN (2009) Effect of risperidone on emotion recognition deficits in antipsychotic-naive schizophrenia: a short-term follow-up study. *Schizophr Res*. Aug; **113**(1):72–76.

CHAPTER 4

The genetics of schizophrenia

James T.R. Walters, Michael O'Donovan and Michael J. Owen

*MRC Centre for Neuropsychiatric Genetics and Genomics,
Cardiff University School of Medicine*

Information Box

- In the last two to three years knowledge of the molecular genetics of schizophrenia has advanced more than at any other time.
- Genome-wide association studies have identified common genetic variants which increase the risk of developing schizophrenia. A number of these variants have been widely replicated as increasing susceptibility to schizophrenia and seem to influence risk across traditional diagnostic boundaries.
- Several rare, large copy number variants (deletions or duplications of segments of DNA) also increase the risk of schizophrenia, as well as other neurodevelopmental disorders such as autism and intellectual disability.
- These and related findings in genetic epidemiology indicate that the genetic architecture of schizophrenia is complex and likely to involve a 'mixed economy' of common variants of small effect and rarer variants typically with larger effects.

INTRODUCTION

Since its earliest description, schizophrenia has been known to be a disorder that runs in families and we now know from family, twin and adoption studies that this is substantially genetic in origin. Based upon genetic linkage analysis and candidate gene association studies, initial attempts to find the genes responsible met with

---

Schizophrenia: Current Science and Clinical Practice, First Edition. Edited by Wolfgang Gaebel.
© 2011 John Wiley & Sons, Ltd. Published 2011 by John Wiley & Sons, Ltd.

limited success. However the field has advanced considerably with the advent of genome-wide association technology and the ability to exploit this for analysis of copy number variation. This chapter will summarise the current state of knowledge and examine the potential impact of the study of genetics on schizophrenia research and clinical practice.

GENETIC EPIDEMIOLOGY OF SCHIZOPHRENIA

Genetic epidemiology refers to a variety of study designs that can be used to establish the extent to which genetic and environmental factors influence traits or disease and how that genetic risk is transmitted across generations – the mode of inheritance. The degree of genetic contribution to a disorder is often described by the term *heritability*; generally referring to the proportion of liability to a disorder in a population that is attributable to genetic factors.

Family, twin and adoption studies of schizophrenia

Conducted over many decades across many countries, based upon a range of diagnostic and ascertainment practices, and using a variety of analytic methodologies, family studies of over 8000 individuals with schizophrenia and their relatives [1], and more recently, population studies of millions of individuals [2,3] have provided unequivocal evidence that the disorder is familial. Overall, risk in the first degree relatives of a proband is about 9%, an approximately 10-fold increase over that in the general population, with a rapid decline as the degree of genetic relatedness to the proband becomes more distant [1] (see Figure 4.1).

Twin and adoption studies are powerful tools to demonstrate the relative contribution of genetic and environmental effects on conditions such as schizophrenia. A large number of twin studies of schizophrenia deploying varying methods of ascertainment, diagnostic practices and methodological sophistication, point clearly to increased phenotypic similarity with respect to schizophrenia in monozygotic (MZ) compared with dizygotic (DZ) twins (Figure 4.1). This chapter will not discuss these findings in detail but interested readers are referred to recent reviews and meta-analyses for in-depth appraisal of this literature and its methodology [4,5]. Importantly from these studies there is agreement in estimates of heritability for schizophrenia at around 80%. There is also consistent support for an influence of both nonshared and shared environments as contributing to risk for schizophrenia.

It is reassuring that the results of adoption studies have largely corroborated the findings of twin studies in confirming a substantial genetic component to the aetiology of schizophrenia [6,7].

In both twin and adoption study approaches there are assumptions in design which can introduce caveats to their interpretation. However the consistency

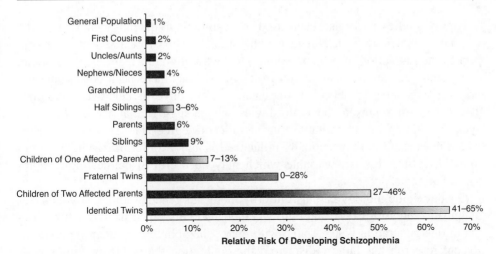

Figure 4.1 Risk of developing schizophrenia in the relatives of a proband with schizophrenia. Based on data from references [1–4]. Shaded areas show range of estimates for values of risk.

of the findings from both approaches, along with recent positive results from molecular genetics, makes redundant the argument against a genetic influence on schizophrenia.

The patterns of inheritance will be discussed in more detail later in this chapter, but the evidence from family studies suggests that schizophrenia is a complex disorder which does not conform to simple, Mendelian inheritance. From these studies the causes of schizophrenia appear to be multifactorial, likely involving many genes and both shared and nonshared environmental influences.

Genetic epidemiology – informing diagnosis?

Whilst the studies described have established a genetic basis for schizophrenia these results cannot be assumed to validate schizophrenia as a categorical diagnosis. In recent years researchers have examined the nosological validity of the diagnosis of schizophrenia by examining the occurrence of spectrum conditions or other related diagnoses in family members of probands.

Family studies have demonstrated that rates of *schizophrenia-spectrum conditions,* characterised by attenuated symptoms, are elevated in the relatives of those with schizophrenia [8]. That genetic factors contribute to such spectrum conditions is implied by a report that the linkage signals for schizophrenia and schizotypy in nonpsychotic relatives show significant correlation [9]. Although there have been positive studies of associations of schizophrenia candidate genes with schizotypy dimensions [10], whether the schizophrenia continuum that may be apparent in relatives extends to the population at large is yet to be conclusively established.

Family studies have also been used to examine sub-diagnoses and particular symptoms that may be useful in genetic studies. This work has lent little support to the dissection of schizophrenia into its traditional categories of paranoid, hebephrenic, catatonic, simple and residual. Nor has there been consistent support for a genetic influence on dimensions of positive or negative symptoms. The exception seems to be twin studies which suggest that the disorganised symptom dimension is heritable to a significant degree [11,12]. Another factor which does seem to be genetically influenced is age of onset of psychotic symptoms [13], thus this is a variable which may be useful in delineating samples for research.

Genetic epidemiology can also inform about the genetic/biological validity of diagnostic categories by examining whether disorders breed true; if schizophrenia in one generation is associated with only schizophrenia in other generations. Recent research has largely disproved the contention that schizophrenia breeds true. In a seminal study Lichtenstein and colleagues [2] addressed the question of whether schizophrenia and bipolar disorder were conditions with a shared or discrete aetiology. The authors linked the Swedish registers to quantify genetic and environmental influences for the two disorders and their co-morbidity (see Figure 4.2). This is the most comprehensive study of its kind to date, involving over 9 million individuals in assessing risk in biological and adoptive families. The study confirmed an increased risk of schizophrenia or bipolar disorder in the families of individuals with these respective disorders. Heritability estimates were 64% for schizophrenia and 59% for bipolar disorder. Furthermore there was an increased risk of schizophrenia in the families of those with bipolar disorder and likewise an increased risk of bipolar disorder in the families of those with schizophrenia. The increased risk of schizophrenia extended to the adopted children of biological parents with bipolar disorder. An additional finding was that the comorbidity between schizophrenia and bipolar disorder was largely genetic in origin [63%].

Another recent study examined the risk for a range of psychiatric disorders in the offspring of parents who both had received a diagnosis of schizophrenia or bipolar disorder [3]. Based upon Danish register data the risk of schizophrenia in children of parents both of whom had schizophrenia [27%] was nearly four times the risk in children with only one parent with schizophrenia [7%] compared with a 0.86% risk for individuals with neither parent having been admitted to psychiatric hospital. When both parents had bipolar disorder the risk to their child of developing schizophrenia was more than 4 times that in the general population [4.8%].

Despite taking different approaches the findings of these studies mirror each other in strongly indicating a genetic overlap between schizophrenia and bipolar disorder. These results have presented a challenge for the next stage of genetic approaches which have sought to find the genes responsible for genetic susceptibility to schizophrenia.

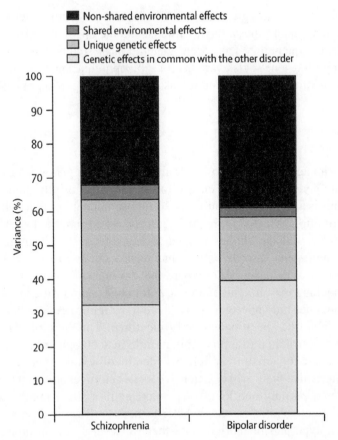

Figure 4.2 Data from Lichtenstein *et al.* [2] population-based family study of schizophrenia and bipolar disorder showing percentage variance explained by genetic and environmental factors. Reproduced from The Lancet [2], Copyright (2009), with permission from Elsevier.

MOLECULAR GENETICS OF SCHIZOPHRENIA

Molecular genetic studies essentially seek correlations between the possession of particular DNA variants and the manifestation of a phenotype. In schizophrenia as in other disorders, the early studies attempted to locate genetic signals by linkage, and this led to the identification of positional candidate genes (genes within regions of potential linkage) which were subsequently tested by genetic association. These studies were complemented by functional candidate gene association studies, that is, studies of genes selected on the basis of encoding proteins relevant to hypotheses of schizophrenia pathogenesis. In addition cytogenetic techniques identified the potential importance of a small number of chromosomal abnormalities.

More recently technological advances have enabled genome-wide association studies of hundreds of thousands of variants, and the upcoming prospect of whole genome DNA sequencing. The recent generation of studies have identified very strongly supported genetic risk variants for schizophrenia, and have also implicated rare structural variation as a factor at least in a small proportion of cases.

Linkage

The aim of linkage analysis is to locate the approximate genomic co-ordinates of susceptibility genes. In its most classic form as applied to fully dominant genetic disorders, this is achieved by identifying chromosomal regions that, within families containing multiple affected individuals, are always co-inherited with a disorder.

In the 1980s, linkage studies proved highly effective in locating pathogenic genes for single-gene disorders. This has turned out not to be so for common disorders, medical or psychiatric, where the transmission patterns do not follow simple Mendelian rules. In schizophrenia, as for most common disorders, promising findings from one study have generally failed to be replicated in other studies, and no linkage signal has been consistently identified. This lack of consistency has generally been attributed to a predominant role in schizophrenia for risk variants whose effects are too small to be reliably identified by linkage in realistic sample sizes. An alternative view evokes extensive locus heterogeneity, in which the effect sizes are large, but any one locus only operates in a small number of families. Both weak effects and/or extensive heterogeneity will result in poor correlation between genotype and phenotype, and thereby severely compromise the power of linkage. Where the explanatory models differ is that the heterogeneity models predict that highly significant linkages should be obtained in studies of individual large pedigrees. Although a number of strong linkages have indeed been observed in single pedigrees this does not appear to be the case for the majority of large kindreds.

Given our earlier comment that no linkage signals have been consistently identified, we do not discuss the previous linkage data in any detail, but instead point interested readers elsewhere [14] and for updated linkage results: http://slep.unc.edu. An important point is that despite these difficulties, promising candidate genes have emerged from linkage studies (next section). Moreover, an initial meta-analysis of schizophrenia linkage studies [15] identified a genome-wide significant signal (that is, a signal that is significant allowing for multiple testing) on chromosome 2q. Unfortunately this 2q locus linkage signal became nonsignificant in an updated meta-analysis based upon over 7000 cases [16], although this study did report an excess of nominally significant linkages over that expected by chance. Therefore although no individual locus was definitively identified, the latter observation strongly supports the existence of many true linkages in the data, and therefore the existence of multiple risk loci. Loci with strongest support included regions of chromosomes 1, 2q, 3q, 4q, 5q, 8p and 10q.

Positional candidate studies

Despite a lack of consistent replication, some of the better linkage signals have been followed up by association mapping in unrelated individuals. Genes mapping to linkage regions are called positional candidate genes, their putative role in the disorder resting primarily on their chromosomal location.

In schizophrenia there are several examples of positional candidate genes for which there is quite strong support, including *regulator of G-protein signalling 4 (RGS4)* [17] as well as *fibroblast growth factor receptor 2 (FGFR2)* [18] and *Protein Kinase C, alpha (PRKCA)* [19] which were recently reported by the present authors. However, those loci which have gained most attention and support are *neuregulin 1 (NRG1), dysbindin (DTNBP1)* and *D-amino acid oxidase activator (DAOA).*

NRG1 was identified as a potential susceptibility gene through association mapping by *deCODE Genetics* of a putative linkage at 8p22-p11 that had been observed in Icelandic pedigrees [20]. The strongest evidence for association was obtained for a haplotype (in this context, a haplotype is a segment of DNA defined by multiple genetic markers) at the 5' end of the gene, a finding that was later exactly replicated in a Scottish population [21] and by ourselves in another UK population [22].

Neuregulin 1 has an enormous range of developmental functions including influencing neuronal migration, synaptic development, oligodendrocyte function and myelination. It is known to interact with the kinase *ErbB4*, the gene of which also shows some weak evidence for association [23].

Variants of *NRG1* have been associated with altered frontal and temporal cortex activation and white matter structure [24,25]. Since those findings are plausibly related to theories of schizophrenia pathogenesis, they have enhanced *NRG1* as a plausible candidate gene.

However, it is important to remember that although there have been positive reports of association; there are also many negative reports. That is not necessarily unexpected (see later discussion about genetic effect size). More troublesome is that most of the follow-up studies, be they positive or negative, have not tested the original associated haplotype, and many of these 'positive' studies, including neuroimaging studies, involve different variants. For these reasons the evidence that *NRG1* is a susceptibility locus for schizophrenia cannot yet be considered conclusive.

DTNBP1 was identified as a potential susceptibility gene after an association mapping study across a putative linkage on the short arm of chromosome 6 [26]. The protein is expressed pre- and post-synaptically, with high levels of expression in the hippocampus and cerebellum. Several reported risk variants/haplotypes at this locus have been additionally associated with reduced *DTNBP1* mRNA and/or protein expression in post-mortem brain [27]. *Dysbindin* has biological plausibility, playing a role in vesicular transport of neurotransmitters as a part of the biogenesis of lysosome-related organelles complex 1 (*BLOC-1*), and perhaps a role in dopamine *D2* receptor internalisation, an action which could explain its role in the pathogenesis of schizophrenia.

Taken as a whole, there is a body of evidence that places *DTNBP1* alongside *NRG1* as among the top schizophrenia candidates from the pre-GWAS era. However, just as is the case with *NRG1* this view of *DTNBP1* must be tempered by the reality that while there have been numerous follow-up studies reported to be supportive for association, the precise associated variants and haplotypes vary, making the genetic data far from unequivocal.

Finally in this section, we consider *DAOA* which was identified as a potential susceptibility gene after an association mapping study across a putative linkage region on the long arm of chromosome 13. Support initially came from a French-Canadian and a Russian sample [28]. Although the biology of this gene/protein is poorly understood *DAOA* interacts with D-amino acid oxidase which may indirectly alter glutamate signalling. The initial result has replicated in other schizophrenia samples, and also in bipolar disorder [29], the latter being compatible with genetic epidemiological data suggesting overlap between the two disorders. Although initial replication data appeared more consistent for the associated alleles, as data have accumulated the evidence has somewhat diminished, and in the most recent and largest published meta-analysis [30], the evidence for association was restricted to Asian samples. Thus, as for the other candidate genes described, questions remain regarding the true relevance of *DAOA* to schizophrenia.

Functional candidate studies

Positional candidate studies adopt an essentially agnostic position with respect to the pathophysiology of schizophrenia. An alternative approach is to look for association with genes involved in mechanisms that have a putative role in disease pathogenesis. The majority of early studies in psychiatric genetics focused on such candidates given the limited capacity of genotyping at the time. As a result the vast functional candidate gene literature consists primarily of studies in relatively small samples using single functional variants or limited sets of variants which fail to systematically cover the common variation in genes. These issues, together with the small genetic effects typical of such variants and our limited knowledge of the underlying pathophysiology, have resulted in often inconsistent findings and limited replication. In an attempt to address these issues the schizophrenia research forum have established the SZGene database (http://www.schizophreniaforum.org/res/sczgene/default.asp) which tracks and collates association study results and performs meta-analyses [31]. This is a valuable resource in what is a fast-changing field.

Table 4.1 outlines results for some of the most popular functional candidate genes which have typically been investigated based upon the perceived importance of neurotransmitter systems in schizophrenia. Those genes presented in table 1

Table 4.1 Summary table of functional candidate genes

Gene	Variant	Supporting evidence	Proposed function	Summary of findings
DRD2 **Dopamine Receptor D2**	Ser311Cys serine to cysteine polymorphism	Positive meta-analysis.	Polymorphism thought to lead to impaired receptor function	Meta-analytic samples not large, but results merit further study, perhaps particularly examining interactions between functional variants
	rs6277	Positive meta-analysis.	Alters RNA stability and receptor expression	Meta-analytic samples not large, but results merit further study
DRD3 **Dopamine Receptor D3**	Serine-Glycine non-synonymous variant	Initial positive reports, negative meta-analysis. Little support from studies with systematic coverage of the gene.	Variant is of questionable functional significance.	Significant association disappeared when meta-analytic samples increased to over 10 000 subjects (typical of size of samples that will be required to authenticate candidate susceptibility variants).
DRD4 **Dopamine Receptor D4**	rs1800955 (521T/C)	Large effect size in initial report, positive meta-analysis (small sample).	SNP located in promoter region of DRD4.	Further investigation required given comparatively large effect size of initial study and limited meta-analysis sample size. Meta-analytic evidence of weak association with novelty seeking.

(Continued)

Table 4.1 (Continued)

Gene	Variant	Supporting evidence	Proposed function	Summary of findings
DAT *Dopamine Transporter SLC6A3*	rs3756450, rs464049	Emerged as strongest candidate in study that systematically examined dopamine related variants	rs3756450 has possible effect on promoter activity	This study represented an advance in the field in its systematic coverage although replication for this dopamine transporter susceptibility variant is required.
HTR2A *(Encoding 5HT2A receptor)*	rs6311 (T102C)	Initial positive reports. The most recent evidence suggests weakly significant association with schizophrenia.	Contradictory evidence that this polymorphism influences *HTR2A* expression.	Study with comprehensive coverage and meta-analysis supports weakly significant association.
Serotonin Transporter gene SLC6A4	VNTR, variable number tandem repeat polymorphism, STin2.12	Contrary findings in meta-analyses regarding association with schizophrenia	No known functional effect.	Contradictory meta-analytic results warrant further study.

Details of original studies and updated meta-analyses can be found at http://www.schizophreniaforum.org/res/sczgene/default.asp

represent a sample of the most widely studied variants, which are dopamine and serotonin candidate genes and should not be considered in any way comprehensive. Although other neurotransmitter systems, such as GABA and glutamate have been implicated in candidate genetic studies in schizophrenia, they generally lack the level of evidence of those presented (either from being examined systematically or in meta-analyses).

We will consider one particular candidate gene in more detail by way of illustration of issues that inform the interpretation of all candidate gene studies.

The *catechol-O-methyl transferase* gene (*COMT*), probably the most widely studied gene in psychiatric genetics, encodes an enzyme which catabolises dopamine. Given the prominence of the dopamine hypothesis of schizophrenia this gene attracted a great deal of early interest. Support for this gene is also provided by its location in a region of chromosome 22q11 which, when deleted, results in a syndrome in which schizophrenia is a common feature (32) (see next section). *COMT*'s status as an ideal functional candidate was further strengthened by reports of a functional valine-to-methionine variant (Val/Met), which alters the enzyme's activity. In schizophrenia studies have reported positive and negative associations for the Val/Met polymorphism, whilst the most up-to-date meta-analysis indicates no significant effect at the Val/Met locus, although there may be significant association at another *COMT* locus (rs737865) (SZGene accessed April 2010).

Despite the apparent lack of association at the Val/Met locus with schizophrenia, investigators pursued the initial positive findings by examining the effects of the Val/Met polymorphism using neurocognitive and neuroimaging paradigms [33]. These studies were the first to use *endophenotypes* in this way by investigating the action of a genetic variant. Endophenotypes are heritable traits, such as cognitive or imaging parameters, that occur more frequently in cases than controls, cosegregate with illness in families and are thought to display a simpler genetic architecture than phenotypes [34]. We have argued elsewhere that caution needs to be exercised in adopting endophenotype approaches [35] and findings with *COMT* illustrate some of these points: [i] the genetic variants to be used in endophenotype studies should be robustly replicated, [ii] endophenotypes will be most useful in exploring the actions of risk variants rather than for gene-finding [iii] efforts should be made to confirm that the endophenotype lies on the pathway between gene and phenotype – if not it is unlikely to be informative about disease mechanisms.

COMT was also one of the first genes to be investigated in studies of gene-environment interaction. Caspi and colleagues [36] found that carriers of the *COMT* Val allele were more likely than carriers of two Met alleles to develop psychosis if they used cannabis, although these results have not been replicated in a subsequent study [37].

Such gene-environment (and gene-gene) interactions have the potential to be informative about disease pathways and mechanisms. However given the inherent complexities of these studies, including the potential for multiple testing, their wholesale adoption requires caution [38] and at the very least genes or environmental exposures that are established risk factors should be selected. Given the potential for such important interactions it seems sensible that appropriate studies should be designed to include reliable data on important environmental exposures.

Chromosomal abnormalities

Prior to the advent of systematic scans of the genome for the structural chromosomal variants known as copy number variants (CNVs – see next section), a small number of rare chromosomal abnormalities had already been implicated in the disorder.

The chromosomal abnormality most strongly implicated is a known cause of DiGeorge syndrome, now more commonly known as Velocardiofacial Syndrome (VCFS). This affects roughly 1 in 4000 births and is characterised by a deletion (typically 1.5-3Mb in size) of chromosome 22q11.2. Individuals with VCFS express a range of phenotypic features involving congenital abnormalities of a number of organs and tissues, particularly those derived from the branchial arches. Common features include cardiac malformations, characteristic facies/dysmorphology, cleft palate [39] and neuropsychiatric phenotypes including reduced cortical brain volume [40]. Borderline learning disability is common and psychotic disorder occurs in around 30% of adults with VCFS, the majority of which satisfies diagnostic criteria for schizophrenia [32]. This finding of considerably increased risk for schizophrenia in VCFS provided a model to investigate the genetic basis of the disorder. The associated 22q11.2 deletion imparts a risk for schizophrenia 25–30 times that of the general population, a risk assumed to be due to haploinsufficiency of one or more of over 40 genes in the deleted region. Many of these genes are functionally plausible candidates, none more so than *COMT* as has been discussed. *PRODH* is another gene in this region and is a strong candidate as it encodes the enzyme proline dehydrogenase and has been shown to modulate sensorimotor gating in mice [41], a deficit also seen in schizophrenia. Whilst there have been positive associations for *PRODH* the data overall do not support association. The development of mouse models of the 22q11.2 deletion and subsequent follow up studies have aided research in this area and implicated two adjacent genes, *TBX1* and *GNB1L*. *TBX1* is a member of the T-Box family of transcription factors and *GNB1L* encodes a G-protein beta-subunit-like polypeptide although its function is unknown. There have been positive reports of association for SNPs in both these genes [42,43] though, whilst the evidence for GNB1L appears stronger, neither finding has been independently replicated.

Although the causative variant, gene or genes have yet to be definitively identified and whilst there is incomplete penetrance for schizophrenia (1 in 4 people with VCFS affected) this locus is seen to be potentially important in providing clues to the aetiology of schizophrenia. It was originally thought that up to 1% of cases of schizophrenia possessed the VCFS deletion although data from larger, more recent studies suggests this figure is between 0.2%-0.4% [44,45]. Nonetheless of all identified risk factors VCFS has the largest effect on risk for schizophrenia other than having a twin or two parents with the disorder.

St Clair and colleagues reported a balanced translocation at chromosome 1:11 (q42.1; q14.3) which co-segregated with schizophrenia in a large Scottish pedigree [46]. However, it is clear that in this family, the translocation influences risk not just of schizophrenia but also of major mood disorders (recurrent unipolar depression and bipolar disorder), a clear demonstration of a genetic lesion whose effects do not conform to traditional diagnostic boundaries. In support of this finding Hamshere and colleagues also reported significant linkage to a mixed psychosis/affective phenotype in the chromosome 1 translocation region [47]. The chromosome 11 region involved in the translocation harbours no genes, but the chromosome 1 breakpoint disrupts two genes, subsequently named disrupted in schizophrenia 1 and 2 (*DISC1 and DISC2*) of which *DISC1* has emerged as the gene most likely to mediate the effects of the translocation. There have since been several reports of association between variants in the vicinity of this gene and schizophrenia and bipolar disorder, but currently, the evidence for this is weak. It should be noted that the failure to show genetic association does not negate the strong evidence for the involvement of this gene that comes from the existence of the co-segregation between the balanced translocation and major mental disorder in one large pedigree.

DISC1 has a plethora of cellular functions, indeed it has been described as a hub protein for neural growth, particularly given its role in both neurite and dendrite outgrowth. In the several mouse models which have sought to mimic the genetic mutation there is evidence for behavioural phenotypes of relevance to schizophrenia [48–50]. Two binding partners of *DISC1, NDEL1* and *NDE1* have been independently associated with schizophrenia [51,52] and in addition *NDE1* is in the chromosome 16p13.1 region implicated by copy number variants that predispose to schizophrenia and neurodevelopmental disorders [53]. *PDE4B* is another gene in this complex with reported interaction effects with *DISC1* in association with schizophrenia [54].

In human studies, *DISC1* variants have been associated with deficits in memory and decreased prefrontal and hippocampal grey matter volume [55]. Intriguing though those studies are, in the absence of clear evidence that those same variants are relevant to schizophrenia susceptibility, it is uncertain that those findings provide insights into the clinical disorder.

Taken together the molecular genetic and biological evidence would suggest that *DISC1* is very likely to be a true risk gene for schizophrenia although the extent of its action in the population with schizophrenia as a whole is as yet unknown.

Genome wide association studies

In the last two to three years, the advent of large-scale genome-wide association studies [GWAS] has enabled more progress to be made in the genetic investigation of common diseases than in all previous years combined. Several developments have made this possible;

(i)   the completion of the human genome project, the identification of millions of polymorphic markers across the genome, and the availability of data from the HapMap project which catalogues genotype frequency of these single nucleotide polymorphisms (SNPs), and the patterns of linkage disequilibrium between them.

(ii) the availability of affordable high-throughput genotyping arrays

(iii) the study of large samples as a result of international collaboration and co-operation between investigators.

GWAS are based on the common disease/common variant hypothesis which postulates that for common diseases such as schizophrenia, much of the genetic risk is due to common risk variants (minor allele frequencies of $>1\%$). GWAS also rely on the phenomenon of linkage disequilibrium between related SNPs, that is, that genotypes at SNPs in varying levels of close proximity are often correlated; therefore it is possible to make inferences about the association status of a high proportion of all SNPs by genotyping a subset of them, although that still requires several hundred thousand variants to be assayed in each person. Until recently, such large scale analyses were not possible, but in the last few years, genotyping on this scale, using what is often called DNA chip or micro-array technology, has become a reality, and at ever decreasing costs. Widely used genotyping platforms currently type between 500 000 and 1 million SNPs, and capture over 80% of all known common variation across the human genome.

The economies allowed by chip technology enable GWAS to be undertaken in extremely large samples, a factor that has been crucial for success since, in most complex diseases, sample sizes of the scale of tens of thousands of individuals (or more) are necessary to identify common variants of small effect at convincing levels of evidence. Prior to considering the results of GWAS, another issue to consider is that of statistical significance, given the burden of multiple testing inherent when investigating association of such large numbers of variants. It is generally accepted that genome-wide significance in GWAS is attained at an approximate p value of 5×10^{-8} [56].

GWAS IN SCHIZOPHRENIA

A number of early GWAS studies of schizophrenia were based on DNA pooling, whereby DNA samples are mixed together to create case and control pools, each containing tens or hundreds of individuals [57–59]. Allele frequencies are then estimated in each pool in a single assay (rather than an assay for each individual person) and the results from case and control pools compared. This approach was taken primarily due to cost implications. One notable finding to emerge from these studies was the identification of *reelin (RELN)* as a potential susceptibility gene for schizophrenia in women, though not quite at genome-wide levels of significance [59]. Given its role in neurodevelopmental processes including corticogenesis, neuronal migration, and neuroplasticity and its reduced expression in schizophrenia [59], *reelin* is a very plausible functional candidate gene for neurodevelopmental disorders. Indeed *reelin* is known to be involved in an autosomal recessive form of lissencephaly, Norman-Roberts syndrome, which is characterised pathologically by abnormal cortical layering and clinically by craniofacial abnormalities and neuropsychiatric symptoms including seizures and profound learning disability [60]. However, at present, the data supporting a role for this gene in schizophrenia are not fully persuasive.

Given the small differences in allele frequencies expected for genes of small effect, even minor inaccuracies in allele frequency estimation from DNA pools can be problematic, and therefore GWAS studies based upon individual sample genotyping are much preferable to those based upon pooling. In schizophrenia, the first study to use individual genotypes was a small study of 178 cases and 144 controls [61]. That study provided strong, but not genome-wide significant support ($p = 3.7 \times 10^{-7}$), equidistant between two genes; *colony stimulating factor 2 receptor alpha (CSF2RA)*, which is a sub-unit of a cytokine receptor and *short stature homeobox isoform b (SHOX),* a putative transcription factor absent in some people with short stature. Significant associations were reported for *CSF2RA* in a very small replication sample (71 cases and 31 controls), although given the low power of the study much more evidence for this locus will be required before it can be accepted as a highly likely susceptibility gene. To date the implicated loci have not received support in subsequent studies.

The first GWAS to report a genome-wide significant result was a study by O'Donovan and colleagues [62]. They performed genome-wide analysis in a relatively modest sample of 479 cases and 2937 control subjects, and followed up the most significant results (those with p value$<1 \times 10^{-5}$) in additional samples of up to 6829 cases with schizophrenia and 9897 controls. Of 12 SNPs followed up from the initial GWAS, the strongest supported (rs1344706) was at 2q32.1 within the gene *ZNF804A*. Even in this large combined schizophrenia dataset, genome-wide significance was not obtained, the meta-analysis p value being 1.6×10^{-7}. However, this threshold was surpassed ($p = 9 \times 10^{-9}$) when the affected phenotype was expanded to include bipolar cases.

ZNF804A has since received additional support for association [63,64], one of these studies also supporting associations with schizophrenia and the broader psychosis phenotype. More recently, Williams and colleagues [65] have provided additional evidence for association through meta-analysis of a larger data set (18 945 cases with schizophrenia/schizoaffective disorder, 21 274 cases combined of schizophrenia and bipolar disorder and 38 675 controls). The meta-analysis provided evidence for association of rs1344706 that surpasses genome-wide significance by several orders of magnitude for both schizophrenia (p $= 2.5 \times 10^{-11}$) and schizophrenia and bipolar disorder combined (p $= 4.1 \times 10^{-13}$). After de novo polymorphism discovery and detailed association analysis, rs1344706 remained the most strongly associated marker in the gene. The allelic association at the *ZNF804A* locus is now one of the most compelling in schizophrenia, and supports the accumulating data suggesting overlapping genetic risk between schizophrenia and bipolar disorder.

Little is known about the biological function of *ZNF804A* although it is a putative transcription factor. Esslinger and colleagues [66] have found that the risk variant is associated with enhanced functional connectivity between the hippocampus and prefrontal cortex in healthy individuals, an imaging finding which the same group has observed in people with schizophrenia [67]. Walters and colleagues [68] have found that the risk allele is associated with better cognitive function in people with schizophrenia but not controls, suggesting that rather than influencing cognitive function per se, the gene may be increasing risk for a psychosis phenotype with relatively preserved cognitive function.

Three GWAS studies of schizophrenia were simultaneously published in the journal *Nature* in 2009. The studies were based upon three large consortia datasets; the Molecular Genetics of Schizophrenia group (MGS) [69], the International Schizophrenia Consortium (ISC) [70] and SGENE [71]. The consortia also exchanged data for the top 1000 or so SNPs of interest from their studies to enable meta-analysis of specific loci. The individual studies were based upon initial GWAS samples of >2000 cases and up to 13500 controls. The only genome-wide significant result in an individual study analysis was observed in the ISC study in the *major histocompatability complex (MHC)* region, 7 kilobases from *NOTCH4*, a gene previously suggested as a candidate for schizophrenia.

In the combined datasets reported by SGENE, which also included additional cases and controls, in total 12945 cases and 34591 controls, seven loci emerged as genome-wide significant. Five loci were located in a broad region of chromosome 6 that includes the *MHC* region (best p value $= 1.4 \times 10^{-12}$). The others were at 11q24.2, upstream of the *neurogranin* gene (*NRGN*) (p $= 2.4 \times 10^{-9}$) and in an intron of *transcription factor 4 (TCF 4)* on 18q21.2 (p $= 4.1 \times 10^{-9}$).

The region on chromosome 6 that was implicated is large, spanning about 5 Mb. Across that region, the genotypes of thousands of SNPs spanning a very large number of genes are highly correlated which means that the signal cannot be yet attributed to a specific gene. The broad region includes many genes that play a role in the immune system, including human leucocyte antigen genes. The potential involvement of immune-related genes is interesting given epidemiological findings suggesting a role for infection in the aetiology of schizophrenia. However, it should be stressed that the associated region also contains genes unrelated to immune function, so it should not be assumed that the finding supports the involvement of immunological processes in schizophrenia aetiology.

NGRN is expressed in the brain, particularly in the hippocampus [72]. It encodes a postsynaptic protein kinase substrate that plays a role in regulating calcium by binding to calmodulin, and by this mechanism, is thought to be involved in regulating glutamate/NMDA receptor signaling. Such a role is consistent with, aberrant glutamate function as a pathophysiological process in schizophrenia.

TCF4, a member of the E-protein family, is involved in neuronal development [73]. Recently mutations in this gene have been found to cause the autosomal dominant condition Pitt-Hopkins syndrome [74] which is characterised by profound learning disability, intermittent hyperventilation, microcephaly, epilepsy and widespread neurological signs.

One further key finding to emerge from this triplet of GWAS studies is the demonstration of a substantial polygenic component to schizophrenia aetiology. The analysis by the ISC [70] examined the influence of common variants en masse by considering any alleles surpassing very relaxed thresholds for association as 'risk' alleles (risk in quotes as the vast majority of those are not expected to be true risk alleles). They next assigned scores to cases and controls in independent datasets based upon the number of the risk alleles carried by each individual. Surprisingly, the scores were able to discriminate (very weakly but highly significantly) between cases and controls, even when risk allele status was based upon a p value threshold as relaxed as $p<0.5$. This implies the existence of a very large number of true risk alleles with very small effects on risk [and therefore very slim evidence for association for most individual loci]. The authors also found that the sets of schizophrenia 'risk' alleles could discriminate between bipolar disorder samples and controls, but not between controls and a variety of non-psychiatric conditions. These analyses led to several conclusions (i) a large number of loci of small effect, probably in the thousands, contribute to the aetiology of schizophrenia and account for at least 30% of the total variation (genetic and non genetic) in its liability (ii) this polygenic risk is substantially shared with bipolar disorder but not with a series of nonpsychiatric conditions. These findings therefore provide further support for (i) the common disease/common variant hypothesis and (ii) common genetic aetiology between schizophrenia and bipolar disorder.

There has been widespread debate about the degree to which GWAS have 'delivered' given the levels of investment necessary to carry out this work. Ultimately, (and it is premature to draw final conclusions as much larger analyses are currently underway), whether they will be considered to have been valuable will depend upon their ability to deliver new insights into mechanisms, diagnosis or nosology. However, what have emerged are robust new candidates which are supported at levels of significance and replication previously unseen in this field. These genetic findings seem both to support novel mechanisms and corroborate previously identified pathways. Despite this some have questioned whether such large scale studies are worthwhile, and there is a common belief that weak risk factors cannot confer insights into pathogenesis and possible therapeutics. However, the utility of a genetic finding in these respects is independent of its effect size. Thus important

novel insights into pathogenesis have already been gained from GWAS of type II
diabetes [75] and Crohn's disease [76] and regarding therapeutics, common alleles
in *PPARG* and *KCNJ11* confer small increments in risk of type II diabetes (OR~
1.14) but both genes encode important targets for drugs used to treat this disorder
[75].

Copy number variation

Recent studies including those applying GWAS technology have also identified
the involvement of structural chromosomal variants in schizophrenia. Structural
variation in this sense includes DNA copy number variants (CNVs) consisting of
deletions and duplications of chromosomal segments. CNVs vary in size, from
insertions or deletions of a thousand bases to those encompassing several million
bases that affect the dosage of large numbers of genes. CNVs have been shown to
be ubiquitous in the general population and to account for a significant degree of
the genomic variation between individuals [77].

Initial studies yielding very promising findings were in relatively small samples
of around a hundred or so cases and controls [78,79], but these have been followed
by two genome wide studies in much larger populations [44,80]. A general finding
is that rare (<1%), large (>100kb) CNVs are present at increased rates in those
with schizophrenia compared to healthy controls. One study has also suggested a
substantially elevated rate of *de novo* CNVs (that is, CNVs arising as a new mutation) in sporadic cases of schizophrenia, although this finding is as yet unconfirmed
[81]. This work followed research in neurodevelopmental disorders indicating that
rare, *de novo* CNVs of 100kb or more contribute to about 10% of cases of sporadic
autism and idiopathic mental retardation [82].

From the perspective of providing insights into pathogenesis, it is more important
to associate specific loci with schizophrenia than to make observations of a general
increase in the rate of CNVs at a general level. Very large samples are required
to unambiguously demonstrate association to rare events (the focus of most of
CNV studies to date) but several studies have been large enough to do this. A
cautionary note when interpreting CNV data is that CNV assays do not yet have
perfect sensitivity or specificity, and this can vary systematically between cases and
controls for many reasons including type of CNV detection method and sample
source (blood, cell lines, buccal DNA) that can vary even within studies. Thus,
there is considerable potential for false positive CNV findings. Nevertheless, some
of the most promising findings are extremely robust and are presented in Table 4.2.

(The following sources provide detailed reviews - Kirov [83], Tam *et al.* [84]
and Sebat [85])

To date, the CNVs that have been implicated in schizophrenia are rare, large
and confer bigger effect sizes than identified SNPs (see Table 4.2 and Figure 4.3).
Given that CNV analyses have focused on this type of CNV, the role of smaller or

Table 4.2 Major CNV findings in schizophrenia

Chromosome region	Type of CNV associated in Schizophrenia	Frequency (%) in Cases/Controls	Odds Ratio [83] (approx.)	Evidence in Related Phenotypes	Further Comments
1q21.1	Deletions [44,79,80]	0.2/0.02	9	Deletions associated with microcepahly, autism, ADHD, neuroblastoma[86]	Early findings suggest duplication associated with macrocephaly[87]
2p16.3 (*NRXN1*)	Deletions [78,79,88]	0.19/0.04	5	Deletions in this gene and the related gene, *CNTNAP2*, associated with phenotype resembling Pitt-Hopkins syndrome and reported in autism [89, 90]	This CNV is promising as it implicates a specific gene – neurexin, which is involved in maintenance of synaptic function with its post-synaptic partner proteins– neuroligins
15q11.2	Deletions [44,91]	0.6/0.22	3	Associated with speech problems, ADHD, OCD, autism, ID[92]	This is the most common of the strongly implicated CNV regions
15q13.3	Deletions[44,80,91]	0.2/0.02	10	Idiopathic generalized epilepsy, ID, ADHD, autism[93,94]	Initial evidence suggesting CNVs in 15q11–13, Prader-Willi/ Angelman syndrome region may be implicated in schizophrenia

(Continued)

Table 4.2 (*Continued*)

Chromosome region	Type of CNV associated in Schizophrenia	Frequency (%) in Cases/Controls	Odds Ratio [83] (approx.)	Evidence in Related Phenotypes	Further Comments
16p13.1	Deletions/Duplications[80,91]	0.3–0.7/ 0.09–0.24	3	Autism, ID, epilepsy[92,95]	Preliminary evidence that duplications are associated with SZ and deletions associated with more severe developmental phenotype of autism, ID[83]
16p11.2	Duplications[97]	0.3/0.03	10	Deletions in this region one of most common identified causes of autism, also increased rate in ID[90,92,96]	Deletion carriers more likely to express severe cognitive phenotype when carrying a second large CNV – *second hit*[98]
22q11.2	Deletions[44,80]	0.15–0.4/0	n.a. (not present in controls)	Broad neurodevelopmental phenotypes – autism, ID, ADHD	Rare duplications of this region reported in controls. See section on chromosomal abnormalities

SZ – schizophrenia; ID – intellectual disability (learning disability); ADHD – attention deficit hyperactivity disorder; OCD – obsessive compulsive disorder.

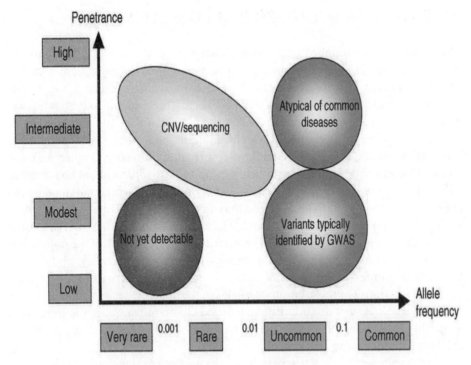

Figure 4.3 Genetic strategies to identify risk variants of different allelic frequency and effect size [99]. Reproduced from 'Current Opinion in Genetics & Development' [5], Copyright (2009), with permission from Elsevier.

more common CNVs is unclear. As is evident from Table 4.2 replicated schizophrenia CNVs are all also associated with a diverse spectrum of neurodevelopmental disorders including learning disability, autism, epilepsy and for some CNVs also with ADHD. Unlike common SNPs, the early evidence does not suggest a major overlap with respect to CNVs for shared risk between schizophrenia and bipolar disorder, suggesting rare CNVs may represent a point of rarity between the two disorders.

It is currently difficult to draw specific inferences about pathophysiology as most of the implicated CNVs span multiple genes. Resolving which individual genes are relevant to pathophysiology might not be straightforward; indeed the question may be based upon a false premise if it transpires that risk requires the involvement of several or all genes within the CNV. The difficulties are clearly illustrated by the longstanding association between schizophrenia and 22q11DEL. That deletion spans many genes, including *COMT* (see above). However, none, *COMT* included, have been confirmed as schizophrenia susceptibility genes. The association of deletions apparently disrupting *NRXN1* alone is the exception and this finding offers fruitful avenues for future research (see Table 4.2).

THE FUTURE OF SCHIZOPHRENIA GENETICS

Recent studies have implicated a number of novel SNP and CNV risk variants for schizophrenia at levels of statistical support and replicability that are unprecedented. As well as identifying novel avenues for mechanistic research, these findings have also identified genetic overlaps between schizophrenia and both bipolar disorder and neurodevelopmental disorders such as autism and mental retardation. This has led some to speculate that schizophrenia and other major psychiatric disorders lie on a spectrum of neurodevelopmental abnormality (Figure 4.4) and refocused attention on how best the phenotype of these disorders should be defined.

Despite these successes the majority of the heritability of schizophrenia remains unaccounted for. The individual SNPs thus far robustly identified account for a small percentage of disease liability and, while statistical modeling of GWAS data suggests that common variants will be responsible for at least 30% of the population variance at risk of schizophrenia (and perhaps 40% or more of its heritability), the small effects conferred by most loci make it unlikely that it will be possible to identify the majority of those common alleles in the next few years with the sample sizes available. As well as currently undetected common variation, the remaining heritability is likely to reflect the operation of CNVs and rare sequence variants for which direct sequencing will probably be required.

Given the advances in CNV research and the promise of sequencing, some commentators have promoted the idea that schizophrenia is a disease caused entirely or predominantly by multiple rare variants [100]. We feel that this fails to acknowledge the contribution of common variation borne out by the confirmed common risk variants to have emerged from GWAS. Furthermore this hypothesis is also inconsistent with evidence from genetic epidemiology indicating that Mendelian patterns of inheritance are unlikely to be the sole cause of the familial nature of schizophrenia [101] and that sporadic cases and familial aggregation can be accounted for by polygenic inheritance [102]. The balance of evidence indicates that schizophrenia results from a combination of common alleles of small effect and rare alleles of larger effect, although the relative contribution of each of these factors remains to be determined.

It is likely that further GWAS and CNV studies over the next few years, employing meta-analyses of existing datasets and increasing sample sizes, will deliver yet more risk loci and this will be enhanced by new analytic approaches based on sets of SNPs and CNVs implicating functionally related sets of genes. Moreover, based on experience from other common diseases, we can expect pathophysiological insights to emerge even with only a small fraction of the total number of common risk loci identified and for these to lead to more focused and hypothesis-driven studies. We also anticipate the application of new generation sequencing methods allowing studies of whole exome (the protein-coding exons) and whole genome sequencing. These will potentially allow the identification of rare sequence variants conferring levels of risk similar in magnitude to those seen in the current CNV studies. It is

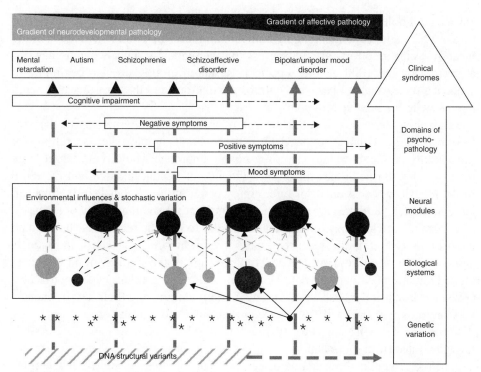

Figure 4.4 Hypothesised model of the relationship between genotype and clinical phenotype. This is a simplified model of a highly complex set of relationships between genotype and clinical phenotype. Starting at the level of genetic variation, we have represented DNA structural variation (hatched shading) as contributing particularly to neurodevelopmental disorders and associated with enduring cognitive and functional impairment. Single gene variants, of which there are many, are shown as asterisks. In general, even single basepair changes in a gene may influence multiple biological systems because genes typically have multiple functions and produce interacting proteins. For simplicity, we have shown only an example of a variant that influences three biological systems (small solid black circle and arrows) and another that influences only one system (black asterisk and arrow). Variation in the relevant biological systems is influenced by genotype at many genetic loci and by environmental exposures. The relevant biological systems influence the neural modules; the key relevant functional elements of the brain (shown as large solid black circles). Typically, multiple biological systems influence each neural module. The (abnormal) functioning of the neural modules together influences the domains of psychopathology experienced and ultimately the clinical syndromes [103]. Reproduced from *British Journal of Psychiatry* [5] with permission from The Royal College of Psychiatrists.

envisaged whole genome sequencing will cost under $1000 within the next three to five years and so sequencing of clinical samples will become possible. In the meantime current efforts are in progress to systematically sequence genomes, led at present by the 1000 genomes project. Research groups are also beginning to sequence the exomes of case and control populations and these results will begin to emerge in the next year or so.

Sequencing based approaches are often presented as alternatives to the collection of large samples required by GWAS. For example when searching for rare, highly penetrant mutations, a reasonable approach would be to target large multiply-affected pedigrees that show evidence of genetic linkage and therefore might plausibly be enriched for rare, highly penetrant mutations [100]. However, large multiplex pedigrees are uncommon, comprising a small minority of all cases, and those in which linkage points unequivocally to specific regions of the genome almost nonexistent. In the absence of clues to their presence in specific individuals and to their location from unequivocal linkage signals, the majority of rare disease-related mutations will also have to be identified through genome-wide approaches. Given the low prior probabilities for any given mutation, and their low frequency, very large sample sizes will be required to provide credible support.

Large samples will also in all probability be required to test the generality of findings generated from endophenotype studies which are considerably more expensive and difficult to collect in a standardised way. Thus all genetic approaches will require collection of data from large samples, but as genetic technology improves and becomes cheaper it will be possible to use these samples to test an increasing number of genetic hypotheses. Attention should now be given to developing the most economical approaches to ascertaining and phenotyping such samples and to making the genetic and phenotype data available to as many researchers as possible.

It is also argued that rare risk alleles, by virtue of having larger effect sizes, will give greater biological insights than common risk alleles of small effect. We have already seen from studies in other common diseases that this distinction is overly simplistic and that there are ample grounds for believing that the identification of common risk alleles will also bring valuable insights to disease mechanisms. One theoretical advantage of identifying higher penetrance alleles is that their effects might be easier to model in cellular and whole animal systems. While this is likely to be true, this must be balanced against the possibility that identification of pathways based upon common alleles might offer greater insights into more common mechanisms and thereby to novel drug targets with wider applicability than those derived from ultra-rare variants.

Throughout this chapter and elsewhere we have pointed out the shortcomings of current diagnostic approaches [103]. Schizophrenia is highly heterogeneous, and it is self-evident that if we could sub-divide it into more homogeneous groups, or define dimensional phenotypes that more closely index pathophysiology, we would increase the power of all aetiological studies including genetics. It is therefore highly encouraging that, despite heterogeneity, risk loci can be robustly identified by GWAS using samples defined by current diagnostic criteria. Moreover, armed with sufficient GWAS data it should be possible to identify categorical and dimensional phenotypes that relate to specific sets of risk alleles, and recent findings suggest that such approaches should not be constrained by the current dichotomous view of the functional psychoses (Figure 4.4) [103]. We have shown one way in which this might be achieved without imposing a further burden of multiple testing, and in doing so, obtained evidence for a relatively selective involvement of multiple SNPs in the GABAergic system in schizoaffective disorder [104]. We have little doubt that other approaches will emerge that will allow more homogeneous patient groups to be identified from large GWAS datasets.

Schizophrenia genetics in the clinic?

With advances in the field of genetics the prospect of genetic testing for disease risk will arise. Indeed private companies have begun to offer personal genetic profiling to assess risk for psychiatric disorders. At this stage such testing seems unfounded considering the current state of knowledge. Given the relatively small effect sizes of the SNP variants thus far discovered, the individual risk of carrying such variants will be minimal. In the future an argument could be made that CNV screening may be informative for families, although with the uncertainties that remain about variable penetrance and the spectrum of phenotypes associated with CNVs, we feel that such testing remains premature. None of the variants identified to date are either necessary or sufficient for schizophrenia and so such genetic tests are open to misinterpretation by individuals or wider society. It is potentially damaging to the field to take such bold and emotive steps in a premature fashion. The knowledge of the genetic architecture of type II diabetes is at a more advanced stage than that of schizophrenia yet research suggests no benefit from adding in a panel of risk genotypes to existing risk prediction measures [105]. We feel that given the small extent of liability to disease accounted for by identified variants this is likely to be the case for schizophrenia for the foreseeable future.

The field of pharmacogenetics examines the utility of genetic variants in informing treatment decisions particularly in predicting adverse events/side effects or response to medication. Studies in this field have to date been in relatively small samples and face problems similar to those of candidate gene studies in this respect. However the potential for this field is demonstrated by the improved survival in cancer patients for treatments aimed at specific genetic subtypes of the disease as well as beneficial, genetically-tailored approaches to treatment in other common, multifactorial medical diseases. Whilst such advances have not yet reached the psychiatric clinic there is the potential for pharmacogenetics to benefit patients with schizophrenia, perhaps particularly through identifying genetic sub-types of the disorder.

Genetic research is likely to have more immediate impact on refashioning existing diagnostic categories. As we have seen the action of genetic risk variants is not confined to current diagnostic categories and may act on symptom dimensions across disorders. In this way genetics has the potential to transform the diagnostic and clinical practice of psychiatry.

CONCLUSIONS

While only small parts of the heritability of any complex disorder have been accounted for, large-scale genetic approaches are already yielding new insights into the pathogenesis of common, non-psychiatric diseases where there was already prior knowledge of disease mechanisms. Underlying the success of these endeavours has been the appreciation that large scale studies will yield the most secure advances, be they relevant to common or rare alleles, and that these can only be achieved through the pooled resources of many investigators. Research into schizophrenia and other psychiatric disorders starts from a much lower level of prior knowledge and therefore has the potential to gain even more from the application of these approaches.

ACKNOWLEDGEMENTS

The authors' work is funded through grants from the Wellcome Trust, MRC, NIH, NARSAD, Stanley Medical Research Institute and the Welsh Assembly. We are members of the MRC Centre for Neuropsychiatric Genetics and Genomics in Cardiff University.

REFERENCES

1. Gottesman II. (1991) *Schizophrenia Genesis: The Origins of Madness*. Freeman: New York.
2. Lichtenstein P, Yip BH, Bjork C, *et al.* (2009) Common genetic determinants of schizophrenia and bipolar disorder in Swedish families: a population-based study. *Lancet* **373**(9659):234–239.
3. Gottesman II, Laursen TM, Bertelsen A, *et al.* (2010) Severe Mental Disorders in Offspring with 2 Psychiatrically Ill Parents. *Arch Gen Psychiatry* **67**(3):252–257.
4. Cardno AG, Gottesman II. (2000) Twin studies of schizophrenia: From bow-and-arrow concordances to star wars mx and functional genomics. *American Journal of Medical Genetics* **97**(1):12–17.
5. Sullivan PF, Kendler KS, Neale MC. (2003) Schizophrenia as a Complex Trait: Evidence From a Meta-analysis of Twin Studies. *Arch Gen Psychiatry* **60**(12):1187–1192.

6. Kety SS, Wender PH, Jacobsen B, *et al.* (1994) Mental-Illness in the Biological and Adoptive Relatives of Schizophrenic Adoptees - Replication of the Copenhagen Study in the Rest of Denmark. *Arch Gen Psychiatry* **51**(6):442–455.

7. Tienari P, Wynne LC, Sorri A, *et al.* (2004) Genotype-environment interaction in schizophrenia-spectrum disorder - Long-term follow-up study of Finnish adoptees. *British Journal of Psychiatry* **184**:216–222.

8. Kendler KS, McGuire M, Gruenberg AM, *et al.* (1993) The Roscommon Family Study. III. Schizophrenia-related personality disorders in relatives. *Arch Gen Psychiatry* **50**(10):781–788.

9. Fanous AH, Neale MC, Gardner CO, *et al.* (2007) Significant correlation in linkage signals from genome-wide scans of schizophrenia and schizotypy. *Molecular Psychiatry* **12**(10):958–965.

10. Stefanis NC, Trikalinos TA, Avramopoulos D, *et al.* (2007) Impact of Schizophrenia Candidate Genes on Schizotypy and Cognitive Endophenotypes at the Population Level. *Biological Psychiatry* **62**(7):784–792.

11. Cardno AG, Sham PC, Murray RM, *et al.* (2001) Twin study of symptom dimensions in psychoses. *British Journal of Psychiatry* **179**:39–45.

12. Cardno AG, Rijsdijk FV, Murray RM, *et al.* (2008) Twin Study Refining Psychotic Symptom Dimensions as Phenotypes for Genetic Research. *American Journal of Medical Genetics Part B-Neuropsychiatric Genetics* **147B**(7):1213–1221.

13. Hare E, Glahn DC, Dassori A, *et al.* (2010) Heritability of Age of Onset of Psychosis in Schizophrenia. *American Journal of Medical Genetics Part B-Neuropsychiatric Genetics* **153B**(1):298–302.

14. Riley B, Riley B (2004) Linkage studies of schizophrenia. *Neurotoxicity Research* **6**(1):17–34.

15. Lewis CM, Levinson DF, Wise LH, *et al.* (2003) Genome Scan Meta-Analysis of Schizophrenia and Bipolar Disorder, Part II: Schizophrenia. *The American Journal of Human Genetics* **73**(1):34–48.

16. Ng MYM, Levinson DF, Faraone SV *et al.* (2009) Meta-analysis of 32 genome-wide linkage studies of schizophrenia. *Molecular Psychiatry* **14**(8):774–785.

17. Chowdari KV, Mirnics K, Semwal P, *et al.* (2002) Association and linkage analyses of RGS4 polymorphisms in schizophrenia. *Hum Mol Genet* **11**(12):1373–1380.

18. O'Donovan MC, Norton N, Williams H, *et al.* (2009) Analysis of 10 independent samples provides evidence for association between schizophrenia and a SNP flanking fibroblast growth factor receptor 2. *Molecular Psychiatry* **14**(1):30–36.

19. Carroll LS, Williams NM, Moskvina V, *et al.* Evidence for rare and common genetic risk variants for schizophrenia at protein kinase C, alpha. *Mol Psychiatry* advance online publication Sep 2009.

20. Stefansson H, Sigurdsson E, Steinthorsdottir V, *et al.* (2002) Neuregulin 1 and susceptibility to schizophrenia. *Am J Hum Genet* **71**(4):877–892.

21. Stefansson H, Sarginson J, Kong A, *et al.* (2003) Association of neuregulin 1 with schizophrenia confirmed in a Scottish population. *Am J Hum Genet* **72**(1):83–87.

22. Williams NM, Preece A, Spurlock G, *et al.* (2003) Support for genetic variation in neuregulin 1 and susceptibility to schizophrenia. *Mol Psychiatry* **8**(5):485–487.

23. Norton N, Moskvina V, Morris DW *et al.* (2006) Evidence that interaction between Neuregulin 1 and its receptor erbB4 increases susceptibility to schizophrenia.

American Journal of Medical Genetics Part B-Neuropsychiatric Genetics **141B**(1): 96–101.

24. Hall J, Whalley HC, Job DE, *et al.* (2006) A neuregulin 1 variant associated with abnormal cortical function and psychotic symptoms. *Nature Neuroscience* **9**(12):1477–1478.

25. McIntosh AM, Moorhead TWJ, Job D, *et al.* (2008) The effects of a neuregulin 1 variant on white matter density and integrity. *Molecular Psychiatry* **13**(11):1054–1059.

26. Straub RE, Jiang YX, MacLean CJ, *et al.* (2002) Genetic variation in the 6p22.3 gene DTNBP1, the human ortholog of the mouse dysbindin gene, is associated with schizophrenia. *Am J Hum Genet* **71**(2):337–348.

27. Weickert CS, Rothmond DA, Hyde TM, *et al.* (2008) Reduced DTNBP1 (dysbindin-1) mRNA in the hippocampal formation of schizophrenia patients. *Schizophr Res* **98**(1–3): 105–110.

28. Chumakov I, Blumenfeld M, Guerassimenko O, *et al.* (2002) Genetic and physiological data implicating the new human gene G72 and the gene for D-amino acid oxidase in schizophrenia. *Proc Natl Acad Sci USA* **99**(21):13675–13680.

29. Hattori E, Liu C, Badner JA, *et al.* (2003) Polymorphisms at the G72/G30 Gene Locus, on 13q33, Are Associated with Bipolar Disorder in Two Independent Pedigree Series. *The American Journal of Human Genetics* **72**(5):1131–1140.

30. Shi J, Badner JA, Gershon ES, *et al.* (2008) Allelic association of G72/G30 with schizophrenia and bipolar disorder: a comprehensive meta-analysis. *Schizophr Res* **98**(1–3): 89–97.

31. Allen NC, Bagade S, McQueen MB, *et al.* (2008) Systematic meta-analyses and field synopsis of genetic association studies in schizophrenia: the SzGene database. *Nat Genet* **40**(7):827–834.

32. Murphy KC, Jones LA, Owen MJ (1999) High rates of schizophrenia in adults with velo-cardio-facial syndrome. *Arch Gen Psychiatry* **56**(10):940–945.

33. Egan MF, Goldberg TE, Kolachana BS, *et al.* (2001) Effect of COMT Val108/158 Met genotype on frontal lobe function and risk for schizophrenia. *Proc Natl Acad Sci USA* **98**(12):6917–6922.

34. Gottesman II, Gould TD (2003) The endophenotype concept in psychiatry: etymology and strategic intentions. *American Journal of Psychiatry* **160**(4):636–645.

35. Walters JT, Owen MJ (2007) Endophenotypes in psychiatric genetics. *Mol Psychiatry* **12**(10):886–890.

36. Caspi A, Moffitt TE, Cannon M, *et al.* (2005) Moderation of the effect of adolescent-onset cannabis use on adult psychosis by a functional polymorphism in the catechol-O-methyltransferase gene: longitudinal evidence of a gene X environment interaction. *Biol Psychiatry* **57**(10):1117–1127.

37. Zammit S, Spurlock G, Williams H, *et al.* (2007) Genotype effects of CHRNA7, CNR1 and COMT in schizophrenia: interactions with tobacco and cannabis use. *Br J Psychiatry* **191**:402–407.

38. Risch N, Herrell R, Lehner T, *et al.* (2009) Interaction between the serotonin transporter gene (5-HTTLPR), stressful life events, and risk of depression: a meta-analysis. *JAMA* **301**(23):2462–2471.

39. Lindsay EA (2001) Chromosomal microdeletions: dissecting del22q11 syndrome. *Nat Rev Genet* **2**(11):858–868.

40. Tan GM, Arnone D, McIntosh AM, *et al.* (2009) Meta-analysis of magnetic resonance imaging studies in chromosome 22q11.2 deletion syndrome (velocardiofacial syndrome). *Schizophr Res* **115**(2–3): 173–181.

41. Gogos JA, Santha M, Takacs Z, *et al.* (1999) The gene encoding proline dehydrogenase modulates sensorimotor gating in mice. *Nat Genet* **21**(4):434–439.

42. Williams NM, Glaser B, Norton N, *et al.* (2008) Strong evidence that GNB1L is associated with schizophrenia. *Hum Mol Genet* **17**(4):555–566.

43. Ma G, Shi Y, Tang W, *et al.* (2007) An association study between the genetic polymorphisms within TBX1 and schizophrenia in the Chinese population. *Neuroscience Letters* **425**(3):146–150.

44. Stefansson H, Rujescu D, Cichon S, *et al.* (2008) Large recurrent microdeletions associated with schizophrenia. *Nature* **455**(7210):232–236.

45. Stone JL, O'Donovan MC, Gurling H, *et al.* (2008) Rare chromosomal deletions and duplications increase risk of schizophrenia. *Nature* **455**(7210):237–241.

46. St Clair D, Blackwood D, Muir W, *et al.* (1990) Association within a Family of a Balanced Autosomal Translocation with Major Mental-Illness. *Lancet* **336**(8706):13–16.

47. Hamshere ML, Bennett P, Williams N, *et al.* (2005) Genomewide linkage scan in Schizoaffective disorder - Significant evidence for linkage at 1q42 close to DISC1, and suggestive evidence at 22q11 and 19p13. *Arch Gen Psychiatry* **62**(10):1081–1088.

48. Hikida T, Jaaro-Peled H, Seshadri S, *et al.* (2007) Dominant-negative DISC1 transgenic mice display schizophrenia-associated phenotypes detected by measures translatable to humans. *Proc Natl Acad Sci USA* **104**(36):14501–14506.

49. Clapcote SJ, Lipina TV, Millar JK, *et al.* (2007) Behavioral phenotypes of Disc1 missense mutations in mice. *Neuron* **54**(3):387–402.

50. Koike H, Arguello PA, Kvajo M, *et al.* (2006) Disc1 is mutated in the 129S6/SvEv strain and modulates working memory in mice. *Proc Natl Acad Sci USA* **103**(10):3693–3697.

51. Hennah W, Tomppo L, Hiekkalinna T, *et al.* (2007) Families with the risk allele of DISC1 reveal a link between schizophrenia and another component of the same molecular pathway, NDE1. *Hum Mol Genet* **16**(5):453–462.

52. Tomppo L, Hennah W, Lahermo P, *et al.* (2009) Association between genes of Disrupted in schizophrenia 1 (DISC1) interactors and schizophrenia supports the role of the DISC1 pathway in the etiology of major mental illnesses. *Biol Psychiatry* **65**(12):1055–1062.

53. Ingason A, Rujescu D, Cichon S, *et al.* Copy number variations of chromosome 16p13.1 region associated with schizophrenia. *Mol Psychiatry* advance online publication Sep 2009.

54. Millar JK, Pickard BS, Mackie S, *et al.* (2005) DISC1 and PDE4B are interacting genetic factors in schizophrenia that regulate cAMP signaling. *Science* **310**(5751): 1187–1191.

55. Cannon TD, Hennah W, van Erp TG, *et al.* (2005) Association of DISC1/TRAX haplotypes with schizophrenia, reduced prefrontal gray matter, and impaired short- and long-term memory. *Arch Gen Psychiatry* **62**(11):1205–1213.

56. Dudbridge F, Gusnanto A (2008) Estimation of significance thresholds for genomewide association scans. *Genet Epidemiol* **32**(3):227–234.

57. Mah S, Nelson MR, DeLisi LE, *et al.* (2006) Identification of the semaphorin receptor PLXNA2 as a candidate for susceptibility to schizophrenia. *Molecular Psychiatry* **11**(5):471–478.

58. Kirov G, Zaharieva I, Georgieva L, *et al.* (2009) A genome-wide association study in 574 schizophrenia trios using DNA pooling. *Molecular Psychiatry* **14**(8):796–803.

59. Shifman S, Johannesson M, Bronstein M, *et al.* (2008) Genome-wide association identifies a common variant in the reelin gene that increases the risk of schizophrenia only in women. *Plos Genetics* **4**(2):e28. doi:10.1371/journal.pgen.0040028.

60. Hong SE, Shugart YY, Huang DT, *et al.* (2000) Autosomal recessive lissencephaly with cerebellar hypoplasia is associated with human RELN mutations. *Nat Genet* **26**(1):93–96.

61. Lencz T, Morgan TV, Athanasiou M, *et al.* (2007) Converging evidence for a pseudoautosomal cytokine receptor gene locus in schizophrenia. *Molecular Psychiatry* **12**(6):572–580.

62. O'Donovan MC, Craddock N, Norton N, *et al.* (2008) Identification of loci associated with schizophrenia by genome-wide association and follow-up. *Nat Genet* **40**(9):1053–1055.

63. Riley B, Thiselton D, Maher BS, *et al.* (2010) Replication of association between schizophrenia and ZNF804A in the Irish Case-Control Study of Schizophrenia sample. *Mol Psychiatry* **15**(1):29–37.

64. Steinberg S, Mors O, Borglum AD, *et al.* Expanding the range of ZNF804A variants conferring risk of psychosis. Mol Psychiatry advance online publication January 2010.

65. Williams HJ, Norton N, Dwyer S, Moskvina V, Nikolov I, Carroll L *et al.* Fine mapping of ZNF804A and genome-wide significant evidence for its involvement in schizophrenia and bipolar disorder. *Mol Psychiatry* advance online publication April 2010.

66. Esslinger C, Walter H, Kirsch P, *et al.* (2009) Neural Mechanisms of a Genome-Wide Supported Psychosis Variant. *Science* **324**(5927): 605.

67. Meyer-Lindenberg AS, Olsen RK, Kohn PD, *et al.* (2005) Regionally Specific Disturbance of Dorsolateral Prefrontal-Hippocampal Functional Connectivity in Schizophrenia. *Arch Gen Psychiatry* **62**(4):379–386.

68. Walters J, Corvin A, Owen M, *et al.* (in press) The psychosis susceptibility gene ZNF804A is associated with less impaired cognitive performance in schizophrenia. *Arch Gen Psychiatry.*

69. Shi J, Levinson DF, Duan J, *et al.* (2009) Common variants on chromosome 6p22.1 are associated with schizophrenia. *Nature* **460**(7256):753–757.

70. Purcell SM, Wray NR, Stone JL, *et al.* (2009) Common polygenic variation contributes to risk of schizophrenia and bipolar disorder. *Nature* **460**(7256):748–752.

71. Stefansson H, Ophoff RA, Steinberg S, *et al.* (2009) Common variants conferring risk of schizophrenia. *Nature* **460**(7256):744–U799.

72. Huang FL, Huang KP, Boucheron C (2007) Long-term enrichment enhances the cognitive behavior of the aging neurogranin null mice without affecting their hippocampal LTP. *Learn Mem* **14**(8):512–519.

73. Flora A, Garcia JJ, Thaller C, *et al.* (2007) The E-protein Tcf4 interacts with Math1 to regulate differentiation of a specific subset of neuronal progenitors. *Proc Natl Acad Sci USA* **104**(39):15382–15387.

74. Amiel J, Rio M, de Pontual L, *et al.* (2007) Mutations in TCF4, encoding a class I basic helix-loop-helix transcription factor, are responsible for Pitt-Hopkins syndrome, a severe epileptic encephalopathy associated with autonomic dysfunction. *Am J Hum Genet* **80**(5):988–993.

75. Prokopenko I, McCarthy MI, Lindgren CM (2008) Type 2 diabetes: new genes, new understanding. *Trends Genet* **24**(12):613–621.

76. Hirschhorn JN (2009) Genomewide association studies–illuminating biologic pathways. *N Engl J Med* **360**(17):1699–1701.

77. McCarroll SA, Kuruvilla FG, Korn JM, *et al.* (2008) Integrated detection and population-genetic analysis of SNPs and copy number variation. *Nat Genet* **40**(10):1166–1174.

78. Kirov G, Gumus D, Chen W, *et al.* (2008) Comparative genome hybridization suggests a role for NRXN1 and APBA2 in schizophrenia. *Hum Mol Genet* **17**(3):458–465.

79. Walsh T, McClellan JM, McCarthy SE, *et al.* (2008) Rare Structural Variants Disrupt Multiple Genes in Neurodevelopmental Pathways in Schizophrenia. *Science* **320**(5875):539–543.

80. Stone JL, O'Donovan MC, Gurling H, *et al.* (2008) Rare chromosomal deletions and duplications increase risk of schizophrenia. *Nature* **455**(7210):237–241.

81. Xu B, Roos JL, Levy S, *et al.* (2008) Strong association of de novo copy number mutations with sporadic schizophrenia. *Nat Genet* **40**(7):880–885.

82. Sebat J, Lakshmi B, Malhotra D, *et al.* (2007) Strong association of de novo copy number mutations with autism. *Science* **316**(5823):445–449.

83. Kirov G (2010) The role of copy number variation in schizophrenia. *Expert Review of Neurotherapeutics* **10**(1):25–32.

84. Tam GWC, Redon R, Carter NP, *et al.* (2009) The Role of DNA Copy Number Variation in Schizophrenia. *Biological Psychiatry* **66**(11):1005–1012.

85. Sebat J, Levy DL, McCarthy SE (2009) Rare structural variants in schizophrenia: one disorder, multiple mutations; one mutation, multiple disorders. *Trends Genet* **25**(12):528–535.

86. Mefford HC, Sharp AJ, Baker C, *et al.* (2008) Recurrent Rearrangements of Chromosome 1q21.1 and Variable Pediatric Phenotypes. *N Engl J Med* **359**(16): 1685–1699.

87. Brunetti-Pierri N, Berg JS, Scaglia F, *et al.* (2008) Recurrent reciprocal 1q21.1 deletions and duplications associated with microcephaly or macrocephaly and developmental and behavioral abnormalities. *Nat Genet* **40**(12):1466–1471.

88. Rujescu D, Ingason A, Cichon S, *et al.* (2009) Disruption of the neurexin 1 gene is associated with schizophrenia. *Hum Mol Genet* **18**(5):988–996.

89. Zweier C, de Jong EK, Zweier M, *et al.* (2009) CNTNAP2 and NRXN1 Are Mutated in Autosomal-Recessive Pitt-Hopkins-like Mental Retardation and Determine the Level of a Common Synaptic Protein in Drosophila. *Am J Hum Genet* **85**(5): 655–666.

90. Weiss LA, Shen Y, Korn JM, *et al.* (2008) Association between Microdeletion and Microduplication at 16p11.2 and Autism. *N Engl J Med* **358**(7):667–675.

91. Kirov G, Grozeva D, Norton N, *et al.* (2009) Support for the involvement of large copy number variants in the pathogenesis of schizophrenia. *Hum Mol Genet* **18**(8):1497–1503.

92. Mefford HC, Cooper GM, Zerr T, *et al.* (2009) A method for rapid, targeted CNV genotyping identifies rare variants associated with neurocognitive disease. *Genome Res* **19**(9):1579–1585.

93. Miller DT, Shen Y, Weiss LA, *et al.* (2009) Microdeletion/duplication at 15q13.2q13.3 among individuals with features of autism and other neuropsychiatric disorders. *J Med Genet* **46**(4):242–248.

94. Sharp AJ, Mefford HC, Li K, *et al.* (2008) A recurrent 15q13.3 microdeletion syndrome associated with mental retardation and seizures. *Nat Genet* **40**(3):322–328.

95. Ullmann R, Turner G, Kirchhoff M, *et al.* (2007) Array CGH identifies reciprocal 16p13.1 duplications and deletions that predispose to autism and/or mental retardation. *Hum Mutat* **28**(7):674–682.

96. Glessner JT, Wang K, Cai G, *et al.* (2009) Autism genome-wide copy number variation reveals ubiquitin and neuronal genes. *Nature* **459**(7246):569–573.

97. McCarthy SE, Makarov V, Kirov G, *et al.* (2009) Microduplications of 16p11.2 are associated with schizophrenia. *Nat Genet* **41**(11):1223–1227.

98. Girirajan S, Rosenfeld JA, Cooper GM, *et al.* (2010) A recurrent 16p12.1 microdeletion supports a two-hit model for severe developmental delay. *Nat Genet*; **42**(3):203–209.

99. Owen MJ, Williams HJ, O'Donovan MC (2009) Schizophrenia genetics: advancing on two fronts. *Curr Opin Genet Dev* **19**(3):266–270.

100. McClellan JM, Susser E, King MC (2007) Schizophrenia: a common disease caused by multiple rare alleles. *Br J Psychiatry* **190:** 194–199.

101. O'Rourke DH, Gottesman, II, Suarez BK, *et al.* (1982) Refutation of the general single-locus model for the etiology of schizophrenia. *Am J Hum Genet* **34**(4):630–649.

102. Yang J, Visscher PM, Wray NR Sporadic cases are the norm for complex disease. *Eur J Hum Genet* advance on-line publication Oct 2009.

103. Craddock N, Owen MJ (2010) The Kraepelinian dichotomy - going, going. . . but still not gone. *The British Journal of Psychiatry* **196**(2):92–95.

104. Craddock N, Jones L, Jones IR, *et al.* (2008) Strong genetic evidence for a selective influence of GABAA receptors on a component of the bipolar disorder phenotype. *Mol Psychiatry* **15**(2):146–153.

105. Talmud PJ, Hingorani AD, Cooper JA, *et al.* (2010) Utility of genetic and non-genetic risk factors in prediction of type 2 diabetes: Whitehall II prospective cohort study. *British Medical Journal* **340:** b4838.

CHAPTER 5

Early recognition and prevention of schizophrenia

Patrick D. McGorry and Sherilyn Goldstone
Centre for Youth Mental Health, Orygen Youth Health Research Centre,
University of Melbourne, Parkville, Melbourne, Australia.

Key statements

- Increasing experimental evidence indicates that the course of the psychotic illnesses is not fixed, and that early therapeutic intervention has the potential to greatly ameliorate outcome.
- Early detection of those at risk of developing a psychotic illness is crucial to allow timely and appropriate therapeutic intervention.
- The therapeutic interventions offered should be determined by the stage of illness, and designed to relieve symptoms and distress as well as preventing secondary morbidity and progression of illness.

THE CONTEXT FOR EARLY RECOGNITION AND PREVENTION

The onset of a psychotic illness brings with it the very real threat of disaster to a young person. These potentially serious and sometimes fatal illnesses typically emerge during late adolescence and early adulthood [1], a period of exquisite developmental sensitivity when psychological, social and vocational pathways are being established as part of the transition to independent adulthood [2]. It is no surprise, then, that all too often the emergence of a mental illness can disrupt the young person's developmental trajectory and cause significant distress and disability, seriously limiting or even blocking their potential. Ample evidence shows that mental illness in young people is associated with high rates of enduring

---

Schizophrenia: Current Science and Clinical Practice, First Edition. Edited by Wolfgang Gaebel.
© 2011 John Wiley & Sons, Ltd. Published 2011 by John Wiley & Sons, Ltd.

disability, including school failure, unstable employment, poor social and family functioning, leading to a spiral of disability and disadvantage that becomes difficult to reverse.

Historically, the prognosis for people with schizophrenia has been considered as bleak, with progressive and inevitable decline being accepted as the norm [3]. This unfortunate perception has engendered widespread therapeutic nihilism, limiting treatment efforts and resulting in delayed and inconsistent palliative care. However, over the last two decades this pessimistic view of schizophrenia has changed. Seminal research studies in first-episode psychosis from the 1980s created a climate in which the distinct clinical needs of young people in the early stages of illness could be appreciated for the first time [4–6]. At the same time, the collateral damage caused by long delays in accessing treatment and the traumatic modes of entry into the existing mental health care services became apparent, and the possibility of avoiding or minimising this began to tantalise a range of clinical researchers around the world. In the 1990s frontline early psychosis clinical services were established, first in Melbourne, Australia, and soon afterwards in many key locations in the UK, Europe, North America and Asia. There are now hundreds of early intervention programs worldwide which focus on the special needs of young people facing the onset of a serious mental illness and their families [7].

The current view of the psychotic disorders is more optimistic, largely as a result of the systematic efforts of clinicians and researchers dedicated to improving the outcome for young people affected by psychosis. An increasingly rich harvest of evidence from large international studies has shown that the course of these disorders is not fixed, with deterioration in social and occupational functioning being the norm and a poor prognosis inevitable, but rather, as fluid and malleable [8–16]. Examination of the risk factors which can influence outcome has revealed that many of these may be reversible, and that attention to these factors as part of treatment has the potential to limit or repair the damage. Hence the explosion of interest in phase-specific treatment and early intervention, with the ultimate aim being primary prevention; that is, preventing the transition from the early (prodromal) stages of illness to full-threshold psychosis, or at the very least, the reduction or prevention of secondary morbidity.

Primary prevention for the psychotic disorders awaits the clear definition of malleable risk factors for onset. To date, therefore, the preventive frontier extends only as far as early intervention, which in current reality means early *secondary* prevention. Current early intervention approaches target three stages in the development of a psychotic illness: the ultra-high risk or prodromal period, the first episode, and the recovery or critical period. The principal reason for these distinctions relates to the underlying risk of developing chronic illness, and the timing and duration for the initial prescription of antipsychotics and other medication, since psychosocial interventions are needed at all stages of illness. Here, we discuss current issues and clinical practice in the assessment and treatment of patients in the earliest stages of the onset of illness: the ultra-high risk prodromal phase.

THE PRODROMAL STAGE: DEFINITION AND ASSESSMENT

Much of the initial research effort into early psychosis was focused on the timely recognition and phase-specific treatment of first-episode psychosis. An important consequence of this was the identification of the duration of untreated psychosis (DUP) as one of the most important risk factors for outcome, with longer DUP being both a marker and independent factor for poor outcome [17,18]. Since it had long been recognised that in most patients a prolonged period of attenuated symptoms and impaired functioning precedes the first psychotic episode [19,20], intervention during the pre-psychotic phase was proposed as a means of minimising the duration of untreated illness and therefore ameliorating, delaying, or even preventing the onset of fully-fledged disorder [21]. However, progress towards this goal presented a major challenge: the prospective identification of the prodrome, a task complicated by the nonspecific nature of prodromal symptoms [22–24].

In general, negative symptoms such as decreased concentration, reduced drive and lack of energy predominate early in this phase, accompanied by general symptoms such as sleep disturbance, anxiety and irritability. Affective symptoms, particularly depression, are also common. These symptoms tend to accumulate exponentially until relatively late in the prodrome, when sub-threshold positive (psychotic) symptoms emerge. Ultimately, the positive symptoms intensify and may culminate in a transition to frank psychosis (see Figure 5.1).

Typically, increasing levels of social and vocational disability accompany the increase in symptomatology, and much of the disability associated with the psychotic disorders, particularly schizophrenia, develops well before the onset of frank psychosis and is difficult to reverse even if the first psychotic episode is successfully treated [25]. Because these symptoms, including sub-threshold psychotic-like experiences, are common in the general population, particularly amongst

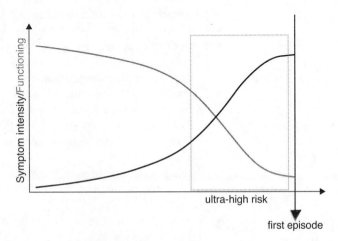

Figure 5.1 The psychosis prodrome

adolescents and young adults, they cannot be considered as diagnostic of a pre-psychotic state in their own right [26,27]. Additional risk factors and specific criteria are necessary to exclude false positive cases to avoid unnecessary treatment and the stigma associated with the diagnosis of a mental illness.

In the mid-1990s we introduced criteria for the prospective identification of individuals at heightened risk of progressing to a first episode of psychosis within a brief time period – that is, as being in the prodromal phase of illness. These 'ultra-high risk' (UHR) criteria are based on a combination of epidemiological evidence and known trait and state risk factors for psychosis ([28,29]; Table 5.1).

Table 5.1   Clinical criteria identifying young people at ultra-high risk of psychosis

Ultra-High Risk Criteria: (i) must be aged between 14 and 29 years, (ii) have been referred to a specialized service for help, and (iii) meet the criteria for one or more of the following three groups:

Group 1: *Attenuated positive psychotic symptoms*	• Presence of at least one of the following symptoms: ideas of reference, odd beliefs or magical thinking, perceptual disturbance, paranoid ideation, odd thinking and speech, odd behaviour and appearance • Frequency of symptoms: at least several times a week • Recency of symptoms: present within the last year • Duration of symptoms: present for at least 1 week and no longer than 5 years
Group 2: *Brief limited intermittent psychotic symptoms*	• Transient psychotic symptoms. Presence of at least one of the following: ideas of reference, magical thinking, perceptual disturbance, paranoid ideation, odd thinking or speech • Duration of episode: less than 1 week • Frequency of symptoms: at least several times per week • Symptoms resolve spontaneously • Recency of symptoms: must have occurred within the last year
Group 3: *Trait and state risk factors*	• Schizotypal personality disorder in the identified individual, or a first-degree relative with a psychotic disorder • Significant decline in mental state or functioning, maintained for at least 1 month and not longer than 5 years • This decline in functioning must have occurred within the past year

They include:

- being aged between 14–30 years of age, since young people in this age range are at greatest risk of developing a psychotic illness *and*
- seeking clinical care, since young people who are not distressed by their symptoms and who have not experienced a decline in functioning are less likely to become seriously unwell in the near future *and*
- having attenuated positive psychotic symptoms *or*
- having experienced brief self-limited psychotic symptoms *or*
- having a family history of psychotic disorder, combined with a recent decline in functioning.

Since then, these criteria have subsequently been validated in a series of international studies [30–35]. As a result, several well-developed screening tools for prodromal symptoms are currently in use; these include the Comprehensive Assessment of the At-Risk Mental State (CAARMS, [36]), the Structured Interview for Prodromal Symptoms (SIPS) and the Scale of Prodromal Symptoms (SOPS) [37] and the Schizophrenia Proneness Instrument (SPI) [38]. The former expand the mild-end psychosis ratings of the BPRS [39] and the CASH [40] together with state and trait risk factors, while the SPI relies on a broad scatter of symptoms and neurocognitive features, dividing the prodrome into early and late stages.

The number of ultra-high risk patients who go on to develop full-threshold psychosis has been reported to be as high as 40.8% in our initial one-year study of 49 prodromal patients [29]. Subsequently, the North American Prodrome Longitudinal Study followed 291 prodromal patients over two years and found a transition rate of 35%, corresponding to a relative risk of transition to full-threshold psychosis of 405 [31]. However, more recent studies have shown transition rates as low as 16%, a relative risk of 200 [41]. The reasons for this reduction in the rate of transition are unclear; this may be a result of earlier detection and more effective intervention, or alternatively, due to the referral of more 'false positive' patients to UHR clinics, or perhaps due to lead-time bias where early referral leads to a longer follow-up time before transition occurs [42]. Regardless, the most common outcome for UHR patients is not psychosis *per se*, but persistence or emergence of a nonpsychotic illness, typically a blend of anxiety and depression [43]. This carries obvious implications for the treatment of UHR patients, who should perhaps be considered as being at risk of severe mental illness more broadly (see below).

Finally, the successful identification of the UHR population has greatly facilitated two important advances in the early psychosis field: firstly, research into the biological processes associated with the onset of psychosis, including psychopathological, neurocognitive and neurobiological variables; and secondly, the implementation of intervention trials aimed at treating existing symptomatic and functional impairment in the UHR population and determining whether specific interventions are able to ameliorate, delay, or even prevent the onset of fully-fledged psychotic disorder in this population.

TREATMENT DURING THE PRODROMAL STAGE

The intervention studies carried out in UHR groups to date are summarised briefly below and in Table 5.2. The first such intervention trial, conducted by our group in Melbourne, Australia, compared combined cognitive behaviour therapy (CBT) and low dose atypical antipsychotic medication (risperidone) (n = 31) with usual case management (n = 28) [44]. Subjects were randomised, but neither the patients nor the investigators were blind to the intervention received. The rate of onset of psychosis was significantly lower than in the treatment group than in the control group at the end of the six-month treatment phase (9.7% v 35%, p = 0.026). However, after a further six-month follow-up this finding was no longer statistically significant due to patients who were not fully adherent to risperidone developing a psychotic disorder during this second follow-up period. Those who were fully adherent during the initial six-month treatment phase all remained nonpsychotic over the follow-up period, even though they had ceased drug treatment. This study demonstrated that the onset of psychosis can at least be delayed, if not prevented, by specific intervention. However, since medication and CBT were combined, the active component of the treatment regime could not be identified. The results also suggested that further benefit may be obtained with a longer treatment time, an outcome reinforced by a longer-term follow up of the sample, which failed to show any persisting benefit over three to four years in the experimental group [43].

A more sophisticated randomised double-blind placebo-controlled trial was then conducted by researchers from Yale University, USA. Low dose olanzapine (n = 31) was compared to placebo (n = 29) for 12 months, followed by a 12-month monitoring period [45]. Although there was a trend towards the olanzapine-treated group having a reduced rate of transition to psychosis, this finding was not significant. There were also some adverse effects associated with olanzapine treatment, leading to a more conservative interpretation of the results. The risk-benefit ratio for olanzapine thus appears to be less favourable than risperidone at this stage of illness.

Open-label trials of aripiprazole [46] and amisulpride [47] have also recently been conducted in UHR cohorts. In the aripiprazole trial, 15 UHR patients were treated with a flexible dose regime of 5–30 mg/day for 8 weeks [46]. Improvements on clinical measures were evident by the first week and no participants transitioned to psychosis. Adverse events were minimal. Similar findings were seen in the amisulpride trial [47] a randomised controlled trial involving a cohort of 124 UHR patients considered to be in the late initial prodromal stage who received either amisulpride (50–800 mg/day) together with a needs-focused intervention, or the needs-focused intervention alone for 12 weeks. At the end

Table 5.2 Clinical trials of therapeutic interventions in young people at ultra-high risk of psychosis

Authors	Intervention	Timeframe of study	Outcome (intervention *vs* control groups)	
McGorry *et al* 2002; Phillips *et al* 2007	RCT of CBT + 1–2 mg/day risperidone vs needs-based psychosocial support	6 months of treatment +6 months of follow-up; Medium-term follow-up at 3-4 years post-baseline	N = 59	Rate of transition to psychosis 9.7% *vs* 35%; p = 0.026
McGlashan *et al* 2006	RCT of 5–15 mg/day olanzapine vs placebo	12 months of treatment + 12 months of follow-up	N = 60	Rate of transition to psychosis 16.1% *vs* 37.9%; p = 0.09
Ruhrmann *et al* 2007	RCT of 50–800 mg/day amisulpride + needs-focused intervention vs needs-focused intervention alone	12 weeks	N = 124	Improvement in both groups, with a significantly greater improvement seen in the aripiprazole group for positive (F(1.98) = 7.83, p<0.01), negative (F(1.98) = 4.85, p<0.05) and general symptoms (F(1.98) = 4.63, p<0.05)
Woods *et al* 2007	Open-label pilot study of 5–30 mg/day aripiprazole	8 weeks	N = 15	Statistically significant reductions in positive, negative and general symptoms (F = 9.2, p<0.001), with 11/15 participants responding to treatment
Cornblatt *et al* 2007	Naturalistic study of antidepressants or atypical antipsychotics	2 years	N = 48	Rate of conversion to psychosis: 43% of those in the antipsychotic group *vs* 0 in the antidepressant group
Morrison *et al* 2004	RCT of CBT vs monitoring of mental state	6 months of treatment + 6 months of follow-up	N = 58	Rate of conversion to psychosis 6% *vs* 26%; p = 0.019
Bechdolf *et al* 2006	Multicentre RCT of CBT vs standard care	12 months	N = 128	Rate of conversion to psychosis 1.6% *vs* 13.8%, p = 0.02
Amminger *et al* 2010	RCT of 1.2 g/day omega-3 fatty acids vs placebo	12 weeks of treatment + 40 weeks of follow-up	N = 81	Rate of conversion to psychosis 4.9% *vs* 27.5%; p = 0.007

of the study period, the amisulpride group showed significantly greater improvements in positive ($F(1.98) = 7.83$, $p<0.01$), negative ($F(1.98) = 4.85$, $p<0.05$), and general symptoms ($F(1.98) = 4.63$, $p<0.05$), as well as in overall functioning ($F(1.98) = 5.70$, $p<0.05$) than the control group. Adverse events were minor, with prolactinaemia and a small weight gain being the most important. Together, these findings indicate a promising efficacy and safety profile for these agents in UHR patients.

More recently, there has been interest in the possibility of using antidepressants to reduce the risk of psychosis in UHR patients. Cornblatt et al. [48] reported a naturalistic study of young people with prodromal symptoms treated either with antidepressants or antipsychotics. Twelve of the 28 patients (43%) who had been prescribed antipsychotics progressed to full-threshold psychosis in the following two years, whereas none of the 20 patients treated with antidepressants subsequently developed psychosis. Similar results are reported by Fusar-Poli et al. [49] on the basis of a file audit study. However, these results need to be interpreted with caution due to the uncontrolled nature of the studies: there may have been differences in baseline symptoms, functioning or other variables between the treatment groups and nonadherence was far more prominent amongst patients prescribed antipsychotics than patients prescribed antidepressants. Our initial trial [44] found that antidepressants, again prescribed according to clinical need, had no influence on the transition rate.

The first treatment trial of a psychological intervention alone in UHR patients was conducted in Manchester, UK [50]. Subjects (n = 58) were randomised to receive cognitive therapy for six months or monitoring of mental state only. The group that received cognitive therapy had a significantly lower rate of transition to full threshold disorder (6% v 26%, $p<0.05$) and a significantly greater reduction in psychiatric symptoms ($p<0.02$) at 12 months. At three-year follow up, cognitive therapy was associated with a significantly lower rate of transition to psychosis and a significantly reduced likelihood of being prescribed antipsychotic medication. Consistent with this, Bechdolf et al. [51] reported that for patients in the early initial prodromal state, as identified by the presence of basic symptoms, CBT was superior to supportive counselling in reducing progression to sub-threshold psychotic symptoms and to full-threshold psychosis over 24 months. The OPUS trial [52] also indicated that transition rates could be reduced in a group of patients with schizotypal disorder by intervening with the OPUS package, which consisted of intensive clinical case management, family involvement, and a psychoeducational approach within a cognitive behavioural framework.

In a recent, more sophisticated double-blind placebo controlled intervention trial, we have compared the combinations of risperidone and CBT with placebo and CBT or placebo and supportive therapy in a group of 115 UHR patients [43]. The six-month transition rates were low in all three treatment groups, suggesting that antipsychotics may not be necessary for UHR patients who are detected early, or that recent UHR cohorts are derived from less 'enriched' samples in terms of the true positive rate [42].

Finally, in an extremely promising trial of a benign intervention, Amminger *et al.* ran a 12-week placebo-controlled randomised trial of the omega-3 fatty acid eicosapentanoic acid (EPA) in a group of 80 UHR adolescents. At the end of the 12-week intervention phase, 8 of 38 (21.1%) individuals in the placebo group and 1 of 38 (2.6%) in the EPA group had progressed to FEP, a statistically significant difference ($p = 0.028$). No clinically significant adverse effects were reported, and EPA was well accepted by this patient group. Most notably, the treatment effect was maintained at six-month follow-up [53]. Previous treatment studies of EPA supplementation in different samples of psychotic patients indicate that the effect of EPA is dependent on stage of illness. EPA has been found to be partially effective in samples with recent onset psychosis [54,55] but have no effect in chronic schizophrenia [56]. There is also good evidence that EPA has a generalised positive effect on mental health complaints [57]. This generalised effect is particularly appropriate for the UHR group, who have been found to have a wide variety of general psychiatric features, not only attenuated psychotic symptoms, and which are a target in their own right.

Early detection and treatment may mean that the more benign interventions, such as EPA or psychosocial interventions, including CBT and supportive therapy, are the most appropriate for UHR patients. These should certainly be offered first; only when symptoms and impairment persist or worsen should other options such as drug therapies be considered. The high rates of psychotic-like experiences in community cohorts [26,27] is consistent with the notion that a staged approach to treatment may be indicated, with antipsychotic agents not being necessary for all individuals with sub-threshold psychotic symptoms. However, the role of antipsychotic medication should not be ignored in this population. Broad spectrum antipsychotics may have a neuroprotective effect, aid in reducing anxiety and depression, and tend to cause minimal side effects. They may still have a place in delaying or preventing the onset of psychosis, especially in those who present late with UHR symptoms or fail to respond to initial intervention with gentler therapies. Symptom severity alone, as we have defined it in the definition of 'transition to psychosis' may not be a perfect guide for the need for antipsychotic medication. Other factors, such as symptom type, and other clinical phenomena, including comorbid substance use, triggers and stressors, genetic and other biomarkers, and so on, will also determine the optimal treatment for a given patient. When antipsychotics are prescribed, the best candidates are those with a more favourable metabolic and neurological safety profile such as quetiapine and aripiprazole [58]. To date, the results of the intervention trials in UHR patients are promising, but remain in clinical equipoise; further research exploring treatment options and sequences via sophisticated clinical trials is necessary to build a solid evidence base to inform future therapeutic strategies.

THE PSYCHOSIS RISK SYNDROME: A NOVEL DIAGNOSTIC ENTITY?

Unlike in physical medicine, the concept of risk and the risk syndrome is relatively new in psychiatry. It stems from conceptual advances made in the 1990s building on the preventative framework of Gordon [59], which initially proposed the idea of targeting preventive interventions to particular population groups (universal measures, selective measures, or indicated prevention) depending on an assessment of the risks, costs and benefits involved in each case. Since we have a relatively poor knowledge of the causal and/or malleable risk factors for the onset of mental illness, authors including Bell [60], Mrazek and Haggerty [61], and Eaton [62] proposed that sub-threshold syndromes be regarded as risk factors for full-threshold disorders such as schizophrenia and major depression, and that these sub-threshold syndromes could be targeted by preventive interventions as a step towards indicated prevention for serious mental illness.

The clinical staging model springs from these ideas [63,64]. This model defines the extent of progression of a disorder at a particular time, and where a person lies on the continuum of the course of illness, thereby providing a diagnostic framework which aims to clarify as quickly as possible which people are at risk of persistent and disabling mental illness. This type of staged approach allows the differentiation of earlier, milder clinical phenomena from those that accompany illness progression, thereby permitting the selection of treatments that are more relevant to the stage of illness and thus more likely to be effective and less likely to be harmful. It also provides the potential to change the course of illness, since appropriate early treatment may prevent illness progression and result in remission or cure (Figure 5.2, Table 5.3).

The proposal to include the 'psychosis risk syndrome' as a new class of disorder for inclusion in DSM V [65,66] has arisen from this recent paradigm shift towards preventive psychiatry. Since we first operationalised the clinical criteria denoting ultra-high risk for an early transition to psychosis [28] there has been substantial progress in confirming the predictive validity of these criteria and in showing that the risk they confer for transition can be reduced by both psychosocial and drug therapies, at least in the short term and while such treatments are being adhered to [41,44,45,50,53,66]. Following on from this research, diagnostic criteria for the psychosis risk syndrome have now been formalised, and are based on the presence of distressing attenuated positive symptoms associated with a decline in functioning that cannot be explained by any other psychiatric diagnosis (see Table 5.4) [65,66]. The evidence to date supports the utility and feasibility of early intervention for the psychoses, and has largely opened the way to a new era of 'pre-emptive psychiatry' [67], where the prediction of risk can be used to facilitate early detection and the strategic targeting of appropriate preventive interventions, not just for the psychoses, but for all serious mental illnesses.

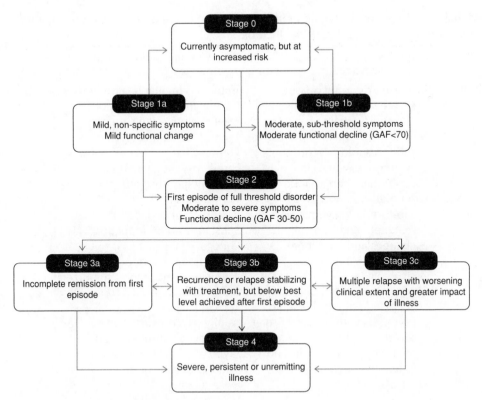

Figure 5.2 The clinical staging model

Another driving force behind the argument for the inclusion of the psychosis risk syndrome as a new diagnostic entity has been the growing awareness that mental disorders in general, and the psychotic disorders in particular, are not static, sharply defined illnesses with separate aetiologies and courses, but rather disorders that overlap and develop in stages [22,68–71]. The current diagnostic infrastructure fails to acknowledge the complex evolution of the onset of serious mental illness; how symptoms are acquired and how they ebb and flow has not been widely considered [62]. We lack clear definitions for distinguishing between benign, self-limiting states and symptoms which represent the early stages of what may become persistent and disabling conditions, despite strong evidence showing that sub-threshold symptoms strongly predict future disorder [24,62,72–74]. Although it is widely accepted that the need for care substantially precedes the point at which a formal diagnosis can be assigned, as yet there are no guidelines to define the initial clinical stages to guide early intervention, let alone the range and sequences of interventions to offer. The proposal to include the psychosis risk syndrome as a new diagnostic entity is a first step towards addressing these issues, although it does raise significant questions that require further consideration.

Table 5.3 The clinical staging model of the onset of the psychotic disorders, with the prodromal phase indicated by the box

Stage	Definition	Potential interventions
0	Increased risk of psychotic or severe mood symptoms but currently asymptomatic	Improved mental health literacy Family and drug education Brief cognitive skills training
1a	Mild non-specific symptoms, sub-threshold psychotic symptoms, with mild functional change or decline	Formal mental health literacy Formal CBT Family psychoeducation Substance misuse reduction
1b	Ultra-high risk: Moderate sub-threshold symptoms with moderate neurocognitive changes and functional decline (GAF < 70)	Formal CBT Family psychoeducation Substance abuse reduction Omega-3 fatty acids Atypical antipsychotics? Antidepressants, mood stabilizers
2	First episode of full-threshold psychosis with moderate to severe symptoms, neurocognitive deficits and functional decline (GAF 30–50)	Formal CBT Family psychoeducation Substance misuse reduction Atypical antipsychotics Antidepressants or mood stabilizers Vocational rehabilitation

Firstly, although the predictive validity of the UHR criteria is reasonable, the most common outcome of the UHR state is not psychosis per se but persistence or emergence of nonpsychotic illness, typically a blend of anxiety and depression [43]. Apart from the ethical implications, which will be discussed below, this lends weight to the idea of a 'common risk syndrome' that precedes the more specific outcomes that may take shape as symptoms persist, progress or intensify. Risk syndromes with greater specificity for schizophrenia or psychosis on the one hand and for severe mood disorders on the other may evolve beyond this common risk syndrome, but prior to reaching full threshold for the target syndrome (See Figure 5.3). Hence, there are also arguments to support the broadening of the 'risk syndrome' category to include this earlier stage, where there is clearly a need for care of a more general type prior to the appearance of more specific symptoms that indicate progression of illness.

Secondly, there is still some debate around the issue of whether preventive strategies for ultra-high risk patients should focus on schizophrenia or the psychotic disorders more broadly. Because the diagnosis of schizophrenia is intrinsically difficult to apply until the patient has been ill for a prolonged period of time,

Table 5.4 Diagnostic criteria for the psychosis risk syndrome proposed for inclusion in DSM-V

Criterion	Note that all six criteria must be met for the diagnosis to be made
A	*Characteristic symptoms*: At least one of the first three DSM-V criteria A for schizophrenia (delusions, hallucinations, disorganized speech) present in an attenuated form (attenuated positive symptoms). The symptom must be of sufficient severity and frequency as to be noticed subjectively, or by others. Reality testing must be retained, however, and the symptom must not interfere substantially with thinking, social relations, or other behaviour
B	*Recency/progression*: The symptom or symptoms meeting criterion A must have been present in the last month and begun or worsened over the previous year.
C	*Frequency/currency*: The symptom or symptoms meeting criterion A must occur at an average frequency of at least once per week over the last month
D	*Distress/disability*: The symptoms are sufficiently distressing to the patient and or others for help to have been sought, and are associated with a decline in social, cognitive or vocational functioning
E	The attenuated positive symptoms cannot be better explained by other DSM-V diagnoses
F	Clinical criteria for any DSM-V frank psychotic disorder have never been met

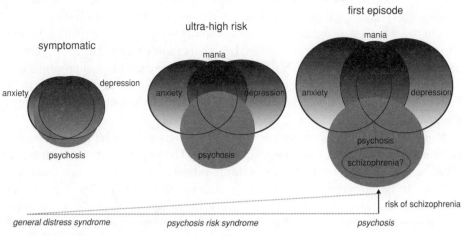

Figure 5.3 Evolution of symptom specificity during the prodromal phase

without intervention during the UHR stage patients may be denied evidence-based treatment at a time when it is particularly necessary. Of the 20–40% of UHR patients who do go on to develop a first episode, only 75% will ultimately receive a diagnosis of schizophrenia, highlighting the need to intervene appropriately earlier rather than later.

A third, and no less important consideration relates to the development of effective interventions for those at ultra-high risk of psychosis. As discussed above, a series of intervention trials have been run over the last decade, with promising, though preliminary results. At this stage, the field is in clinical equipoise; much remains to be discovered, and active exploration of the treatment options and sequences for this crucial stage of illness via sophisticated clinical trials is necessary. Regardless, endorsement of the psychosis risk syndrome as a formal diagnostic category provides a further step towards the establishment of a clear framework for early detection and preventive intervention, and consequently, the development of evidence-based treatments for the early stages of serious mental illnesses such as the psychoses.

ETHICAL ISSUES

It is important to be aware of the pitfalls and the potential for harm arising from the use of risk syndromes, most notably the assumption that the treatment needs are the same as for the fully-fledged disorders. This has been controversial particularly because of confusion between the issue of defining the boundary for care on the one hand, and the timing of commencement of antipsychotic medication on the other. Clearly, over-medicalisation is a real danger, and while manifest symptoms should be treated on their merits, treatment choices should be made with the maxim 'first, do no harm' firmly in mind. Thus, benign therapies such as EPA or psychosocial interventions, including CBT or supportive therapy are most appropriate as a first line treatment in UHR patients, with the prescription of antipsychotic medication being reserved for those who respond poorly, or not at all, to the gentler therapies.

Stigma is all too often another important consequence of a psychiatric diagnosis, particularly a diagnosis that implies psychosis. The question of stigmatising by labelling young people with an 'at risk for psychosis' diagnosis is indeed realistic, and has to be answered. One answer, which we favour, is to broaden the risk syndrome concept, as we have argued above, to include pluripotential risk syndrome which simply indicates a need for care, rather than indicating an outcome that may or may not eventuate. Another crucial factor in the reduction of stigma is the provision of an appropriate culture and context of care [75]. Given the demographics of this patient group, the best service models promote collaborative care within a respectful, youth-friendly setting that emphasises optimism and hope for the future.

SUMMARY AND CONCLUSIONS

'I feel certain that many incipient cases might be arrested before the efficient contact with reality is completely suspended.' Henry Stack Sullivan, 1927 [76].

Almost a century ago, Henry Stack Sullivan aptly presaged the aims of today's pre-emptive psychiatry. Although neglected until relatively recently, research into the psychotic disorders has shown that the course of these illnesses is not fixed, with deteriorating function and increasing disability the inevitable outcome, but rather, as fluid and malleable. Research has also shown that certain of the risk factors identified to date (for example, duration of untreated illness, co-morbid anxiety and depression, substance abuse for example) can be modified, and attention to these factors as part of the treatment has the potential to limit or repair the damage associated with the onset of illness. This has sparked an explosion of interest in early intervention and its ultimate aim of primary prevention, not only for the psychotic disorders, but for mental illness in general, and led to a paradigm shift in psychological medicine: pre-emptive psychiatry, with its aims of personalised, preventive care.

While there is now a substantial body of evidence backing the value of early intervention for the psychotic disorders in terms of the human, social, and economic outcomes produced [77–81], many important issues remain to be addressed. At the most basic level, the clinical and trait/state risk factors that form the basis of our current predictive criteria are still relatively crude. The identification of endophenotypes and biomarkers that provide an accurate assessment of risk is of crucial importance not only for the design of better therapeutic approaches, but also for a better understanding of the biological mechanisms that underlie the onset of illness. The intervention studies that have been conducted to date are promising and have provided proof of concept. However, the optimal types and sequences of interventions to be offered at each stage of the onset of illness remains to be established, and sophisticated large-scale clinical trials, informed by ongoing biological research, are necessary to resolve these questions.

Various models exist for the provision of early psychosis services, though all offer one to two years of specialised care aimed at maximising engagement, adherence to treatment, appropriate lifestyle changes, family support, vocational recovery and progress. However, the first five years post-diagnosis are crucial for long-term recovery and outcome, and there is evidence to suggest that some of the gains provided by the initial care in specialised services are eroded after the transition to generic services. To minimise the risk of disengagement, relapse and suicide, a substantial subset of patients may need specialised care for a longer period of up to five years.

In conclusion, the last two decades have seen a radical transformation in our understanding of mental disorders. The research effort dedicated towards a better understanding of the psychoses and better clinical care for patients with psychotic disorders has largely contributed to the current transformation of psychiatry towards a more preventive focus, analogous to the approach widespread in physical medicine. Early intervention, a keystone of pre-emptive psychiatry, is now being adopted across the full diagnostic spectrum, and this exciting new field promises human, economic, and public health benefits on a much larger scale than could have been envisioned in psychiatry even a decade ago.

REFERENCES

1. Kessler RC, Berglund P, Demler O, Jin R, Merikangas KR, Walters EE (2005) Lifetime prevalence and age-of-onset distributions of DSM-IV disorders in the National Comorbidity Survey Replication. *Arch Gen Psychiatry* **62**, 593–602.
2. Arnett JJ (2004) *Emerging adulthood: the winding road from the late teens through the twenties.* Oxford University Press, New York.
3. Cohen P, Cohen J (1984) The clinician's illusion. *Arch Gen Psychiatry* **41**, 1178–1182.
4. Crow TJ, MacMillan JF, Johnson AL, Johnstone EC (1986) A randomised controlled trial of prophylactic neuroleptic treatment. *Br J Psychiatry* **148**, 120–127.
5. Kane JM, Rifkin A, Quitkin F, Nayak D, Ramos-Lorenzi J (1982) Fluphenazine vs placebo in patients with remitted, acute first-episode schizophrenia. *Arch Gen Psychiatry* **39**, 70–73.
6. Lieberman JA, Alvir JM, Woerner M, Degreef G, Bilder RM, Ashtari M, *et al.* (1992) Prospective study of psychobiology in first-episode schizophrenia at Hillside Hospital. *Schizophr Bull* **18**, 351–371.
7. Edwards J, McGorry PD (2002) *Implementing early intervention in psychosis: a guide to establishing early psychosis services.* Martin Dunitz, London.
8. Craig TK, Garety P, Power P, Rahaman N, Colbert S, Fornells-Ambrojo M, *et al.* (2004) The Lambeth Early Onset (LEO) Team: randomised controlled trial of the effectiveness of specialised care for early psychosis. *BMJ* **329**, 1067.
9. Crumlish N, Whitty P, Clarke M, Browne S, Kamali M, Gervin M, *et al.* (2009) Beyond the critical period: longitudinal study of 8-year outcome in first-episode non-affective psychosis. *Br J Psychiatry* **194**, 18–24.
10. Henry L, Harris M, Amminger GP, Jackson HJ, Yuen HP, Harrigan SM, *et al.* (2007) The EPPIC long term follow-up study of first episode psychosis: clinical and functional long term outcome. *Schizophr Bull* **33**, s590.
11. Johannessen JO, Larsen TK, Joa I, Melle I, Friis S, Opjordsmoen S, *et al.* (2005) Pathways to care for first-episode psychosis in an early detection healthcare sector: part of the Scandinavian TIPS study. *Br J Psychiatry Suppl* **48**, s24–s28.
12. Larsen TK, Melle I, Auestad B, Friis S, Haahr U, Johannessen JO, *et al.* (2006) Early detection of first-episode psychosis: the effect on 1-year outcome. *Schizophr Bull* **32**, 758–764.
13. Melle I, Johannesen JO, Friis S, Haahr U, Joa I, Larsen TK, *et al.* (2006) Early detection of the first episode of schizophrenia and suicidal behavior. *Am J Psychiatry* **163**, 800–804.
14. Melle I, Larsen TK, Haahr U, Friis S, Johannessen JO, Opjordsmoen S, *et al.* (2004) Reducing the duration of untreated first-episode psychosis: effects on clinical presentation. *Arch Gen Psychiatry* **61**, 143–150.

15. Petersen L, Nordentoft M, Jeppesen P, Ohlenschaeger J, Thorup A, Christensen TO, *et al.* (2005) Improving 1-year outcome in first-episode psychosis: OPUS trial. *Br J Psychiatry Suppl* **48**, s98–s103.

16. Thorup A, Petersen L, Jeppesen P, Ohlenschlaeger J, Christensen T, Krarup G, *et al.* (2005) Integrated treatment ameliorates negative symptoms in first episode psychosis–results from the Danish OPUS trial. *Schizophr Res* **79**, 95–105.

17. Marshall M, Lewis S, Lockwood A, Drake R, Jones P, Croudace T (2005) Association between duration of untreated psychosis and outcome in cohorts of first-episode patients: a systematic review. *Arch Gen Psychiatry* **62**, 975–983.

18. Perkins DO, Gu H, Boteva K, Lieberman JA (2005) Relationship between duration of untreated psychosis and outcome in first-episode schizophrenia: a critical review and meta-analysis. *Am J Psychiatry* **162**, 1785–1804.

19. an der Heiden W, Hafner H (2000) The epidemiology of onset and course of schizophrenia. *Eur Arch Psychiatry Clin Neurosci* **250**, 292–303.

20. Yung AR, McGorry PD (1996) The prodromal phase of first-episode psychosis: past and current conceptualizations. *Schizophr Bull* **22**, 353–370.

21. Yung AR, Phillips LJ, McGorry PD, McFarlane CA, Francey S, Harrigan S, *et al.* (1998) Prediction of psychosis. A step towards indicated prevention of schizophrenia. *Br J Psychiatry Suppl* **172**, 14–20.

22. Huber G (1997) The heterogeneous course of schizophrenia. *Schizophr Res* **28**, 177–185.

23. McGorry PD, Yung AR, Phillips LJ (2003) The 'close-in' or ultra high-risk model: a safe and effective strategy for research and clinical intervention in prepsychotic mental disorder. *Schizophr Bull* **29**, 771–790.

24. Yung AR, Phillips LJ, Mcgorry PD (2004) *Treating schizophrenia in the prodromal phase*. Taylor and Francis, London.

25. Hafner H, Maurer K, Loffler W, an der Heiden W, Hambrecht M, Schultze-Lutter F (2003) Modeling the early course of schizophrenia. *Schizophr Bull* **29**, 325–340.

26. van Os J, Hanssen M, Bijl RV, Vollebergh W (2001) Prevalence of psychotic disorder and community level of psychotic symptoms: an urban-rural comparison. *Arch Gen Psychiatry* **58**, 663–668.

27. Yung AR, Nelson B, Baker K, Buckby JA, Baksheev G, Cosgrave EM (2009) Psychotic-like experiences in a community sample of adolescents: implications for the continuum model of psychosis and prediction of schizophrenia. *Aust N Z J Psychiatry* **43**, 118–128.

28. Yung AR, McGorry PD (1996) The initial prodrome in psychosis: descriptive and qualitative aspects. *Aust N Z J Psychiatry* **30**, 587–599.

29. Yung AR, Phillips LJ, Yuen HP, Francey SM, McFarlane CA, Hallgren M, *et al.* (2003) Psychosis prediction: 12-month follow up of a high-risk ('prodromal') group. *Schizophr Res* **60**, 21–32.

30. Addington J, Cadenhead KS, Cannon TD, Cornblatt B, McGlashan TH, Perkins DO, *et al.* (2007) North American Prodrome Longitudinal Study: a collaborative multisite approach to prodromal schizophrenia research. *Schizophr Bull* **33**, 665–672.

31. Cannon TD, Cadenhead K, Cornblatt B, Woods SW, Addington J, Walker E, *et al.* (2008) Prediction of psychosis in youth at high clinical risk: a multisite longitudinal study in North America. *Arch Gen Psychiatry* **65**, 28–37.

32. Mason O, Startup M, Halpin S, Schall U, Conrad A, Carr V (2004) Risk factors for transition to first episode psychosis among individuals with 'at-risk mental states'. *Schizophr Res* **71**, 227–237.

33. Miller TJ, McGlashan TH, Rosen JL, Somjee L, Markovich PJ, Stein K, *et al.* (2002) Prospective diagnosis of the initial prodrome for schizophrenia based on the Structured Interview for Prodromal Syndromes: preliminary evidence of interrater reliability and predictive validity. *Am J Psychiatry* **159**, 863–865.

34. Riecher-Rossler A, Gschwandtner U, Aston J, Borgwardt S, Drewe M, Fuhr P, *et al.* (2007) The Basel early-detection-of-psychosis (FEPSY)-study–design and preliminary results. *Acta Psychiatr Scand* **115**, 114–125.

35. Ruhrmann S, Schultze-Lutter F, Klosterkotter J (2003) Early detection and intervention in the initial prodromal phase of schizophrenia. *Pharmacopsychiatry* **36**, s162–s167.

36. Yung AR, Yuen HP, McGorry PD, Phillips LJ, Kelly D, Dell'Olio M, *et al.* (2005) Mapping the onset of psychosis: the Comprehensive Assessment of At-Risk Mental States. *Aust N Z J Psychiatry* **39**, 964–971.

37. Miller TJ, McGlashan TH, Rosen JL, Cadenhead K, Cannon T, Ventura J, *et al.* (2003) Prodromal assessment with the structured interview for prodromal syndromes and the scale of prodromal symptoms: predictive validity, interrater reliability, and training to reliability. *Schizophr Bull* **29**, 703–715.

38. Schultze-Lutter F, Addington J, Ruhrmann S, Klosterkotter J (2007) *Schizophrenia Proneness Instrument, Adult version*. Giovanni Fioriti, Rome.

39. Overall JE, Gorham DR (1962) The Brief Psychiatric Rating Scale. *Psychol Rep* **10**, 799–812.

40. Andreasen N (1987) *The Comprehensive Assessment of Symptoms and History (CASH) interview*. The University of Iowa, Iowa City.

41. Yung AR, Nelson B, Stanford C, Simmons MB, Cosgrave EM, Killackey E, *et al.* (2008) Validation of 'prodromal' criteria to detect individuals at ultra high risk of psychosis: 2 year follow-up. *Schizophr Res* **105**, 10–17.

42. Yung AR, Yuen HP, Berger G, Francey S, Hung TC, Nelson B, *et al.* (2007) Declining transition rate in ultra high risk (prodromal) services: dilution or reduction of risk? *Schizophr Bull* **33**, 673–681.

43. Phillips LJ, McGorry PD, Yuen HP, Ward J, Donovan K, Kelly D, *et al.* (2007) Medium term follow-up of a randomized controlled trial of interventions for young people at ultra high risk of psychosis. *Schizophr Res* **96**, 25–33.

44. McGorry PD, Yung AR, Phillips LJ, Yuen HP, Francey S, Cosgrave EM, *et al.* (2002) Randomized controlled trial of interventions designed to reduce the risk of progression to first-episode psychosis in a clinical sample with subthreshold symptoms. *Arch Gen Psychiatry* **59**, 921–928.

45. McGlashan TH, Zipursky RB, Perkins D, Addington J, Miller T, Woods SW, *et al.* (2006) Randomized, double-blind trial of olanzapine versus placebo in patients prodromally symptomatic for psychosis. *Am J Psychiatry* **163**, 790–799.

46. Woods SW, Tully EM, Walsh BC, Hawkins KA, Callahan JL, Cohen SJ, *et al.* (2007) Aripiprazole in the treatment of the psychosis prodrome: an open-label pilot study. *Br J Psychiatry Suppl* **51**, s96–s101.

47. Rurhmann S, Bechdolf A, Kuhn KU, Wagner M, Schultze-Lutter F, Janssen B *et al.* (2007) Acute effects of treatment for prodromal symptoms for people putatively in a late initial prodromal state of psychosis. *Br J Psychiatry* **51**, s88–s95.

48. Cornblatt BA, Lencz T, Smith CW, Olsen R, Auther AM, Nakayama E, *et al.* (2007) Can antidepressants be used to treat the schizophrenia prodrome? Results of a prospective, naturalistic treatment study of adolescents. *J Clin Psychiatry* **68**, 546–557.

49. Fusar-Poli P, Valmaggia L, McGuire P (2007) Can antidepressants prevent psychosis? *Lancet* **370**, 1746–1748.

50. Morrison AP, French P, Walford L, Lewis SW, Kilcommons A, Green J, *et al.* (2004) Cognitive therapy for the prevention of psychosis in people at ultra-high risk: randomised controlled trial. *Br J Psychiatry* **185**, 291–297.

51. Bechdolf A, Wagner M, Klosterkotter J (2006) Cognitive behaviour therapy (CBT) in the early initial prodromal state of psychosis: concept and practical approach. *Schizophr Res* **86**, s96.

52. Nordentoft M, Thorup A, Petersen L, Ohlenschlaeger J, Melau M, Christensen TO, *et al.* (2006) Transition rates from schizotypal disorder to psychotic disorder for first-contact patients included in the OPUS trial. A randomized clinical trial of integrated treatment and standard treatment. *Schizophr Res* **83**, 29–40.

53. Amminger GP, Schafer MR, Papageorgiou K, Klier CM, Cotton SM, Harrigan S, *et al.* (2010) Long-chain omega-3 fatty acids for indicated prevention of psychotic disorders: a randomized, placebo-controlled trial. *Arch Gen Psychiatry* **67**, 146–154.

54. Berger GE, Proffitt TM, McConchie M, Yuen H, Wood SJ, Amminger GP, *et al.* (2007) Ethyl-eicosapentaenoic acid in first-episode psychosis: a randomized, placebo-controlled trial. *J Clin Psychiatry* **68**, 1867–1875.

55. Emsley R, Myburgh C, Oosthuizen P, van Rensburg SJ (2002) Randomized, placebo-controlled study of ethyl-eicosapentaenoic acid as supplemental treatment in schizophrenia. *Am J Psychiatry* **159**, 1596–1598.

56. Fenton WS, Dickerson F, Boronow J, Hibbeln JR, Knable M (2001) A placebo-controlled trial of omega-3 fatty acid (ethyl eicosapentaenoic acid) supplementation for residual symptoms and cognitive impairment in schizophrenia. *Am J Psychiatry* **158**, 2071–2074.

57. Freeman MP, Hibbeln JR, Wisner KL, Davis JM, Mischoulon D, Peet M, *et al.* (2006) Omega-3 fatty acids: evidence basis for treatment and future research in psychiatry. *J Clin Psychiatry* **67**, 1954–1967.

58. Kahn RS, Fleischhacker WW, Boter H, Davidson M, Vergouwe Y, Keet IP, *et al.* (2008) Effectiveness of antipsychotic drugs in first-episode schizophrenia and schizophreniform disorder: an open randomised clinical trial. *Lancet* **371**, 1085–1097.

59. Gordon RS, Jr. (1983) An operational classification of disease prevention. *Public Health Rep* **98**, 107–109.

60. Bell RQ (1992) Multiple-risk cohorts and segmenting risk as solutions to the problem of false positives in risk for the major psychoses. *Psychiatry* **55**, 370–381.

61. Mrazek PJ, Haggerty RJ (1994) *Reducing the risks for mental disorder: frontiers for preventive intervention research.* National Academy Press, Washington DC.

62. Eaton WW, Badawi M, Melton B (1995) Prodromes and precursors: epidemiologic data for primary prevention of disorders with slow onset. *Am J Psychiatry* **152**, 967–972.

63. McGorry PD, Hickie IB, Yung AR, Pantelis C, Jackson HJ (2006) Clinical staging of psychiatric disorders: a heuristic framework for choosing earlier, safer and more effective interventions. *Aust N Z J Psychiatry* **40**, 616–622.

64. McGorry PD, Purcell R, Hickie IB, Yung AR, Pantelis C, Jackson HJ (2007) Clinical staging: a heuristic model for psychiatry and youth mental health. *Med J Aust* **187**, s40–s42.

65. Carpenter WT. (2009) Anticipating DSM-V: should psychosis risk become a diagnostic class? *Schizophr Bull* **35**, 841–843.

66. Woods SW, Addington J, Cadenhead KS, Cannon TD, Cornblatt BA, Heinssen R, *et al.* (2009) Validity of the prodromal risk syndrome for first psychosis: findings from the North American Prodrome Longitudinal Study. *Schizophr Bull* **35**, 894–908.

67. Insel TR (2007) The arrival of preemptive psychiatry. *Early Interven Psychiatry* **1**, 5–6.

68. Crow TJ (1990) Nature of the genetic contribution to psychotic illness–a continuum viewpoint. *Acta Psychiatr Scand* **81**, 401–408.

69. Docherty JP, Van Kammen DP, Siris SG, Marder SR (1978) Stages of onset of schizophrenic psychosis. *Am J Psychiatry* **135**, 420–426.

70. Hafner H (2000) Onset and early course as determinants of the further course of schizophrenia. *Acta Psychiatr Scand Suppl* **44**, 8.

71. Johannesen JO, Martindale BV, Cullberg J (2006) *Evolving psychosis: different stages, different treatments.* Routledge Mental Health, Hove.

72. Harrington R, Clark A (1998) Prevention and early intervention for depression in adolescence and early adult life. *Eur Arch Psychiatry Clin Neurosci.* **248**, 32–45.

73. Hetrick S, Simmons M, Merry S (2008) SSRIs and depression in children and adolescents: the imperative for shared decision-making. *Australas Psychiatry* **16**, 354–358.

74. Seeley JR, Stice E, Rohde P (2009) Screening for depression prevention: identifying adolescent girls at high risk for future depression. *J Abnorm Psychol* **118**, 161–170.

75. Yung AR, McGorry PD, Francey SM, Nelson B, Baker K, Phillips LJ, *et al.* (2007) PACE: a specialised service for young people at risk of psychotic disorders. *Med J Aust* **187**, s43–s46.

76. Sullivan HS (1927) The onset of schizophrenia. *Am J Psychiatry* **6**, 105–134.

77. McCrone P, Craig TK, Power P, Garety PA (2010) Cost-effectiveness of an early intervention service for people with psychosis. *Br J Psychiatry* **196**, 377–382.

78. McGorry P (2010) Evidence, early intervention and the tipping point. *Early Interv Psychiatry* **4**, 1–3.

79. McGorry P, Johanessen JO, Lewis S, Birchwood M, Malla A, Nordentoft M, *et al.* (2010) Early intervention in psychosis: keeping faith with evidence-based health care. *Psychol Med* **40**, 399–404.

80. Mihalopoulos C, Harris M, Henry L, Harrigan S, McGorry P (2009) Is early intervention in psychosis cost-effective over the long term? *Schizophr Bull* **35**, 909–918.

81. Singh SP (2010) Early intervention in psychosis. *Br J Psychiatry* **196**, 343–345.

CHAPTER 6

Pharmacological treatment

Jonathan E. Sherin

Mental Health and Behavioral Science, Miami VA Healthcare System 1201 NW Miami, Florida and Psychiatry and Behavioral Science, University of Miami, 1120 NW, FLorida

Stephen R., Marder

Semel Insitute for Neuroscience at UCLA, The VA Greater Los Angeles Healthcare Center, and the VA Desert Pacific Mental Illness Research, Education, and Clinical Center, Los Angeles, California, USA.

Information Box

- *Antipsychotics are recommended for nearly every person experiencing an episode of schizophrenia.*
- *In the near future, genetic or other information may provide information that will aid clinicians in making rational decisions about which medication is most likely to be effective for a particular individual.*
- *Medication effects can be seen and efficacy predicted within the first two weeks of treatment in many cases.*
- *Both the PORT and NICE guidelines recommend clozapine for patients who have not responded after adequate trials of at least two antipsychotics.*
- *A number of drugs that target negative symptoms and or cognitive impairments are currently in various stages of development. These agents target receptor sites other than D2 and are likely to have qualitatively different effects than available compounds.*

INTRODUCTION

The past decade has seen a re-assessment of the role of pharmacology in treating schizophrenia. Large clinical trials in Europe and the US have revealed the limits of

---

Schizophrenia: Current Science and Clinical Practice, First Edition. Edited by Wolfgang Gaebel.
© 2011 John Wiley & Sons, Ltd. Published 2011 by John Wiley & Sons, Ltd.

the current group of antipsychotics. That is, these agents are effective for attenuating and often eliminating psychotic symptoms such as hallucinations or delusions. Unfortunately, these drugs – all of them targeting dopamine D_2 receptors – are relatively ineffective for treating other psychopathological domains such as negative symptoms and cognitive impairments. This limitation has led to a search for new approaches for managing schizophrenia. This chapter will review the current state of antipsychotic treatment and will look into approaches for improving pharmacological treatments. This chapter will refer to evidence-based guidelines such as the US 2009 Schizophrenia PORT (Patient Outcome Research Team) [1] or the UK NICE (National Institute for Clinical Excellence) guidelines [2].

CURRENT STATE OF PHARMACOLOGICAL TREATMENT

A large body of research conducted over more than 50 years has confirmed that antipsychotic medications are effective in schizophrenia. These agents are effective for reducing the severity of psychotic symptoms in individuals experiencing an acute episode of schizophrenia and they are effective for decreasing the risk of a psychotic relapse in patients who are stable [1,2]. There is also evidence suggesting that delaying treatment with an antipsychotic can have long-term consequences in agreement with research indicating that a longer duration of untreated psychosis is associated with a worse functional and symptom outcome [3]. This set of findings has led to the suggestion that treatment with antipsychotics during a prodromal period before psychosis develops may prevent or delay the onset of schizophrenia. At this point, most studies suggest that this strategy may be effective [4,5].

However, antipsychotics are not 'anti-schizophrenic'. They are effective for treating nearly every form of psychosis that has been described including psychosis in bipolar illness, major depression, dementia, drug-induced psychosis, Huntington's Psychosis, and other psychoses in medical conditions. Moreover, they are only effective for treating the psychotic component of schizophrenia. Patients who are treated with antipsychotics commonly experience other serious impairments that have important effects on their functioning and their quality of life. Often, although psychotic symptoms are reduced, residual symptoms remain.

After the introduction of second generation antipsychotics (SGAs), early studies led to a widespread belief that these agents had advantages in efficacy and adverse effects when compared with first generation antipsychotics (FGAs). This belief was examined in a number of large trials including the NIMH CATIE (Clinical Antipsychotic Trials of Intervention Effectiveness study) [6] and CUtLASS from the UK (Cost Utility of the Latest Antipsychotics in Schizophrenia) [7]. Both of these trials failed to find a difference favouring the SGAs. There were suggestions that the SGAs were associated with less extrapyramidal side effect (EPS), but certain SGAs had substantial metabolic effects. Both studies did, however, find efficacy advantages for clozapine in patients who were partially responsive to other antipsychotics [8,9].

Although data from these large trials do not support an efficacy advantage for SGAs, there are suggestions from meta-analyses that certain antipsychotics may have advantages. For example Leucht and colleagues [10] analysed studies that directly compared SGAs. They found advantages for olanzapine when compared to aripiprazole, quetiapine, risperidone and ziprasidone; advantages for risperidone over quetiapine and ziprasidone; and advantages for clozapine over zotepine and risperidone (see Figure 6.1). The advantages for these agents were confined to positive symptoms. However, the differences calculated as effect sizes were relatively small and would need to be weighed against side effect differences among agents which are substantial.

Although the findings comparing one antipsychotic to another are unclear, the comparisons to placebos are not ambiguous. As a result, antipsychotics are recommended for nearly every person experiencing an episode of schizophrenia [1,2]. In addition, antipsychotic medications are effective for reducing the risk of a psychotic relapse in stabilised patients [1]. Nevertheless, the substantial side effects have led to a search for better medications and new approaches for managing the illness.

PHASES OF SCHIZOPHRENIA

The management of schizophrenia should correspond to the phase of an individual's illness. The American Psychiatric Association guidelines [11] have divided the illness into three discernable stages: An *acute psychotic phase* of schizophrenia occurs when an individual experiences a first episode or an exacerbation of their illness. Following the acute phase – which commonly lasts from four to eight weeks – patients will usually enter a *stabilisation phase*. In this phase, acute symptoms have been controlled, but patients remain at risk for another episode if they experience stress or if medications are abruptly discontinued. This phase may last as long as six months following recovery from acute symptoms. The third stage is the *stable or maintenance phase* when the illness is in a relative stage of remission. The goals during this phase are to prevent psychotic relapse and to assist patients in improving their level of functioning.

Acute phase treatment

During an acute exacerbation of schizophrenia, treatment usually focuses on managing the most severe psychotic symptoms including hallucinations, delusions and suspiciousness. Severe symptoms may lead to agitated behaviours that can, on occasion, be dangerous. The focus of pharmacological treatment during the acute

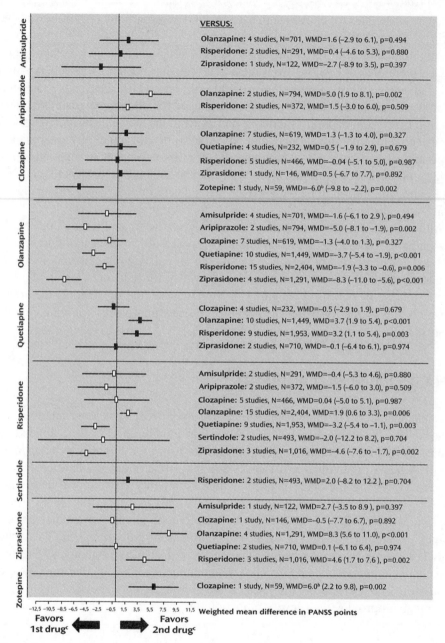

Figure 6.1 Results of comparisons of PANSS total score in meta-analysis of second-generation antipsychotics[a–d]

[a]Numbers in parentheses are 95% confidence intervals. WMD = weighted mean difference.
[b]Data based on Brief Psychiatric Rating Scale.
[c]The first drug is the one written vertically on the left side, and the second is the one written horizontally on the right side of the graph.
[d] Figure from Leucht et al., 2007 [10]

phase is on finding an antipsychotic that is well tolerated at an effective dose. Agitation can be managed with oral or intramuscular antipsychotics. The advantage of oral medications is that patients may fear injections which can temporarily increase agitation. However, intramuscular medications have the advantage of a more rapid onset of action. Intramuscular administration of most antipsychotics results in peak plasma levels in about 30 minutes with clinical effects emerging within 15 to 30 minutes. Orally administered antipsychotics result in a peak plasma level in one to four hours following administration. Injected medications can be the only alternative when patients refuse to take oral medication and treatment is urgent. Rapid dissolve medications are available if there is concern that patients will refuse to swallow medication. Although intramuscular FGAs are effective, they are often associated with serious acute side effects. For example, high potency FGAs such as intramuscular haloperidol can cause akathisia or acute dystonias. Low potency drugs such as intramuscular chlorpromazine can cause severe hypotension.

In the past there was a widespread belief that acutely ill patients would respond more quickly if they were treated with higher medication doses. This has not been supported by evidence from clinical trials. As a result, it is recommended that patients receive a moderate and well tolerated dose of an antipsychotic until there is evidence of response or nonresponse. The Schizophrenia PORT [1] recommends treatment with moderate doses of an antipsychotic other than clozapine. The selection should be based on individual preference; prior treatment response and side effect experience; adherence history; relevant medical history and risk factors; individual medication side effect profile; and long-term treatment planning. Moderate doses are 300–1000 mg of chlorpromazine or the equivalent for other FGAs, 10–30 mg of aripiprazole; 10-20 of olanzapine; 3–15 mg of paliperidone; 300–750 mg of quetiapine; 2–8 mg of risperidone; and 80–160 mg of ziprasidone. The NICE guidelines [2] provide similar advice. They suggest that patients be started on the low end of the approved dose range and that clinicians should document a justification for prescribing outside of this range. Neither guideline supports combining antipsychotics.

Both the PORT and NICE [2] guidelines recommend clozapine for patients who have not responded after adequate trials of at least two antipsychotics. This recommendation was reinforced by recent trials such as NIMH CATIE [8] which found that patients who were discontinued from an antipsychotic for lack of efficacy were more likely to improve on clozapine than other antipsychotics in the trial.

There is some evidence that early treatment response can be useful for predicting drug response. Until recently, most clinicians believed that trials lasting four or more weeks were necessary for determining an antipsychotic was effective. This view was challenged by a meta-analysis [12] which found that nearly all of the improvement on an antipsychotic tended to occur during the first two weeks. This suggests that a trial of only two weeks may be sufficient – in most cases – for determining whether an individual will respond to that agent. This was tested in a trial [13] in which patients were treated with risperidone. Patients who failed to meet response criteria after two weeks were randomly assigned to staying on risperidone or switching to olanzapine. The early nonresponders who changed to olanzapine had significantly better outcomes than those who stayed on risperidone. However the actual difference was relatively small. Both groups did much worse than the individuals who improved during the first week. This indicates that a clinician can learn a substantial amount about a patient's drug responsiveness during a two-week period.

Stabilization phase treatment

There are no clear guidelines for managing patients during the stabilisation phase. Since patients are at a greater vulnerability for an exacerbation than during the stable phase, it is reasonable to maintain the person on the same drug and dose that was effective in treating the acute episode.

Maintenance phase treatment

As patients enter the maintenance phase the goals and challenges shift. The goal of maintenance phase treatment is to prevent the patient from experiencing a psychotic relapse and to engage the person in psychosocial treatments or rehabilitation that will permit functional recovery. Antipsychotic medications are highly effective for preventing relapse. Well controlled studies have found that about 75% of stable patients will relapse in a year if they are changed from an antipsychotic to a placebo. On the other hand, only about 25% will relapse off medication. The Schizophrenia PORT [1] recommends that multiple episode patients receive continuous antipsychotic medication. A number of studies have focused on the possibility that stable patients could be treated intermittently with antipsychotic. In this strategy, medications are gradually discontinued and then restarted when patients show early signs of an exacerbation. A study from Germany [14] found that this strategy may be useful in a subgroup of recent onset patients who are closely monitored and who have easily detected prodromes. The NICE guideline [2] recommends intermittent or targeted treatment for patients who refuse continuous medication or for those who are highly sensitive to the side effects of all antipsychotics.

Nonadherence with taking antipsychotics is the most common cause of psychotic relapse in schizophrenia. Since it is estimated that 40–50% of schizophrenia patients will become nonadherent it becomes clear that assuring medication adherence is critical for adequate management. There are a number of logical approaches for improving adherence including patient and family education, minimising side effects, and simplifying medication regimes. Another approach is to prescribe a long-acting injectable antipsychotic medication. These medications can be administered once every one to four weeks and sometimes less often. Overall, controlled studies support the use of long-acting medications as an alternative to oral medication. The results from double-blind studies tend to favour long-acting medications over oral [15] although this advantage was not found in all studies. However, patients who are at the greatest risk for nonadherence are underrepresented in these controlled trials. There is a consensus that long-acting medications are preferred for patients who are at risk for nonadherence.

New formulations of injectable long-acting antipsychotics may convince clinicians to increase the use of this effective treatment. Paliperidone palmitate is an injectable sustained release form of paliperidone that is usually administered once each month. Since paliperidone is released the first day after an injection of paliperidone palpitate it can be initiated without a cross titration from the oral form. Patients can be started with two injections one week apart followed by injections every month. Side effects will resemble those of oral paliperidone. Since paliperidone is a metabolite of risperidone, patients can be directly converted from oral risperidone to paliperidone palmitate.

Olanzapine pamoate is an injectable formulation that can maintain effective plasma concentrations for two to four weeks. It has a similar liability for metabolic effects as oral olanzapine. In addition olanzapine pamoate is associated with a risk of a post-injection delirium sedation syndrome which resembles an overdose of oral olanzapine. Because these events can occur in a manner that cannot be predicted, patients are required to remain in a medical setting under observation for three hours after each injection.

The availability of these new long-acting medications raises the question as to whether they have advantages in side effects or effectiveness when compared with older depot medications. Unfortunately, there are no direct comparisons at this date to help clinicians decide among these medications.

TREATMENT RESISTANT PATIENTS

Patients with schizophrenia vary in how well they respond to an antipsychotic medication. On one end of a continuum, some individuals can achieve full remission of psychotic symptoms when they are stable; on the other end of the continuum are unfortunate patients who derive little or no benefit from antipsychotics. A majority of patients experience substantial relief although they may have persistent psychotic symptoms that may or may not affect the quality of their community adjustment.

There is strong evidence indicating that clozapine is the preferred antipsychotic for patients who are unresponsive to other antipsychotics [16]. Nearly all of these patients should have a trial of clozapine. Other studies [17] indicate that clozapine is also effective for patients who are only partially responsive to an antipsychotic. This was well demonstrated in the NIMH CATIE study [8] where patients who discontinued another antipsychotic for lack of efficacy showed greater improvement when they were switched to clozapine in comparison to other antipsychotics. Clozapine was also found to be more effective than other drugs in the UK CUtLASS study [7] which evaluated a population similar to CATIE. Unfortunately, clinicians have little guidance for managing patients who still have disturbing psychotic symptoms after an adequate clozapine trial. Other studies have evaluated supplementing clozapine with risperidone and have had mixed results, for example,[18]. Recent, unpublished reports suggest that partially responsive clozapine patients can improve with electroconvulsive treatments.

MANAGING FIRST EPISODES

Managing first episodes of schizophrenia is a particular challenge. The diagnosis can be difficult to establish and the clinical picture may be complicated by substance abuse and other factors. Fortunately, first episode patients have high response rates and they tend to respond to lower doses of antipsychotics. Unfortunately, first episode patients can be more sensitive to the side effects of medications. Recent data indicates that younger patients tend to be particularly sensitive to the metabolic effects of olanzapine [19]. As a result, the PORT recommends that antipsychotics other than olanzapine and clozapine be first line treatments for first episodes of psychosis in younger patients [1].

A recent large European First Episode Study [EUFEST] [20] randomised patients to haloperidol, olanzapine, amisulpride, quetiapine, or ziprasidone. Once patients were randomised, the treatment condition was known to the prescriber and the patient. The rates of discontinuation were higher for haloperidol than the other medications. However, the amount of symptomatic improvement was similar for all of the medications. A reasonable interpretation of these results is that haloperidol shows similar efficacy to the other agents. However, patients and their clinicians find this medication difficult to tolerate.

NEWER ANTIPSYCHOTICS

A number of new antipsychotics have been introduced during the past five years. In addition, long-acting depot formulations of other drugs have also become available. Although these agents target the same D_2 target as all of the other available antipsychotics, they provide alternatives for clinicians.

Paliperidone is actually 9 hydroxy risperidone, the major active metabolite of risperidone. It resembles risperidone in its binding properties, its side effect profile, and its efficacy. Paliperidone has substantial antagonist activity at both D_2 and $5HT_{2A}$ receptors as well as activity at α_1, α_2, and H_1 receptors. A number of studies have found that it is more effective than placebo and it has similar efficacy to olanzapine [21]. These same studies indicate that it causes less weight gain than olanzapine and is more likely to increase prolactin. Unfortunately, there are no direct comparisons between paliperidone and risperidone.

Paliperidone is administered as an extended release tablet. Clinical trials indicate that it is more effective than placebo at doses between 3 and 15 mg [22]. Since doses between 6 and 9 mg result in 70–80% D_2 occupancy [23], a starting dose of 6 mg administered daily in the morning will probably be effective for most patients.

Asenapine is an antagonist at $5HT_{2A}$, $5HT_{2B}$, $5HT_{2C}$, $5HT_6$ and $5HT_7$, α_{1A}, α_{2A}, α_{2B} and α_{2C}, and D_2, D_3 and D_4 receptors. It is administered as a sublingual tablet with a recommended starting dose of 5 mg bid. Clinical trials support its efficacy with one trial – but not all – suggesting that asenapine had an efficacy advantage compared with risperidone [24]. Overall, it appears to cause less weight gain than olanzapine and similar QT effects as quetiapine.

Iloperidone has a similar receptor profile to risperidone and paliperidone. A relatively high $5-HT_{2A}$ to D_2 ratio may explain its relatively low risk of EPS and the high affinity for $\alpha 1$ explains its risk for orthostatic hypotension. Due to hypotension, iloperidone should be started at a dose of 1 mg bid and gradually increased to a target dose of 12 to 24 mg bid. Although hypotension is a concern for iloperidone, it has the advantage of a very low risk of EPS [25].

PERSONALISING DRUG TREATMENT IN SCHIZOPHRENIA

One of the vexing problems for clinicians who treat schizophrenia is the difficulty of matching an antipsychotic to a patient. Aside from the advantages of clozapine over other antipsychotics, the available antipsychotics have similar effectiveness. The important differences are in adverse effects and available formulations (and sometimes cost). The only way for a clinician to know if a particular agent is effective and well tolerated is to initiate a trial which may take several weeks.

Attention has also focused on whether genetic information may be helpful in selecting an antipsychotic. One approach has focused on identifying polymorphisms that are associated with the response to a particular antipsychotic. For example, during the development of iloperidone the predictive value of a 6-marker genotype combination was evaluated. Patients were divided into groups depending on their genotype. For the 'optimal' genotype, 75% of iloperidone-treated patients showed a 20% or greater improvement, whereas only 37% of patients with other genotypes responded. Other studies have suggested that polymorphisms in the genes controlling CYP 450 enzymes may be helpful in predicting the dose or the effectiveness of certain antipsychotics. Although a number of studies have found associations, this strategy is not at a stage where it is likely to be clinically useful [26].

Another approach focuses on genes that are associated with an identified molecular target. The most studied gene has been the catechol O-methyltransferase (COMT) gene which affects dopamine inactivation in the prefrontal cortex. Studies suggest that functionally important polymorphisms in this gene are associated with cognitive impairments as well as drug responses [27,28]. Other polymorphisms that appear to have functional significance are currently being studied. For example, a number of studies have pointed to an association between SNPS (single nucleotide polymorphisms) in the area of the neuregulin 1 (NRG1)/ErbB4 gene and the risk of schizophrenia. Since Nrg1 plays a role in a number of important functions such as myelination, glial cell development, and neuronal plasticity understanding its signaling pathway may serve as a guide to development of a new class of antipsychotic medications.

COGNITION AND NEGATIVE SYMPTOMS AS THERAPEUTIC TARGETS

As mentioned above, available antipsychotic medications are limited in what they can do. These agents are highly effective for reducing the severity of psychotic symptoms in schizophrenia. As a result patients with auditory hallucinations, delusions and suspicious misinterpretations of things in their environment will usually experience considerable relief. However, patients with schizophrenia commonly experience other disabling symptoms including negative symptoms and cognitive impairments. Unfortunately, antipsychotic medications have minimal effects on these symptom domains. For example, patients with schizophrenia on average perform 1.5 standard deviations below the mean on neuropsychological tests. Treatment with a first or second generation antipsychotic medication can result in improvements of less than half of a standard deviation, leaving nearly all patients with schizophrenia with substantial deficits. Moreover, these impairments have important consequences. The ability of patients with schizophrenia to function in areas such as work, education and social relationships is related to the severity of their cognitive impairments and their negative symptoms. The relation of positive symptoms to functioning is much weaker. This explains, in part, why the widespread use of antipsychotics has not led to substantial improvements in functioning.

The recognition that antipsychotics are relatively ineffective for improving function has led to a search for pharmacological agents that are effective for treating cognitive and negative symptoms. The search has focused on co-medications that could be added to an antipsychotic or medications that have a broad spectrum and are effective for psychosis and other psychopathological domains.

In the United States, the search for medications for cognitive impairments has been facilitated by an NIMH initiative termed MATRICS (Measurement and Treatment Research to Improve Cognition in Schizophrenia) (www.matrics.ucla.edu). Through a collaborative effort between representatives from the pharmaceutical industry, academia and government – including NIMH and the FDA – a number of obstacles for drug development were addressed. These included obtaining an FDA opinion that a drug could be approved for cognitive impairment associated

Table 6.1 POTENTIAL TARGETS FOR IMPROVING NEGATIVE SYMPTOMS AND COGNITION IN SCHIZOPHRENIA[a]

Transmitter System	Target	Action	Example	Status
Dopamine	D1	agonist[b]	dihydrexidine	proof of concept
	D4	antagonist	sonepiprazole	limited clinical effect
	COMT	inhibitor	tolcopone	effective in PD
Serotonin	5-HT2a	antagonist	M100907	modest clinical effect
	5-HT1a	agonist	tandospirone	+/− clinical effect
Acetyl-choline	AchE[c]	inhibitors	donezepil	+/− clinical effect
	Nicotinic a7	agonist	DMXB-A	proof of concept
	Muscarinic 1	agonist	NDMC	modest clinical effect
Amino Acid	NMDA	enhancer	glycine	+/− clinical effect
	Glycine T	inhibitor	ORG-24598	proof of concept
	GABA A	agonist	TPA-023	proof of concept

[a]Adapted directly from Ref # [Gray and Roth]
[b]Denotes partial agonist
[c]Acetyl-cholinesterase [AchE]

with schizophrenia as an indication; the development of a consensus battery for measuring cognition in clinical trials; guidelines for the design of registration trials; and potential molecular targets for drug development. MATRICS guidelines and products are currently being widely used in a large number of trials of promising innovative agents.

The search for drugs to improve negative symptoms has also been facilitated by a number of activities including the development of new instruments for negative symptoms, the funding of an NIMH collaboration, and the development of guidelines for trial design. As will be noted in the following sections, the search for drugs that impact negative symptoms and cognitive impairments has focused on some of the same targets.

GLUTAMATERGIC TARGETS

A substantial amount of evidence points to glutamate as a promising target [29] [30]. Drugs that antagonise NMDA glutamate receptors – including phencyclidine and ketamine – can exacerbate the symptoms of schizophrenia. In addition, ketamine can induce cognitive impairments and negative symptoms as well as psychotic symptoms in healthy control subjects that are similar to the symptoms that occur in schizophrenia [31,32]. These observations have led to the development of a number of strategies for addressing a possible hypoglutamatergic hypothesis of schizophrenia.

Direct NMDA agonists are probably not clinically feasible because of potentially serious excitatory effects. As a result, drug development has focused on allosteric modulators that enhance NMDA transmission. Drugs that act on the glycine modulatory site of NMDA the receptor – including glycine, d-cycloserine, d-serine and d-alanine have attracted the most attention. Although some studies have found that these agents are effective for cognition and negative symptoms [33], this has not been the case for all studies [34].

Another approach to increasing NMDA activity focuses on the glycine transporter [35]. Two glycine transporters, GlyT1 and GlyT2, are located on neuronal and glial cells where they regulate extracellular glycine. Inhibiting this transporter appears to increase the concentration of glycine at the glycine modulatory site of the NMDA receptor. Promising results have been reported with sarcosine, a low potency inhibitor of the glycine transporter. Small double-blind trials indicate that sarcosine is effective as an antipsychotic [36,37]. It has not been adequately evaluated as an agent for cognitive impairment. Other glycine transport inhibitors are currently under development.

Other studies have focused on allosteric modulators of the AMPA receptor. In rodent studies, these ampa receptor modulators – or ampakines – improve learning and memory. However a trial of an ampakine in humans did not find that this drug had effects on cognition [38].

Metabotropic glutamate receptors (MGluRs) are located pre- and post synaptically. Eight subtypes of MGluR receptors have been identified at this time. Some of these are co-localised with NMDA receptors and may enhance NMDA activity. For this reason, certain subtypes – for example MGluR1 and 5 are promising for enhancing cognition in schizophrenia. Other preclinical studies have pointed to mGluR3 as an interesting target. For example, studies have found an association between mGluR3 polymorphisms and psychosis. Moreover, there is evidence that these same polymorphisms are associated with cognitive endophenotypes associated with schizophrenia [39]. An mGluR2/3 agent was evaluated in a large phase II study [40]. This was a three arm study in which LY2140023 was compared to both olanzapine and placebo in acute schizophrenia. The mGluR2/3 agonist was more effective than placebo for treating both positive and negative symptoms. A second study failed to find this effect. However, this was a failed study in which olanzapine failed to separate from placebo. Other studies with LY2140023 are currently underway.

DOPAMINE TARGETS

The likelihood that abnormalities in dopaminergic transmission are fundamental to, if not the central features of, the pathophysiology of schizophrenia has been suspected for many years [41,42]. More and more direct evidence mounts over time to support this relationship [43,44]. The specific nature of these abnormalities is not completely clear but at a minimum seems to involve dopaminergic hyper-activity in subcortical dopaminergic systems including the striatum as well as dopaminergic hypo-activity in frontal cortex and perhaps hippocampus [45]. For the most part, dopaminergic hyper-activity is thought to account for the excess symptom domain of schizophrenia (positive or psychotic symptoms), whereas dopaminergic hypo-activity is thought to account for the deficit symptom domains of schizophrenia (negative and cognitive symptoms). Not surprisingly, as mentioned earlier in the chapter, pharmacologic approaches to treating schizophrenia have focused primarily on the 'normalization' of dopaminergic transmission.

To date, the core pharmacologic treatments for schizophrenia, and psychotic illnesses in general, rely on the fact that psychotic (positive) symptoms improve with blockade of dopamine D2-like receptors (D2, D3, D4), which are located predominantly in sub-cortical structures such as the striatum. This therapeutic effect is thought to result from an effective decrease in the amount of dopamine signaling that presumably results from overactive mesolimbic afferents. Of note, clozapine, an SGA with a known impact not only on positive psychotic symptoms but deficit symptoms as well, has particular affinity for the D4 dopamine receptor. Although a mechanism for this additional therapeutic impact of clozapine is not known, there is some evidence that clozapine and other agents which have an action specifically at the D4 receptor might promote cognitive function via modulation of gaba-ergic signaling in the prefrontal cortex. In addition, clozapine may have a pro-cognitive therapeutic effect though a non-D4 mediated mechanism, by indirectly increasing the release of acetylcholine and dopamine from nerve terminals in the temporal lobe [46].

More recent approaches focus on developing treatments for the deficit symptom domains which plague patients with schizophrenia from a functional standpoint, namely negative and cognitive symptoms. These efforts are specifically aimed at increasing the effective amount of signaling through dopamine receptors in frontal cortex, mostly via an indirect mechanism of action. However, efforts to stimulate dopamine receptors in frontal cortex directly are also ongoing. These efforts capitalise on the fact that D1-like (D1, D5) dopamine receptors are predominant in this brain region [47] and seem to have a significant role in cognitive function [48]. In effect, by developing pharmacologic agents that selectively promote signaling through D1-like dopamine receptors, it is possible to differentially simulate dopaminergic transmission in frontal cortex. Several medications have been developed along these lines [49,50], one of which, dyhydrexidine [51], was shown to impact cognitive performance in nonhuman primates [52].

Another approach to boosting dopaminergic transmission in the frontal cortex capitalises on the fact that catechol-O-methyltransferase (COMT), one of the enzymes responsible for deactivating synaptic dopamine (by methylation), appears to be preferentially active in this region [53]. A selective reversible inhibitor of

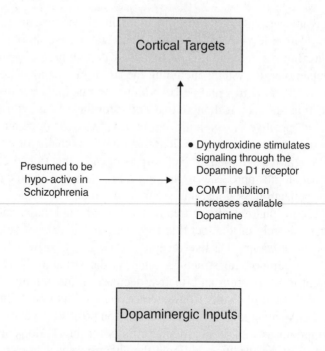

Figure 6.2 Compounds that facilitate dopaminergic transmission in prefrontal cortex, and perhaps hippocampus, may improve cognition and function in patients with Schizophrenia.

COMT, tolcopone, has been shown to improve measures of performance memory in rats [54], and restore cognitive function in subjects with late-stage Parkinson's Disease. However, the use of tolcopone is complicated by its risk for hepatotoxicity and variable effects on executive function in normal human subjects depending on genotype. The usefulness of COMT inhibitors in treating the deficit symptom domains in schizophrenia, remains to be determined.

CHOLINERGIC TARGETS

The extensive nature of the brain's cholinergic innervation and its role in cognition has been a topic of great interest for many years. For some time, it has been recognised that interference with the cholinergic system within the human CNS has a dramatic impact on cognitive function. In particular, blockade of acetyl-choline receptors can cause attentional deficits and even frank delirium. More recently, it has been established that augmentation of cholinergic transmission can improve cognition in subjects with dementing illnesses such as Alzheimer's Disease, presumably by improving attentional function. Not surprisingly, there has been a significant interest in exploring the possibility that boosting transmission at cholinergic synapses might have a beneficial impact on cognition. This interest spans from the general, aging population to numerous disease states that have associated cognitive impairment, with schizophrenia and its deficit symptom domains a prime example.

There are several 'pro-cognitive' medications with FDA approved indications for Alzheimer's Disease. Although it is not clear that these medications improve cognitive function per se in the subject with dementia, they do clearly slow the progression of decline. In theory, these medications might prevent decline by normalising otherwise depleted attentional resources, thereby enabling the baseline neuronal activity that is necessary to maintain circuit integrity. To date, the bulk of pro-cognitive cholinergic compounds that have become available for treatment are designed to interfere with the metabolism of acetylcholine through the inhibition of the cholinesterase enzyme [55]. By blocking the metabolism of acetylcholine, these compounds, known as acetylcholinersterase inhibitors (AchEIs), increase the amount of active transmitter that can stimulate cholinergic receptors.

Although there has been great hope for the use of AchEIs to improve cognitive impairment in schizophrenia, the results to date have been unsatisfying. Open label studies using both donepezil [56] and rivastigmine [57] suggested benefits for cognition. However, larger studies with appropriately rigorous controls in place have failed to demonstrate any effect on cognitive function in subjects with schizophrenia [58,59]. On the other hand, another AchEI, galantamine, has been shown to improve certain measures of cognition in subjects with schizophrenia, notably processing speed and verbal memory [60]. However, in addition to being an AchEI, galantamine has additional actions on cholinergic transmission that may explain its apparently superior, though limited, and debated efficacy (see Figure 6.3). In particular, galantamine is a positive allosteric modulator of nicotinic receptors. As such, galantamine might increase acetylcholine release through presynaptic nicotinic receptor mechanisms and also increase sensitivity to acetylcholine through a post-synaptic nicotinic receptor mechanism. Lastly, the allosteric modulatory effect of galantamine on nicotinic receptors may increase the release of dopamine in prefrontal cortex as well as hippocampus and account for its possible impact on cognition [61].

Aside from galantamine, there is significant interest in the development of other compounds which impact nicotinic receptors directly. One such compound, an anabaseine alkaloid known as DMXB-A, is a partial agonist at nicotinic receptors. In contrast to nicotine itself, which is not useful as a cognitive enhancing agent due to the problem of tachyphylaxis, preliminary studies with DMXB-A suggest that it results in improvement on cognitive measures [62]. Tropisetron, another agonist at the nicotinic receptor, has likewise been shown to have some efficacy in improving measures of cognition (inhibition of P50 responses) in subjects with schizophrenia.

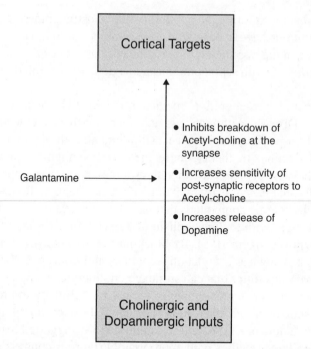

Figure 6.3 Galantamine may promote normalization of deficit symptom domains in Schizophrenia via several separate mechanisms that facilitate both Acetyl-choline and Dopamine transmission in cortex.

HISTAMINE TARGETS

Histamine is a neurotransmitter in the brain which, much like norepinephrine, derives from a small group of neurons with extensive axonal arborisations that ramify broadly throughout the neuraxis [63,64]. Although neuronal histamine is well known to play a critical role in neuro-vegetative functions such as sleeping and eating, histaminergic neurotransmission is also considered critical in cognition and as such may provide a target for treating non-psychotic symptoms of schizophrenia [65]. Histamine acts through at least four receptor subtypes [H1-4], each of which has a documented regional distribution and which could, in theory, be manipulated for clinical benefit [66].

There is no compelling likelihood of a role for H2 and H4 receptors in the central nervous system in large part because of their concentration in the periphery. Of note, however, the H4 receptor is found in bone marrow and may play a role in mediating clozapine-induced agranulocytosis; clozapine stimulates the H4 receptor specifically. The H1 receptor, in contrast, has a widespread localisation in cortical regions but is most often associated with wakefulness and arousal. Medications such as diphenhydramine, that blocks H1 receptors, cause drowsiness

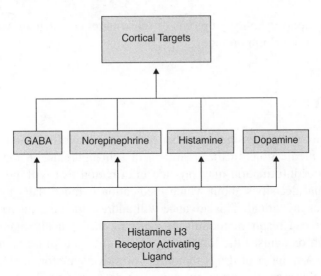

Figure 6.4 Histamine H3 receptor activation of multiple transmitter systems may promote improved cognition and function in patients with Schizophrenia.

and sedation. Not much is known regarding the potential of stimulating H1 receptors as a pro-cognitive strategy, presumably due to the fact that the autonomic and immune effects of H1 receptor stimulation across organ systems would not be tolerated.

The H3 receptor, on the other hand, is of particular interest as a target for treating the cognitive impairments in schizophrenia [67]. H3 receptors are present in brain regions that are associated with hypothesised abnormalities in schizophrenia, including the cortex and ventral striatum. Further, H3 receptors have a significant impact not only on histamine synthesis and release [64; as auto-receptors] but also noradrenergic, cholinergic, dopaminergic and gabaergic transmission. Given the presumed roles outlined in this chapter for each of these neurotransmitter systems in the major symptom domains of schizophrenia, efforts are afoot to develop H3 receptor ligands to treat or augment the treatment of schizophrenia. As a simple example, the hypothesised 'hypodopaminergia' in the prefrontal cortex of patients with schizophrenia might be normalised by H3 hetero-receptor activation in this brain region [69].

Aside from human studies, which have been problematic due to cross-species variability in receptor affinity (that is, medications developed in rats with limited comparable activity in humans) and side effects, one such compound (BF2.649) was shown in a mouse model of schizophrenia to normalise methamphetamine-induced locomotor hyperactivity without altering baseline measures [70]. This same compound was also demonstrated to normalise pre-pulse inhibition deficits generated in mice by exposure to apomorphine [70]. H3 receptor ligands may constitute a psychopharmacologic approach that will prove to have a therapeutic impact on the nonpsychotic symptoms of schizophrenia which are well known to have major functional importance.

SUMMARY

Clinical research is addressing a number of the important limitations of available psychotropic medications in the treatment of schizophrenia. In the near future, genetic or other information may provide information that will aid clinicians in making rational decisions about which medication is most likely to be effective for a particular individual. This advance will address the current 'trial and error' approach that can result in months or years of inadequately managed illness. Other research recognises the limitations of current agents that target dopamine D_2 receptors. A number of drugs that target negative symptoms and or cognitive impairments are currently in various stages of development. These agents target receptor sites other than D2 and are likely to have qualitatively different effects than available compounds.

REFERENCES

1. Buchanan RW, Kreyenbuhl J, Kelly DL, Noel JM, Boggs DL, Fischer BA, Himelhoch S, Fang B, Peterson E, Aquino PR, Keller W (2010) The 2009 schizophrenia PORT psychopharmacological treatment recommendations and summary statements. *Schizophr Bull* **36**(1):71–93.
2. National Institute for Health and Clinical Excellence (2009) Schizophrenia: Core interventions in the treatment and management of schizophrenia in adults in primary and secondary care, National Institute for Health and Clinical Excellence, pp 1–41.
3. Wyatt RJ (1991) Neuroleptics and the natural course of schizophrenia. *Schizophr Bull* **17**(2):325–351.
4. McGlashan TH, Zipursky RB, Perkins D, Addington J, Miller TJ, Woods SW, Hawkins KA, Hoffman R, Lindborg S, Tohen M, Breier A (2003) The PRIME North America randomized double-blind clinical trial of olanzapine versus placebo in patients at risk of being prodromally symptomatic for psychosis. I. Study rationale and design. *Schizophr Res* **61**(1):7–18.
5. McGorry PD, Yung AR, Phillips LJ, Yuen HP, Francey S, Cosgrave EM, Germano D, Bravin J, McDonald T, Blair A, Adlard S, Jackson H (2002) Randomized controlled trial of interventions designed to reduce the risk of progression to first-episode psychosis in a clinical sample with subthreshold symptoms. *Arch Gen Psychiatry* **59**(10):921–928.
6. Lieberman JA, Stroup TS, McEvoy JP, Swartz MS, Rosenheck RA, Perkins DO, Keefe RS, Davis SM, Davis CE, Lebowitz BD, Severe J, Hsiao JK (2005) Effectiveness of antipsychotic drugs in patients with chronic schizophrenia. *N Engl J Med* **353**(12):1209–1223.

7. Jones PB, Barnes TR, Davies L, Dunn G, Lloyd H, Hayhurst KP, Murray RM, Markwick A, Lewis SW (2006) Randomized controlled trial of the effect on Quality of Life of second- vs first-generation antipsychotic drugs in schizophrenia: Cost Utility of the Latest Antipsychotic Drugs in Schizophrenia Study (CUtLASS 1). *Arch Gen Psychiatry* **63**(10):1079–1087.

8. McEvoy JP, Lieberman JA, Stroup TS, Davis SM, Meltzer HY, Rosenheck RA, Swartz MS, Perkins DO, Keefe RS, Davis CE, Severe J, Hsiao JK (2006) Effectiveness of clozapine versus olanzapine, quetiapine, and risperidone in patients with chronic schizophrenia who did not respond to prior atypical antipsychotic treatment. *Am J Psychiatry* **163**(4):600–610.

9. Lewis SW, Barnes TR, Davies L, Murray RM, Dunn G, Hayhurst KP, Markwick A, Lloyd H, Jones PB (2006) Randomized controlled trial of effect of prescription of clozapine versus other second-generation antipsychotic drugs in resistant schizophrenia. *Schizophr Bull* **32**(4):715–723.

10. Leucht S, Komossa K, Rummel-Kluge C, Corves C, Hunger H, Schmid F, Asenjo Lobos C, Schwarz S, Davis JM (2009) A meta-analysis of head-to-head comparisons of second-generation antipsychotics in the treatment of schizophrenia. *Am J Psychiatry* **166**(2):152–163.

11. Lehman AF, Lieberman JA, Dixon LB, McGlashan TH, Miller AL, Perkins DO, Kreyenbuhl J (2004) Practice guideline for the treatment of patients with schizophrenia, second edition. *Am J Psychiatry* **161**(2 Suppl):1–56.

12. Agid O, Kapur S, Arenovich T, Zipursky RB (2003) Delayed-onset hypothesis of antipsychotic action: a hypothesis tested and rejected. *Arch Gen Psychiatry* **60**(12):1228–1235.

13. Kinon BJ, Chen L, Ascher-Svanum H, Stauffer VL, Kollack-Walker S, Zhou W, Kapur S, Kane JM (2010) Early response to antipsychotic drug therapy as a clinical marker of subsequent response in the treatment of schizophrenia. *Neuropsychopharmacology* **35**(2):581–590.

14. Gaebel W, Jänner M, Frommann N, Resea S (2002) First vs multiple episode schizophrenia: twoyear outcome of intermittent and maintenance medication strategies. *Schizophr Res* **53**:145–159.

15. Hogarty GE, Schooler NR, Ulrich R, *et al.* (1979) Fluphenazine and social therapy in the aftercare of schizophrenic patients. Relapse analyses of a two-year controlled study of fluphenazine decanoate and fluphenazine hydrochloride. *Arch Gen Psychiatry* **36**:1283–1294.

16. Kane JM, Honigfeld G, Singer J, Meltzer H (1988) Clozapine for the treatment-resistant schizophrenic. A double-blind comparison with chlorpromazine. *Arch Gen Psychiatry* **45**(9):789–796.

17. Kane JM, Marder SR, Schooler NR, Wirshing WC, Umbricht D, Baker RW, Wirshing DA, Safferman A, Ganguli R, McMeniman M, Borenstein M (2001) Clozapine and haloperidol in moderately refractory schizophrenia: a 6-month randomized and double-blind comparison. *Arch Gen Psychiatry* **58**(10):965–972.

18. Freudenreich O, Henderson DC, Walsh JP, Culhane MA, Goff DC (2007) Risperidone augmentation for schizophrenia partially responsive to clozapine: a double-blind, placebo-controlled trial. *Schizophr Res* **92**(1–3):90–94.

19. Sikich L, Frazier JA, McClellan J, *et al.* (2008) Double-blind comparison of first- and secondgeneration antipsychotics in early-onset schizophrenia and schizo-affective disorder:Findings from the treatment of early-onset schizophrenia spectrum disorders (TEOSS) study. *Am J Psychiatry* **165**:1420–1431.

20. Kahn RS, Fleischhacker WW, Boter H, Davidson M, Vergouwe Y, Keet IP, Gheorghe MD, Rybakowski JK, Galderisi S, Libiger J, Hummer M, Dollfus S, Lopez-Ibor JJ, Hranov LG, Gaebel W, Peuskens J, Lindefors N, Riecher-Rossler A, Grobbee DE (2008) Effectiveness of antipsychotic drugs in first-episode schizophrenia and schizophreniform disorder: an open randomised clinical trial. *Lancet* **371**(9618):1085–1097.

21. Nussbaum A, Stroup TS (2008) Paliperidone for schizophrenia. *Cochrane Database Syst Rev* (2):CD006369

22. Meltzer HY, Bobo WV, Nuamah IF, Lane R, Hough D, Kramer M, Eerdekens M (2008) Efficacy and tolerability of oral paliperidone extended-release tablets in the treatment of acute schizophrenia: pooled data from three 6-week, placebo-controlled studies. *J Clin Psychiatry* **69**(5):817–829.

23. Arakawa R, Ito H, Takano A, Takahashi H, Morimoto T, Sassa T, Ohta K, Kato M, Okubo Y, Suhara T (2008) Dose-finding study of paliperidone ER based on striatal and extrastriatal dopamine D2 receptor occupancy in patients with schizophrenia. *Psychopharmacology* (Berl) **197**(2):229–235.

24. Potkin SG, Cohen M, Panagides J (2007) Efficacy and tolerability of asenapine in acute schizophrenia: a placebo- and risperidone-controlled trial. *J Clin Psychiatry* **68**(10):1492–1500.

25. Citrome L (2009) Iloperidone for schizophrenia: a review of the efficacy and safety profile for this newly commercialised second-generation antipsychotic. *Int J Clin Pract* **63**(8):1237–1248.

26. Fleeman N, McLeod C, Bagust A, Beale S, Boland A, Dundar Y, Jorgensen A, Payne K, Pirmohamed M, Pushpakom S, Walley T, de Warren-Penny P, Dickson R (The clinical effectiveness and cost-effectiveness of testing for cytochrome P450 polymorphisms in patients with schizophrenia treated with antipsychotics: a systematic review and economic evaluation. *Health Technol Assess*; **14**(3):1–157, iii.

27. Bertolino A, Caforio G, Blasi G, De Candia M, Latorre V, Petruzzella V, Altamura M, Nappi G, Papa S, Callicott JH, Mattay VS, Bellomo A, Scarabino T, Weinberger DR, Nardini M (2004) Interaction of COMT (Val(108/158)Met) genotype and olanzapine treatment on prefrontal cortical function in patients with schizophrenia. *Am J Psychiatry* **161**(10):1798–1805.

28. Weickert TW, Goldberg TE, Mishara A, Apud JA, Kolachana BS, Egan MF, Weinberger DR (2004) Catechol-O-methyltransferase val108/158met genotype predicts working memory response to antipsychotic medications. *Biol Psychiatry* **56**(9):677–682.

29. Gray JA, Roth BL (2007) Molecular targets for treating cognitive dysfunction in schizophrenia. *Schizophr Bull* **33**(5):1100–1119.

30. Javitt DC (2004) Glutamate as a therapeutic target in psychiatric disorders. *Mol Psychiatry* **9**(11):984–997, 979

31. Rowland LM, Astur RS, Jung RE, Bustillo JR, Lauriello J, Yeo RA (2005) Selective cognitive impairments associated with NMDA receptor blockade in humans. *Neuropsychopharmacology* **30**(3):633–639.

32. Honey GD, Honey RA, Sharar SR, Turner DC, Pomarol-Clotet E, Kumaran D, Simons JS, Hu X, Rugg MD, Bullmore ET, Fletcher PC (2005) Impairment of specific episodic memory processes by sub-psychotic doses of ketamine: the effects of levels of processing at encoding and of the subsequent retrieval task. *Psychopharmacology* (Berl) **181**(3):445–457.

33. Javitt DC (2007) Glutamate and schizophrenia: phencyclidine, N-methyl-D-aspartate receptors, and dopamine-glutamate interactions. *Int Rev Neurobiol* **78**:69–108.

34. Buchanan RW, Javitt DC, Marder SR, Schooler NR, Gold JM, McMahon RP, Heresco-Levy U, Carpenter WT (2007) The Cognitive and Negative Symptoms in Schizophrenia Trial (CONSIST): the efficacy of glutamatergic agents for negative symptoms and cognitive impairments. *Am J Psychiatry* **164**(10):1593–1602.

35. Javitt DC (2009) Glycine transport inhibitors for the treatment of schizophrenia: symptom and disease modification. *Curr Opin Drug Discov Devel* **12**(4):468–478.

36. Lane HY, Chang YC, Liu YC, Chiu CC, Tsai GE (2005) Sarcosine or D-serine add-on treatment for acute exacerbation of schizophrenia: a randomized, double-blind, placebo-controlled study. *Arch Gen Psychiatry* **62**(11):1196–1204.

37. Lane HY, Liu YC, Huang CL, Chang YC, Liau CH, Perng CH, Tsai GE (2008) Sarcosine (N-methylglycine) treatment for acute schizophrenia: a randomized, double-blind study. *Biol Psychiatry* **63**(1):9–12.

38. Goff DC, Lamberti JS, Leon AC, Green MF, Miller AL, Patel J, Manschreck T, Freudenreich O, Johnson SA (2008) A placebo-controlled add-on trial of the Ampakine, CX516, for cognitive deficits in schizophrenia. *Neuropsychopharmacology* **33**(3):465–472.

39. Harrison PJ, Lyon L, Sartorius LJ, Burnet PW, Lane TA (2008) The group II metabotropic glutamate receptor 3 (mGluR3, mGlu3, GRM3): expression, function and involvement in schizophrenia. *J Psychopharmacol* **22**(3):308–322.

40. Patil ST, Zhang L, Martenyi F, Lowe SL, Jackson KA, Andreev BV, Avedisova AS, Bardenstein LM, Gurovich IY, Morozova MA, Mosolov SN, Neznanov NG, Reznik AM, Smulevich AB, Tochilov VA, Johnson BG, Monn JA, Schoepp DD (2007) Activation of mGlu2/3 receptors as a new approach to treat schizophrenia: a randomized Phase 2 clinical trial. *Nat Med* **13**(9):1102–1107.

41. Meltzer HY, Stahl SM (1976) The dopamine hypothesis of schizophrenia: a review. *Schizophr Bull* **2**(1):19–76.

42. Carlsson A (1977) Does dopamine play a role in schizophrenia? *Psychol Med* **7**(4):583–597.

43. Abi-Dargham A, Gil R, Krystal J, Baldwin RM, Seibyl JP, Bowers M, van Dyck CH, Charney DS, Innis RB, Laruelle M (1998) Increased striatal dopamine transmission in schizophrenia: confirmation in a second cohort. *Am J Psychiatry* **155**(6):761–767.

44. Kegeles LS, Abi-Dargham A, Frankle WG, Gil R, Cooper TB, Slifstein M, Hwang DR, Huang Y, Haber SN, Laruelle M (2010) Increased synaptic dopamine function in associative regions of the striatum in schizophrenia. *Arch Gen Psychiatry* **67**(3):231–239.

45. Lodge DJ, Grace AA (2007) Aberrant hippocampal activity underlies the dopamine dysregulation in an animal model of schizophrenia. *J Neurosci* **27**(42):11424–11430.

46. Chung YC, Li Z, Dai J, Meltzer HY, Ichikawa J (2004) Clozapine increases both acetylcholine and dopamine release in rat ventral hippocampus: role of 5-HT1A receptor agonism. *Brain Res* **1023**(1):54–63.

47. De Keyser J, Ebinger G, Vauquelin G (1989) Evidence for a widespread dopaminergic innervation of the human cerebral neocortex. *Neurosci Lett* **104**(3):281–285.
48. Sawabuchi T, Suzuki S, Iwase K, Ito C, Mizuno D, Togari H, Watanabe I, Talukder SR, Chida J, Kido H (2009) Boost of mucosal secretory immunoglobulin A response by clarithromycin in paediatric influenza. *Respirology* **14**(8):1173–1179.
49. Lovenberg TW, Brewster WK, Mottola DM, Lee RC, Riggs RM, Nichols DE, Lewis MH, Mailman RB (1989) Dihydrexidine, a novel selective high potency full dopamine D-1 receptor agonist. *Eur J Pharmacol* **166**(1):111–113.
50. Knoerzer TA, Nichols DE, Brewster WK, Watts VJ, Mottola D, Mailman RB (1994) Dopaminergic benzo(a)phenanthridines: resolution and pharmacological evaluation of the enantiomers of dihydrexidine, the full efficacy D1 dopamine receptor agonist. *J Med Chem* **37**(15):2453–2460.
51. Mottola DM, Brewster WK, Cook LL, Nichols DE, Mailman RB (1992) Dihydrexidine, a novel full efficacy D1 dopamine receptor agonist. *J Pharmacol Exp Ther* **262**(1):383–393.
52. Castner SA, Williams GV, Goldman-Rakic PS (2000) Reversal of antipsychotic-induced working memory deficits by short-term dopamine D1 receptor stimulation. *Science* **287**(5460):2020–2022.
53. Gogos JA, Morgan M, Luine V, Santha M, Ogawa S, Pfaff D, Karayiorgou M (1998) Catechol-O-methyltransferase-deficient mice exhibit sexually dimorphic changes in catecholamine levels and behavior. *Proc Natl Acad Sci U S A* **95**(17):9991–9996.
54. Liljequist R, Haapalinna A, Ahlander M, Li YH, Mannisto PT (1997) Catechol O-methyltransferase inhibitor tolcapone has minor influence on performance in experimental memory models in rats. *Behav Brain Res* **82**(2):195–202.
55. Cummings JL (2000) Cholinesterase inhibitors: A new class of psychotropic compounds. *Am J Psychiatry* **157**(1):4–15.
56. Buchanan RW, Summerfelt A, Tek C, Gold J (2003) An open-labeled trial of adjunctive donepezil for cognitive impairments in patients with schizophrenia. *Schizophr Res* **59**(1):29–33.
57. Lenzi A, Maltinti E, Poggi E, Fabrizio L, Coli E (2003) Effects of rivastigmine on cognitive function and quality of life in patients with schizophrenia. *Clin Neuropharmacol* **26**(6):317–321.
58. Keefe RS, Bilder RM, Davis SM, Harvey PD, Palmer BW, Gold JM, Meltzer HY, Green MF, Capuano G, Stroup TS, McEvoy JP, Swartz MS, Rosenheck RA, Perkins DO, Davis CE, Hsiao JK, Lieberman JA (2007) Neurocognitive effects of antipsychotic medications in patients with chronic schizophrenia in the CATIE Trial. *Arch Gen Psychiatry* **64**(6):633–647.
59. Sharma T, Reed C, Aasen I, Kumari V (2006) Cognitive effects of adjunctive 24-weeks Rivastigmine treatment to antipsychotics in schizophrenia: a randomized, placebo-controlled, double-blind investigation. *Schizophr Res* **85**(1–3):73–83.
60. Buchanan RW, Conley RR, Dickinson D, Ball MP, Feldman S, Gold JM, McMahon RP (2008) Galantamine for the treatment of cognitive impairments in people with schizophrenia. *Am J Psychiatry* **165**(1):82–89.
61. Schilstrom B, Ivanov VB, Wiker C, Svensson TH (2007) Galantamine enhances dopaminergic neurotransmission in vivo via allosteric potentiation of nicotinic acetylcholine receptors. *Neuropsychopharmacology* **32**(1):43–53.

62. Freedman R, Olincy A, Buchanan RW, Harris JG, Gold JM, Johnson L, Allensworth D, Guzman-Bonilla A, Clement B, Ball MP, Kutnick J, Pender V, Martin LF, Stevens KE, Wagner BD, Zerbe GO, Soti F, Kem WR (2008) Initial phase 2 trial of a nicotinic agonist in schizophrenia. *Am J Psychiatry* **165**(8):1040–1047.

63. Watanabe T, Taguchi Y, Hayashi H, Tanaka J, Shiosaka S, Tohyama M (1983) Evidence for the presence of a histaminergic neuron system in the rat brain: an imunohistochemical analysis. *Neuroscience Letter* **39**:249–254.

64. Panula P, Revuelta AV, Cheney DL, Wu JY, Costa E (1984) An immunohistochemical study on the location of GABAergic neurons in rat septum. *J Comp Neurol* **222**(1):69–80.

65. Brown RE, Stevens DR, Haas HL (2001) The physiology of brain histamine. *Prog Neurobiol* **63**(6):637–672.

66. Parson M, Ganellin C (2006) Histamine and its receptors. *British Journal of Pharmacology* **147**:s127–s132.

67. Ito C (2009) Histamine H3-receptor inverse agonists as novel antipsychotics. *Cent Nerv Syst Agents Med Chem* **9**(2):132–136.

68. Schlicker E, Malinowska B, Kathmann M, Gothert M (1994) Modulation of neurotransmitter release via histamine H3 heteroreceptors. *Fundam Clin Pharmacol* **8**(2):128–137.

69. Esbenshade T, Bowman K, Bitner R, Strakhova M, Cowart M, Brioni J (2008) The histamine H3 receptor: an attractive target for the treatment of cognitive disorders. *British Journal of Pharmacology* **154**:1166–1181.

70. Ligneau X, Landais L, Perrin D, Piriou J, Uguen M, Denis E, Robert P, Parmentier R, Anaclet C, Lin JS, Burban A, Arrang JM, Schwartz JC (2007) Brain histamine and schizophrenia: potential therapeutic applications of H3-receptor inverse agonists studied with BF2. 649. *Biochem Pharmacol* **73**(8):1215–1224.

CHAPTER 7

Cognitive-behavioural interventions

Suzanne Jolley and Philippa Garety

Academic affiliation: King's College London, Institute of Psychiatry, Department of Psychology.

Information Box - Cognitive Behavioural Therapy for Psychosis (CBTp)

- CBTp draws on normative models of psychological functioning to make sense of psychosis and identify areas for intervention
- Interventions centre around change in appraisal and behaviour, often focused on the impact of experiences, rather than the veracity of the experience itself
- There is consistent evidence for effectiveness over the last 20 years, but further development is needed
- Identifying and effectively changing mechanisms and dissemination of interventions are the current challenges

---

INTRODUCTION

The last 20 years have seen cognitive behavioural interventions for schizophrenia spectrum psychosis (CBTp) progress from innovation to international recommendation [1–4]. Therapy techniques have developed both hand in hand with advances in the psychological understanding of psychosis, and by adapting techniques from cognitive approaches to other disorders. Most recently, cognitive models have begun to embrace biological factors, as the complex interplay between the person and the environment becomes more clearly understood. However, the heterogeneity of presentation in psychosis means that treatment approaches are similarly diverse, and the challenge currently is the distillation of effective techniques for intervening

---

Schizophrenia: Current Science and Clinical Practice, First Edition. Edited by Wolfgang Gaebel.
© 2011 John Wiley & Sons, Ltd. Published 2011 by John Wiley & Sons, Ltd.

with different aspects of the disorder, and the establishment of a clearer under-standing of the mechanisms by which these techniques work in order to refine and improve therapy.

THE DEVELOPMENT OF COGNITIVE BEHAVIOURAL APPROACHES TO SCHIZOPHRENIA-SPECTRUM PSYCHOSIS

With the exception of a small number of case studies and case series [5–7], cogni-tive therapy approaches were not systematically applied to psychosis until the late 1980s/early 1990s. The early studies focused primarily on people with delusions and evaluated reappraisal techniques, particularly examination of the evidence for beliefs [8–10], adoption of a normalising approach to psychotic experiences [11], and behavioural problem solving and coping strategy based interventions [12]. Further advances drew more heavily on psychological research into psy-chosis. Increased understanding of the roles of affect (reviewed in Freeman and Garety [13]), life events [14], and particular cognitive biases (reviewed in Garety and Freeman [15]) in the onset and maintenance of psychosis led to the devel-opment of more complex approaches, designed to target psychotic symptoms, associated affect and schematic beliefs. Techniques developed to treat depression [16] were adapted to take account of the complexity and heterogeneity of the difficulties facing people with psychosis, with particular attention on engagement issues [10]. Centres of excellence developed in London/East Anglia; Birming-ham, Manchester, Newcastle and Southampton, with several groups developing treatment manuals emphasising particular aspects of the work [17–19]. A number of successful randomised controlled treatment trials followed, targeting persist-ing positive symptoms of psychosis [20–23]. Attempts to integrate findings from psychological research and from these effective treatment approaches led to the subsequent publication of a number of cognitive models of psychosis, emphasising the roles of biopsychosocial vulnerability, life events, schematic beliefs, anomalous experiences, affective changes, appraisal and behaviour in the development of psy-chosis [24–27]. Over the last 10 years there has been increasing interest in the development of cognitive models and cognitive behavioural approaches interna-tionally, in centres across Europe and the US, encompassing research into psycho-logical mechanisms, development and evaluation of treatment approaches, and the dissemination and wider implementation of treatment.

COGNITIVE BEHAVIOURAL MODELS OF PSYCHOSIS

Biopsychosocial vulnerability

Cognitive models of psychosis adopt a stress-vulnerability stance [28,29], hypothesising a multifactorial vulnerability comprising social, biological and psychological factors with life events acting as triggering stressors [25,30,31]. Within cognitive models, vulnerability factors are assumed to be continuously distributed in the general population and to represent individual differences rather than deficits or disorders. The notion of a continuum of vulnerability to psychosis predates the development of cognitive approaches, and the evidence that core factors of psychotic symptomatology, namely positive symptoms, negative symptoms, and cognitive disorganisation [32] can be identified in attenuated form in the general population, is now powerful, with prevalence estimates varying from 1% to over 30% in nonclinical samples, depending on the experiences being assessed and the measures used [33,34]. These characteristics are seen as arising from individual differences in nervous system organisation, resulting from polygenetic and environmental interactions [35–38,30] and might also give rise to characteristic patterns of neuropsychological performance, which have been demonstrated to be present in nonclinical groups including relatives of people with psychosis [39] and high schizotypes [34], suggesting a degree of continuous distribution. The individual differences are viewed as contributing to a potential vulnerability to developing psychosis but as longitudinal studies indicate that only between 5 and 25% of people with low level symptomatology go on to develop psychosis [33], the correspondence is not high, and indicates multiple, commonly occurring potential vulnerability factors and stressors, which only relatively rarely combine to result in the development of psychosis [40].

Life events and schematic beliefs

The role of life events in the onset of psychosis, in relapse and in exacerbating existing symptomatology [14,41] is now well established. Traumatic events and victimisation events appear particularly significant [42] and recent research suggests that adverse life events contribute cumulatively to the development of psychosis [43]. Other social factors such as urban living [44] and migration [45,46] have been associated with an increased incidence of psychosis. Chronic social disadvantage, adversity and isolation have been considered as the common pathway between these factors and life events [47]. Van Os and colleagues [38,48] have highlighted a mechanism of stress sensitivity through which vulnerability to future stressors is determined by the early interplay of genes and stressful life events. Within cognitive models of psychosis, these environmental factors are also considered to contribute to the development of schematic beliefs [49]. In all cognitive models of mental health problems, early learning through life experiences is considered to shape schematic beliefs and assumptions about the self, the world and other people [50]. Such beliefs are hypothesised to influence the direction of attention; bias the interpretation of material, both that retrieved from memory and new material; and to influence behavioural strategies [51]. Schematic beliefs have only recently been examined in psychosis, but initial findings suggest that they are congruent with psychotic symptomatology, with persecutory beliefs charac-terised by generally negative underlying beliefs about both self and others, and grandiose beliefs characterised by generally positive views of self [52,53]. Except-ing grandiosity, beliefs about the self are usually negative in people with psychosis [54,55] and form an important target for intervention [56,10,57].

The role of affect

Alongside the notion that psychotic symptoms themselves can be conceptualised as part of normal experiences and cognition, has been the developing understanding of the role of affect in psychosis. In contrast to the early separation of neurosis and psychosis [58,59], more recent work emphasises affect in both the development and maintenance of psychosis, and as a response to a psychotic episode [13,60,61]. Of particular interest for cognitive models of psychosis is the identification of cogni-tive processes and behaviours common to both psychosis and affective disorders, as these mechanisms provide routes both to formulating and to intervening with diffi-culties. The focus has been primarily on trauma, depression and anxiety processes.

A history of trauma, and co-morbid post-traumatic symptomatology, are com-mon in psychosis [62]. Trauma reactions have been considered both as a result of psychosis [63] and as implicated in the onset of psychosis [64–66]. In terms of shared mechanisms, trauma-related intrusions and flashbacks, avoidance, hyper-arousal, trauma-influenced schematic beliefs and the impact of trauma on depth of processing have all been considered as contributory to the development and maintenance of psychotic symptomatology [64,67–71].

Depression has been examined as a reaction to psychosis, with appraisals of shame, entrapment, loss and self-blame receiving particular attention [72]. Cog-nitive factors associated with depression in psychosis have not been much inves-tigated in relation to positive symptoms, but recent work on negative symptoms draws heavily on models of depression, emphasising the role of beliefs about failure [73,74].

There is significant co-morbidity in psychosis across the anxiety spectrum [75]. Freeman [76] has examined anxiety in relation to persecutory beliefs, identifying roles for avoidance and safety behaviours [77]; worry processes [78–80] and social evaluative concerns [81]. Birchwood and colleagues have also considered social anxiety as a reaction to psychosis associated with beliefs about the evaluation of oneself by others, following a psychotic episode [82].

The research suggests that the majority of people with psychosis, even those with grandiose presentations, present with explicit affect congruent with their psychotic experiences, indicating potential benefit from a direct psychotherapeutic approach to associated affect in psychosis [53,83–85]. There is little evidence for 'underlying' or 'defensive' incongruent negative affective processes, concurrent with explicit positive or neutral affect, although this might apply in a minority of cases [55,76].

Most recently, specific interventions have been designed to target affective processes in psychosis including worry in people with persecutory beliefs [86], social anxiety [87,88], particularly in early psychosis [89] and trauma in people with severe mental illness [90] and with psychosis [91]. Outcomes suggest that affective processes can be successfully targeted in people with psychosis, and that change in affective processes can have a positive impact on psychotic symptomatology [86].

The central role of appraisal

Within cognitive models, the onset of psychosis is seen as a result of the conjunction of biopsychosocial vulnerability factors, triggering life events and emotional changes. In most cases, there is also an exacerbation of pre-existing unusual perceptual experiences or their occurrence de novo. However, it is the *appraisal* of the combined life events, affective changes and anomalous experiences which determines whether these changes result in psychosis. While Morrison [26] emphasises the personal and sociocultural unacceptability of the appraisal, Garety and colleagues [24,25] consider an appraisal of experiences as externally caused, personally relevant and usually threatening to be central (see Figure 7.1). Freeman [27], with specific reference to persecutory delusions, describes a similar appraisal pattern, but emphasises the role of the discomfort of 'not knowing' and a process of searching for meaning in order to reduce uncertainty-induced anxiety.

Evidence is accruing to support the causal role of appraisal in the development and maintenance of psychosis. Morrison and colleagues have examined metacognitive beliefs relating to the unacceptability of thought content [92] and found some

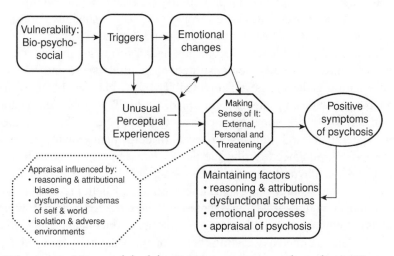

Figure 7.1 A cognitive model of the positive symptoms of psychosis (Garety *et al.*, 2001; 2007)

evidence for more negative appraisals in clinical and at-risk groups. Brett *et al.* [93] investigated appraisals of anomalous experience in clinical and non-clinical groups and found that the clinical group was more likely to consider the experiences to be negative and distressing, to attribute them to an external agency, and to adopt cognitive control and avoidance coping strategies. Birchwood and colleagues have identified particular appraisals concerning the perceived power, malevolence, intrusiveness and controllability of voices driving distress and impairment of functioning [94–96] and change in these appraisals as key to improvement in voices [97].

Reasoning biases

In cognitive models, unhelpful appraisals are viewed as arising not solely from life events, but also from biases in reasoning processes. Therefore, one mechanism for changing distressing or dysfunctional construals of experiences is to develop more impartial appraisals by recognizing and compensating for reasoning biases. Multiple factors are hypothesised to impact on appraisal in both clinical and nonclinical groups, including pre-existing beliefs, affective state, motivational factors and cognitive ability and functioning. In the general population, numerous normative cognitive heuristics and characteristic deviations from logic in human information processing have been identified [98–102]. While similar biases have been demonstrated to operate in people with psychosis [103], there is currently no evidence to suggest that they are more common in people with psychosis [104] than in the general population. Some variables relating to information processing style have, however, been hypothesised to be more pronounced in people with psychosis. Three biases have been argued to be particularly characteristic of, but not exclusive to, people with psychosis. These are the jumping to conclusions data-gathering bias (JTC), attributional biases and theory of mind deficits [15,76].

The JTC bias is a tendency to consider less information before reaching a decision. The bias is usually demonstrated on neutral tasks, and applies only when information gathering is self-directed. The JTC bias has been consistently found in people with current delusions [76], with about 50% demonstrating a bias compared to 10% of nonclinical controls. JTC appears to be associated with delusions specifically and with higher levels of delusional conviction [105–108] and to be more pronounced during the acute state, but still present on recovery [109]. JTC has been hypothesised to be associated with anxiety driven processing [110,111] and there is some empirical support for this. Ellett, Freeman and Garety [112] reported an increase in JTC associated with increased anxiety following a trip down a busy street in people with persecutory beliefs. Lincoln and colleagues have also recently demonstrated associations between experimentally induced increases in anxiety, JTC and paranoid ideation [113]. Demonstrations of the presence of JTC in nonclinical groups, increasing with delusion proneness [114,115] and in at risk groups [116] implicate the bias in the development of delusions as well as the maintenance of established beliefs. The JTC bias has not yet been experimentally investigated with delusion relevant material, but has been shown to be associated with delusional conviction, mediated by belief flexibility, or willingness to consider the possibility that one is mistaken [106], and with being able to generate an alternative to the delusional belief [117].

Attributional style is the tendency to explain events in a particular way and was initially investigated in the study of depression as a cognitive representation of learned helpless [118]. There has been discussion over its status as a state or trait phenomenon [119] and whether it is associated with clinical change [120] in depression. In psychosis, it has been argued that there is a bias towards blaming others for negative events particularly associated with persecutory beliefs, however, the evidence for this has been mixed [76] and affective processes appear to be a strong influence. Depression moderates an externalising attributional style [121] and recent studies suggest the presence of a bias only in more specific subgroups of people with persecutory beliefs such as those with concurrent grandiose beliefs [122] and those who see their persecution as undeserved [123].

Research interest has also recently focused on deficits in social cognition in schizophrenia [124] and particularly impaired mentalising ability (poor theory of mind, ToM) as a possible factor implicated in both the development [125] and maintenance [126] of persecutory beliefs.

Clinically, careful assessment of appraisal and information gathering processes is required to ascertain which biases are contributing to a particular individual's difficulties. Although addressing biased appraisals is a key component of CBTp approaches, very few studies have reported on the specific efficacy of techniques designed to change cognitive processes. Kinderman and Bentall [127] report a successful attributional style intervention with a single case. Moritz and colleagues have developed a metacognitive training designed to modify multiple reasoning biases in a group format [128]. A recent study, adapting some of this material, has shown that it is possible to intervene with people with delusions to correct the tendency to JTC and improve data gathering, with some indications that this may have a direct beneficial effect on reducing delusional conviction [129].

Anomalous experiences

Appraisal processes are also hypothesised to be influenced by unusual perceptual experiences. Systematic research into the role of anomalous experiences in the development of delusions has been limited [76,130] but unusual experiences have been found to be the most commonly cited evidence for delusional beliefs [117] and, clinically, continued unusual experiences often contribute to the persistence of beliefs. However, cognitive models allow for the development of psychosis without anomalous experiences [24,25], a pathway which is clinically reported although not rigorously demonstrated [130]. In support of this, people with delusions without hallucinations have been found to experience similar levels of anomalous experience to a non-clinical group [130]. Thus, in CBTp, while assessing and understanding the role of anomalous experiences is important, it is distressing appraisals of these experiences which are targeted for change, rather than the frequency of occurrence.

The role of behaviour

A small but growing literature supports the role of behaviour in maintaining both hallucinations and delusions. Trower, Birchwood and colleagues highlight the role of compliance responses as safety behaviours in response to command hallucinations, preventing learning that feared consequences will not arise [97]. Morrison and colleagues similarly emphasise the role of avoidance strategies in response to hearing voices, thus preventing learning that the experience is itself innocuous [26]. Delusions are associated with a number of protective behaviours [131], and 'safety behaviours' designed to protect the person from threat are particularly found with persecutory delusions [77]. Behaviour change is a common focus of intervention and often progresses hand in hand with appraisal change.

Insight and illness appraisals

Appraisals of the developing problem and understanding of the implications of this also form an important target for therapy. Recognition of illness, a core aspect of most measures of insight, has mixed effects on adjustment and outcome [132,133] depending on the meaning of insight to the person, and the coping strategies (such as taking medication) it facilitates. Appraisals of illness/problems resulting in a decreased sense of personal blame [49,134] and higher perceived controllability of difficulties [135] are associated with better outcome. Appraisals resulting in a strong sense of engulfment and loss are associated with increased depression [136]. Most recently, illness perception measures have been adapted from physical healthcare for use with people with psychosis [137–140] and studies indicate that perceptions of greater consequences of difficulties, longer duration of problems and a reduced sense of control or hope for cure, are reliably associated with poorer affective adjustment [138,141]. This means that there should be a focus in therapy on developing an adaptive view of difficulties, which allows a sense of personal control and hope of improvement, without inculcating a sense of self-blame or loss and without increasing the sense of negative impact on the person's life. This might or might not involve ideas about illness – it is the implied meaning of the understanding to the individual which is important.

COGNITIVE BEHAVIOURAL THERAPY IN SCHIZOPHRENIA

Cognitive behavioural therapeutic approaches to psychosis (CBTp) draw on this body of work to develop individualised formulations of psychosis and to identify areas to target for intervention. While heterogeneous, the approaches hold in common basic tenets [142] (see Table 7.1). The first is an explicit focus directly on what the client presents as the source of distress, and what they would like to change. Client and therapist engage together in an actively collaborative approach to try to reduce distress and work towards the client's goals. This often involves a particular way of working with client beliefs which can counter the therapist's worldview. An open mindedness towards these beliefs as possibilities, and empathy with the difficulties they engender is essential to a CBTp approach.

Mental health staff and novice CBTp therapists often express discomfort with this approach, feeling the need to point out to clients in a number of more or less subtle ways that they are wrong – for example by immediately expressing counter arguments or alternatives, by requesting the evidence or justification for a particular view, by referring to experiences and beliefs as 'illness' (when this is not the view held by the client), and by 'watering down' the client's report (for example, using language like 'felt', 'thought' rather than 'experienced', 'knew'). While each of these might have a useful place in a collaborative approach adopted later in therapy, their application early on without a collaboratively agreed focus jeopardises engagement.

The second common thread is that of normalisation. The evidence base demonstrates that clients' beliefs and experiences are understandable through normal psychological processes. The therapeutic stance emphasises the understandability of the client's position by drawing on the roles of vulnerability factors, life events, affect, unusual experiences, appraisal and behaviour. Each of these factors will contribute to particular problems in a different way for each individual client – the

Table 7.1 Core components of CBTp interventions

Core components of CBTp interventions (Summarised from Morrison & Barratt, 2010)
Explicit, collaborative goal focus
Engagement and therapeutic style
Normalisation
Individualised formulation based on cognitive model
Appraisal and behaviour targeted for change
Change occurs through new learning (facilitated through monitoring, guided discovery, testing out)
Strategies for change implemented both within and outside sessions
Aim to reduce distress and improve quality of life

task of the therapist is to build a tailored understanding, based on careful and detailed assessment, of the factors which are maintaining distress and preventing the client progressing in the way they would wish. A very simple understanding or formulation might be used early on in therapy, which can be developed as the work progresses [143]. Figures 7.2 and 7.3 in the illustrative case provide an example of this approach. Fundamental to the formulation process is the link to the client's goals and the identification of strategies for change – formulation alone, particularly complex, developmental formulation, is useful for therapists but can be perceived as unhelpful by clients [144,145]. Finally, as the essence of all CBT approaches, is the joint emphasis on appraisal and behaviour as the key to understanding both the development and persistence of the problem. Making changes in behaviour and appraisal, through new learning, remains the main tool of change in CBTp. Central to the acquisition of new learning is the concept of homework – as a session comprises a very small part of a single day, the potential for learning is maximised by the therapist and client developing between session activities to gather new information or to reinforce and progress new ideas. The use of homework assignments has been associated with improved outcome in CBTp [90,146] and greater satisfaction with therapy [147].

Box 7.1   An illustrative case example – John*

John was worried that he was going to be attacked in the street (the onset of his difficulties followed an actual assault). On assessment, he described being absolutely certain that his attackers were still out there and very likely to attack him. As he had not really seen the faces of the men who attacked him, he felt that anybody of similar height and build might be them, and might be liable to attack him. He described a number of 'near misses', where individuals had looked very aggressive (he could tell this by the way they walked and whether they looked at him), or had made what he felt were aggressive gestures towards him, but he had avoided incident by going into a shop, or running home. He found it very difficult to leave his flat, and felt like a failure for having no job, relationship or children. He spent a lot of time thinking about this, feeling angry about the attack and his own reactions to it. The goals John initially stated were to get a job and find a partner. These were carefully broken down into steps to identify a suitable target for a time limited therapy – John agreed that a good first step would be to be able to get out of his flat more easily, to use the bus, and to take up some of the activities that he used to enjoy doing indoors.

John was initially very sensitive to any suggestion that part of the difficulties might be his perception of what was happening. He had a history of disengagement with mental health services and poor relationships with mental health professionals because they thought he was 'paranoid'. Early formulations with John therefore focused mainly on how the difficulties were affecting him. He was able to see how lack of activity and rumination fuelled his low mood. He was also able to see how rumination and avoidance made his worry about being attacked worse. This led to activity scheduling (reading, cooking, watching movies and websurfing at home were particularly enjoyable activities); graded exposure to going out, starting off with a trip out with the therapist, and gradually building up the time he spent outside. The initial formulation shared with John is illustrated in Figure 7.2.

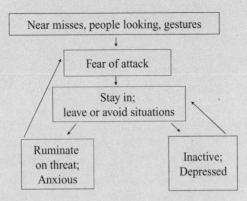

Figure 7.2 John - early (coping) formulation

The trips out which John did manage were used to further assess the threat of attack. The criteria John used to determine the risk of attack with each person were identified, and using guided discovery, John was able to note that not everyone was a risk, and that his judgements about risk varied depending on how anxious he felt. Reminding himself that his own mood state might exaggerate his concern allowed him to slow down enough when he was uncertain, to check people out more to see whether he really needed to remove himself from the situation. John also became aware of his tendency to be 'on guard' and on the lookout for attack. He could see that while this kept him safe, and was understandable given his adverse experience, it could also make him 'jumpier' and less able to get out. He experimented with not immediately trusting his 'instinct' for threat, and taking an extra moment to check situations out. This more complex formulation developed with John is illustrated in Figure 7.3.

Gradually John came to an alternative view, that although his attackers had not been imprisoned, and were likely to still be alive, the chances of them being where he was at any given time were not that high. During further discussion of the likelihood of them attacking him again even if they did see him, John noted that as he had not seen their faces, it was possible they had not

(continued)

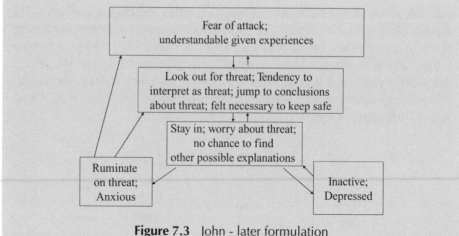

Figure 7.3   John - later formulation

seen his, and therefore that it was a random attack rather than deliberate and personally directed. Although he did not hold this view with much conviction, the possibility did make him feel a bit safer, and allowed him to increase the amount of time he spent outside.

> —(*John is an amalgamation of two genuine clinical cases, with biographical and clinical features changed to protect anonymity)

PSYCHOTHERAPY IN SCHIZOPHRENIA: MORE THAN UNSPECIFIC LEARNING?

The basic tenets of cognitive behavioural approaches shape the structure of therapy and the interventions adopted. Alongside engagement, interventions focus on appraisals of life events, anomalous experience, affective change, and of the problem itself as it develops. Emotional and behavioural reactions, and their role in maintaining difficulties are carefully assessed, and also targeted for change. Concurrent affective and anxiety disorders are addressed using CBT approaches adapted to take account of the presence of anomalous experiences and unusual, strongly held beliefs.

In the early stages, strategies for coping with distressing symptoms, or with their consequences (such as amotivation and avoidance) are identified and tested out by the client. Variation in symptomatology, especially when contingent on the client's behaviour, can be used to moderate catastrophic appraisals about experiences – particularly hopelessness and powerlessness. More detailed assessment of experiences and beliefs continues alongside this process – with the emphasis on the therapist understanding what is maintaining the client's difficulties, and sharing this with the client to reach an agreed model of the problem or formulation. Often this will involve in vivo assessment – for example walking down the street with a client or getting on the bus, so they can point out what they are noticing and how they are interpreting this. Cognitive change is gently facilitated through wondering together with the client about possible exceptions and alternatives for specific situations (was *everybody* intent on harming you when you went to the shop; was there any other reason why that particular person in the shop might have looked at you on that occasion), generating possible alternative explanations and gradually building up to testing out particular fears. The emphasis is on reducing distress and meeting the client's goals, rather than the necessity of major belief change. A minor change to a belief ('it is not quite as unsafe as I thought') can permit sufficient behaviour change to allow the client to meet their goals.

The generation of acceptable alternative beliefs, rather than simply inculcating doubt, appears crucial, and doubt in the absence of plausible alternatives is associated with lower self-esteem [117]. Less catastrophic appraisals of the impact of experiences, and alternative explanations for particular instances are identified in the early stages of CBTp. During the course of therapy, formulations are developed collaboratively with the client and can themselves provide alternative explanations. For example, identifying that the client has learnt to be sensitive to threat because of being in a number of threatening situations throughout their life, might lead to the alternative explanation for perceived threat 'I was just being over-alert'. Later in therapy, work on modifying and compensating for characteristic thinking patterns helps address the possibility of future relapse and maintaining positive changes in the face of new stressors.

COMBINING PSYCHOTHERAPY AND PHARMACOTHERAPY

CBTp is usually delivered alongside medication, and the majority of outcome studies address its effectiveness in combination with medication [148]. The evidence that the addition of CBTp to treatment with medication results in improved outcomes is strong [149,150] and includes both studies showing effects of CBTp where improvement on a regime including medication was already occurring [22,151] and those showing improvement in participants whose symptoms had not responded to medication [10,12,20,21,23,152–154]. A recent pilot study indicates change resulting from CBTp even in a group resistant to clozapine [155]. There is very little evidence concerning the effectiveness of CBT without medication. However, as non-adherence to medication regimes, ranging from cessation of all medication to variation of dose or occasional forgetting, is estimated to be high in people with psychosis [156], all CBTp trials to date are likely to include some participants who do not take medication. Two small case series provide preliminary evidence for effectiveness in these circumstances [157,158].

It is not yet clear from the literature how CBTp and medication work together. There is no good evidence that CBTp increases medication adherence, even where this is a target of therapy [2]. Further, medication has not been found to predict outcome in CBT studies [159] and medication use tends not to differ between treatment groups across trials [160]. A number of neurophysiological models of psychosis have outlined the role of dopamine in driving anomalies of experience and particularly salient experiences [161,162]. Antipsychotic medication is hypothesised to act to reduce hyperdopaminergia and thus to reduce aberrant salience [163,164]. However, anomalies of experience are not the only factor contributing to belief maintenance, and the more complex, heterogeneous elements of cognitive behavioural models – specific appraisals and patterns of behaviour – are not likely to change in response to simple neurochemical changes, particularly where there is evidence implicating these as vulnerability factors, or trait phenomena. Nevertheless, it is possible that some of the additional factors influencing appraisal and behaviour are responsive to medication. There has been some recent evidence that the JTC bias changes following medication [165] with a dose response relationship, but the effect was found with salient material only, suggesting a role of affect rather than purely cognitive processes. A similar investigation of attributional style found that an internalising attributional style mediated poorer outcome in response to medication, but there was little impact of antipsychotic medication on attributional style [166]. It is plausible that medication could act on other contributory factors such as reactivity to stress, and on associated affective difficulties, which would, in turn, impact on cognitive processes. This requires carefully tailored and individualised prescribing in much the same way as psychological therapies are tailored, and is an area for further development. The evidence to date indicates that a combination of pharmacotherapy and psychological therapy is likely to be most effective, and that synergy in the effects of medication and CBTp on anomalous experiences and possibly reasoning biases could be harnessed and specifically addressed in therapy.

EFFICACY OF COGNITIVE BEHAVIOURAL THERAPY FOR PSYCHOSIS (CBTp)

Since the early RCTs focusing on reducing distress for people with medication resistant positive symptoms, approaches have diversified and more recent studies have evaluated the effectiveness of CBTp for different stages of the illness [for example, 167,168] including at risk mental states [169,170]; delivered in group or individual formats [for example, 171]; and delivered by nonexpert therapists [172]. The range of outcomes has also broadened to include relapse reduction [160,173], social functioning [173,167], and associated affective difficulties [89,91]. Findings are summarised in Table 7.2.

A series of metaanalyses has confirmed an overall small but significant positive impact [174–179]. The most recent UK NICE guideline review included 31 controlled trials, and found improvements in frequency and duration of hospitalisation,

Table 7.2 Summary of CBTp outcome analyses

	Subgroups investigated	Summary of findings
1. Target group	At-risk mental state (ARMS), early psychosis (first episode), acute psychosis, persisting symptoms	Best evidence for persisting symptoms group, but acceptable at any stage including acute inpatient (NICE, 2009; Wykes *et al.*, 2008). Emerging evidence for intervention with ARMS - suggestion that CBTp reduces transition in the short term; effects reduced at follow-up. (Morrison *et al.*, 2004, 2007).
2. Key outcome	Psychotic symptoms, social functioning, relapse, affective disturbance	Rehospitalisation reduced in number and length; reduction in overall symptoms; stronger effects for hallucinations and negative symptoms, mixed for delusions. Improved mood and functioning (NICE, 2009; Wykes *et al.*, 2008).
3. Mode of delivery	Group vs. individual; expert therapist vs. brief training	Individual delivery favoured (NICE, 2009). Insufficient data on required therapist training (NICE, 2009; Wykes *et al.*, 2008)
4. Control group	Other active therapy; standard care; non-standard care	Improvements found with CBT compared to any control group; but effects stronger in comparison to standard care (NICE, 2009; Tarrier & Wykes, 2004).

psychotic symptoms, depression, negative symptoms and social functioning. The economic evaluation found that CBTp is cost effective, largely based on the reductions in hospital stays [2]. Since then, Haddock *et al.* [180] have found advantages for CBT over social activity in reducing violent behaviour and delusions, Jackson *et al.* [91] have shown reductions in post-traumatic symptomatology in an early psychosis group, but no changes in depression and self esteem and Fowler *et al.* [89] have demonstrated increases in activity in a nonaffective early psychosis subgroup. Subgroup analyses within the NICE metaanalyses indicated greater effects in the persisting symptoms group compared to acute and first episode groups, and particularly for hallucinations rather than delusions. Indirect evidence supported delivery on an individual basis, over at least 16 sessions [2] (see Table 7.3).

Table 7.3 National Institute of Clinical Excellence UK CBTp recommendations

NICE (UK) CBTp recommendations (2009)	
Target group	Offer to all people with schizophrenia
Mode of delivery	Individual
Duration	At least 16 sessions
Treatment emphasis	Manual-based; approach tested in outcome trial
Components of CBTp	• Monitoring and formulating thought, feeling, behaviour links with respect to symptoms and/or functioning • Re-evaluation of experiences/appraisals • Improving coping • Reducing distress • Improving functioning
Training required	Clinical psychologists or other accredited psychological therapist most common trial therapists
Supervision	Two thirds of trials included regular clinical supervision
Areas requiring further research	• Effect of different duration and session numbers • Training required for CBTp therapists • Core competencies required to deliver CBTp

Despite the overall positive findings, effect sizes are characteristically small [174], and change is heterogeneous and occurs for a subgroup of clients only. Trials have been criticised for their methodology, particularly maintaining blind assessments and loss of follow-up data, and effect sizes are smaller in the most methodologically robust studies (effect size of 0.2 reported by Wykes *et al.* [174]). Comparison treatments vary from treatment as usual [160] to control psychotherapeutic approaches, such as 'befriending' [23]; supportive counseling [151]; or social activity [180]. Greater effects are found in comparison to treatment as usual [2] and while these studies can be criticised for failing to control for nonspecific aspects of therapy, such as time spent talking with a professional, 'control' therapies can often have unexpectedly positive effects [23], the reasons for which are not yet well understood.

There is a clear need to improve the effectiveness of CBTp, but the existing evidence base permits only limited conclusions about the specific improvements required. Much of the evidence to date concerns complex composite CBT approaches for heterogeneous groups of patients – attempting to address psychotic symptoms, affective disturbance, schemas, social functioning and relapse, and measuring multiple outcomes. This approach is necessary given the selection of participants for most trials by a broad diagnostic group rather than for particular problems, but limits any assessment of what works for whom and potentially masks what is and what is not being dealt with effectively in therapy.

In terms of therapy content, although most studies draw on a manualised approach, adherence to the approach is rarely comprehensively assessed, over and above basic competence checks, and the actual content of the therapy received by each individual, within the broad approach adopted, tends not to be specified. Wykes *et al.* [174] reported a rough analysis of treatment emphasis – comparing primarily behavioural approaches with historical/schema-focused interventions, and found an advantage for more behavioural interventions. Rollinson *et al.* [181] reported a more careful assessment of therapy content, but this has not yet been examined in relation to outcome or predictors of outcome. Outcome measurement in itself is a difficulty: the goals of CBTp should be highly individualised (for example, getting to the shop on my own twice a week or feeling less distressed when hallucinating in social situations) and good outcomes in terms of personal goals will not necessarily be evident on standardised measures, particularly not those designed to measure global symptom reduction [182].

Factors identified as influencing outcome in CBTp trials vary between studies [148] and between indices of outcome [183]. They include belief flexibility [184]; insight and higher levels of symptomatology [159]; gender and lower levels of conviction [185]. Therapeutic alliance has also been associated with outcome, most recently in the Socrates trial [186], but with client ratings rather than therapist ratings showing a relationship. Therapist training and competence is likely to be a factor [174], but very little information on this is given in most studies. Measures to assess competence vary, with most having no empirically validated competence criterion, and this is an area requiring further investigation [148,2].

An alternative approach to measuring what is delivered and what changes within multicomponent therapies delivered to a heterogeneous group is to focus on a specific problem or symptom and a particular component of therapy. Recent studies targeting concurrent emotional disorders [86], cognitive biases [128,129], and specific psychotic symptoms [97] have reported positive effects. These studies have the advantages of a more homogeneous client group, at least with respect to the target problem, a more limited range of prescribed interventions, and the potential to include hypothesised mechanisms of change as outcome measures, allowing clearer investigation of what is changing during therapy. There is a suggestion that more carefully targeted approaches achieve a larger effect size [174], but this requires replication.

FUTURE DEVELOPMENTS

The progress made over the past ten years in building up a robust evidence base demonstrating that CBTp is effective for people with psychosis is remarkable, and

Table 7.4 Areas for future development

Improvement of therapy	Assessment of therapy content within trials
	Assessment of therapist competence within trials
	Development of appropriate individualised outcome measures
	Investigation of mechanisms of change
	Development and evaluation of techniques to change mechanisms
Training and competence	Specification of core components of CBTp
	Standardisation of measures of competence and adherence
	Identification of minimum training standards
Dissemination	Development and evaluation of 'low intensity' interventions
	Provision and evaluation of dedicated training programmes
	Education within services to ensure best use of provision

has resulted in its recommendation in national guidelines. However, the recommendation of widespread delivery of CBTp to people with psychosis brings its own difficulties (see Table 7.4). Insufficient numbers of therapists are trained in using these approaches to work with people with psychosis. We do not, as yet, know the essential components of effective CBTp for psychosis for particular problems, although we are progressing towards this goal. This makes it difficult to specify the core competencies that therapists working in the field ought to have, and, in turn, minimum training standards, hampering attempts at implementation [187]. The innovative recent development of specific treatments or computer assisted packages (for command hallucinations or delusional reasoning biases respectively) might assist with this effort, and allow successful delivery by less expert staff. Such packages could form part of 'low intensity' interventions, paralleling those developed as part of the UK Increasing Access to Psychological Therapies (IAPT) programme, designed to increase availability of CBT for people with anxiety and depression. 'Low intensity' approaches would require a less demanding training programme, and more readily attainable core competencies. However, training attempts, at all levels of expertise, are often thwarted by the multiple demands on the time of mental health workers and the absence of supervision and support for trained staff in their home services [188–190]. Even where therapists are abundant, mental health services remain cautious in making referrals [191] indicating the need for wider programmes of training and education of service providers in psychological approaches.

CONCLUSIONS

Over the last 20 years the development of complex multifactorial cognitive behavioural models of psychosis and the evaluation and refinement of cognitive behavioural interventions for psychosis have progressed hand in hand. Psychosis can be understood as driven by normal, understandable cognitive processes, and there is a consistent evidence base indicating positive effects of the treatment approaches drawing on this understanding. However, effect sizes are modest and delivery is limited, and further development of both therapy and therapist training and support is required. Furthermore, the specific mechanisms of change in CBTp are not yet well understood, and progress in this area is essential to continue to develop cognitive behavioural approaches.

ACKNOWLEDGEMENTS

Both authors are part of the PRP (Psychosis Research Partnership) group of researchers (Paul Bebbington, Graham Dunn, David Fowler, Daniel Freeman, Elizabeth Kuipers) which is funded by the Wellcome Trust [085396].

REFERENCES

1. NICE (2003) *Schizophrenia: core interventions in the treatment and management of schizophrenia in primary and secondary care (full guideline).* Gaskell and The British Psychological Society, London.
2. NICE (2009) *Schizophrenia: core interventions in the treatment and management of schizophrenia in primary and secondary care (update).* National Institute of Clinical and Health Excellence, London.
3. Lehman AF, Kreyenbuhl J, Buchanan RW, Dickerson FB, Dixon LB, Green-Paden LD, Boerescu D, Tek C & Steinwachs DM (2003) The Schizophrenia Patient Outcomes Research Team (PORT): Updated Treatment Recommendations. *Schizophrenia Bulletin* **30**, 193–217.
4. Gaebel W, Weinmann S, Sartorius N, Rutz W & McIntyre JS (2005) Schizophrenia practice guidelines: international survey and comparison. *British Journal of Psychiatry* **187**, 248–255.
5. Beck AT (1952) Successful outpatient psychotherapy of a chronic schizophrenic with a delusion based on borrowed guilt. *Psychiatry* **15**, 305–312.
6. Watts FN, Powell GE and Austin SV (1973) The modification of abnormal beliefs. *British Journal of Medical Psychology* **46**, 359–363.
7. Milton F, Patwa VE and Hafner RJ (1978) Confrontation vs. belief modification in persistently deluded patients. *British Journal of Medical Psychology* **51**, 127–130.
8. Chadwick PD & Lowe CF (1990) Measurement and modification of delusional beliefs. *Journal of Consulting Clinical Psychology* **58**, 225–232.

9. Fowler D & Morley S (1989) The cognitive behavioural treatment of hallucinations and delusions: A preliminary study. *Behavioural Psychotherapy* **17**, 267–282.

10. Garety P, Kuipers E, Fowler D, Chamberlain & Dunn G (1994) Cognitive behavioural therapy for drug-resistant psychosis. *British Journal of Medical Psychology* **67**, 259–271.

11. Kingdon DG & Turkington D (1991) The use of cognitive behaviour therapy with a normalizing rationale in schizophrenia. *Journal of Nervous and Mental Disease* **179**, 207–211.

12. Tarrier N, Beckett R, Harwood S, Baker A, Yusupoff L & Ugarteburu I (1993) A trial of two cognitive behavioural methods of treating drug-resistant residual psychotic symptoms in schizophrenic patients: I. Outcome. *British Journal of Psychiatry* **162**, 524–532.

13. Freeman D & Garety PA (2003) Connecting neurosis and psychosis: the direct influence of emotion on delusions and hallucinations. *Behaviour Research & Therapy* **41**, 923–947.

14. Bebbington PE, Bowen J, Hirsch SR and Kuipers L (1995) Schizophrenia and psychosocial stressors. In: Hirsch SR and Weinberger D (Eds). *Schizophrenia*. Blackwell Science, Oxford, Pp. 587–604.

15. Garety PA & Freeman D (1999) Cognitive approaches to delusions: A critical review of theories and evidence. *British Journal of Clinical Psychology* **38**, 113–154.

16. Beck AT, Rush AJ, Shaw BF & Emery G (1979) *Cognitive Therapy of Depression*. Guilford Press, New York.

17. Chadwick PDJ, Birchwood M & Trower P (1996) *Cognitive therapy for delusions, voices and paranoia*. Wiley, New York.

18. Fowler D, Garety P & Kuipers E (1995) *Cognitive behaviour therapy for psychosis: theory and practice*. Wiley, New York.

19. Kingdon D & Turkington D (1994) *Cognitive-behavioral therapy of schizophrenia*. Lawrence Erlbaum Associates, Hove.

20. Kuipers E, Garety PA, Fowler D, Dunn G, Bebbington P, Freeman D & Hadley C (1997) The London-East Anglia randomised controlled trial of cognitive-behaviour therapy for psychosis. I: Effects of the treatment phase. *British Journal of Psychiatry* **171**, 319–327.

21. Tarrier N, Yusupoff L, Kinney C, McCarthy E, Gledhill A, Haddock G, Morris J (1998) Randomized controlled trial of intensive cognitive behaviour therapy for patients with chronic schizophrenia. *British Medical Journal* **317**, 303–307.

22. Pinto A, La Pia S, Mannella R, Domenico G, DeSimone L (1999). Cognitive behavioural therapy and clozapine for clients with treatment-refractory schizophrenia. *Psychiatric Services* **50**, 901–904.

23. Sensky T, Turkington D, Kingdon D, Scott JL, Scott J, Siddle R, O'Carroll M & Barnes TRE (2000) A randomized controlled trial of cognitive behavioural therapy for persistent symptoms in schizophrenia resistant to medication. *Archives of General Psychiatry* **57**, 165–172.

24. Garety PA, Kuipers E, Fowler D, Freeman D & Bebbington PE (2001) A cognitive model of the positive symptoms of psychosis. *Psychological Medicine* **31**, 189–195.

25. Garety PA, Bebbington P, Fowler D, Freeman D & Kuipers E (2007) Implications for neurobiological research of cognitive models of psychosis: a theoretical paper. *Psychological Medicine* **37**, 1377–1392.

26. Morrison AP (2001) The interpretation of intrusions in psychosis: An integrative cognitive approach to hallucinations and delusions. *Behavioural and Cognitive Psychotherapy* **29**, 257–276.

27. Freeman D, Garety PA, Kuipers E, Fowler D & Bebbington PE (2002) A cognitive model of persecutory delusions. *British Journal of Clinical Psychology* **41**, 331–347.

28. Zubin J & Spring B (1977) Vulnerability: A New View on Schizophrenia. *Journal of Abnormal Psychology* **86**, 103–126.

29. Gottesman I & Shields J (1982) *Schizophrenia: The Epigenetic Puzzle.* Cambridge University Press, Cambridge.

30. van der Gaag M (2006) A neuropsychiatric model of biological and psychological processes in the remission of delusions and auditory hallucinations. *Schizophrenia Bulletin* **32**, S113-S122.

31. Broome MR, Woolley JB, Tabraham P, Johns LC, Bramon E, Murray GK, Pariante C, McGuire PK & Murray RM (2005) What causes the onset of psychosis? *Schizophrenia Research* **79**, 23–34.

32. Liddle P (1987) The symptoms of chronic schizophrenia: A re-examination of the positive-negative dichotomy. *British Journal of Psychiatry* **151**, 221–234.

33. van Os J, Linscott RJ, Myin-Germeys I, Delespaul P & Krabbendam L (2009) A systematic review and meta-analysis of the psychosis continuum: evidence for a psychosis proneness–persistence–impairment model of psychotic disorder. *Psychological Medicine* **39**, 179–195.

34. Raine A (2006) Schizotypal personality: Neurodevelopmental and psychosocial trajectories. *Annual Review of Clinical Psychology* **2**, 291–326.

35. Claridge G (1972) The schizophrenias as nervous types. *British Journal of Psychiatry* **121**, 1–17.

36. Claridge G (1987) 'The schizophrenias as nervous types' revisited. *British Journal of Psychiatry* **151**, 735–743.

37. Claridge G (1994) Single indicator of risk for schizophrenia: Probable fact or likely myth? *Schizophrenia Bulletin* **20**, 151–168.

38. van Os J, Rutten BP and Poulton R (2008) Gene-Environment Interactions in Schizophrenia: Review of Epidemiological Findings and Future Directions. *Schizophrenia Bulletin* **34**, 1066–1082.

39. Reichenberg A & Harvey PD (2007) Neuropsychological impairments in schizophrenia: Integration of performance-based and brain imaging findings. *Psychological Bulletin* **133**, 833–858.

40. van Os J and Kapur S (2009) Schizophrenia. *The Lancet* **374**, 635–645.

41. Bebbington P & Kuipers E (2008) Psychosocial factors. Chapter 8 in Mueser KT and Jeste DV (eds) *Clinical Handbook of Schizophrenia.* Guilford Press, New York, pp 74–81.

42. Bebbington P, Bhugra D, Brughra T, Singleton N, Farrell M, Jenkins R, Lewis G & Meltzer H (2004) Psychosis, victimisation and childhood disadvantage. *British Journal of Psychiatry* **185**, 220–226.

43. Shevlin M, Houston JE, Dorahy MJ, Adamson G (2008) Cumulative traumas and psychosis: an analysis of the national comorbidity survey and the British Psychiatric Morbidity Survey. *Schizophrenia Bulletin* **34**, 193–199.

44. Krabbendam L & van Os J (2005) Schizophrenia and Urbanicity: A Major Environmental Influence—Conditional on Genetic Risk. *Schizophrenia Bulletin* **31**, 795–799.

45. Cantor-Graae E & Selten JP (2005) Schizophrenia and Migration: A Meta-Analysis and Review. *American Journal of Psychiatry* **162**, 12–24.

46. Boydell J, van Os J, McKenzie K, Allardyce J, Goel R, McCreadie R, *et al.* (2001) Incidence of schizophrenia in ethnic minorities in London: ecological study into interactions with environment. *British Medical Journal* **323**, 1336–1338.

47. Morgan C, Kirkbride J, Hutchinson G, Craig T, Morgan K, Dazzan P, Boydell J, Doody GA, Jones PB, Murray RM, Leff J & Fearon P (2008) Cumulative social disadvantage, ethnicity and first-episode psychosis: A case-control study. *Psychological Medicine* **38**, 1701–1715.

48. van Winkel R, Stefanis NC & Myin-Germeys I (2008) Psychosocial stress and psychosis. A review of the neurobiological mechanisms and the evidence for gene-stress interaction. *Schizophrenia Bulletin* **34**, 1095–1105.

49. Birchwood M, Iqbal Z, Chadwick P and Trower P (2000) Cognitive approach to depression and suicidal thinking in psychosis. 1. Ontogeny of post-psychotic depression. *British Journal of Psychiatry* **177**, 516–521.

50. Beck AT (1967) *Depression: Causes and treatment*. University of Pennsylvania Press, Philadelphia.

51. Beck AT, Freeman A *et al.* (1990) *Cognitive therapy of personality disorders*. Guilford, New York.

52. Fowler D, Freeman D, Smith B, Kuipers E, Bebbington P, Bashforth H, Coker S, Hodgekins J, Gracie A, Dunn G, Garety P (2006) The Brief Core Schema Scales (BCSS): psychometric properties and associations with paranoia and grandiosity in non-clinical and psychosis samples. *Psychological Medicine* **36**, 749–759.

53. Smith B, Fowler DG, Freeman D, Bebbington P, Bashforth H, Garety P, Dunn G and Kuipers E (2006) Emotion and psychosis: Links between depression, self-esteem, negative schematic beliefs and delusions and hallucinations. *Schizophrenia Research* **86**, 181–188.

54. Barrowclough C, Tarrier N, Humphreys L, Ward J, Gregg L and Andrews B (2003) Self-esteem in schizophrenia: relationships between self-evaluation, family attitudes and symptomology. *Journal of Abnormal Psychology* **112**, 92–99.

55. Freeman D, Garety P, Fowler D, Kuipers E, Dunn G, Bebbington P & Hadley C (1998) The London-East Anglia randomised controlled trial of cognitive-behaviour therapy for psychosis IV: Self-esteem and persecutory delusions. *British Journal of Clinical Psychology* **37**, 415–430.

56. Hall PL & Tarrier N (2003) The cognitive – behavioural treatment of low self-esteem in psychotic patients: a pilot study. *Behaviour ResearchTherapy* **41**, 317–332.

57. Borras L, Boucherie M, Mohr S, Lecomte T, Perroud N, Huguelet Ph (2009) Increasing self-esteem: efficacy of a group intervention for individuals with severe mental disorders. *European Psychiatry: the journal of the Association of European Psychiatrists* **24**, 307–316.

58. Jaspers K (1913/1959) *General Psychopathology*. (J.Hoenig & M.W. Hamilton, trans). Manchester University Press, Manchester.

59. Schneider K (1959) *Clinical Psychopathology*. Grune and Stratton, New York.
60. Birchwood M (2003) Pathways to emotional dysfunction in first-episode psychosis. *British Journal of Psychiatry* **182**, 373–375.
61. Krabbendam L and van Os J (2005) Affective processes in the onset and persistence of psychosis. *European Archives of Psychiatry and Clinical Neuroscience* **255**, 185–189.
62. Mueser KT, Salyers MP, Rosenberg SD, Goodman LA, Essock SM, Osher FC *et al.* (2004) Interpersonal trauma and posttraumatic stress disorder in patients with severe mental illness: Demographic, clinical, and health correlates. *Schizophrenia Bulletin* **30**, 45–57.
63. Jackson C, Knott C, Skeate A & Birchwood M (2004) The trauma of first episode psychosis: the role of cognitive mediation. *Australian & New Zealand Journal of Psychiatry* **38**, 327–333.
64. Read J, van Os J, Morrison AP & Ross CA (2005) Childhood trauma, psychosis and schizophrenia. *Acta Psychiatrica Scandinavica* **112**, 330–350.
65. Morgan C & Fisher H (2007) Environmental factors in schizophrenia: Childhood trauma–A critical review. *Schizophrenia Bulletin* **33**, 3–10.
66. Freeman D & Fowler D (2009) Routes to psychotic symptoms: trauma, anxiety and psychosis-like experiences. *Psychiatry Research* **169**, 107–112.
67. Mueser K, Rosenberg SD, Goodman LA & Trumbetta SL (2002) Trauma, PTSD, and the course of severe mental illness: an interactive model. *Schizophrenia Research* **53**, 123–143.
68. Morrison AP, Frame L & Larkin W (2003) Relationships between trauma and psychosis: a review and integration. *British Journal of Clinical Psychology* **42**, 331–353.
69. Gracie A, Freeman D, Green S, Garety PA, Kuipers E, Hardy A, Ray K, Dunn G, Bebbington P, Fowler D (2007) The association between traumatic experience, paranoia and hallucinations: a test of the predictions of psychological models. *Acta Psychiatrica Scandinavica* **116**, 280–289.
70. Hardy A, Fowler D, Freeman D, Smith B, Steel C, Evans J, Garety P, Kuipers E, Bebbington P & Dunn, G (2005) Trauma and hallucinatory experience in psychosis. *Journal of Nervous and Mental Disease* **193**, 501–507.
71. Steel C, Fowler D & Holmes EA (2005) Trauma-related intrusions and psychosis: An information processing account. *Behavioural and Cognitive Psychotherapy* **33**, 139–152.
72. Birchwood M, Iqbal Z and Upthegrove R (2005) Psychological pathways to depression in schizophrenia: Studies in acute psychosis, post psychotic depression and auditory hallucinations. *European Archives of Psychiatry & Clinical Neuroscience* **255**, 202–212.
73. Rector NA, Beck AT, Stolar NM (2005) The negative symptoms of schizophrenia: a cognitive perspective. *Canadian Journal of Psychiatry* **50**, 247–257.
74. Grant PM and Beck AT (2009) Defeatist beliefs as a mediator of cognitive impairment, negative symptoms, and functioning in schizophrenia. *Schizophrenia Bulletin* **35**, 798–806.
75. Braga RJ, Petrides G & Figueira I (2004) Anxiety disorders in schizophrenia. *Comprehensive Psychiatry* **45**, 460–468.
76. Freeman D (2007) Suspicious minds: the psychology of persecutory delusions. *Clinical Psychology Review* **27**, 425–457.

77. Freeman D, Garety PA, Kuipers E, Fowler D, Bebbington PE & Dunn G (2007) Acting on persecutory delusions: The importance of safety seeking. *Behaviour Research and Therapy* **45**, 89–99.
78. Freeman D & Garety PA (1999) Worry, worry processes and dimensions of delusions: an exploratory investigation of a role for anxiety processes in the maintenance of delusional distress. *Behavioural & Cognitive Psychotherapy* **27**, 47–62.
79. Startup H, Freeman D, Garety PA (2007) Persecutory delusions and catastrophic worry in psychosis: Developing the understanding of delusion distress and persistence. *Behaviour Research and Therapy* **45**, 523–538.
80. Freeman D, Pugh K, Antley A, Slater M, Bebbington P, Gittins M, Dunn G, Kuipers E, Fowler D & Garety P (2008). Virtual reality study of paranoid thinking in the general population. *British Journal of Psychiatry* **192**, 258–263.
81. Freeman D, Gittins M, Pugh K, Antley A, Slater M & Dunn G (2008) What makes one person paranoid and another person anxious? The differential prediction of social anxiety and persecutory ideation in an experimental situation. *Psychological Medicine* **38**, 1121–1132.
82. Birchwood M, Trower P, Brunet K, Gilbert P, Iqbal Z & Jackson C (2007) Social anxiety and the shame of psychosis: a study in first episode psychosis. *Behaviour Research and Therapy* **45**, 1025–1037.
83. Smith N, Freeman D & Kuipers E (2005) Grandiose delusions: an experimental investigation of the delusion as defense. *Journal of Nervous and Mental Disease* **193**, 480–487.
84. Humphreys L & Barrowclough C (2006) Attributional style, defensive functioning and persecutory delusions: Symptom-specific or general coping strategy? *British Journal of Clinical Psychology* **45**, 231–246.
85. Drake RJ, Pickles A, Bentall RP, Kinderman P, Haddock G, Tarrier N *et al.* (2004) The evolution of insight paranoia and depression during early schizophrenia. *Psychological Medicine* **34**, 285–292.
86. Foster C, Startup H, Potts L & Freeman D (2010) A randomised controlled trial of a worry intervention for individuals with persistent persecutory delusions. *Journal of Behavior Therapy and Experimental Psychiatry* **41**, 45–51.
87. Halperin S, Nathan P, Drummond P & Castle D (2000) A cognitive-behavioural, group-based intervention for social anxiety in schizophrenia. *Australian and New Zealand Journal of Psychiatry* **34**, 809–813.
88. Kingsep P, Nathan P & Castle D (2003) Cognitive behavioural group treatment for social anxiety in schizophrenia. *Schizophrenia Research* **63**, 121–129.
89. Fowler D, Hodgekins J, Painter M, Reilly T, Crane C, Macmillan I, Mugford M, Croudace T and Jones PB (2009) Cognitive behaviour therapy for improving social recovery in psychosis: a randomised controlled trial (Improving Social Recovery in Psychosis). *Psychological Medicine* **39**, 1627–1636.
90. Mueser K, Rosenberg SD, Xie H, Jankowski MK, Bolton EE, Lu W, Hamblen JL, Rosenberg HJ, McHugo GJ and Wolfe R (2008) A randomized controlled trial of cognitive-behavioral treatment for posttraumatic stress disorder in severe mental illness. *Journal of Consulting and Clinical Psychology* **76**, 259–271.
91. Jackson C, Trower P, Reid I, Smith J, Hall M, Townend M, Barton K, Jones J, Ross K, Russell R, Newton E, Dunn G and Birchwood M (2009) Improving psychological

adjustment following a first episode of psychosis: A randomised controlled trial of cognitive therapy to reduce post psychotic trauma symptoms. *Behaviour Research and Therapy* **47**, 454–462.

92. Morrison AP, French P and Wells A (2007) Metacognitive beliefs across the continuum of psychosis: comparisons between patients with psychotic disorders, patients at ultra-high risk and non-patients. *Behaviour Research & Therapy* **45**, 2241–2246.

93. Brett CMC, Peters EP, Johns LC, Tabraham P, Valmaggia LR & Mcguire PM (2007) Appraisals of Anomalous Experiences Interview (AANEX): A multidimensional measure of psychological responses to anomalies associated with psychosis. *British Journal of Psychiatry*, **191** (S51), S23-S30.

94. Birchwood M, Meaden A, Trower P, Gilbert P & Plaistow J (2000) The power and omnipotence of voices: Subordination and entrapment by voices and significant others. *Psychological Medicine* **30**, 337–344.

95. Fannon D, Hayward P, Thompson N, Green N, Surguladze S & Wykes T (2009) The self or the voice? Relative contributions of self-esteem and voice appraisal in persistent auditory hallucinations. *Schizophrenia Research* **112**, 174–180.

96. Mawson A, Cohen K & Berry K (2009) Reviewing evidence for the cognitive model of auditory hallucinations: the relationship between cognitive voice appraisals and distress during psychosis. *Clinical Psychology Review*, doi:10.1016/j.cpr.2009.11.006

97. Trower P, Birchwood M, Meaden A, Byrne S, Nelson A & Ross K (2004) Cognitive therapy for command hallucinations: randomized controlled trial. *British Journal of Psychiatry* **184**, 312–320.

98. Wason PC (1960) On the failure to eliminate hypotheses in a conceptual task. *Quarterly Journal of Experimental Psychology* **12**, 129–140.

99. Wason P (1966) Reasoning. In *New Horizons in Psychology*. Penguin, Hammondsworth, UK.

100. Wason P & Johnson-Laird P (1972) *Psychology of Reasoning: Structure and Content*. Harvard University Press, Cambridge, MA.

101. Tversky A & Kahneman D (1974) Judgments under uncertainty: Heuristics and biases. *Science* **185**, 1124–1131.

102. Evans J St BT, Barston JL & Pollard P (1983) On the conflict between logic and belief in syllogistic reasoning. *Memory and Cognition* **11**, 295–306.

103. Corcoran R, Cummins S, Rowse G, Moore R, Blackwood N, Howard R, Kinderman P & Bentall RP (2006) Reasoning under uncertainty: heuristic judgments in patients with persecutory delusions or depression. *Psychological Medicine* **36**, 1109–1118.

104. Kemp R, Chua S, McKenna P & David A (1997) Reasoning and delusions. *British Journal of Psychiatry* **170**, 398–405.

105. Peters ER, Thornton P, Siksou L, Linney Y & MacCabe JH (2008) Specificity of the jump-to-conclusions bias in deluded patients. *British Journal of Clinical Psychology* **47**, 239–244.

106. Garety PA, Freeman D, Jolley S, Dunn G, Bebbington PE, Fowler DG Kuipers, E, Dudley R (2005) Reasoning, emotions and delusional conviction in psychosis. *Journal of Abnormal Psychology* **114**, 373–384.

107. Moritz S & Woodward TS (2005) Jumping to conclusions in delusional and non-delusional schizophrenic patients. *British Journal of Clinical Psychology* **44**, 193–207.

108. Freeman D, Pugh K & Garety P (2008) Jumping to conclusions and paranoid ideation in the general population. *Schizophrenia Research* **102**, 254–260.

109. Peters E and Garety P (2006) Cognitive functioning in delusions: A longitudinal analysis. *Behaviour Research & Therapy* **44**, 481–514.

110. Dudley REJ & Over DE (2003) People with delusions jump to conclusions: a theoretical account of research findings on the reasoning of people with delusions. *Clinical Psychology & Psychotherapy* **10**, 263–274.

111. Fine C, Gardner M, Craigie J & Gold I (2007) Hopping, skipping or jumping to conclusions? Clarifying the role of the JTC bias in delusions. *Cognitive Neuropsychiatry* **12**, 46–77.

112. Ellett L, Freeman D and Garety PA (2008) The psychological effect of an urban environment on individuals with persecutory delusions: the Camberwell walk study. *Schizophrenia Research* **99**, 77–84.

113. Lincoln TM, Lange J, Burau J, Exner C and Moritz S (in press) The effect of state anxiety on paranoid ideation and jumping to conclusions. An experimental investigation. *Schizophrenia Bulletin.* doi:10.1093/schbul/sbp029

114. Van Dael F, Versmissen D, Janssen I, Myin-Germeys I, van Os J & Krabbendam L (2006) Data gathering: Biased in psychosis? *Schizophrenia Bulletin* **32**, 341–351.

115. Colbert SM & Peters ER (2002) Need for closure and jumping-to-conclusions in delusion-prone individuals. *Journal of Nervous and Mental Disease* **190**, 27–31.

116. Broome MR, Johns LC, Valli I, Woolley JB, Tabraham P, Brett C, Valmaggia L, Peters E, Garety PA & McGuire PK (2007) Delusion formation and reasoning biases in those at clinical high risk for psychosis. *British Journal of Psychiatry* **51** (S), 38–42.

117. Freeman D, Garety P, Fowler D, Kuipers E, Bebbington P & Dunn G (2004) Why do people with delusions fail to choose more realistic explanations for their experiences? An empirical investigation. *Journal of Consulting and Clinical Psychology* **72**, 671–680.

118. Abramson LY, Seligman MEP & Teasdale JD (1978) Learned helplessness in humans: Critique and reformulation. *Journal of Abnormal Psychology* **87**, 49–74.

119. DeRubeis RJ & Hollon SD (1995) The role of explanatory style in the cognitive therapy of depression. In G Buchanan & MEP Seligman (Eds.), *Explanatory style*, pp. 99–111. Lawrence Erlbaum, Hillsdale, NJ.

120. Moore MT and Fresco DM (2007) The relationship of explanatory flexibility to explanatory style. *Behavior Therapy* **38**, 325–332.

121. Candido CL & Romney DM (1990) Attributional style in paranoid vs. depressed patients. *British Journal of Medical Psychology* **63**, 355–363.

122. Jolley S, Garety PA, Bebbington PE, Dunn G, Freeman D, Kuipers E, Fowler D, Hemsley D (2006) Attributional style in psychosis – the role of affect and belief type. *Behaviour Research and Therapy* **44**, 1597–1607.

123. Fornells-Ambrojo M & Garety PA (2009) Understanding attributional biases, emotions and self-esteem in 'poor me' paranoia: Findings from an early psychosis sample. *British Journal of Clinical Psychology* **48**, 141–162.

124. Couture SM, Penn DL, Addington J, Woods SW and Perkins DO (2008) Assessment of social judgments and complex mental states in the early phases of psychosis. *Schizophrenia Research* **100**, 237–241.

125. Versmissen D, Janssen I, Myin-Germeys I, Mengelers R, a Campo J, van Os J & Krabbendam L (2008) Evidence for a relationship between mentalising deficits and paranoia over the psychosis continuum. *Schizophrenia Research* **99**, 103–110.

126. Corcoran R, Cahill C & Frith CD (1997) The appreciation of visual jokes in people with schizophrenia: a study of 'mentalizing' ability. *Schizophrenia Research* **24**, 319–327.

127. Kinderman P & Bentall RP (1997) Attribution therapy for paranoid delusions: a case study. *Behavioural and Cognitive Psychotherapy* **25**, 269–280.

128. Moritz S & Woodward TS (2007) Metacognitive training in schizophrenia: from basic research to knowledge translation and intervention. *Current Opinion in Psychiatry* **20**, 619–625.

129. Ross K, Freeman D, Dunn G & Garety P (2009) A randomised experimental investigation of reasoning training for people with delusions. *Schizophrenia Bulletin*, Advance Access published on June 11, 2009; doi: doi:10.1093/schbul/sbn165

130. Bell V, Halligan PW & Ellis HD (2008) Are anomalous perceptual experiences necessary for delusions? *The Journal of Nervous and Mental Disease* **196**, 3–8.

131. Buchanan A, Reed A, Wessely S, Garety P, Taylor P, Grubin D & Dunn G (1993) Acting on delusions. II: The phenomenological correlates of acting on delusions. *The British Journal of Psychiatry* **163**, 77–81.

132. Cooke MA, Peters ER, Greenwood KE, Fisher PL, Kumari V, Kuipers E (2007) Insight in psychosis: Influence of cognitive ability and self-esteem. *British Journal of Psychiatry* **191**, 234–237.

133. Hasson-Ohayon I, Kravetz S, Roe D, David AS & Weiser M (2006) Insight into psychosis and quality of life. *Comprehensive Psychiatry* **47**, 265–269.

134. Iqbal Z, Birchwood M, Chadwick P & Trower P (2000) Cognitive approach to depression and suicidal thinking in psychosis. 2. Testing the validity of a social ranking model. *British Journal of Psychiatry* **177**, 522–528.

135. Birchwood M, Mason R, MacMillan F & Healy J (1993) Depression, demoralization and control over psychotic illness: a comparison of depressed and non-depressed patients with a chronic psychosis. *Psychological Medicine* **23**, 387–395.

136. Rooke O and Birchwood M (1998) Loss, humiliation and entrapment as appraisals of schizophrenic illness: a prospective study of depressed and non-depressed patients. *British Journal of Clinical Psychology* **37**, 259–268.

137. Lobban F, Barrowclough C & Jones S (2003) A review of the role of illness models in severe mental illness. *Clinical Psychology Review* **23**, 171–196.

138. Lobban F, Barrowclough C & Jones S (2004) The impact of beliefs about mental health problems and coping on outcome in schizophrenia. *Psychological Medicine* **34**, 1165–1176.

139. Lobban F, Barrowclough C and Jones S (2005) Assessing cognitive representations of mental health problems. I. The illness perception questionnaire for schizophrenia. *British Journal of Clinical Psychology* **44**, 147–162.

140. Jolley S & Garety PA (2004) Insight and delusions, a cognitive psychological approach. Chapter 5 in Amador, XF and David AS (eds) *Insight and Psychosis*. Oxford University Press, New York.

141. Watson PWB, Garety PA, Weinman J, Dunn G, Bebbington PE, Fowler D, Freeman D & Kuipers E (2006) Emotional dysfunction in schizophrenia spectrum psychosis: The role of illness perceptions. *Psychological Medicine* **36**, 761–770.

142. Morrison AP and Barratt S (2010) What are the components of CBT for psychosis? A Delphi Study. *Schizophrenia Bulletin* **36**, 136–142.

143. Kinderman P & Lobban F (2000) Evolving formulations; sharing complex information with clients. *Behavioural and Cognitive Psychotherapy* **28**, 307–310.

144. Chadwick P, Williams C & Mackenzie J (2003) Impact of case formulation in cognitive behaviour therapy for psychosis. *Behaviour Research and Therapy* **41**, 67–80.

145. Morberg Pain C, Chadwick P & Abba N (2008) Clients' experience of case formulation in cognitive behaviour therapy for psychosis. *British Journal of Clinical Psychology* **47**, 127–138.

146. Glaser N, Kazantzis N, Deane F & Oades L (2000) Critical issues in using homework assignments within cognitive-behavioral therapy for schizophrenia. *Journal of Rational-Emotive & Cognitive-Behavior Therapy* **18**, 247–261.

147. Miles H, Peters E & Kuipers E (2007) Service-User Satisfaction with CBT for Psychosis. *Behavioural and Cognitive Psychotherapy* **35**, 109–116.

148. Tarrier N & Wykes T (2004). Is there evidence that cognitive behaviour therapy is an effective treatment for schizophrenia? A cautious or cautionary tale? *Behaviour Research and Therapy* **42**, 1377–1401.

149. Kingdon D, Rathod S, Hansen L, Naeem F & Wright JH (2007) Combining Cognitive Therapy and Pharmacotherapy for Schizophrenia. *Journal of Cognitive Psychotherapy* **21**, 28–36.

150. Friedman ES & Thase ME (2009) Combining cognitive-behavioral therapy with medication. In Gabbard GO (Ed). (2009). *Textbook of psychotherapeutic treatments*. (pp. 263–285). xx, 876 pp. American Psychiatric Publishing, Inc., Arlington, VA, US.

151. Lewis S, Tarrier N, Haddock G, Bentall R, Kinderman P, Kingdon D, Siddle R, Drake R, Everitt J, Leadley K, Benn A, Grazebrook K, Haley C, Akhtar S, Davies L, Palmer S, Faragher B & Dunn G (2002). Randomised controlled trial of cognitive behavioural therapy in early schizophrenia: acute phase outcomes. *British Journal of Psychiatry* **181**, S91–S97.

152. Valmaggia LR, van der Gaag M, Tarrier N, Pignenborg M & Slooff CF (2005) Cognitive behavioural therapy for refractory psychotic symptoms of schizophrenia resistant to atypical antipsychotic medication. *British Journal of Psychiatry* **186**, 324–330.

153. Durham RC, Guthrie M, Morton V, Reid DA, Treliving LR, Fowler D & Macdonald RR (2003) Tayside-Fife clinical trial of cognitive behavioural therapy for medication-resistant psychotic symptoms. *British Journal of Psychiatry* **182**, 303–311.

154. Cather C, Penn D, Otto MW, Yovel I, Mueser KT & Goff DC (2005) A pilot study of functional cognitive-behavioural therapy (fCBT) for schizophrenia. *Schizophrenia Research* **74**, 201–209.

155. Barretto EM, Kayo M, Avrichir BS, Sa AR, Camargo MG, Napolitano IC, Nery FG, Pinto JA Jr. Bannwart S, Scemes S, Di Sarno E & Elkis H (2009) A preliminary

controlled trial of cognitive behavioral therapy in clozapine-resistant schizophrenia. *Journal of Nervous & Mental Disease* **197**, 865–868.

156. Kikkert MJ, Barbui C, Koeter MW, David AS, Leese M, Tansella M, Gieler A, Puschner B, Schene AH (2008) Assessment of medication adherence in patients with schizophrenia: the Achilles heel of adherence research. *Journal of Nervous & Mental Disease* **196**, 274–281.

157. Christodoulides T, Dudley R, Brown D, Turkington D & Beck AT (2008) Cognitive behaviour therapy in patients with schizophrenia who are not prescribed antipsychotic medication: A case series. *Psychology and Psychotherapy: Theory, Research and Practice* **81**, 199–207.

158. Morrison A (2001) Cognitive therapy for auditory hallucinations as an alternative to antipsychotic medication: A case series. *Clinical Psychology and Psychotherapy* **8**, 136–147.

159. Naeem F, Kingdon D & Turkington D (2008) Predictors of response to Cognitive Behaviour Therapy in the treatment of Schizophrenia: a comparison of brief and standard interventions *Cognitive Therapy and Research* **32**, 651–656.

160. Garety PA, Fowler D, Freeman D, Bebbington P, Dunn G & Kuipers E (2008) A randomised controlled trial of cognitive behavioural therapy and family intervention for the prevention of relapse and reduction of symptoms in psychosis. *British Journal of Psychiatry* **192**, 412–423.

161. Gray JA, Feldon J, Rawlins JPN, Hemsley DR and Smith AD (1991) The Neuropsychology of schizophrenia. *Behavioural and Brain Sciences* **14**, 1–20.

162. Kapur S (2003) Psychosis as a state of aberrant salience: a framework linking biology, phenomenology, and pharmacology in schizophrenia. *American Journal of Psychiatry* **160**, 13–23.

163. Kapur S (2004) How antipsychotics become anti- 'psychotic' – from dopamine to salience to psychosis. *Trends in Pharmacological Sciences* **25**, 402–406.

164. Kapur S, Agid O, Mizrahi R and Li M (2006) How antipsychotics work - from receptors to reality. *Experimental Neurotherapeutics* **3**, 10–21.

165. Menon M, Mizrahi R & Kapur S (2008) 'Jumping to conclusions' and delusions in psychosis: relationship and response to treatment. *Schizophrenia Research* **98**, 225–331.

166. Mizrahi R, Addington J, Remington G & Kapur S (2008) Attribution style as a factor in psychosis and symptom resolution. *Schizophrenia Research* **104**, 220–227.

167. Startup M, Jackson MC & Bendix S (2004) North Wales randomized controlled trial of cognitive behaviour therapy for acute schizophrenia spectrum disorders: outcomes at 6 and 12 months. *Psychological Medicine.* **34**: 413–422.

168. Startup M, Jackson MC, Evans KE, Bendix S (2005) North Wales randomized controlled trial of cognitive behaviour therapy for acute schizophrenia spectrum disorders: Two-year follow-up and economic evaluation. *Psychological Medicine* **35**, 1307–1316.

169. Morrison AP, French P, Walford L, Lewis SW, Kilcommons A, Green J, Parker S, Bentall RP (2004). Cognitive therapy for the prevention of psychosis in people at ultra-high risk: Randomised controlled trial. *British Journal of Psychiatry* **185**, 291–297.

170. Morrison AP, French P, Parker S, Roberts M, Stevens H, Bentall RP, Lewis SW (2007b) Three-year follow-up of a randomized controlled trial of cognitive therapy for the prevention of psychosis in people at ultrahigh risk. *Schizophrenia Bulletin* **33**, 682–687.

171. Bechdolf A, Knost B, Kunterman C, Schiller S, Klosterkotter J, Hambrecht M & Pukrop R (2004) A randomized comparison of group cognitive behavioural therapy and group psycho-education in patients with schizophrenia. *Acta Psychiatrica Scandinavica.* **110**: 21–28.

172. Turkington D, Kingdon D & Turner T (2002) Effectiveness of a brief cognitive behavioural therapy intervention in the treatment of schizophrenia. *British Journal of Psychiatry* **180**, 523–527.

173. Gumley A, O'Grady M, McNay L, Reilly J, Power K & Norrie J (2003) Early intervention for relapse in schizophrenia: results of a 12-month randomized controlled trial of cognitive behavioural therapy. *Psychological Medicine.* **33**: 419–431.

174. Wykes T, Steel C, Everitt B & Tarrier N (2008) Cognitive behaviour therapy for schizophrenia: effect sizes, clinical models, and methodological rigor. *Schizophrenia Bulletin* **34**, 523–537.

175. Pfammater M, Junghan UM & Brenner HD (2006) Efficacy of psychological therapy in schizophrenia: Conclusions from meta-analyses. *Schizophrenia Bulletin* **32**, S64-80.

176. Zimmerman G, Favrod J, Trieu VH & Pomini V (2005) The effect of cognitive behavioural treatment on the positive symptoms of schizophrenia spectrum disorders: A meta-analysis. *Schizophrenia Research* **77**, 1–9.

177. Jones C, Cormac I, Silveira da Mota Neto JI, Campbell C (2004) Cognitive behaviour therapy for schizophrenia. *Cochrane Database of Systematic Reviews*, Issue 4. Art. No.: CD000524.

178. Pilling S, Bebbington P, Kuipers E, Garety P, Geddes J, Orbach G & Morgan C (2002) Psychological treatments in schizophrenia: I. Meta-analysis of family intervention and cognitive behaviour therapy. *Psychological Medicine* **32**, 763–782.

179. Gould RA, Mueser KT, Bolton E, Mays V & Goff D (2001) Cognitive therapy for psychosis in schizophrenia: an effect size analysis. *Schizophrenia Research* **48**, 335–342.

180. Haddock G, Barrowclough C, Shaw JJ, Dunn G, Novaco RW, Tarrier N (2009) Cognitive-behavioural therapy v. social activity therapy for people with psychosis and a history of violence: Randomised controlled trial. *British Journal of Psychiatry* **194**, 152–157.

181. Rollinson R, Smith B, Steel C, Jolley S, Onwumere J, Garety PA, Kuipers E, Freeman D, Bebbington PE, Dunn G, Startup M, Fowler D (2008) Measuring adherence in CBT for psychosis: A psychometric analysis of an adherence scale. *Behavioural and Cognitive Psychotherapy* **36**, 163–178.

182. Birchwood M, Trower P (2006) The future of cognitive-behavioural therapy for psychosis: not a quasi-neuroleptic. *British Journal of Psychiatry* **188**, 107–108.

183. Granholm E, Auslander LA, Gottlieb JD, McQuaid JR and McClure FS (2006) Therapeutic factors contributing to change in cognitive-behavioral group therapy for older persons with schizophrenia. *Journal of Contemporary Psychotherapy*, **36**, 31–41.

184. Garety PA, Fowler D, Kuipers E, Freeman D, Dunn G, Bebbington PE, Hadley C & Jones S (1997) The London-East Anglia randomised controlled trial of cognitive behaviour therapy for psychosis II: Predictors of outcome. *British Journal of Psychiatry*, **171**, 420–426.

185. Brabban A, Tai S, Turkington D (2009) Predictors of outcome in brief cognitive behavior therapy for schizophrenia. *Schizophrenia Bulletin*. **35**, 859–864.

186. Bentall RP, Lewis S, Tarrier N, Haddock G, Drake R, & Day J (2003) Relationships matter: the impact of the therapeutic alliance on outcome in schizophrenia. *Schizophrenia Research*, **60** (Suppl. 1), 319.

187. Shafran R, Clark DM, Fairburn CG, Arntz A, Barlow DH, Ehlers A, Freeston M, Garety PA, Hollon SD, Ost LG, Salkovskis PM, Williams JMG and Wilson GT (2009) Mind the gap: Improving the dissemination of CBT. *Behaviour Research and Therapy*, **47**, 902–909.

188. Pilling S & Price K (2006) Developing and implementing clinical guidelines: lessons from the NICE schizophrenia guideline. *Epidemiologia e Psichiatria Sociale* **17**, 349–357.

189. Berry K & Haddock, G (2008) The implementation of the NICE guidelines for schizophrenia: Barriers to the implementation of psychological interventions and recommendations for the future. *Psychology and Psychotherapy: Theory, Research and Practice* **81**, 419–436..

190. Brooker C & Brabban A (2004) *Measured Success: A Scoping Review of Evaluated Psychosocial Interventions Training for Work with People with Serious Mental Health Problems.* NIMHE / Trent WDC.

191. Kingdon DG & Kirschen H (2006). Who does not get cognitive-behavioral therapy for schizophrenia when therapy is readily available? *Psychiatry Services* **57**, 1792–1794.

CHAPTER 8

Management, rehabilitation, stigma

Wulf Rössler

Professor of Clinical and Social Psychiatry and Head, Department of General and Social Psychiatry, University of Zurich

---

Information Box

The Management of Schizophrenia rests on three Pillars:

- Medication to relieve symptoms and prevent relapses
- Psychosocial interventions help patients and families to cope with the illness
- Rehabilitation helps patients to reintegrate and regain occupational functioning

---

INTRODUCTION

More than 100 years of research have not been able to resolve the puzzle that schizophrenia represents. There is no cure for schizophrenia. Thus, the treatment of schizophrenia rests pragmatically on three main pillars. Firstly, there are medications to relieve symptoms and prevent relapse. Secondly, psychosocial interventions help patients and families cope with the illness and aim at preventing relapse. Thirdly, rehabilitation helps patients to reintegrate into the community and regain occupational functioning.

The Schizophrenia Patients Outcomes Research Team (PORT) regularly provides updated recommendations of evidence-based psychosocial treatment interventions for persons with schizophrenia adjunctive to pharmacotherapy [1]. Assertive community treatment supported employment, cognitive behavioural therapy, family-based services, token economy, skills training, psychosocial

---

Schizophrenia: Current Science and Clinical Practice, First Edition. Edited by Wolfgang Gaebel.
© 2011 John Wiley & Sons, Ltd. Published 2011 by John Wiley & Sons, Ltd.

interventions for alcohol and substance use disorders and psychosocial interventions for weight management were recommended for implementation in clinical practice settings for persons with schizophrenia. Medication adherence, cognitive remediation, psychosocial treatments for recent onset schizophrenia and peer support and peer delivered services were identified as emerging areas of interest but yet having not enough evidence to merit a treatment recommendation. Similar recommendations were provided by the National Institute for Health and Clinical Excellence in the UK though these recommendations and the PORT recommendations are not necessarily equivalent. Considering the vast literature concerning the management and the rehabilitation of persons with schizophrenia, the chapter provided here expresses inevitably the opinions and convictions of the author.

MANAGING SCHIZOPHRENIA: INTEGRATIVE APPROACHES

The management of such a complex and long-lasting disease touches many domains relevant for the lives of the affected persons. It is not only the illness itself, which must be mastered but also the consequences on the lives of the affected. In a hierarchy of needs securing existential needs is of paramount importance. But naturally, the most affected long for social integration and specifically for intimate relationships. Managing schizophrenia also has to take into account that the relevance of single needs can vary over the life span. During young adulthood starting a family or job entry is of more importance than in later life when the affected person looks back on their lives and reflects if they were able to realise their life plans. The therapists also have to bear in mind that all management and rehabilitation approaches must be adapted to the respective cultural and ethnic environment.

Overall management approaches refer among other things to the burden on patients and caregivers, to differential treatment aspects with respect to gender, as well as to legal problems or to premature death.

Burden for patients, families and communities

Affected individuals suffer primarily from the distressing symptoms of disorders. They also lack self-esteem because they are unable to participate in work and leisure activities, often not only as a result of disability, but also of stigma and discrimination. Although usually unjustified, they additionally worry about being a burden for others.

As a consequence of deinstitutionalisation the burden of care has increasingly fallen on the relatives of the mentally ill. Informal care-giving significantly contributes to healthcare and rehabilitation [2]. Fifty to 90% of disabled persons live with their relatives following acute psychiatric treatment [3]. This is a task many families do not choose voluntarily. Caregiving imposes a significant burden on families. If one converts relatives' time and effort of caring for their affected during acute illness into money value, the sum of money amounts roughly to the expenses of inpatient treatment [3].

The burden on families ranges from emotional reactions to the illness, the stress of coping with disturbed behaviour, the disruption of household routine, the stigma they are also confronted with, the restriction of social activities to economic difficulties. A cross-European study [EPSILON, 4] found caregiver burden in *schizophrenia* to be almost identical across five countries. Scores were higher when caregivers had more contact with patients, when patients lived with their family, when patients were older, and in regions with fewer psychiatric beds.

Restriction of involuntary hospital admission and reduced lengths of hospital stay can further increase burden on relatives. But the most important predictor of burden for relatives is the distress and changes in the relationship between caregiver and the affected occurring during acute illness [3]. Threats, nuisances, time spent with the affected, and restricted social life and leisure activities are additional predictors. Despite their burden, relatives do not complain much, although they sometimes receive little support, advice or information from the professionals engaged in treating the respective patient [5].

Additionally, not all families are equally capable of giving full support for their disabled member and not willing to replace an insufficient healthcare system [6]. Caregivers regularly experience higher levels of burden when they have poor coping resources and reduced social support [7]. But families also represent support systems, which provide natural settings for context-dependent learning important for recovery of functioning [8]. As such there has been a growing interest in helping affected families since the beginning of care reforms [9].

One area of interest deals with the expectations of relatives concerning the provision of care. Relatives quite often feel ignored, not taken seriously and also feel insufficiently informed by health professionals. They also may feel that their contribution to care is not appreciated or that they will be blamed for any patient problems. It certainly is no surprise that there is a lot of frustration and resentment among relatives considering the physical, financial and emotional family burden.

Box 8.1   Family Burden

- As a consequence of deinstitutionalization the burden of care has increasingly fallen on the relatives of the mentally ill
- The most important predictor of burden for relatives are changes in the relationship between caregivers and the affected
- Family intervention is effective in lowering relapse rates and in improving psychosocial functioning

The social and emotional environment within the family has been found to correlate with relapses in schizophrenia. Family intervention programs have produced promising results for a long time. Family intervention is effective in lowering relapse rate and also in improving outcome, for example, psychosocial functioning [10]. Possibly, family intervention can reduce family burden. Furthermore, the treatment gains are fairly stable [11]. But we also have to appreciate that it is not clear what the effective components of the different models are [12]. Additionally, family interventions differ in frequency and length of treatment. There are also no criteria for the minimum amount of treatment necessary.

In a study conducted by [14] (reduced) family burden was associated with professional and social network support received by the family. Thus, professional and social network support, represent crucial resources to reduce family burden in schizophrenia. Mental health services should therefore aim to assist key caregivers of people with chronic schizophrenia to manage stress, whether or not the patient lives in the same household as the caregiver [15].

Gender issues

Gender differences in schizophrenia are well known. In particular, differences in age at onset have been confirmed in many studies. Women seem to have a more favourable *course* and a better psychosocial *'outcome'* than men [16]. They were shown to have fewer and shorter hospital stays, better social adjustment and a better living situation than men, whereas the *symptom-related* course seems to be similar

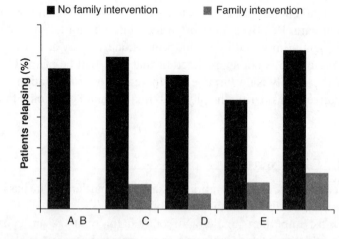

A = Goldstein et al. Arch Gen Psychiatry 1978   B = Leff et al. Br J Psychiatry 1981
C = Falloon et al. N Engl J Med 1982   D = Hogarty et al. Arch Gen Psychiatry 1986
E = Tarrier et al. Br J Psychiatry 1988

Figure 8.1   Effect of family intervention on relapse rate, from 13

for both genders. Women's mortality is also lower, mainly due to their significantly lower suicide rate. The tendency for the course to be better in women could have to do with their later age of onset, which is associated with a better social integration [17,18].

The *burden* of the disease can be very different for men and women. As such, the later age of onset in women means that they frequently have to cope with losses, for example, in relationships or in the professional sphere. Men, due to their younger age, have typically not established themselves in these respects to the same extent at the onset of the condition. This means that for women the focus in therapy has to be the maintenance or reestablishment of certain roles, whereas for men the goal is often to attain certain roles for the very first time.

Also gender specific social roles, social status, social stress or social support can influence the course of the disease. For example, significantly more women than men with schizophrenia care for children [19]. The care for these children can be an enormous burden for which these women to date get far too little help. In most European countries there is a severe lack of assessment and treatment facilities for these mothers with their children, although the need for such facilities is well documented [19–21] .

There are times with enhanced risk for an exacerbation of psychosis in women, dramatically so after parturition [22] but also in perimenopause or perimenstrually [23]. This puts a specific burden on women and needs a gender-sensitive therapeutic approach.

Box 8.2   Gender Issues

- Gender specific social roles, social status, social stress or social support can influence the course of the illness
- Consideration needs to be given to the large field of gender-specific pharmacotherapy

---

Consideration needs also to be given to the large field of gender-specific pharmacotherapy for example, the sex-specific treatment- and side effects of neuroleptics [24]. Hyperprolactinaemia-inducing neuroleptics for example, can have severe short- and long-term consequences in women such as premature menopause, osteopenia and so on [23]. It is not clear yet to which extent men are also affected by hyperprolactinaemia-induced side effects.

Men on the other hand not only need higher doses of neuroleptics [24], they also have specific needs in terms of psychosocial care. We have to be aware of their higher comorbidity, especially with respect to drugs and alcohol, their higher risk of self-neglecting behaviour or suicide [18].

Mortality

Globally, schizophrenia reduces an affected individual's lifespan by on average 10 years [25,26] analysed case register data of 9156 patients with schizophrenia. They found that compared to the age-standardised general population the relative mortality risk of male schizophrenia patients was 4.7 fold and that of female patients 2.3 fold increased [27] recorded an increased risk of dying from homicide in men with schizophrenia. But the increased mortality seems to be mainly due to suicide. Studies showed that 30% to 40% of patients diagnosed with schizophrenia had attempted suicide at least once during their lifetime [28,29]. The risk for suicide during inpatient treatment is about 50 times higher than in the general population [30]. About 10% to 13% of the patients die from suicide [31]. Palmer [32] and colleagues recently calculated that 'only' 4.9% of schizophrenia patients commit suicide.

Box 8.3   Mortality

- Schizophrenia reduces an affected individual's life span by on average 10 years
- The increased risk is mainly due to suicide
- Risk factors increasing the suicide risk are under-treatment due to non-adherence to therapy, multiple relapses, social isolation and loss of faith in treatment

---

Managing schizophrenia patients at risk for suicide is a difficult area for clinical psychiatrists. There are well known risk factors for suicide [33]. Younger males with a high premorbid educational level, a high socio-economic background on one side and psychotic symptoms, a clinical depression associated with hopelessness, comorbid substance abuse on the other side increase the risk for suicide. There are also some important treatment factors increasing the risk: undertreatment due to nonadherence to therapy, multiple relapses and frequent rehospitalisation, social isolation and finally loss of faith in treatment.

The risk factors also point to possible preventive measures: suitable pharmacological treatment (medication status is the strongest predictor for relapse; discontinuation of medication seems to increase relapse risk about 5-fold [34], preventing substance abuse, psychosocial programs for the prevention of hospitalisation as well as adequate aftercare programs. In particular patients who become aware that they will hardly be able to realise their life plans, urgently need new goals for their lives. Accompanying psychotherapy will be helpful for those patients. In this context the concept of recovery has gained importance. Already in 1993 Anthony defined 'recovery' as a unique process of changing one's attitudes, values, feelings, goals, skills and roles. Recovery is a way of living a satisfying, hopeful and contributing life even within the limitations caused by the illness. The major objective of recovery is that an affected person should be given support to build their own life in the way they want to [35].

Box 8.4   Personaly Recovery Tasks [35]

- Developing a positive identity
- Framing the "mental illness"
- Self-managing the mental illness
- Developing valued social roles

Furthermore, individuals with schizophrenia show an increased morbidity from natural causes [36,37], which certainly also contributes to their increased mortality. In connection with the psychopharmacological treatment, the specific risks of the metabolic syndrome have to be discussed. The metabolic dysfunction is an important source for the risk of type 2 diabetes mellitus and for cardiovascular diseases in schizophrenia [38]. In particular, cardiovascular deaths are a significant cause of mortality among patients with schizophrenia. It is recommended, that all schizophrenia patients obtain routine metabolic monitoring. Antipsychotic medication with limited metabolic risks should be preferentially prescribed and the use of medication with known effects on insulin resistance should be considered.

Weight should be routinely monitored in all patients with schizophrenia. Patients should be encouraged to monitor their own weight and report changes to their treating clinician [39]. Individuals with schizophrenia who are overweight or obese should be offered a psychosocial weight loss intervention to promote weight loss. The key elements of psychosocial interventions for weight loss include psycho-education focused on nutritional counselling, caloric expenditure, and portion control and behavioural self-management [1]. Patients and relatives organisations consider somatic health as a priority. Promoting specific health care programmes can be useful for intensifying the therapeutic alliance with patients.

Legal problems

It is a longstanding public belief that schizophrenia is associated with an increased risk of violence. In fact [40] in a meta-analysis of studies from the 1990s found that there is an increased risk of violence in terms of odds ratios between 4 and 8 predominantly for men with schizophrenia. This risk is even more elevated if there is a comorbid substance abuse. A recent longitudinal study using Swedish register data from psychiatric admissions and criminal convictions confirmed these results insofar as the risk is elevated in schizophrenia mainly in connection with comorbid substance abuse. There is no relevant increased risk without comorbid substance abuse [41].

Box 8.5   Violence

- There is an increased risk of violence predominantly for men
- The risk is more elevated if there is a comorbid substance abuse

---

Nevertheless, there is only a negligible – but possibly growing – proportion [42] of the community's violence, which could be attributed to schizophrenia. In a representative survey in Switzerland we could show that this is in line with the general public's attitude: about 70% of the respondents agreed to compulsory admissions in case of serious mental illness [43]. These attitudes are reflected in legislative actions and in the public's expectations about the role of mental health professionals in ensuring the safety of the community. Nevertheless, there are considerable differences in rates of compulsory admission between different European countries [44], [45], which is by no means justified by objective reasons, but more due to differing legislation and regional health care policies (Table 8.1).

Despite the long-standing public interest in and criticism of the ability of mental health professionals to assess and predict violence, there have been few efforts to develop or evaluate interventions to improve decision making in predicting violence. Assessment and management of violence risk should be prioritised in patients with schizophrenia and comorbid substance abuse. Whether it is necessary to assess violence risk in all schizophrenia patients, as recommended in the current guidelines of the American Psychiatric Association [46] depends on a variety of individual factors concerning the respective regional or national service provision. Persons with schizophrenia and a comorbid substance use disorder should be

Table 8.1   Rates of involuntary placements for mental disorder in European Union countries per 100 000 population (Data source: Salize & Dressing (2004) from [13])

Austria	175 (1999)
Belgium	47 (1998)
Denmark	34 (2000)
Finland	218 (2000)
Germany	175 (2000)
Ireland	74 (1999)
Luxembourg	93 (2000)
The Netherlands	44 (1999)
Portugal	6 (2000)
Sweden	114 (1998)
United Kingdom	48 (1999)

offered a specific treatment programme. The key elements of such a programme include motivational enhancement, behavioural strategies that focus on engagement in treatment, coping skills training and a relapse prevention training [1].

HEALTH CARE SETTINGS FOR SCHIZOPHRENIA PATIENTS: WHICH SETTING IS OPTIMAL?

The recent history of mental health services can be divided into three periods, covering the rise of the asylum and traditional hospital care; the decline of the asylum; and the appearance of balanced care. Balanced care comprises a range of services in a defined region. The balanced care approach [47] seeks to provide services that:

- are close to home, including modern hospitals for acute admissions and long-term residential facilities in the community;
- are mobile, including services that provide home treatment;
- address disabilities as well as symptoms;
- provide treatment and care specific to the diagnosis and needs of each individual;
- adhere to international conventions on human rights;
- reflect the priorities of the service users themselves; and
- are coordinated among mental health care providers and agencies.

No other patient group than those with schizophrenia were and still are more concerned by these health care developments. In the era of the asylums or even in the times of the transition to community care persons with schizophrenia were the dominating patient group in inpatient care. Today schizophrenia patients are one group among others during acute inpatient treatment [48].

Effective psychiatric management requires individualised and specialised treatment, which has to be embedded in a comprehensive and coordinated system of rehabilitative services. In particular this is indispensable for the so-called heavy users, who are in need of ongoing treatment and care by a multitude of services. Although heavy users with a diagnosis of schizophrenia only account for 1 in 10 of all patients with a recent onset of schizophrenia, these persons consume about half of the inpatient capacity of this patient group [49].

The components of balanced care need to be well integrated. But even when a variety of services are available, they are often poorly linked in many cases, and costly duplication may occur. A recent cost study of schizophrenia in six European countries demonstrated remarkable differences in direct costs of patients with schizophrenia across Europe. This is mainly due to differing care philosophies and differing resource allocation to mental health care [50].

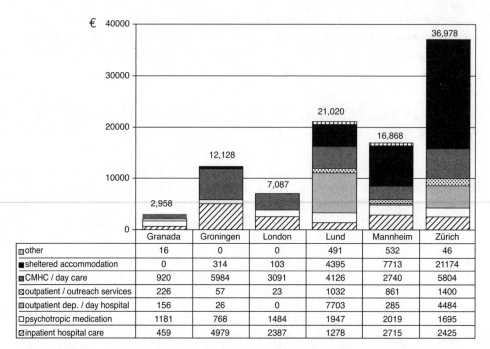

	Granada	Groningen	London	Lund	Mannheim	Zürich
other	16	0	0	491	532	46
sheltered accommodation	0	314	103	4395	7713	21174
CMHC / day care	920	5984	3091	4126	2740	5804
outpatient / outreach services	226	57	23	1032	861	1400
outpatient dep. / day hospital	156	26	0	7703	285	4484
psychotropic medication	1181	768	1484	1947	2019	1695
inpatient hospital care	459	4979	2387	1278	2715	2425

Figure 8.2   Cost of treatment of schizophrenia in six European countries [50]

With respect to the delivery of treatment and care, the process of deinstitutional-isation has led to fragmentation of services in the community. Lack of coordination and cooperation between services is the result and one of the main reasons for the revolving door phenomenon. A better coordination and cooperation is the major objective of case management. However, research on case management is not con-clusive. This might amongst others be due to the fact that a significant influence of national culture is evident both in the acceptability of case management and in approaches to researching it [51].

While developing community support systems it became obvious that there is a need to coordinate and integrate the services provided as each involved profes-sional concentrates on different aspects of the same patient. Therefore, as a key coordinating and integrating mechanism, the concept of case management (CM) originated. CM focuses on all aspects of the physical and social environment. The core elements of CM are the assessment of patient needs, the development of com-prehensive service plans for the patients and arrangement of service delivery [52].

Over the past two decades a variety of different models of CM have been developed which exceed the original idea that CM mainly intends to link the patient to needed services and to coordinate those services. Today, most clinical case managers also provide direct services in the patient's natural environment. This model is called Intensive Case Management (ICM). ICM on its part is difficult to distinguish from Assertive Community Treatment (ACT).

Stein and Test have developed the basic compounds of ACT in the 1970s [53]. The original programme was designed as a community based alternative to hospital treatment for persons with severe mental illnesses. A comprehensive range of treatment, rehabilitation and support services in the community is provided through a multidisciplinary team. ACT is characterised by an assertive outreach approach, that is, interventions are mainly provided in the natural environment of the disabled individuals [54].

Research on CM and ACT yielded 'mixed' results [51]. While the traditional office-based CM approach obviously is less successful, the ACT model was found to be more beneficial when compared with standard care [55]. ACT can reduce time in hospital [56], but has moderate or only little effects on improving symptomatology and social functioning [57]. The differing features of the respective services might explain the international variation. Six regularly occurring features of successful services were identified: smaller case loads, regularly visiting at home, a high percentage of contacts at home, responsibility for health and social care, multidisciplinary teams and a psychiatrist integrated in the team [58].

PSYCHIATRIC REHABILITATION

The goal of psychiatric rehabilitation is to help individuals with persistent and serious mental illness to establish the emotional, social and intellectual skills needed to live, learn and work in the community with the least amount of professional support [59]. Even though psychiatric rehabilitation does not deny the existence or the impact of mental illness, rehabilitation practice has changed the perception of mental illness. Enabling persons with persistent and serious mental illness to live a normal life in the community causes a shift away from a focus on an illness model towards a model of functional disability [60]. As such, other outcome measures apart from clinical conditions become relevant. Especially social role functioning including social relationship, work and leisure as well as quality of life and family burden is of major interest for the mentally disabled individuals living in the community.

The international classification of functioning, disability and health

Long-term consequences of major mental disorders might be described using different dimensions. A useful tool was provided by the International Classification of Impairment, Disability and Handicaps (ICIDH), first published by the World Health Organization in 1980 [61]. The ICIDH has been recently revised. The revision process has taken place since the mid 1990s and has resulted in many changes to the original classification, including a change of name.

The revised 'International Classification of Functioning, Disability and Health' (ICF) [25] includes a change from negative descriptions of impairments, disabilities and handicaps to neutral descriptions of body structure and function, activities and participation. A further change has been the inclusion of a section on environmental factors as part of the classification. This is in recognition of the importance of the role of environmental factors in either facilitating functioning or creating barriers for people with disabilities. Environmental factors interact with a given health condition to create a disability or restore functioning, depending on whether the environmental factor is a facilitator or barrier.

Box 8.6   Foundations of the ICF

• Human Functioning	*not*	*merely disability*
• Universal Model	*not*	*a minority model*
• Integrative Model	*not*	*merely medical or social*
• Interactive Model	*not*	*linear progressive*
• Context – inclusive	*not*	*person alone*
• Cultural applicability	*not*	*western concepts*
• Life span coverage	*not*	*adult driven*

The ICF is a useful tool to comprehend the chronically mentally ill in all their dimensions including impairments at the structural or functional level of the body, at the person level concerning activity limitations and at the societal level with respect to restrictions of participation. Each level encompasses a theoretical foundation on which a respective rehabilitative intervention can be formulated. Interventions can be classified as rehabilitative in the case that they are mainly directed towards a *functional improvement* of the affected individual. As such the *nature of an intervention is defined by the goal*, which is addressed by the intervention.

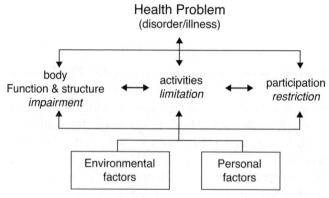

Figure 8.3   International classification of functioning, disability and health [25]

Target population

The majority of the chronically mentally ill targeted by psychiatric rehabilitation have a diagnosis of schizophrenia. The core group is drawn from patients with:

- persistent psychopathology;
- marked instability characterised by frequent relapse; and
- social maladaptation [62]

Many of the patients with schizophrenia carry dual diagnoses especially in combination with substance abuse [63]. The so-called young adult chronic patients constitute an additional category that is diagnostically more complicated [64]. These patients present complex pictures of symptomatology difficult to categorise within our diagnostic and classification systems. We have to acknowledge that many of these patients display psychotic symptoms without reaching the threshold of a full diagnosis of schizophrenia. Persons with subclinical psychotic disorders regularly indicate problems in all areas of their lives [65]. All in all they represent the most difficult-to-treat patient population.

CONCEPTUAL FRAMEWORK

The overall philosophy of psychiatric rehabilitation in psychiatric disorders comprises two intervention strategies: The first strategy is individual-centred and aims at developing the patient's skill in interacting with a stressful environment. The second strategy is an ecological approach and is directed towards developing environmental resources to reduce potential stressors. Most disabled persons need a combination of both approaches.

In any event the starting point for an adequate understanding of rehabilitation is that it is concerned with the individual person in the context of his or her specific environment. Psychiatric rehabilitation is regularly carried out under real life conditions. Thus rehabilitation practitioners have to take into consideration the realistic life circumstances that the affected person is likely to encounter in their day-to-day living [66].

> **Box 8.7   Rehabilitation: Conceptual Framework**
>
> - Two intervention strategies
>   - Developing patient's skills (individual-centered)
>   - Developing environmental resources (ecological approach)
> - Identify personal goals
> - Focus on patient's strengths
> - Concentrate on person's rights as a respected partner

A necessary second step is helping disabled persons to identify their personal goals. This is not a process where those persons simply list their needs. Motivational interviews provide a more sophisticated approach to identify the individuals' personal costs and benefits associated with the needs listed [67]. This also makes it necessary to assess the individuals' readiness for change [68], [69].

Subsequently the rehabilitative planning process focuses on the patient's strengths [66]. Irrespective of the degree of psychopathology of a given patient, the practitioner must work with the 'well part of the ego' as 'there is always an intact portion of the ego to which treatment and rehabilitation efforts can be directed' [70]. This leads to a closely related concept: the aim of restoring hope to people who suffered major setbacks in self-esteem because of their illness. As Bachrach [66] states 'it is the kind of hope that comes with learning to accept the fact of one's illness and one's limitations and proceeding from there'.

Psychiatric rehabilitation cannot be enforced. Quite the contrary, psychiatric rehabilitation concentrates on peoples' rights as a respected partner and endorses their involvement and self-determination concerning all aspects of the treatment and rehabilitation process. These rehabilitation values are also incorporated in the concept of recovery [71]. Within the concept of recovery, the therapeutic alliance plays a crucial role in engaging the patient in his or her own care planning [72]. It is essential that the patient can rely on his or her therapist's understanding and trust [73] as most of the chronically mentally ill and disabled persons lose close, intimate and stable relationships in the course of the disease [74]. Recent research has suggested that social support is associated with recovery from chronic diseases, greater life satisfaction and enhanced ability to cope with life stressors [75]. Corrigan and colleagues [76] have found that the most important factor facilitating recovery is the support of peers. Therefore, psychiatric rehabilitation is also an exercise in network building [77].

Finally, people with mental disorders and their caregivers prefer to see themselves as consumers of mental health services with an active interest in learning about psychiatric disorders and in selecting the respective treatment approaches. Consumerism allows the taking of the affected persons' perspective and seriously considering courses of action relevant for them [78]. In this context physicians should also acknowledge that disagreement about the illness between patient and him or her is not always the result of the illness process [79].

CURRENT APPROACHES

Individual-centred rehabilitation

Pharmacological treatment from a rehabilitative perspective

Antipsychotic medication has proven useful in reducing, and often eliminating, acute symptoms of schizophrenia such as hallucinations and delusions [80]. In addition, maintenance treatment is essential to prevent recurrence of symptoms and to protect the brain from the cognitive decline associated with relapse [82]. The interactions between medication and psychosocial interventions appear to be more than merely additive, since each can enhance the effects of the other. Recent studies using newer antipsychotics suggest that these agents improve the participation of patients in psychosocial treatments [81].

There is evidence of a neuroprotective effect of medication adherence, which has implications for prognosis and long-term cognitive functioning [82]. But adherence to antipsychotic medication is often poor. Within a year, 50% of patients started on medication will quit treatment, and virtually all stop medication within two years or take medication only sporadically [80]. Non-adherence is associated with psychotic relapse, hospitalisation, and other adverse outcomes.

Pharmacotherapy in psychiatric rehabilitation needs some special consideration. Symptom control does not necessarily have the highest priority as some side effects of pharmacological treatment can weaken a person's ability to perform his social roles, and impair vocational rehabilitation. As such, it is no surprise that nonadherence with medication-taking is one of the most serious problems in the long term treatment of persons with serious mental illness [83]. Many patients living in the community want to take responsibility for their medication themselves. Training in self-management of medication [84] emphasises patients' autonomy and increases acceptance of and responsibility for treatment. This also includes the varying of medication without consultation within certain limits.

Most interventions to enhance adherence have been pragmatic. A variety of strategies have been tested to improve medication adherence. Many studies tested the effects of patient education on enhancing adherence in patients with schizophrenia using group and individual educational methods. But research provides only mixed support for educational approaches [1]. Interventions based on motivational interviewing and cognitive behavioural therapy seem to be promising [80] as well as the provision of environmental support for medication adherence [1].

However, at this point, there is insufficient evidence to recommend any specific intervention to promote adherence to antipsychotic medications among persons with schizophrenia [1].

COGNITIVE BEHAVIOURAL THERAPY

Controlled studies of cognitive behavioural therapie (CBT) with individuals with schizophrenia who have persistent psychotic symptoms despite adequate pharmacotherapy have shown benefits in reducing the severity of delusions, hallucinations, positive and negative symptoms, and in improving social functioning [85,86]. The effects of CBT on depression, suicidality, hopelessness, illness insight, relapse, and rehospitalisation have not been clearly established [1].

Table 8.2 Mean effect sizes for randomised, controlled and experimental studies of social skills trainings for patients with schizophrenia arranged by outcome and proximity of the outcome to the effects of the intervention (adapted from Kurtz & Mueser (2008) [89])

Outcome measures	Number of studies	Number of clients	Effect sizes
Social skills	7	330	1.20
Daily living skills	7	481	0.52
Psychosocial functioning	7	371	0.52
Negative symptoms	6	363	0.40
Other symptoms	10	604	0.15
Relapse/rehospitalisation	9	485	0.23

The key elements of CBT include the identification of target problems or symptoms and the development of specific cognitive and behavioural strategies to cope with these problems or symptoms. All CBT approaches focus on the patient's view of his or her symptoms or problems and the development of more rationale coping responses. Other strategies focus exclusively on cognitive and behavioural approaches in combination with social skills training. CBT may be provided either in a group or on an individual basis. The intensity and duration of the therapies studied vary from 6 to more than 50 sessions; weekly or biweekly sessions over a treatment period of 4–9 months [1].

SOCIAL SKILLS TRAINING

In recent years, social skills training in psychiatric rehabilitation has become very popular and has been widely promulgated. The most prominent proponent of skills training is Robert Liberman who has designed systematic and structured skills

Table 8.3 Mean effect sizes for randomised studies of cognitive behaviour therapy for psychosis arranged by outcome measures (adapted from Wykes et al. (2008) [86])

Outcome measures	Number of studies	Number of clients	Effect sizes
Target symptoms	33	1964	0.400
Positive symptoms	32	1918	0.372
Negative symptoms	23	1268	0.437
Functioning	15	867	0.378
Mood	15	953	0.363
Social anxiety	2	61	0.353

training since the mid 1970s [87]. Liberman and his colleagues packaged the skill training in the form of modules with different topics. The modules focus on medication management, symptom management, substance abuse management, basic conversational skills, interpersonal problem solving, friendship and intimacy, recreation and leisure, workplace fundamentals, community (re-)entry and family involvement. Each module is composed of skill areas. The skills areas are taught in exercises with demonstration videos, role-play and problem solving exercises and in vivo and homework assignments [87,88].

The results of several control studies suggest that disabled individuals can be taught a wide range of social skills [89]. Social and community functioning improve when the trained skills are relevant for the patient's daily life and the environment perceives and reinforces the changed behaviour. Unlike medication effects, benefits from skills training occur more slowly. Furthermore, long term training has to be provided for positive effects [91–93]. Overall, social skills training has been shown to be effective in the acquisition and maintenance of skills and their transfer to community life [94,88].

Ecological approach to rehabilitation

As a general rule people with psychiatric disabilities tend to have the same life aspirations as people without disabilities in their society or culture [95]. They want to be respected as autonomous individuals and lead a life as normal as possible. As such they mostly desire (i) their own housing, (ii) an adequate education and a meaningful work career, (iii) satisfying social and intimate relationships.

HOUSING

The objective of psychiatric reforms since the mid 1950s has been to resettle chronically mentally ill persons from large custodial institutions to community settings. Providing sheltered housing in the community for the long-term patients of the old asylums was one of the first steps in the process of deinstitutionalisation. Most long-stay patients can successfully leave psychiatric hospitals and live in community settings [74].

Ideally, a residential continuum with different housing options should be provided. A residential continuum ranges from round-the-clock staffed sheltered homes to more independent and less staffed sheltered apartments which eventually allow individuals to move to independent housing in the community [96]. Critics of the residential continuum contended that (i) up to now a residential continuum is rarely available in communities, (ii) that a residential continuum does not meet the varying and fluctuating needs of persons with serious mental illnesses, and (iii) that a residential continuum does not account for individual preferences and choices. Supported housing, that is, independent housing coupled with the provision of support services [97] emerged in the 1980s as an alternative to RC. Supported housing offers flexible and individualised services depending on the individual's demands. In the meantime, rehabilitation research could demonstrate that supported housing is a realistic goal for the majority of people with psychiatric disabilities [98]. Once in supported housing the majority stay in housing and are less likely to become hospitalised. Other outcomes do not yield consistent results [99,98].

WORK

The beneficial effects of work on mental health have been known for centuries [100]. Therefore, vocational rehabilitation has been a core element of psychiatric rehabilitation since its beginning. Vocational rehabilitation is based on the assumption that work does not only improve activity, social contacts and so on, but may also promote gains in related areas such as self-esteem and quality of life, as work and employment are a step away from dependency and a step to integration into society. Enhanced self-esteem in turn improves adherence to rehabilitation of individuals with impaired insight [101].

Box 8.8   Vocational Rehabilitation

- Beneficial effects of work on mental health known for centuries
- Sheltered workshops quite often prove a dead end for the disabled
- Today the most promising vocational rehabilitation model is supported employment

---

Vocational rehabilitation originated in psychiatric institutions where the lack of activity and stimulation led to apathy and withdrawal of their inpatients. Long before the introduction of medication occupational and work therapy contributed to sustainable improvements in long-stay inpatients. Today occupational and work therapy are no longer hospital-based but represent the starting point for a wide variety of rehabilitative techniques teaching vocational skills [102].

Vocational rehabilitation programmes in the community provide a series of graded steps to promote job entry or re-entry. For less disabled persons brief and focused techniques are used to teach how they can find a job, fill out applications and conduct employment interviews [103]. In transitional employment a temporary work environment is provided to teach vocational skills, which should enable the affected person to move on to competitive employment. But all too often the gap between transitional and competitive employment is so wide that the mentally disabled individuals remain in a temporary work environment. Sheltered workshops providing pre-vocational training and also quite often prove a dead end for the disabled persons.

One consequence of the difficulties in integrating mentally disabled individuals into the common labour market has been the steady growth of cooperatives, which operate commercially with disabled and nondisabled staff working together on equal terms and sharing in management. The mental health professionals work in the background providing support and expertise [60].

Today, the most promising vocational rehabilitation model is supported employment. The work of Robert Drake and Deborah Becker decisively influenced the conceptualisation of supported employment (SE). In their 'Individual Placement Model' disabled persons are placed in competitive employment according to their choices as soon as possible and receive all support needed to maintain their position [91,104]. The support provided is continued indefinitely. Participation in supported employment programmss is followed by an increase in the ability to find and keep employment [105–107]. Links were also found between job tenure and nonvocational outcomes, such as improved self-esteem, social integration, relationships and control of substance abuse [104,108,109]. It was also demonstrated that those who had found long-term employment through supported employment had improved cognition, quality of life and better symptom control [104,110,109].

Although findings regarding SE are encouraging, some critical issues remain to be answered. Many individuals in supported employment obtain unskilled part-time jobs. Since most studies only evaluated short (12–18 months) follow-up periods, the long-term impact remains unclear. Currently we do not know which individuals benefit from supported SE and which do not [56]. After all, we have to realise that the integration into the labour market does by no means only depend on the ability of the persons affected to fulfil a work role and on the provision of sophisticated vocational training and support techniques, but also on the willingness of society to integrate its most disabled members.

PARTICIPATION IN COMMUNITY LIFE WITH FULL RIGHTS

As practitioners we often are confronted with the deleterious effects of stigma and discrimination in the lives of people with serious mental illnesses. Numerous studies have examined stigmatising attitudes toward people with mental illness [111–118]. In particular negative attitudes towards the mentally ill, especially towards persons with schizophrenia, are widespread [114]. Individuals with schizophrenia are frequently looked at as dangerous and unpredictable [117]. Many media reports reflect this fear even if in reality a possible risk is mainly directed to the closest relatives. This and other stigmata attached to schizophrenia create a vicious cycle of discrimination – leading to social isolation, unemployment, drug abuse, long lasting institutionalisation or even homelessness – all factors which further decrease the chances of recovery and reintegration into normal life in addition to the often deleterious consequences of the illness itself.

In recent years, the scientific interest in the perspective of the labelled individual has increased too. There is extensive empirical evidence of the negative consequences of labelling and perceived stigmatisation. These include demoralisation, low quality of life, unemployment and reduced social networks [119–123]. Once assigned the label 'mental illness' and having become aware of the related negative stereotypes, the affected individuals expect to be rejected, devaluated or discriminated against. This vicious cycle decreases the chance of returning to normal life.

Box 8.9   Stigma and Discrimination

- Numerous studies have examined stigmatizing attitudes toward the mentally ill
- In particular negative attitudes toward persons with schizophrenia are widespread
- There is extensive empirical evidence of the negative consequences of stigma and discrimination
- Well-integrated people with mental illness exhibit better outcomes

---

On the other hand, well-integrated people with mental illness exhibit better outcomes regarding psychopathology and quality of life [124]. The importance of social integration is underlined even more when considering the subjective availability of support: perceived social support predicts outcome in terms of recovery from acute episodes of mental illness [125], community integration [126], and quality of life [127,128,108].

On the basis of comprehensive research in this area during the last decade, several strategies have been developed to fight the stigma and discrimination suffered by those who have mental illnesses [129]. Different research centres developed interventions directed at specific target groups relevant for de-stigmatisation, for example, students [130] or police officers [131]. Persons in contact with mentally ill individuals quite often have a more positive attitude. Contact with the mentally ill persons also reduces social distance [118], which is a strong argument in favour of community psychiatry [118].

Other initiatives have targeted stigma by means of more comprehensive programmes. The World Psychiatric Association launched one of the internationally best-known programmss in 1996 (www.openthedoors.com). All these initiatives make clear that efforts in re-integrating persons with serious mental illness into community life must be accompanied by measures on the societal level.

THE CONTRIBUTION OF MENTAL HEALTH PROFESSIONALS TO STIGMA AND DISCRIMINATION

Mental health professionals hold much power over the lives of mentally ill persons. Current laws in most countries around the world allow involuntary civil commitment to inpatient treatment and often to outpatient treatment as well. Additionally, there is a remaining broad spectrum of informal coercive measures that are imposed on psychiatric patients outside judicious compulsory practices. Reasons for informal coercive interventions which use threats of negative sanctions to compel the patient to accept treatment [132], refer to the concept of paternalism in order to take the responsibility for patients' health [133] and/or the concept of social control as a mandate by society to prevent or reduce undesired and disruptive behaviour [134]. Hence the efficient use of treatment approaches very much depends on mental health professionals' attitudes and views about their patients. Informal coercive practices are likely to increase perceived coercion in person with psychotic disorders [135].

Most of us consider ourselves basically as partners of our patients with respect to decisions about management and rehabilitation. Concerning public representation we intuitively follow the idea that we predominantly act as agents for our patients who often are not capable of formulating their needs. Thus, most research intended to reduce stigma and discrimination because of mental illness is in principal directed to the general public. We rarely ask what our 'contribution' as mental health professionals could be to diminish stigma and discrimination because of mental illness. Norman Sartorius [136] gives a possible answer to it: 'First, we should examine our own attitudes . . .'.

For many years mental health professionals have not been considered as an important source for discrimination because of mental illness. But we could demonstrate in several studies that mental health professionals, in particular psychiatrists, do not hold better attitudes towards the mentally ill as compared to the general population [137–139]. It is not immoderate to expect more accepting attitudes and more understanding for the mentally ill among mental health professionals compared to the general population. We know from many studies with lay persons that contact with the mentally ill improves attitudes and social closeness for all concerned [118]. Why should this not work with mental health professionals? And finally, we were trained for many years to better understand and deal with the disorders our patients suffer from. Nonetheless, many professionals hold the pessimistic notion that persons with severe mental illnesses are doomed to poor outcomes.

Holding negative attitudes towards the mentally ill can have serious implications for the lives of the people all the more mental health professionals hold the power to have significant influence on the treatment and rehabilitation of the severely mentally ill. Persons that endorse the stigma of mental illness are not going to support an individual's right to self-determination, the right to determine the kind of job they should pursue, the neighbourhood they want to live in, and the people with whom they want to keep company.

We as psychiatrists often wonder why many of our patients do not like us (particularly inpatients) – in contrast to almost all other medical disciplines. The answer is not so difficult: Many patients simply do not think that they were treated with fairness, concern and respect [135]. We use paternalistic approaches and do not believe in their ability to take responsibility for themselves. Thus we do not contribute to our patients' self-esteem and self-efficacy, which is a significant part of the recovery process.

PW Corrigan [140] has proposed a heuristic model of how to improve treatment and community outcomes:

- Establishing a provider attitude of recovery and developing collaborative treatment plans will lead to a better use of medication and rehabilitation services;
- Replacing self-stigma with recovery expectations will lead to more self-efficacy which makes it more likely for our patients to pursue work and independent living opportunities;
- Challenging stigmatising attitudes and discriminatory behaviour will alleviate the chances of our patients finding reasonable accommodation and facilitate work and independent living opportunities.

The findings about the recovery process and the factors which impact on this process, challenge our current policies and the institutional practices developed to care for people with mental illnesses. All the progress we have made and will make in our field will be in vain if we do not find an alliance with those people affected.

THE ROLE OF THE PSYCHIATRIST IN THE MANAGEMENT AND REHABILITATION OF SCHIZOPHRENIA PATIENTS

Management and rehabilitation is by its very nature multidisciplinary because of the many different competencies required [141]. As a matter of course most psychiatrists have not acquired all the relevant skills needed in psychiatric rehabilitation during their training, which is predominantly hospital-based. Young psychiatrists today are primarily trained in diagnostic procedures and prescription of medication directed almost exclusively to symptom control and not trained in integrating pharmacological and psychosocial training [69]. Another side effect of hospital-based training is that young psychiatrists are confronted with the negative developments of difficult-to-treat patients who are frequently re-hospitalised. This is possibly one of the reasons why we found that psychiatrists in institutional settings do not hold fewer stereotypes of mentally ill people than the general population, nor display a greater willingness to closely interact with mentally ill people [139]. Therefore, it would be beneficial if the community training of young psychiatrists could take priority over hospital-based training. More training opportunities to experience the patients in the 'real world' would allow psychiatrists in institutional settings to develop a more positive perspective and better understanding of persons with severe and persistent mental disorders.

OUTLOOK

Management and rehabilitation is the most visible part of psychiatric care and as such represents the link to society. The attitude of the public towards psychiatry is mostly influenced by what management and rehabilitation accomplishes or not. Comparably the US President's Commission on Mental Health [142] declared that helping affected persons to achieve functional recovery is the main purpose of the mental health care system.

The refinement of psychiatric rehabilitation has achieved a point where it should be made readily available for every disabled person. But we have to be aware that there is a long way between research and practice. Lehman and colleagues [143] for example assessed the patterns of usual care for schizophrenic patients and examined the conformance rate with the treatment recommendations based on existing scientific evidence. The conformance rate was modest, generally below 50%. As such, it is obvious that current treatment and rehabilitation practice have to be substantially improved in the light of the rehabilitation research available.

REFERENCES

1. Dixon LB, Dickerson F, Bellack AS *et al.* (2009) The 2009 schizophrenia PORT psychosocial treatment recommendations and summary statements. *Schizophr Bull* **36**, 48–70.
2. Schulze B & Rössler W (2005) Caregiver burden in mental illness: review of measurement, findings and interventions in 2004–2005. *Current Opinion in Psychiatry* **18**, 684–691.
3. Lauber C, Eichenberger A, Luginbuhl P *et al.* (2003) Determinants of burden in caregivers of patients with exacerbating schizophrenia. *Eur Psychiatry* **18**, 285–289.
4. Thornicroft G, Tansella M, Becker T *et al.* (2004) The personal impact of schizophrenia in Europe. *Schizophr Res* **69**, 125–132.
5. Fadden G, Bebbington P & Kuipers L (1987) The burden of care: the impact of functional psychiatric illness on the patient's family. *Br J Psychiatry* **150**, 285–292.
6. Johnson D (1990) The family's experience of living with mental illness. In: Lefley H & Johnson D (eds.) *Families as allies in treatment of the mentally ill: New directions for mental health professionals.* American Psychiatric Press, Inc., Washington, DC.
7. Magliano L, Fadden G, Madianos M *et al.* (1998) Burden on the families of patients with schizophrenia: results of the BIOMED I study. *Soc Psychiatry Psychiatr Epidemiol* **33**, 405–412.

8. Schooler NR (1995) Integration of family and drug treatment strategies in the treatment of schizophrenia: a selective review. *Int Clin Psychopharmacol* **10 Suppl 3**, 73–80.

9. Strachan AM (1986) Family intervention for the rehabilitation of schizophrenia: toward protection and coping. *Schizophr Bull* **12**, 678–698.

10. Koukia E & Madianos MG (2005) Is psychosocial rehabilitation of schizophrenic patients preventing family burden? A comparative study. *J Psychiatr Ment Health Nurs* **12**, 415–422.

11. Pilling S, Bebbington P, Kuipers E *et al.* (2002) Psychological treatments in schizophrenia: I. Meta-analysis of family intervention and cognitive behaviour therapy. *Psychol Med* **32**, 763–782.

12. Barbato A & D'Avanzo B (2000) Family interventions in schizophrenia and related disorders: a critical review of clinical trials. *Acta Psychiatr Scand* **102**, 81–97.

13. Rössler W, Salize HJ, van Os J *et al.* (2005) Size of burden of schizophrenia and psychotic disorders. *European Neuropsychopharmacology* **15**, 399–409.

14. Magliano L, Marasco C, Fiorillo A *et al.* (2002) The impact of professional and social network support on the burden of families of patients with schizophrenia in Italy. *Acta Psychiatr Scand* **106**, 291–298.

15. Laidlaw TM, Coverdale JH, Falloon IR *et al.* (2002) Caregivers' stresses when living together or apart from patients with chronic schizophrenia. *Community Ment Health J* **38**, 303–310.

16. Riecher-Rossler A & Hafner H (2000) Gender aspects in schizophrenia: bridging the border between social and biological psychiatry. *Acta Psychiatr Scand Suppl*, 58–62.

17. Navarro F, van Os J, Jones P *et al.* (1996) Explaining sex differences in course and outcome in the functional psychoses. *Schizophr Res* **21**, 161–170.

18. Riecher-Rossler A & Rossler W (1998) The course of schizophrenic psychoses: what do we really know? A selective review from an epidemiological perspective. *Eur Arch Psychiatry Clin Neurosci* **248**, 189–202.

19. Seeman MV (2004) Relational ethics: when mothers suffer from psychosis. *Arch Womens Ment Health* **7**, 201–210.

20. Mowbray CT, Oyserman D, Bybee D *et al.* (2001) Life circumstances of mothers with serious mental illnesses. *Psychiatr Rehabil J* **25**, 114–123.

21. Oyserman D, Mowbray CT & Zemencuk JK (1994) Resources and supports for mothers with severe mental illness. *Health Soc Work* **19**, 132–142.

22. Kendell RE, Chalmers JC & Platz C (1987) Epidemiology of puerperal psychoses. *Br J Psychiatry* **150**, 662–673.

23. Riecher-Rossler A (2003) [Estrogens and the gonadal axis. Implications for women with schizophrenia]. *Nervenarzt* **74**, 398–405.

24. Goldstein JM, Cohen LS, Horton NJ *et al.* (2002) Sex differences in clinical response to olanzapine compared with haloperidol. *Psychiatry Res* **110**, 27–37.

25. WHO (2001) *International Classification of Functioning, Disability and Health (ICF)*, Geneva.

26. Mortensen PB & Juel K (1993) Mortality and causes of death in first admitted schizophrenic patients. *Br J Psychiatry* **163**, 183–189.

27. Hiroeh U, Appleby L, Mortensen PB *et al.* (2001) Death by homicide, suicide, and other unnatural causes in people with mental illness: a population-based study. *Lancet* **358**, 2110–2112.

28. Breier A, Schreiber JL, Dyer J *et al.* (1991) National Institute of Mental Health longitudinal study of chronic schizophrenia. Prognosis and predictors of outcome. *Arch Gen Psychiatry* **48**, 239–246.

29. Radomsky ED, Haas GL, Mann JJ *et al.* (1999) Suicidal behavior in patients with schizophrenia and other psychotic disorders. *Am J Psychiatry* **156**, 1590–1595.

30. Ajdacic-Gross V, Lauber C, Baumgartner M *et al.* (2009) In-patient suicide - a 13-year assessment. *Acta Psychiatr Scand.*

31. Caldwell CB & Gottesman, II (1990) Schizophrenics kill themselves too: a review of risk factors for suicide. *Schizophr Bull* **16**, 571–589.

32. Palmer BA, Pankratz VS & Bostwick JM (2005) The lifetime risk of suicide in schizophrenia: a reexamination. *Arch Gen Psychiatry* **62**, 247–253.

33. Roy A & Pompili M (2009) Management of schizophrenia with suicide risk. *Psychiatr Clin North Am* **32**, 863–883.

34. Robinson D, Woerner MG, Alvir JM *et al.* (1999) Predictors of relapse following response from a first episode of schizophrenia or schizoaffective disorder. *Arch Gen Psychiatry* **56**, 241–247.

35. Slade M (2009) 100 ways to support recovery A guide for mental health professionals. rethink. 32.

36. Hewer W, Rossler W, Fatkenheuer B *et al.* (1995) Mortality among patients in psychiatric hospitals in Germany. *Acta Psychiatr Scand* **91**, 174–179.

37. Hewer W & Rossler W (1997) [Mortality of patients with functional psychiatric illnesses during inpatient treatment]. *Fortschr Neurol Psychiatr* **65**, 171–181.

38. Meyer JM & Stahl SM (2009) The metabolic syndrome and schizophrenia. *Acta Psychiatr Scand* **119**, 4–14.

39. Monteleone P, Martiadis V & Maj M (2009) Management of schizophrenia with obesity, metabolic, and endocrinological disorders. *Psychiatr Clin North Am* **32**, 775–794.

40. Angermeyer MC (2000) Schizophrenia and violence. *Acta Psychiatr Scand Suppl*, 63–67.

41. Fazel S, Langstrom N, Hjern A *et al.* (2009) Schizophrenia, substance abuse, and violent crime. *JAMA* **301**, 2016–2023.

42. Munk-Jorgensen P (1999) Has deinstitutionalization gone too far? *Eur Arch Psychiatry Clin Neurosci* **249**, 136–143.

43. Lauber C, Nordt C, Sartorius N *et al.* (2000) Public acceptance of restrictions on mentally ill people. *Acta Psychiatr Scand Suppl*, 26–32.

44. Riecher-Rossler A & Rossler W (1993) Compulsory admission of psychiatric patients–an international comparison. *Acta Psychiatr Scand* **87**, 231–236.

45. Salize HJ & Dressing H (2004) Epidemiology of involuntary placement of mentally ill people across the European Union. *Br J Psychiatry* **184**, 163–168.

46. Lehman AF, Lieberman JA, Dixon LB *et al.* (2004) Practice guideline for the treatment of patients with schizophrenia, second edition. *Am J Psychiatry* **161**, 1–56.

47. Thornicroft G & Tansella M (2003) What are the arguments for community-based mental health care? WHO Regional office for Europe's Health Evidence Network (HEN). 1–24.

48. Lay B, Nordt C & Rossler W (2007) Trends in psychiatric hospitalisation of people with schizophrenia: a register-based investigation over the last three decades. *Schizophr Res* **97**, 68–78.

49. Lay B, Lauber C & Rossler W (2006) Prediction of in-patient use in first-admitted patients with psychosis. *Eur Psychiatry* **21**, 401–409.

50. Salize H, McCabe R, Bullenkamp J *et al.* (2009) Cost of treatment in schizophrenia in six European countries. *Schizophrenia Research* **Jun 2009**, 70–77.

51. Burns T, Fioritti A, Holloway F *et al.* (2001) Case management and assertive community treatment in Europe. *Psychiatr Serv* **52**, 631–636.

52. Rossler W, Loffler W, Fatkenheuer B *et al.* (1992) Does case management reduce the rehospitalization rate? *Acta Psychiatr Scand* **86**, 445–449.

53. Stein LI & Test MA (1980) Alternative to mental hospital treatment. I. Conceptual model, treatment program, and clinical evaluation. *Arch Gen Psychiatry* **37**, 392–397.

54. Scott JE & Dixon LB (1995) Assertive community treatment and case management for schizophrenia. *Schizophr Bull* **21**, 657–668.

55. Marshall M (1996) Case management: a dubious practice. *BMJ* **312**, 523–524.

56. Mueser KT, Bond GR, Drake RE *et al.* (1998) Models of community care for severe mental illness: a review of research on case management. *Schizophr Bull* **24**, 37–74.

57. Killaspy H, Bebbington P, Blizard R *et al.* (2006) The REACT study: randomised evaluation of assertive community treatment in north London. *BMJ* **332**, 815–820.

58. Burns T, Catty J & Wright C (2006) De-constructing home-based care for mental illness: can one identify the effective ingredients? *Acta Psychiatr Scand Suppl*, 33–35.

59. Anthony W (1979) *The principles of psychiatric rehabilitation*. University Park Press, Baltimore.

60. Grove B (1994) Reform of mental health care in Europe. Progress and change in the last decade. *Br J Psychiatry* **165**, 431–433.

61. WHO (1980) *International Classification of Impairments, Disabilities and Handicaps*, Geneva.

62. Royal College of Psychiatrists (1992) *Occupational therapy and mental disorders. A consensus statement by the Royal College of Psychiatrists and the College of Occupational Therapists*, London.

63. Cuffel BJ (1996) Comorbid substance use disorder: prevalence, patterns of use, and course. *New Dir Ment Health Serv*, 93–105.

64. Schwartz S, Goldfinger S, Ratener M *et al.* (1983) *The young adult patient and the care system: fragmentation prototypes. New Directions for Mental Health Services.* Jossey-Bass, San Francisco.

65. Rossler W, Riecher-Rossler A, Angst J *et al.* (2007) Psychotic experiences in the general population: a twenty-year prospective community study. *Schizophr Res* **92**, 1–14.

66. Bachrach LL (2000) Psychosocial rehabilitation and psychiatry in the treatment of schizophrenia–what are the boundaries? *Acta Psychiatr Scand Suppl*, 6–10.

67. Corrigan PW, McCracken SG & Holmes EP (2001) Motivational interviews as goal assessment for persons with psychiatric disability. *Community Ment Health J* **37**, 113–122.

68. Rogers ES, Martin R, Anthony W *et al.* (2001) Assessing readiness for change among persons with severe mental illness. *Community Ment Health J* **37**, 97–112.

69. Liberman RP, Wallace CJ & Hassell J (2004) Rehab rounds: Predicting readiness and responsiveness to skills training: the Micro-Module Learning Test. *Psychiatr Serv* **55**, 764–766.

70. Lamb HR (1982) *Treating the long-term mentally ill: beyond deinstitutionaliation.* Jossey-Bass, San Francisco.

71. Farkas M, Gagne C, Anthony W *et al.* (2005) Implementing recovery oriented evidence based programs: identifying the critical dimensions. *Community Ment Health J* **41**, 141–158.

72. Priebe S, McCabe R, Bullenkamp J *et al.* (2002) The impact of routine outcome measurement on treatment processes in community mental health care: approach and methods of the MECCA study. *Epidemiol Psichiatr Soc* **11**, 198–205.

73. Tuttman S (1997) Protecting the therapeutic alliance in this time of changing healthcare delivery systems. *Int J Group Psychother* **47**, 3–16.

74. Barbato A, D'Avanzo B, Rocca G *et al.* (2004) A study of long-stay patients resettled in the community after closure of a psychiatric hospital in Italy. *Psychiatr Serv* **55**, 67–70.

75. Rogers ES, Anthony W & Lyass A (2004) The nature and dimensions of social support among individuals with severe mental illnesses. *Community Ment Health J* **40**, 437–450.

76. Corrigan PW, Slopen N, Gracia G *et al.* (2005) Some recovery processes in mutual-help groups for persons with mental illness; II: qualitative analysis of participant interviews. *Community Ment Health J* **41**, 721–735.

77. Cutler DL (1985) Clinical care update. The chronically mentally ill. *Community Ment Health J* **21**, 3–13.

78. Kopelowicz A & Liberman RP (1995) Biobehavioral treatment and rehabilitation of schizophrenia. *Harv Rev Psychiatry* **3**, 55–64.

79. Bebbington PE (1995) The content and context of compliance. *Int Clin Psychopharmacol* **9 Suppl 5**, 41–50.

80. Gray R, White J, Schulz M *et al.* (2010) Enhancing medication adherence in people with schizophrenia: An international programme of research. *International Journal of Mental Health Nursing*, 9.

81. Marder SR (2000) Integrating pharmacological and psychosocial treatments for schizophrenia. *Acta Psychiatr Scand Suppl*, 87–90.

82. Lieberman JA, Stroup TS, McEvoy JP *et al.* (2005) Effectiveness of antipsychotic drugs in patients with chronic schizophrenia. *N Engl J Med* **353**, 1209–1223.

83. Dencker SJ & Liberman RP (1995) From compliance to collaboration in the treatment of schizophrenia. *Int Clin Psychopharmacol* **9 Suppl 5**, 75–78.

84. Eckman TA, Liberman RP, Phipps CC *et al.* (1990) Teaching medication management skills to schizophrenic patients. *J Clin Psychopharmacol* **10**, 33–38.

85. Tarrier N (2005) Cognitive behaviour therapy for schizophrenia – a review of development, evidence and implementation. *Psychother Psychosom* **74**, 136–144.

86. Wykes T, Steel C, Everitt B *et al.* (2008) Cognitive behavior therapy for schizophrenia: effect sizes, clinical models, and methodological rigor. *Schizophr Bull* **34**, 523–537.

87. Liberman R (1988) *Psychiatric rehabilitation of chronic mental patients.* American Psychiatric Press, Washington DC.

88. Liberman RP, Glynn S, Blair KE *et al.* (2002) In vivo amplified skills training: promoting generalization of independent living skills for clients with schizophrenia. *Psychiatry* **65**, 137–155.

89. Kurtz MM & Mueser KT (2008) A meta-analysis of controlled research on social skills training for schizophrenia. *J Consult Clin Psychol* **76**, 491–504.

90. Penn DL & Mueser KT (1996) Research update on the psychosocial treatment of schizophrenia. *Am J Psychiatry* **153**, 607–617.

91. Wallace CJ (1998) Social skills training in psychiatric rehabilitation: recent findings. *International Review of Psychiatry* **19**, 9–19.

92. Glynn SM, Marder SR, Liberman RP *et al.* (2002) Supplementing clinic-based skills training with manual-based community support sessions: effects on social adjustment of patients with schizophrenia. *Am J Psychiatry* **159**, 829–837.

93. Bellack AS (2004) Skills training for people with severe mental illness. *Psychiatr Rehabil J* **27**, 375–391.

94. Roder V, Zorn P, Muller D *et al.* (2001) Improving recreational, residential, and vocational outcomes for patients with schizophrenia. *Psychiatr Serv* **52**, 1439–1441.

95. Onken SJ, Dumont JM, Ridgway P *et al.* Mental health recovery: What helps and what hinders? A national research project for the development of recovery facilitating system performance indicators. Alexandria, VA: www.rfmh.org/csipmh/projects/rc10.shtm; 2002.

96. Ridgway P & Zipple AM (1990) The paradigm shift in residential services: From linear continuum to supported housing approaches. *Psychosocial Rehabilitation Journal* **13**, 11–32.

97. Carling PJ (1992) Housing, community support, and homelessness: Emerging pollicy in mental health systems. *New England Journal of Public Policy* **8**, 281–295.

98. Rog DJ (2004) The evidence on supported housing. *Psychiatr Rehabil J* **27**, 334–344.

99. Berger G, Bernhardt T, Schramm U *et al.* (2004) No effects of a combination of caregivers support group and memory training/music therapy in dementia patients from a memory clinic population. *Int J Geriatr Psychiatry* **19**, 223–231.

100. Harding CM, Strauss JS, Hafez H *et al.* (1987) Work and mental illness. I. Toward an integration of the rehabilitation process. *J Nerv Ment Dis* **175**, 317–326.

101. McElroy EM (1987) Sources of distress among families of the hospitalized mentally ill. *New Dir Ment Health Serv*, 61–72.

102. Royal College of Psychiatrists (1996) *Psychiatric Rehabilitation. Revised.* Gaskell, London.

103. Jacobs H, Kardashian S, Kreinbring R *et al.* (1988) A skills-oriented model for facilitating empoyment in psychiatrically disabled persons. *Rehabilitation Counseling Bulletin* **27**, 96–97.

104. Bond GR (2004) Supported employment: evidence for an evidence-based practice. *Psychiatr Rehabil J* **27**, 345–359.

105. Baronet AM & Gerber GJ (1998) Psychiatric rehabilitation: efficacy of four models. *Clin Psychol Rev* **18**, 189–228.

106. Cook JA, Leff HS, Blyler CR *et al.* (2005) Results of a multisite randomized trial of supported employment interventions for individuals with severe mental illness. *Arch Gen Psychiatry* **62**, 505–512.

107. Cook JA, Lehman AF, Drake R *et al.* (2005) Integration of psychiatric and vocational services: a multisite randomized, controlled trial of supported employment. *Am J Psychiatry* **162**, 1948–1956.

108. Ruesch P, Graf J, Meyer PC *et al.* (2004) Occupation, social support and quality of life in persons with schizophrenic or affective disorders. *Soc Psychiatry Psychiatr Epidemiol* **39**, 686–694.
109. Salyers MP, Becker DR, Drake RE *et al.* (2004) A ten-year follow-up of a supported employment program. *Psychiatr Serv* **55**, 302–308.
110. McGurk SR & Mueser KT (2003) Cognitive functioning and employment in severe mental illness. *J Nerv Ment Dis* **191**, 789–798.
111. Bhugra D (1989) Attitudes towards mental illness. A review of the literature. *Acta Psychiatr Scand* **80**, 1–12.
112. Jorm AF (2000) Mental health literacy. Public knowledge and beliefs about mental disorders. *Br J Psychiatry* **177**, 396–401.
113. Lauber C, Nordt C, Falcato L *et al.* (2001) Lay recommendations on how to treat mental disorders. *Soc Psychiatry Psychiatr Epidemiol* **36**, 553–556.
114. Stuart H & Arboleda-Florez J (2001) Community attitudes toward people with schizophrenia. *Can J Psychiatry* **46**, 245–252.
115. Gaebel W, Baumann A, Witte AM *et al.* (2002) Public attitudes towards people with mental illness in six German cities: results of a public survey under special consideration of schizophrenia. *Eur Arch Psychiatry Clin Neurosci* **252**, 278–287.
116. Lauber C, Nordt C, Falcato L *et al.* (2002) Public attitude to compulsory admission of mentally ill people. *Acta Psychiatr Scand* **105**, 385–389.
117. Angermeyer MC & Matschinger H (2003) The stigma of mental illness: effects of labelling on public attitudes towards people with mental disorder. *Acta Psychiatr Scand* **108**, 304–309.
118. Lauber C, Nordt C, Falcato L *et al.* (2004) Factors influencing social distance toward people with mental illness. *Community Ment Health J* **40**, 265–274.
119. Link BG, Struening EL, Rahav M *et al.* (1997) On stigma and its consequences: evidence from a longitudinal study of men with dual diagnoses of mental illness and substance abuse. *J Health Soc Behav* **38**, 177–190.
120. Mechanic D, McAlpine D, Rosenfield S *et al.* (1994) Effects of illness attribution and depression on the quality of life among persons with serious mental illness. *Soc Sci Med* **39**, 155–164.
121. Rosenfield S (1997) Labeling mental illness: The effects of received services and perceived stigma on life satisfaction. *American Sociological Review* **62**, 660–672.
122. Graf J, Lauber C, Nordt C *et al.* (2004) Perceived stigmatization of mentally ill people and its consequences for the quality of life in a Swiss population. *J Nerv Ment Dis* **192**, 542–547.
123. Mueller B, Nordt C, Lauber C *et al.* (2006) Social support modifies perceived stigmatization in the first years of mental illness: a longitudinal approach. *Soc Sci Med* **62**, 39–49.
124. Becker T, Leese M, Clarkson P *et al.* (1998) Links between social network and quality of life: an epidemiologically representative study of psychotic patients in south London. *Soc Psychiatry Psychiatr Epidemiol* **33**, 229–304.
125. George LK, Blazer DG, Hughes DC *et al.* (1989) Social support and the outcome of major depression. *Br J Psychiatry* **154**, 478–485.

126. Hall GB & Nelson G (1996) Social networks, social support, personal empowerment, and the adaptation of psychiatric consumers/survivors: path analytic models. *Soc Sci Med* **43**, 1743–1754.

127. Yanos PT, Rosenfield S & Horwitz AV (2001) Negative and supportive social interactions and quality of life among persons diagnosed with severe mental illness. *Community Ment Health J* **37**, 405–419.

128. Rossler W, Salize HJ, Cucchiaro G *et al.* (1999) Does the place of treatment influence the quality of life of schizophrenics? *Acta Psychiatr Scand* **100**, 142–148.

129. Rusch N, Angermeyer MC & Corrigan PW (2005) Mental illness stigma: concepts, consequences, and initiatives to reduce stigma. *Eur Psychiatry* **20**, 529–539.

130. Meise U, Sulzenbacher H, Kemmler G *et al.* (2000) ["...not dangerous, but nevertheless frightening". A program against stigmatization of schizophrenia in schools]. *Psychiatr Prax* **27**, 340–346.

131. Pinfold V, Huxley P, Thornicroft G *et al.* (2003) Reducing psychiatric stigma and discrimination–evaluating an educational intervention with the police force in England. *Soc Psychiatry Psychiatr Epidemiol* **38**, 337–344.

132. Monahan J, Bonnie RJ, Appelbaum PS *et al.* (2001) Mandated Community Treatment: Beyond Outpatient Commitment. *Psychiatr Serv 52* **52**, 1198–1205.

133. Veatch R (1994) Against paternalism in the patient-physician relationship. In: Gilon R (eds.) *Principles of health care ethics*. John Wiley, Chichester, pp. 409–419.

134. Lovell AM (1996) Coercion and social control. A framework for research on aggressive strategies in community mental health. In: Dennis DL & Monahan J (eds.) *Coercion and Aggressive Community Treatment: A new Frontier in Mental Health Law*. Plenum Press, New York.

135. Jager M & Rossler W (2009) [Informal coercion to enhance treatment adherence among psychiatric patients]. *Neuropsychiatr* **23**, 206–215.

136. Sartorius N (1998) Stigma: what can psychiatrists do about it? *Lancet* **352**, 1058–1059.

137. Lauber C, Anthony M, Ajdacic-Gross V *et al.* (2004) What about psychiatrists' attitude to mentally ill people? *European Psychiatry* **19**, 423–427.

138. Lauber C, Nordt C & Rossler W (2006) Attitudes and mental illness: consumers and the general public are on one side of the medal, mental health professionals on the other. *Acta Psychiatr Scand* **114**, 145–146; author reply 146–147.

139. Nordt C, Rossler W & Lauber C (2006) Attitudes of mental health professionals toward people with schizophrenia and major depression. *Schizophr Bull* **32**, 709–714.

140. Corrigan PW (2002) Empowerment and serious mental illness: treatment partnerships and community opportunities. *Psychiatr Q* **73**, 217–228.

141. Liberman RP, Hilty DM, Drake RE *et al.* (2001) Requirements for multidisciplinary teamwork in psychiatric rehabilitation. *Psychiatr Serv* **52**, 1331–1342.

142. Health PsNFCoM. Achieving the promise: Transforming mental health care in America. Washington DC: www.mentalhealthcommission.gov/reports/ Finalreport/toc_exec.html; 2003.

143. Lehman AF & Steinwachs DM (1998) Patterns of usual care for schizophrenia: initial results from the Schizophrenia Patient Outcomes Research Team (PORT) Client Survey. *Schizophr Bull* **24**, 11–20; discussion 20–32.

Index

Schizophrenia: Current Science and Clinical Practice, First Edition. Edited by Wolfgang Gaebel.
© 2011 John Wiley & Sons, Ltd. Published 2011 by John Wiley & Sons, Ltd.